HISTORY OF CIVILISATION

The Peoples of the Hills

The Peoples of the Hills

ANCIENT ARARAT AND CAUCASUS

CHARLES BURNEY
Lecturer in Near Eastern Archaeology
University of Manchester

DAVID MARSHALL LANG
Professor of Caucasian Studies
School of Oriental and African Studies
University of London

WEIDENFELD AND NICOLSON
5 WINSLEY STREET LONDON W1

ISBN 0 297 00495 6

Printed in Great Britain by
Ebenezer Baylis and Son Ltd.
The Trinity Press, Worcester, and London

CONTENTS

LIST OF ILLUSTRATIONS

Between pages 144 and 145

ACKNOWLEDGEMENTS

The authors have collaborated in this work over nearly five years, and are especially grateful to the staff of Weidenfeld and Nicolson for their help and understanding; and one author (CAB) would like to add a special word of appreciation of their patience in the face of delays, largely arising from the bulk of new data collected during his visit, with his co-author, to the Soviet Union in April 1968.

Thanks for help during this visit and for books and offprints are especially due to A. A. Martirosian, Emma V. Khanzadian, B. N. Arakelian, S. A. Sardarian, K. L. Oganesian, A. O. Mnatsakanian, S. A. Esayan and T. Khacharian (Armenia); to O. M. Japaridze, T. N. Chubinishvili, G. A. Melikishvili, R. Abrahamishvili and A. Gobinishvili (Georgia); to Dr Yampolski, O. Abibullaev, and I. Narimanov (Azerbaijan: Baku). Without the active help and information so willingly provided by these and many others whom it is impossible to name, the month spent in the Trans-Caucasian republics of the Soviet Union would have been far less fruitful.

Both authors must record their gratitude to the Calouste Gulbenkian Foundation for a generous grant towards the expenses of their visit to the USSR in 1968.

For many of the photographs taken in Turkey, Iran and the USSR the authors must thank Mrs Burney. Among others who have kindly supplied photographs, special thanks are due to Dr R. D. Barnett (Figs. 61, 64, 65); Professor Vakhtang Beridze (5, 47, 78, 80, 87, 102, 108, 109); the Trustees of the British Museum (71, 77); Michael Burrell (6, 10, 74); Chester Beatty Library, Dublin (110, 111); Mestia Regional Museum, Georgia (101, 103, 104); Russian Historical Museum, Moscow (43, 44).

C. A. Burney
D. M. Lang

LIST OF MAPS

PREFACE

The subtitle of this book suggests the task facing the authors in their endeavour to trace the successive stages from prehistory to civilisation in the highlands from the upper Euphrates to the Caucasus and to Lake Reza'iyeh (formerly Urmia). In some periods it has been far easier to discern an underlying unity throughout this zone than at other times. The modern political frontiers (indicated in Map 1) do not simplify research. In Chapter II, owing to the sparseness of material before *c.* 3,000 BC in the highland zone, a wider geographical horizon was thought desirable, including the Anatolian plateau.

It is hoped that this book will be approached as an introduction to a wide subject and as an attempt to span the gulf all too frequently found to divide prehistory, Assyriology and Urartology, Graeco–Roman history and the study of Armenia and Georgia in the early centuries of the Christian era. Specialists in each field are sure to find themselves frustrated by lack of detail to help their particular enquiries. If they are stimulated to pursue such problems by the text of this book and through the footnotes, one of the authors' purposes will have been achieved. The other purpose is to bring a relatively little known aspect of the ancient and early medieval world to the attention of a wider public.

It should be emphasised that the illustrations and maps are intended to support and enliven the argument in the text, not even to begin to provide a complete record of any part of the relevant material.

CHAPTER 1

THE ENVIRONMENT

Anatolia has been described as the bridge uniting the Near East and Europe; but it has always been much more than that. The Caucasus range is at once a barrier and a funnel leading from the steppes of southern Russia to the highland zone of the Near East. It is this zone, especially eastern Anatolia and the Urmia basin of north-western Iran, as well as Trans-Caucasia, which falls within the compass of this book. No brief or facile summary can possibly provide an adequate understanding of the physical geography of these regions, yet no grasp of their past is conceivable without such an understanding. During certain periods the zone from the Caucasus to Lake Urmia and westward to the upper Euphrates enjoyed a cultural and sometimes also a political unity which justifies the geographical limits of this book. At other times no such cohesion is apparent.

Geology is ever present to the eye of the traveller through Anatolia and Iran, in most of which the hillsides are bare and eroded, exposing the variegated colours of the rocks. This is especially true of the central plateau of Anatolia, of the eastern Urmia basin and of the Araxes valley and much of Soviet Azerbaijan. But it was not always so, and it is one of the tasks of the student of the ancient Near East to make use of all available evidence, however tentative, to reconstruct the natural environment of earlier periods.[1] This book will take in material dating back to about 7,000 BC, if the evidence of radio-carbon dates is accepted. These dates do offer a mainly consistent pattern. During the subsequent millennia slight changes in climate and thus also in environment have indeed occurred: man-made changes certainly have wrought their havoc on the landscape. The efforts of modern governments, including notices urging public awareness and appreciation of forests, seem to have come almost too late to have any significant effect, though this may be too pessimistic an assessment. Meanwhile the forces of erosion, unleashed by centuries of deforestation and by the depredations of the goat, still continue to take toll of the irreplaceable resources of soil.

The annual rainfall of most of the Anatolian plateau is low, with a poor distribution over the year as a whole, the wet season being from March to mid-May. There is also a considerable fluctuation in rainfall from year to year, so that areas which in some years yield a good harvest in others become marginal for cultivation: this is especially so in central Anatolia, where recent extensions of arable farming with tractors and deep ploughing have brought the risk of a dust bowl.[2] But such conditions cannot have obtained in prehistoric times, not even today do they apply to more than a part of the Anatolian plateau. In all the coastal regions, in the highlands of eastern Anatolia and in most of Trans-Caucasia annual rainfall is higher than in central Anatolia, and vegetation and general ecology are accordingly different. Only in Iranian Azerbaijan, centred round Lake Urmia, are conditions more closely comparable with those of the semi-arid regions of Turkey.

The highland zone from the Euphrates eastwards, though rightly reckoned as within the Near East, enjoys, or suffers, extremes of seasonal temperatures more appropriate to central Asia. Much of this zone lies within the critical limit of winter, with an annual minimum of thirty days of frost in terms of mean daily temperatures. In the region of Kars, Erzurum and Van winter is longer and far more extreme than the comparatively moderate heat of summer which seldom lasts as much as three whole months from the middle of June. The Black Sea littoral enjoys, in contrast, a maritime climate with rain all the year round and with, towards the south-east corner of the Black Sea, an almost subtropical luxuriance surpassed only on the southern shores of the Caspian Sea. This verdure extends to Abkhazia, and to a lesser degree into central Georgia. The Taurus range provides a sharp frontier along the north for the Atlantic storms of winter and spring sweeping east across the Mediterranean and Syria. A similar contrast can be seen near Bayburt, on the road from Trabzon to Erzurum, where the plateau is bathed in hot sunshine in July and August but the clouds from the Black Sea to the north reach the very crest of the mountains and almost spill over. Summer there ends with the incursion of the cold wet winds from the north, eventually bringing snow. The same occurs in Azerbaijan, especially north of Lake Urmia, a region with one of the widest ranges of temperature from summer to winter of any part of the world; here, however, as in the Van region, the presence of a large lake must exercise at least a slight moderating influence on the continental climate.

Some attempt must be made to reconstruct the natural environment during the last nine or ten millennia. The sheer weight of evidence makes the physical conditions of today, except where altered by man, the prime source for reconstruction of those of earlier periods. From the results of palaeo-climatology it seems apparent that during the last glaciation the climatic snowline was as much as 2,700 ft lower than that of today, though in places only 2,000 ft lower. With this went an alpine vegetation in the highlands of eastern Anatolia and in Caucasia, with meadows and scrub and some glaciers. Two radio-carbon dates show that loess ceased to be deposited by about 9,000 BC, suggesting that by then the dry northerly winds, blowing during the glacial periods from the steppes of Eurasia, were not so prevalent. In post-glacial times climatic conditions do not seem to have fluctuated very significantly in the Near East.[3]

Relatively small climatic changes could have disproportionately wide effects on the climate of a whole region, especially from the growth and shrinkage of lakes. Such changes may well have affected Lake Urmia, today nowhere more than one hundred feet deep and with wide areas of salt flats under water only in the spring. Large areas of inland drainage are also comprised within the confines of the Anatolian plateau, among these being the Konya Plain, the Salt Lake basin and the catchment areas of the lakes along the northern foothills of the Taurus. Some evidence exists to support the theory that large lakes, since then either drastically shrunk or completely vanished, existed in early post-glacial times over much of these areas, with consequent deposition of alluvium.[4] Such extensive sheets of water suggest a lower rate of evaporation than today, appropriate to a lower average temperature, and their effect on the climate would have been considerable. Only a slight decline in average annual precipitation would, however, have been quite sufficient to cause, with a slight rise in average temperature, the drying up of much of the land previously under water perennially or seasonally. If the annual rainfall should fall below twelve inches the growth of even deep-rooted trees will cease, bringing about another factor making for aridity and erosion. Thus contemporary environmental conditions obtaining over most of central Anatolia would come into being, perhaps with surprising rapidity. The balance between aridity and a sufficiency of rainfall for plant and tree growth, between semi-desert or steppe conditions and those suitable for primitive village cultivation, has always been a delicate one in much of the Near East, certainly throughout post-glacial times.

This delicate balance must have affected the extent of forests over much of Anatolia and Caucasia, though in the mountainous regions the work of tree-felling and the subsequent grazing by goats must have played the main part in deforestation and consequent erosion. Once started, this process tends to gather momentum, as the soil becomes less capable of retaining moisture and is no longer anchored to the hillsides by the roots of trees, scrub and grasses. Archaeological evidence, such as the occurrence of stag antlers at the Hittite capital of Boğazköy (Hattusas), may provide indications of forest where none survives now. Even clearer evidence is to be seen in the massive diameter and great quantity of timbers used in such buildings as the burnt palace of Beycesultan Level v, in south-western Anatolia.[5] Wooden frame construction is still widely used in the highland zone of the Near East, with an in-filling of mud brick or of stones set in mud; but the dimensions of the timbers used today are modest compared with those in prehistoric buildings, and poplar, so easily and quickly grown along the banks of streams and irrigation ditches, is far the commonest type of wood used. One of the most impressive monuments surviving to attest the skill in carpentry of the early peoples of Anatolia is the tomb-chamber of the great tumulus at Gordion, opened up in 1957.[6] These are but some of the indications which lead to one general conclusion, that the forest-covered acreage of Anatolia and probably that of the Zagros mountains also, has much diminished during the last three or four millennia, more especially since the Hellenistic period. Along the Pontic ranges and in Caucasia, however, vast forests still survive, in a zone blessed with a far higher rainfall than that of the now treeless Anatolian plateau or of the Urmia basin.

The pattern of settlements in the highland zone during successive periods, and the varying importance of arable farming and of sheep and cattle, are subjects as yet hardly studied at all, save in the Soviet Union. The direct evidence of animal bones from excavations is the most tangible criterion, without which theories on the evolution and changes of patterns of settlement are liable to be mainly speculative. It is in the study of animal bones from prehistoric sites that Soviet archaeologists have so far made one of their outstanding contributions, directly relevant to sites in Trans-Caucasia.[7]

Palaeo-botany has provided evidence illuminating the earliest stages of the cultivation of emmer and einkorn wheat and two-row barley, with subsequent mutations resulting in improved strains; but still the problem of the ultimate geographical sources of the wild grains found in the earliest excavated settlements awaits solution, and is likely still to do so until a very extensive programme of botanical research directed to this end has been completed.[8] While the occurrences of wild wheat far to the east, including Afghanistan, might be taken to suggest at least one nucleus of early agriculture thereabouts, the absence to date of discoveries of sites of an antiquity comparable with that of Çatal Hüyük in the Konya Plain, let alone Jericho, reduces the significance of these discoveries. Plant remains other than those of cereals can also be of great interest. Pollen analyses are of immense use not only for relative chronology and palaeo-climatology but also for detailed recording of the flora of a given site.

It is a commonplace that any settlement must be near a reliable source of water, whether river, lake or spring, the last being most favoured by the Anatolian peasant today, who is surprisingly fastidious concerning the quality of his drinking water.[9] Who is to say that his ancestors, even as early as neolithic times, were not similarly appreciative of clear cold springs? The importance of these in the religion of prehistoric Anatolia, with the veneration of so many divinities attached to source of fresh water, suggests that such an appreciation prevailed at least as early as the second millennium BC. Since such springs are more often to be found along the edges of mountain-girt plains than in the middle, it is there that most sites are found.

Apart from water, the demands of primitive agriculture, of stock-breeding and of a continued reliance to a large degree on hunting all dictated the location of early sites. In later periods, more specifically in the Iron Age, the needs of defence, whether of one isolated site or of a chain of fortified sites deliberately arranged, often led to the construction of settlements on spurs and in commanding and relatively impregnable positions. Nearly all sites in such locations are found, on examination, to yield surface pottery and sometimes other evidence pointing to a date in the Iron Age. On the whole there was more continuity from the early first millennium BC into later centuries, in Anatolia into Hellenistic and Roman times, than from the Late Bronze Age into the Iron Age, when in many regions there was a great change in the distribution and type of settlements. In some parts of Anatolia, however, many mounds with earlier occupation are crowned by Iron Age levels whose extent and depth make excavation of the underlying levels likely to be prohibitive in expense, time and effort: frequently such sites have flat summits but steep sides, suggesting fortifications. In contrast to these mounds are the many which scarcely protrude above the level of the surrounding plain or valley, and which must usually represent one period of occupation with subsequent and final abandonment. Commonly the stratified levels of such sites are found, on excavation, to continue down to some depth below the modern level of the plain: accumulation of alluvium can be very rapid.[10] Therefore there must be many, perhaps very many, prehistoric mounds now completely buried beneath subsequent alluvium: such sites are likely to remain long, if not for ever, undetected. It is permissible to hazard a guess that a large proportion of them will be of fourth millennium BC and earlier date.

The incompleteness of many surveys must be emphasized. It is especially difficult to discover ancient settlements in forest-clad hills, though these were in some regions numerous from quite early times: for example, little or nothing of pre-Classical date has been found along the Pontic littoral east of the districts of Samsun and Bafra, though there the easy access from central Anatolia makes the presence of prehistoric settlements hardly remarkable. In the fertile land down by the Black

Sea coast of Turkey traces of sites have probably largely been buried or washed away long since. In Abkhazia it is not settlement sites but the stone-lined cist-graves, or dolmens, which form the major class of monument. Summer encampments in mountain pastures, resembling those termed *yayla* in modern Turkey, must likewise be hard to detect. Hill fortresses, however, such as those of Urartu around Lake Van, are often quite easy to detect, from their predictable positions on spurs commanding a plain or valley. These had a permanent function; but on inaccessible mountain tops only the crudest defences are normally found, for such were built for purely temporary use as refuges. Many hill sites must await the time and energy of archaeologists prepared to spend days tramping over hills with little or no results. The archaeologist carrying out a survey must be ready to find sites of widely differing periods and of various types, largely depending on the nature of the terrain. No survey can ever be definitive, and an immense amount of reconnaissance work remains to be done in areas already surveyed in preliminary fashion. Social anthropology may help in suggesting solutions to questions of the patterns of settlement during successive cultural periods; but in the absence of written records the answers must necessarily be largely tentative.

Not only local conditions of water supply, soil, vegetation, fauna and climate influenced the birth and development of villages and towns: there was also the influence, so often intangible in the surviving record, of contacts with other settlements, near and far off. Such contacts depended on natural routes across mountain ranges, the plains and valleys of the Anatolian plateau, the Urmia basin and Trans-Caucasia and also the obstacles of the coasts. It is not surprising that the courses of many modern highways still follow these prehistoric routes. Passes over the Taurus, for example, must always have been in certain defined places;[11] further east, the Malatya-Maraş road was always important, linking the eastern highlands with Cilicia and the Amuq. The Caucasus is crossed in the centre by the Daryal Pass; the Zigana Pass over the less formidable Pontic range is likewise important, even though there is no proof that this was a route used before Xenophon.[12] River valleys in the highland zone tend, however, to be more in the nature of barriers than natural routes: with their long, winding and precipitous gorges and their rapids inhibiting navigation, with their wide seasonal fluctuation in flow and their drop in altitude in a relatively short distance to the coastal plains, such rivers as the Kizil Irmak (the ancient Halys, now the Red River) and the Ceyhan (Pyramos), flowing into the Black Sea and the Mediterranean respectively, in no way provided routes for communication in any direction. The upper Euphrates, in its northern branch (Kara

6

Su) and below the confluence with its southern branch (Murat), has many deep gorges. Both the Kura and the Araxes are too dangerous for navigation, though their valleys do provide means of communication by land. So likewise does the Murat valley, the route taken by several Assyrian kings on their campaigns into the heart of Urartu.[13] Save only on the greater lakes, the highland zone gives little scope for navigation of any kind,[14] nor are the coasts of Turkey well supplied with natural harbours. Movement across the highland plateaux in most directions has long been relatively easy, though the presence of large areas of forest and scrub must have inhibited movement in a manner not found today.

East of the northern Euphrates (Kara Su) the general altitude increases from west to east, and the mountain ranges draw closer together, with a predominantly east-west direction, so that movement from east to west tends to be easier than from north to south. Only two natural east-west routes exist across eastern Anatolia: a northern one from Doğubayazit via Karaköse (Agri) to Erzurum and thence to Erzincan and from there over a mountain chain to Suşehri and, after another highland passage, to Sivas and the central plateau; and a southern route from the north end of Lake Urmia via the Kotur valley to Van, and thence across or round Lake Van and on via the Muş plain and the lower Murat valley to the crossing of the Euphrates and beyond to Malatya. From this city there is a route south-west to Maraş and the Mediterranean, another route west to Kayseri and a third north-west to Sivas. More important in the history of migrations from the east and north-east is the northerly route, joined at Horasan, some thirty-five miles east of Erzurum on the upper Araxes, by a route from the north-east through Kars, leading in from Georgia. From Aşkale, twenty-five miles west of Erzurum, runs the route through Bayburt, a major Seljuk fortress in the Middle Ages, to Gümüşhane and thence over the Zigana Pass to the Black Sea at Trabzon. The easiest route to the southern shores of the Black Sea is from the central plateau via Çorum down to the coast at Samsun: there are several other routes, such as that via Şebinkarahisar, but they are for the most part arduous. To the east, the Urmia basin is relatively easily reached from Trans-Caucasia, and it lay athwart the road of successive migrations, including those of the Iranian tribes from the late second millennium BC onwards. The fact that its geographical position, between the south-west shores of the Caspian Sea and the mountains now providing a natural frontier between Turkey and Iran, made it a funnel through which all invaders from the Caucasus southwards into Iran were obliged to pass, may account for the ethnic and cultural diversity apparent at least by the early first millennium BC.[15] To this day, moreover, settled agriculture and nomadism exist side by side, if not always without friction.

7

Contacts and connections between neighbouring regions and over much greater distances were possible from the earliest times, along the natural routes largely above-mentioned. Mountains formed obstacles to political unity, but trade was a different matter. Artifacts thought or known to originate elsewhere, and usually easily portable, and substances not existing naturally in the area of the site, give proofs of trade or diffusion. Before the introduction of copper-working, different types of stone comprise most of these imported materials. On the mechanics of this early trade, whether or not it was really organized and if so by whom, it is rather fruitless to speculate.[16] One thing, however, needs emphasis: travel over long distances was perfectly possible even in neolithic times, as analogies with the period just before the introduction of the steam engine indicate. Nomads in the nineteenth century AD are known to have moved, with their sheep, all the way up from the Aleppo region in the spring to the Sivas region of central Anatolia and back again in the autumn, an annual return journey of about seven hundred miles. How much easier would travel without flocks of sheep have been! Archaeologists have sometimes tended to exaggerate the deterrent effect of geographical obstacles to movement and trade. It was also erroneously believed that a long period, even of centuries, should often be allowed for the diffusion of prehistoric cultures. But early man could move as far and as fast as his feet and his determination would take him.

The demands of trade necessitated knowledge of and access to the sources of the relevant raw materials, both in neolithic times and later. Anatolia and Trans-Caucasia are rich in minerals and other materials. The Turkish villager of today has a keen eye for any ores that he may pick up. Copper, tin and antimony all occur in good quantities in Trans-Caucasia, the presence of tin being of special importance: it is not found in Anatolia, nor apparently in Iran, though it may occur in or near Afghanistan.[17] The number of deposits worked in antiquity must be beyond reckoning, largely because so many were too small to be of any interest for commercial purposes nowadays, or are too remote to be accessible or to repay the expense of road-building. The copper deposits of Turkey include Ergani Madeni in the south-east and sources near Kastamonu and in the extreme north-east, in ancient Colchis; iron occurs near Divriği and Hasançelebi, both in east central Anatolia; gold and silver occur in the Taurus near Bulgarmadeni, and silver also at places where it is noted in the name (Turkish: *gümüş*), at Gümüşhane, on the Trabzon-Erzurum road, and at Gümüşhacıköy, west of Amasya and south-west of Samsun; there is also silver in the Ergani Maden area. Antimony is found at Turhal, near Amasya. Alluvial gold must be

8

available in many places in Anatolia, and copper is known from the Kültepe tablets to have been one of the major exports of the native Anatolian cities to Ashur, by means of the Assyrian caravans; but the precise sources of this copper remain unknown. Tin (*anakum* in the Akkadian tongue) was imported by the Assyrian merchants to Kanesh (Kültepe) and the other trading posts which they had set up:[18] its absence in Anatolia may be associated with the lack of granite, with which cassiterite, or tin ore, is almost always found. The Hittites were supposedly the earliest masters of iron-working, but whence they obtained their iron ore is unknown: one possibility would be from Divriği, though rather far from the centre of their territory. Until less secrecy surrounds the results of the various geological surveys and until these are made readily available to archaeologists the whole subject of the prehistoric sources of metals in the highland zone must remain largely obscure. In addition to metals other minerals were exploited in antiquity, one of these being salt, readily found in and around Lake Urmia and the Salt Lake of central Anatolia.

In neolithic times obsidian, ranging from transparency to an opaque jet black, was an important item of trade, prized for its cutting qualities and thus used for all manner of tools and weapons. Recent studies have shown the sources of much of the obsidian found at widely separated sites, from Jericho to Ali Kosh in Khuzistan.[19] Yet it would be safer to say that certain possible sources have been located, and others eliminated for certain, by using spectographic analysis of trace elements. This method has led to the distinguishing of at least two regions providing obsidian, central Anatolia and the eastern highlands from Lake Van to Armenia, but it cannot tell the archaeologist whether the recorded sources are the only ones producing obsidian with those particular trace elements. There are so many small occurrences of natural, unworked obsidian, perhaps especially in eastern Anatolia, that it would be rash to try to pinpoint the sources of individual specimens very precisely.[20] Nemrut Dağ, the extinct volcano overlooking Lake Van, is the best known source in that region. Tilkitepe, in the shadow of the castle-rock of Van, has produced some of the largest known cores of obsidian, from which flakes had been struck.

Apart from mineral resources, Anatolia and Trans-Caucasia are rich in plant life. Anatolia is situated at the meeting of three principal zones of distribution of plants: these are the so-called Euro-Siberian zone (Europe, Russia and Siberia), the Irano-Turanian zone (the steppes of central Asia, Iran and central Anatolia) and the Mediterranean zone. The Black Sea littoral belongs to the first zone, the Anatolian plateau to the second and the south coast of Turkey to the third. Recent work has shown a large percentage of plants which are endemic, that is, confined

9

to Turkey: this is particularly true of the Taurus ranges, where the Irano-Turanian and Mediterranean botanical zones meet.[21] The distribution of trees is also relevant to prehistory. Deciduous forests of oak, ash and beech cover large areas of the Pontic coast including Abkhazia, and extend up the lower slopes of the mountains, with coniferous forest above, the forest line coming just below 6,000 ft. Above this altitude are open alps, or mountain pastures. The slopes of the Caucasus are likewise wealthy in timber. The Urmia basin, however, is now at least relatively treeless, somewhat comparable with that other region surrounding a lake of heavily saline water, the basin of the Salt Lake. To the south, in the Konya Plain, even as early as the neolithic town of Çatal Hüyük houses were being built of mud brick but in imitation of wooden framed buildings: already, therefore, timber may have been becoming scarcer in that part of Anatolia. On the north side of the Pontic range the tree cover is less dense than on the side facing the Black Sea, and the conditions of the plateau are soon reached. Scrub-oak and juniper are among the few trees on the plateau, though nowadays poplars have been planted along many miles of stream banks and irrigation ditches: these are in great demand for roof beams for village houses, and have the advantage of rapid growth. Cedars, black pines and silver firs are common in the Mediterranean zone.

Even more important than the different varieties of timber available for building were the species of edible plants. Of these of course the most important are the cereals, but also the most problematical because of the unsolved questions of their origins. The wild prototype of einkorn wheat apparently occurs in the Marmara region and in most of Turkey and in the Levant, but not in the highlands of eastern Anatolia nor in the Caucasus; the wild prototype of emmer wheat occurs in the Levant and in the Zagros foothills; the wild prototype of barley occurs over most of the highland zone, except in the Araxes valley and northward.[22] Too much emphasis should not, however, be placed on the precise habitats of these wild prototypes today.

Leguminous and orchard plants and trees have been and still are abundant and ubiquitous in the highland zone, except in the semi-arid regions. Citrus fruits occur only in the Aegean and Mediterranean coastal regions; but apples, plums, apricots, peaches and mulberries are common in the eastern highlands, including the districts round Lake Van, where they are hardy enough to survive the severe winters. Today they are also abundantly grown in the Pontic region. Woody plants in general grow much more rapidly in the Near East than in Europe, so that orchard farming must have been more obviously profitable. It goes without saying that for all foods demand and supply would always have been strictly localized.

The vine is a hardy plant at home in much of Anatolia, Trans-Caucasia and the Urmia basin, the grape-bearing type being *vitis vinifera*, thought to have originated around the Caspian Sea. It requires long dry summers, mild or hot, and cool winters; but it will not survive either humid summers, which bring fungi, or very cold winters, with temperatures below about − 18 centigrade. Viticulture may well have begun either near the Caspian or in a region including Colchis, where at two sites dating to the fourth millennium BC the earliest material evidence has been found, in the form of grape-pips, in accumulations associated with stores of chestnuts, hazelnuts and acorns, these too being for food, at the same sites.[23] These accumulations could indeed have been the outcome of food-gathering rather than of harvesting of cultivated vines, but this seems rather unlikely. A modification to the theory that viticulture originated in the Caucasus or in the sheltered parts of eastern Anatolia is that, side by side with the distribution of the wild vine in the same regions, viticulture originated in the Zagros foothills of northern Mesopotamia and in Syria and Palestine, and that thence it followed the cultivation of cereals all over the eastern Mediterranean and Aegean.[24] The later history of the westward spread of viticulture does not decisively favour either postulated homeland, though the balance of archaeological and also linguistic evidence might seem slightly in favour of the traditional theory of an origin in Caucasia.

Natural belts of vegetation have been distinguished for the period *c*. 8,000–*c*. 5,000 BC, in the climatic conditions of post-glacial times and before serious impact by human settlements.[25] The greatest area was covered by deciduous or mixed forest and is classified as 'warm temperate'; predominantly coniferous forest, 'cool temperate', covered the slopes of the Pontic and Caucasian ranges; along the Pontic and Caspian shores and in a narrow piedmont strip of the Fertile Crescent the vegetation was subtropical in its luxuriance; round the estuary of the Araxes was an area of galeria woodland, also subtropical, but not far upstream were semi-desert, shrub and grass; conditions in the Urmia basin were probably similar to those in central Anatolia, with semi-arid grasslands and parklands, or steppes. If correct, this reconstruction of vegetational cover indicates a generally higher rainfall than today, for the disappearance of trees from so much of the highland zone and central Anatolia cannot be ascribed entirely to man. Generalizations on any main region must take into account local peculiarities.

The fauna of the highland zone remains quite varied even today, with leopard and bear in the mountains, as well as wolves, and with boar in surviving swamps. Fish still abound in rivers and fresh water lakes. Partridge, little shot, occur over wide regions. Larger birds include the stork, pelican, and crane, the last being shy and confined to the remoter highlands; there is also a great variety of birds of prey and of vultures. Nevertheless undoubtedly in early post-glacial times the fauna was both more varied and more abundant. The men of Çatal Hüyük hunted aurochs, wild pig, red deer, wild sheep, roe deer, two species of wild ass, fallow deer and more rarely also gazelle, fox, wolf and leopard.[26] This abundance of game was then not universal, even in areas relatively close to the wide grasslands of the Konya Plain in which Çatal Hüyük stood.[27] Jarmo, in the Zagros foothills, has provided a long list of fauna.[28] Until such lists are available for early settlements in the intervening highland zone, it seems premature to try to reconstruct the fauna of Anatolia and Trans-Caucasia as a whole for early post-glacial times.

The domestication of animals is too wide a subject for discussion here.[29] Sheep and goats, whose bones are generally indistinguishable, provided much of the food for the earliest settlements; but they also provided wool and skins for clothing. Textiles were primarily woollen, but wild flax, though not found at Çatal Hüyük, is native to the Zagros region, and was cultivated at an early period.

The great wealth of the highland zone in natural resourses was at times counteracted by varied climatic conditions and difficulties of access. A rather better natural environment, with much greater forest cover, was, however, a general feature. Slow deterioration of the climate has combined with the shortsightedness of man, only at this late hour restrained by governmental control and reafforestation, to turn far wider regions than before into treeless, semi-arid steppe. Much of the highlands has more in common today with central Asia than with either the Russian plains or the Mediterranean littoral: it was not always so.

A brief comment on terminology – for it is quite impossible to omit a number of special terms used by archaeologists, particularly those used to differentiate successive periods of cultural development. In the nineteenth century classification by form, method of manufacture and material of artifacts of stone and metal led to the introduction of the familiar terms 'palaeolithic', 'neolithic', 'bronze age' and 'iron age', to which were in due course added 'mesolithic' and 'chalcolithic'. This last is often referred to as 'eneolithic', as in the Soviet literature. The term 'copper age' has also been used for parts of Anatolia, especially the central plateau. Some of these terms have more meaning than others, 'neolithic' representing in one word a recognizable cultural stage, as does 'palaeolithic' before it. The unsatisfactory character of these terms has long been recognized, and various alternatives have been suggested.[30] Some of these are long-winded, while others imply acceptance of the traditional terms. If it is admitted that many chronological terms have become mere labels of convenience, the reader needs not be troubled too much by such complexities, which are of the archaeologists' own making. To abolish all existing terms without international agreement risks adding to the confusion. A recent scheme based on radio-carbon dates and referring to successive millennia has much to commend it for the earlier periods;[31] but no such arrangement can properly be applied to later periods, when finer subdivisions are required. In Trans-Caucasia the Soviet archaeological terminology has been developed without any regard to terms used in Turkey and Iran, and vice versa. With no possibility of applying the Soviet periods to the whole zone dealt with in this book, and with the manifold regional variations and local cultural provinces, new terms have been applied wherever justifiable by the context, as in the third millennium BC. Elsewhere existing terms have been as much as possible synthesized into a comprehensible whole, though complete consistency cannot be achieved.

CHAPTER 2

THE EARLIEST SETTLEMENTS

Man the hunter was forced to roam far and wide in pursuit of his food supply, and was at the mercy of changes in the habits of his quarry, in turn affected by climatic changes. Man the cultivator and herdsman was equally dependent on an adequate rainfall and vulnerable to the fluctuations of the harvest. The life of the earliest villagers, in Anatolia and elsewhere in the Near East, can never have been easy: the return for hours worked must usually have been meagre. Flocks and herds often perished in seasons of drought. Yet in spite of all these hazards these first villagers had taken that decisive step which has been appropriately given the name of the Neolithic Revolution. It was indeed a revolution, for they had begun the long process of bringing their natural environment under control, instead of being in all essentials controlled by their environment. This perhaps explains the much more rapid cultural advancement than during the long succession of palaeolithic cultures. Once man had begun, however tentatively, to mould his environment to his own ends, the scale of time becomes quite suddenly shortened: advances no longer take thousands of years but only centuries.

Reference to the scale of time in these remote periods has been made possible by the application of nuclear physics to archaeology in the form of radio-carbon (carbon 14) dating.[1] The accuracy of this method has greatly improved over the last twenty years. Most significant is the pattern of relative chronology emerging from the radio-carbon dates.[2]

Physical anthropology, in spite of its severe limitations in the face of paucity and poor preservation of skeletons, shows that the Near East was at first peopled entirely by long-headed races, the so-called Eurafrican and the Proto-Mediterranean. Gradually, during the periods following the Neolithic Revolution, round-headed groups came into the Near East and mingled with the earlier races.[3] Certain common features, however, suggest that during the formative period, when the first essays in agriculture and stock-breeding were being made, the population of much of the Near East shared the same ancestry. Upper Palaeolithic people were

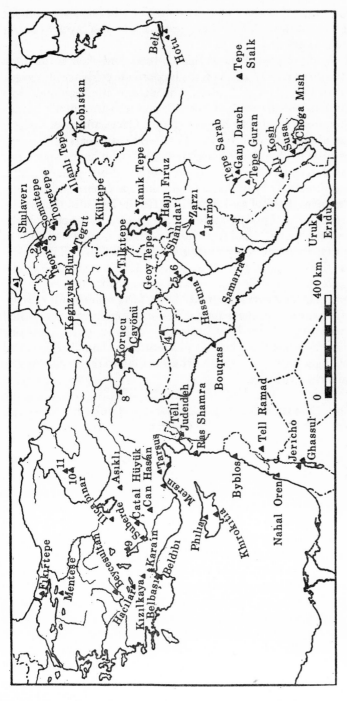

1 *Significant sites of the earliest periods untill late fourth millennium BC.*

Key to numbered sites: 1 Samelé Klde 2 Aruchlo 3 Sadachlo 4 Tell Chagar Bazar 5 Tell Arpachiyah 6 Tepe Gawra 7 Tell as-Sawwan 8 Arslantepe (Malatya) 9 Çukurkent 10 Alaca Hüyük 11 Büyük Güllücek

NOTE: Modern political frontiers are shown by broken line.

of modest stature, five feet eight inches for men and five feet one inch for women being the average. It was their descendants who brought about the Neolithic Revolution.

Knowledge of the Upper Palaeolithic cultures and their immediate successors in the Near East is based on the incomplete evidence at present available from widely scattered areas. Throughout the highland zone from the Anatolian plateau to the Caucasus and into Iran much fundamental investigation remains to be carried out. Caves and rock shelters in the districts above Antalya, on the Mediterranean coast of Turkey, have been investigated by Turkish archaeologists, who have carried out excavations and recorded rock paintings visible above ground: long sequences from Lower Palaeolithic to Neolithic have been found here, the major sites being Beldibi and Kara'in.[4] The lack of obsidian in the Belbaşi industry of the Antalya region suggests little contact with the Anatolian plateau during Mesolithic times, perhaps c. 10,000–9,000 BC. The Antalya sites were probably always relatively isolated. The search for parallels with the paintings at Beldibi must lead to reference to the rock paintings in the far south-east of Turkey, near Siirt, or even further to the great group of rock carvings at Kobistan, forty miles south of Baku and near the Caspian shore: there the earliest drawings have been termed Mesolithic, a dating defended by indicating deposits up against one carved rock face, in which had been found a sequence of flint artifacts and evidence of changes in the rupestrian art according to the height up the rock of an individual drawing.[5]

Even Palaeolithic man moved over considerable distances when the need arose, and when there was a demand for a particular raw material, such as obsidian. This stone, popularly called volcanic glass and varying from opaque black to virtual transparency, is found very widely at early sites in the Near East. Through spectographic analyses of the impurities, or trace elements, the general region of origin can be located; and thus significant evidence for trade and for cultural contacts affecting perhaps the whole life of Neolithic and earlier sites has come to light.[6] One of the main sources was Nemrut Dağ, the extinct volcano at the west end of Lake Van; but innumerable sources still unrecorded assuredly await discovery in eastern Anatolia, even if all those from one region exhibit generally uniform and identifiable characteristics. Obsidian artifacts of Middle Palaeolithic type have been found in the Hakkâri, Van and Kars provinces of eastern Turkey. The earliest stratified occurrence of obsidian in the Near East is in Layer c of the Shanidar cave, dated by radiocarbon samples to 30,000 years before the present day; obsidian also occurs in the Zarzi cave, about eighty miles further south in the Zagros mountains.[7] Even at a time when metal-working had reached an advanced stage at sites of the Halaf culture, during the fifth millennium BC, there was a flourishing trade in obsidian between the Van region and upper Mesopotamia.

In Caucasia climatic conditions were especially severe in Upper Palaeolithic times, but this is not the earliest period represented. Lower Palaeolithic hand-axes of Acheulean type and flakes have been found on the Black Sea coast and inland in the Georgian districts of Imereti and Kartli; and flake tools said to be Mousterian (Middle Palaeolithic) come from the same areas. The Upper Palaeolithic sequence is represented by blades, scrapers, borers and flakes of flint and a few only of obsidian. In the cave of Sakazhia, near Kutaisi, cave bear, cave lion, elk and bison have been distinguished in the bones recovered, indicating a cold climate in keeping with the last glaciation.[8] In the Mingrelian district of Georgia the lower layer of a camping place at Odishi has yielded flint and obsidian microliths of the very end of the Upper Palaeolithic or its immediate sequel. In Armenia, especially round Mount Artin and along the Hrazdan River, artifacts attributable to a succession of Lower, Middle and Upper Palaeolithic cultures comparable with their equivalents in western Europe have been found.[9]

Palaeolithic hunters did not dwell in the damp and murky depths of their caves but on platforms immediately inside or outside the entrance. Open air sites were also inhabited by hunting groups, if only seasonally. In Russia, where natural caves are lacking, there are widespread Upper Palaeolithic shelters dug into the loess, the wind-blown soil deposited in the dry conditions of glacial times.[10] The discovery of similar open sites in Anatolia and elsewhere in the Near East must surely come, though not easily: it is most unlikely that such sites, contemporary with the caves and rock shelters, did not exist.

Evidence for the transition from a pattern of living predominantly in caves and rock shelters to one mainly in open sites must be sought outside Anatolia and Caucasia. This transition was a salient feature of the Neolithic Revolution, though a consequence rather than a cause. The sites investigated in the Zagros region suggest that this phase may be dated approximately 10,000–9,000 BC. Unfortunately most of the Zagros sites seem to provide not so much a continuous sequence as isolated, chronologically overlapping but widely disparate cultures belonging to the formative centuries of the Neolithic Revolution and the preceding phases.[11] Of comparable significance for the transition from food collection to food production is the Natufian culture of Palestine, from whose earliest phase, the Lower Natufian, derived the precocious community of Pre-Pottery Neolithic A Jericho.[12]

The development of cultivation of cereals and other food plants and the domestication of certain animal species need have required no more than a few centuries, though clearly these were not achieved overnight.

Moreover, much of the Upper Palaeolithic way of life persisted on the Anatolian plateau and elsewhere in the Near East. It is to Anatolia that the discussion must next turn, before further consideration of the highlands of eastern Turkey and Caucasia.

For the understanding of the achievements of Neolithic man the relatively meagre remains of relevant date in eastern Turkey, Trans-Caucasia and north-west Iran provide inadequate evidence. The site of greatest interest, although of limited relevance, owing to its situation on the Anatolian plateau, is Çatal Hüyük. Study of its inhabitants as hunters, farmers, builders, artists, craftsmen and inventors, together with some attempt to understand their religion, can assist comprehension of contemporary settlements in widely separated regions. Çatal Hüyük was not the earliest settlement on the Anatolian plateau: the site of Suberde by Lake Suğla, some sixty miles west-south-west of Çatal Hüyük, and the unexcavated Aşikli Hüyük near the Salt Lake are both probably slightly older; so too is the aceramic site of Hacilar, near Lake Burdur, showing a far westward extension of early settled communities not later than c. 7,000 BC.[13] Though there was much typical of its time, probably more than the available evidence can prove, the uniqueness of Çatal Hüyük is incontestable.[14]

Hunting was no mere antiquated survival at Çatal Hüyük, as the numerous large obsidian lanceheads, the most distinctive type in the chipped stone industry, indicate. There are also many arrowheads, of two sizes, possibly used with a long and a short bow. Very large scrapers suggest the skinning of animals and the cleaning of hides. Whatever the meaning of many of the wall paintings which are the most arresting element in the achievements of this community, some undoubtedly depict hunting and the ritual and magic closely associated with it in the religion of this people. Such must be the explanation of the great red bull covering most of the north wall of one shrine in Level III and surrounded by puny little men, none of whom is shown attacking it: the extraordinary scenes of baiting found on the walls of a shrine in Level v, with men pulling at the animals' tongues, must likewise be seen in this context. The association of the leopard, much hunted, with the female figure called by the excavator, on the basis of much later analogies, the Mistress of Animals may indeed symbolize the submission of wild creatures to the advancing forces of agriculture and stock-breeding.

The town beside the Çarşamba River, thirty-two acres in extent, could never have been founded with the support of hunting alone. The palaeo-botanical evidence is rather clearer than that for the domestication of animals. By the time of Çatal Hüyük vi at least fourteen food plants were being cultivated.[15] Some plants were used for their oil; fruit and nut seeds were probably brought from the Taurus foothills. The absence of direct proof of digging or turning the soil, in the form of picks and hoes, has little significance, for such implements may well have been made of wood. Numerous querns, rubbing stones, pestles and mortars provide typical indications of agriculture. The evidence as a whole suggests that the women of Çatal Hüyük played a very great role in farming, while hunting was left entirely to the men, who may also have had sole responsibility for the flocks and herds. The lack of paintings depicting agricultural scenes must be set against the prominence of the female in the reliefs and figurines.

The town of Çatal Hüyük exhibits a certain uniformity, not only in the plan of the buildings but also in building materials and methods; but it would be anachronistic to refer to town planning at this time. Tradition and force of habit, not centralized authority, must have been the factors resulting in architectural continuity at Çatal Hüyük. An artist's vision of the whole town may perhaps be discernible in the wall painting in which either the units making up the town or the individual buildings forming one unit are shown against a background of a volcano in eruption. The problems of construction and repair of contiguous buildings, of necessity terraced up the sides of the large mound, dictated some of the solutions. Perhaps the most distinctive feature is the absence of doorways at ground level into the individual houses and shrines, which had much in common. Access was by way of the roof and down a wooden ladder set against the wall, a means of entry with modern parallels in widely separated parts of the world, wherever security or climate make this appropriate. Architectural construction at Çatal Hüyük was not static and unchanging, but reflected a growing confidence in the use of mud brick and a correspondingly diminished reliance on timber: before Level v the buildings were of wood construction, the frame having only a flimsy filling of mud bricks; not until Level ii was the wooden frame abandoned, with engaged brick piers replacing the vertical posts. Decorative as well as structural innovations and repairs often resulted in numerous layers of paint, whether on a flat mural or over a plastered relief: the scheme of the decoration might change or remain much the same. In Level vii at Çatal Hüyük there were up to 120 layers of plaster made from the white earth used for this purpose, and for floors and ceilings as well as walls; in Level vi b there were up to one hundred layers. The number of layers of plaster in buildings of the same level tends to be approximately the same. All this evidence serves to stress the fallacy of the suggestion that mud brick buildings, properly maintained, cannot last more than a few years. It is not unreasonable to suggest that at Çatal Hüyük walls were replastered annually, thus providing evidence of the minimum duration of each level.

For paints the artists used an assortment of minerals, including iron oxides, copper ores, mercury oxide, manganese and galena. Different shades of red are the predominant colours, obtained from iron ore, cinnabar and perhaps also haematite. The plaster reliefs cannot have presented many technical problems, though different techniques were used for different subjects. Animal bones and horns were much used for attachments to fix the reliefs more firmly to the walls. Not only mural paintings but also reliefs in plaster, painted or plain, sculpture in stone and modelling in clay gave opportunities for the display of the talents of this precocious community. Although a painted black bull occurs as early as Level ix, relief decoration is the special hallmark of the earlier shrines, in one of which were found only reliefs, with no paintings. Reliefs may perhaps be associated with clay statuettes, since both are the product of modelling, of manipulating a soft material into the shape required. After Level v reliefs disappear, no longer fashionable at Çatal Hüyük; at about the same time clay supplanted stone as the most popular material for statuettes. Stone-carving had at first been the usual method of fashioning such figurines, very probably cult-statues and often heirlooms from earlier shrines, carefully preserved when the time to destroy and rebuild arrived, and when the fixed images on the walls were deliberately defaced. These contrast with relatively crude human and animal figurines of clay, many found in pits outside the shrines. The evidence for continuity of cult is reinforced by traces of wear and repairs on some stone statuettes. Towards the end of the history of Çatal Hüyük, in Level ii, one shrine yielded nine statuettes, eight being of clay. These are in some respects comparable with the rather later figurines from Hacilar vi, a fact suggesting that by this time (c. 5,600 BC) the artistic traditions of Çatal Hüyük, at least in sculpture in the round, had spread over a wide zone of the Anatolian plateau.[16] This was the artistic form most likely to be diffused, simply because the statuettes were so easily portable. The wall paintings and reliefs can hardly have been seen by so many outsiders, who may have been debarred from entering the shrines.

Much of the achievement of the artists of Çatal Hüyük can be appraised in relation to technical precocity and standard of craftsmanship in a number of materials. Wood, bone, textiles and even metals received their attention. Clay was used for pottery, though on a limited scale and for a rather restricted and conservative range of forms. Vessels for cooking, eating, drinking and storage were in later periods normally of pottery; but here other materials were equally or more popular, especially wood and basketry. Though the beginnings of pottery in Anatolia could lie in the Konya Plain, the quantity at Çatal Hüyük is too small for any firm conclusions: it has been excavated in a small sounding right down to Level xii, where straw-tempered and cream burnished wares were recovered. The forms are primitive, the commonest being the hole mouth jar, but the quality is such as hardly to suggest the first faltering work of the earliest potters. Çatal Hüyük can be compared with those other settlements elsewhere in the Near East, such as Jericho, which long flourished without need of pottery.[17]

Wood was used for many purposes at Çatal Hüyük, among others as an alternative medium for vessels, proof of which is apparent from a truly remarkable series of vessels and boxes from Levels VI B and VI A, including dishes 50 cm long perhaps for meat, 'egg-cups', round bowls and dishes and oval bowls with ledge handles. Fire is the ally of the excavator, and these vessels, made without aid of nails or glue, were preserved on house floors and in burials through carbonization. Fir and perhaps other soft woods were roughed and gouged out with obsidian scrapers and other tools, much of the abundant obsidian industry at Çatal Hüyük being in all probability devoted to this craft. In making vessels emery and sand must have been used in the final process of smoothing the surface. A modern parallel is the type of handled jar termed in Turkish *cam bardak*, or 'pine glass', a deep, narrow-necked jar carved out of a section of tree-trunk: to keep these watertight and to prevent splitting they have to be kept full of liquid. Harder woods, oak and juniper, were used in building; timbers were squared, greenstone axes, adzes and chisels being employed. This skill seems not to have been surpassed in Anatolia, at least in surviving material, until the eighth century BC, when the Phrygians made the elaborately ornate furniture found in the tumuli at Gordion.[18]

Chipping, grinding, polishing and drilling were techniques all used by the artisans of Çatal Hüyük in the production of tools, weapons, vessels, statuettes and ornaments of stone. Numerous types of stone were used, save only the hard igneous rocks such as granite. Obsidian mirrors found in burials were set in lime plaster and polished by an unknown technique. The perforation of large objects like maceheads presented no difficulty; but it was another matter with the drilling of some of the stone beads, including those of obsidian, which have perforations too fine for a modern steel needle. It is quite uncertain how this was achieved: the use of copper drills seems doubtful.

The discovery of both copper and lead at Çatal Hüyük, from Level IX upwards, is indeed of the first importance for the history of technology, all the more so from the analysis of what seemed a lump of copper from Level VI as in fact copper slag. The ability to smelt ores to remove their natural impurities implies the mastery of metallurgy as early as the seventh millennium BC, a possibility which cannot be indisputably proved without some additional evidence. The lead at Çatal Hüyük, however, suggests smelting as early as Level IX, since in Anatolia it is found only in the form of the ore galena, which cannot be used in its natural state. The absence of metal implements at Çatal Hüyük may be fortuitous, in the light of the finding of a copper awl, 4 cm long, at Suberde.[19]

Such materials as bone, used for a variety of articles, and rushes, coiled and tied together to make baskets, presented no technical difficulties. A developed bone industry was an almost universal feature at Neolithic sites throughout the Near East. Baskets were all the more important before pottery had come into general use. Mats and woven rush carpets were found in many buildings. Belt-hooks and fasteners, spatulae and miniature vessels, these last made also of antler, characterize the bone industry.

Weaving of rush mats and coiling of baskets were simple processes compared with the weaving of textiles, of which Çatal Hüyük affords abundant evidence, direct and indirect. The same good chance which, through fire, preserved the wooden vessels has brought about the survival in carbonized state of woven cloth. Some fragments of this were of amazingly fine two-ply yarn, spun from two very fine threads of wool. These are far the oldest known textiles, at least a millennium older than the linen from the Fayum villages in Egypt.[20] The balance of evidence seems strongly in favour of wool rather than linen as the material, wool being abundant, whereas there is a complete absence of flax seeds among the many seeds found in the excavations. As for indirect evidence, the disappearance of wall paintings may well have been the outcome of a change in fashion to the use of textile hangings as mural decoration, towards the very end of the history of Çatal Hüyük. Most probably the wall paintings preceded and inspired the textiles, not vice versa; but by the Early Chalcolithic period at Hacilar the fine painted pottery so characteristic of that site was surely imitating textile patterns, not inspiring them.[21] Some of the paintings of Çatal Hüyük, however, certainly betray direct imitations of textiles, even the stitching along the borders sometimes being depicted. A suggestion that the stamp-seals found here could have been used for printing patterns on textiles is attractive but surely anachronistic.

Life and death, birth and burial, seem to be the dominant themes of the religion of this remarkable Neolithic community, on whose precise theological beliefs lengthy speculation must be tempting but idle. The timespan from the seventh millennium BC until classical times is too great for any direct comparisons to be treated without caution, even though the links between the religion of Anatolia in the Bronze Age and in Hellenistic and Roman times are beyond dispute. Continuity of population from the Early Neolithic period till the Early Bronze Age cannot, in the nature of available evidence, be proved, but may well have been significant. The weird imagery of so many of the rooms led Mellaart from the first to describe them as shrines and to distinguish them from mere houses. The evidence supports this distinction. The shrines are marked out by a combination of a number of features, seldom found at all in the houses, comprising wall paintings, reliefs, cattle horns set into benches, rows of bull's heads, cult statuettes in the principal room, ochre burials, human skulls on platforms and perhaps also obsidian mirrors and bone belt-fasteners. The absence of animal sacrifices within these rooms is hardly remarkable, given the lack of any access from the roof except by ladder.

It must remain largely an enigma what exactly happened inside the shrines, whether, for example, the worshippers were entirely of a priestly caste or whether they include the laity. The excavations have provided indications of how the shrines, once built, were subsequently maintained and embellished. Hands are a feature of the wall paintings frequently recurring in various forms: normally they are of adults but sometimes of children, more often the right hand than the left. To this day the hand is widespread as an amulet to ward off the evil eye, and red-painted hands even occur in the modern Küçükköy, the village close to Çatal Hüyük, on either side of some doorways. This is a remarkable coincidence, copying of the Early Neolithic paintings being ruled out by the existence of these modern parallels before the excavations began in 1961. Inside the shrines hands wet with paint could be laid on sacred reliefs of animal heads or of a goddess, presumably to draw strength therefrom. Where many hands occur together the idea of 'all hands' may indeed be intended, and this is sometimes shown in association with a net pattern, probably depicting a hunting net or snare and suggesting the purpose of the muster. Within the sacred walls many births may have taken place; and the dying may perhaps have been brought there. After each new set of burials, as Mellaart suggests perhaps restricted to certain seasons of the year, the platforms would have had to be rebuilt. Spring and autumn are two seasons for refurbishing of houses in Anatolia today. In Çatal Hüyük, in those days of fleeting youth, disease and early death, the afterlife and provisions for it figured no less prominently in the popular mind than in other communities in the prehistoric Near East.

The care taken with burials is exemplified by one which had the brain removed from the cranium and a ball of cloth inserted in its place. Most lie in the contracted position on the left side. Individual burials are rare, and frequently successive generations seem to have shared a common grave beneath the platform of the shrine or house, with consequent disturbance of the skeletons and grave-goods of the earlier burials. Paintings which cast light on events between death and final burial give additional evidence on funerary customs: in one shrine scenes of vultures attacking headless corpses can have but one interpretation, that the bones had first to be stripped of all flesh by these scavengers. These were indeed vultures, not priests or other persons dressed as such.[22] But the argument for a priestly caste as inhabitants of the quarter uncovered by the excavations seems to be reinforced by the greater wealth of grave-goods with burials in the shrines compared with those in the houses. Red ochre was used to paint either the skull only or the whole skeleton of some burials, though only a small percentage of the total of almost five hundred excavated. Ochre burials give a link both with the Upper Palaeolithic and with later cultures elsewhere in the Near East.[23] Among these was one with the skull painted in red ochre and two large sliced cowrie shells, of a type found in the Red Sea, dropped from the eye sockets. Long-distance trade is thus suggested, and there is a clear parallel with Pre-Pottery Neolithic B Jericho, with its famous plastered skulls; similar to these are red-plastered skulls with cowrie-shell eyes found in Level II at Tell Ramad in southern Syria.[24] Trade is also indicated by beads, including those of dentalium shell from the Mediterranean: none of the materials used is to be found near Çatal Hüyük, and many come from afar. Grave-goods naturally constituted the principal source of small finds, the women having an assortment of jewellery and cosmetic equipment, including obsidian mirrors; the men were given hunting weapons, particularly a flint dagger, and belts with fasteners of polished bone.

The people of Çatal Hüyük lived and died amid scenes bearing little relation to the humdrum activities of daily life, their religion finding expression through strange devices of bull and ram, dancing hunter and solid symbol of maternity. The incomprehensible character of many of the paintings, reliefs and statuettes must not be overlooked in any over-zealous espousal of one or other theory attempting to explain their significance in terms familiar to the anthropologist or to the student of comparative religion. These works of art, the paintings especially posing unprecedented problems of conservation, naturally raise more questions than they answer.

Seeing through a glass darkly is surely better than not seeing at all, a restriction forced on the student of the continuity, changes and diffusion of material cultures on the Anatolian plateau outside Çatal Hüyük. Only two excavated sites, Hacilar and Can Hasan, cast strong light on the early village economy of Anatolia, and that almost entirely on periods later than Çatal Hüyük. Artistic and technical achievements comparable with those of the town in the Konya Plain may well have flourished in several unknown localities; but this is necessarily conjecture.

The obsidian industry, a deciding factor in the choice of Çatal Hüyük for excavation, gives the clearest link between that site and the smaller, less advanced but longer known site of Mersin, in the Cilician plain. Here

a radio-carbon sample from close to the base of the mound gave a date of
c. 6,000 BC: with adjustment to the half-life of 5,730 BC any discrepancy is
reduced.[25] Mersin came within the limits of a Syro-Cicilian cultural
province providing the link between the cultures of the Levant and those
of the Konya Plain and remoter regions of the Anatolian plateau.[26] The
distribution of the dark-faced burnished pottery distinctive of this province
is very wide, extending as far east as the Mosul region of the Tigris valley,
at Tell Hassuna, where in Level ia three successive layers of a camping
site were uncovered. This occupation was of a temporary character and
distinguished from the following levels by the absence of painted pottery.[27]
This illustrates the ease of movement across the grasslands of the Fertile
Crescent, a phenomenon repeated in later periods. Thus there may
theoretically have been contact between the Anatolian plateau and the
Zagros highlands and Urmia region far to the east, via the Cilician plain,
north Syria and upper Mesopotamia. No such contact is apparent across
the highlands of eastern Turkey, though the evidence is too meagre for
any sound conclusions. Hassuna ia in any case falls in the sixth millennium BC: for any much earlier connections the sites of Bouqras, on the
Euphrates near the confluence of the Khabur, and Çayönü, near
Diyarbakir, may perhaps prove significant.[28]

Early Neolithic sites in the Konya Plain and eastwards as far as the
area of Kayseri have yielded surface finds making them broadly comparable with Çatal Hüyük, even though local or regional peculiarities
are revealed at Aşikli Hüyük. To the west of the Konya Plain two sites
on the shores of Lake Beyşehir, Çukurkent and Alan Hüyük, and
Kizilkaya, a mound north of Antalya on the road over the Taurus to
Burdur, are the most important of a number of settlements attributable
broadly to the Early Neolithic period, the seventh and early sixth
millennia BC.[29]

The Late Neolithic period in Anatolia seems to have been relatively
brief, at Hacilar ending c. 5,600 BC. Evidence for this stage is most firmly
based on the stratified material from Mersin XXVI-XXV and Hacilar
IX-VI. The very term 'Late Neolithic' is little more than a useful label
for a phase in which the two marked advances on the previous period
were an improvement in the pottery and a greater talent in modelling
clay figurines, apparent almost exclusively at Hacilar.

The people of Hacilar relied less on hunting than their predecessors to
the east at Çatal Hüyük. Though only a village, Hacilar displays significant architectural advances in Level VI in the construction and layout of
houses since the time of Çatal Hüyük. Buildings were on a larger scale,
wide doorways from the courtyards replacing the rooftop access of the
Çatal Hüyük houses and shrines. The thickness of the walls at Hacilar,
together with evidence in one house of a staircase with balustrade, indicate

an upper storey. In the same district of Burdur today two-storeyed houses have a roofed verandah facing south and small rooms opening off it; the upper rooms would scarcely have been used in winter. The settlement of Hacilar VI, larger than that of Hacilar II in the Early Chalcolithic period and perhaps fortified, can fairly be described as the most prosperous phase in the history of the site.

It is for its clay statuettes that Hacilar VI is best known, a remarkable collection being found in three houses next to one another, thirty-five of a much larger total being restorable. These were modelled round a core, and were finished with a fine red or cream slipped and burnished surface. The absence of heads is the result of their being made as a separate piece formed with a peg for insertion into the body. Eyes and hair were incised, but the mouth was never shown. The fact that some statuettes remained unbaked shows that they were the work of local artists. As the excavator says, the goddess is found standing, seated, kneeling, squatting, reclining and enthroned. His theory that two ethnic groups are represented among the statuettes is supported by provisional conclusions on the physical anthropology of the inhabitants of Hacilar, in which two dolichocephalic races have been distinguished, the Proto-Mediterranean stock so widespread as the basic ethnic stratum of the earliest settlements in the Near East and a sturdier Eurafrican race. The brachycephalic element present at Çatal Hüyük seems lacking at Hacilar, suggesting that those newcomers in the preceding period to the Konya Plain had even by the Late Neolithic period not penetrated that far west. The differences among the statuettes may, however, reflect different ages and ranks rather than distinct races. The statuettes from Hacilar of the Mistress of Animals, the finest of which shows the goddess seated on a leopard and holding a leopard cub in her arms, reveal an improvement in modelling on the similar statuettes from Çatal Hüyük; but more significant is their indication of religious continuity from the earlier and larger site to the later village 150 miles to the west. There was to be no other urban community, able to support professional artists and craftsmen, in Anatolia for many centuries after the abandonment of Çatal Hüyük.

Mersin XXVI-XXV is by contrast obscure and of minor interest except as a link in the long sequence of levels giving that site its importance. The obsidian industry of the Lower Neolithic levels continued to decline and the ground stone industry to develop, indicating the general replacement of food gathering by food production as the mainstay of the economy.

The common denominator of all cultures ascribed to the Early Chalcolithic period in different parts of the Near East is the appearance and development of painted pottery. Hacilar most clearly shows this phenomenon as a local achievement, gradually emerging to maturity. At Mersin the pattern is complicated by the mingling of influences from north Syria and further east with those from the Konya Plain, in an area at no period noted for its cultural originality but rather as a meeting place for elements from beyond the Cilician plain. Present evidence shows fairly clearly that there was an Early Chalcolithic culture, as such based on a village economy, with a broadly comparable style of painted pottery extending from upper Mesopotamia westwards across the Euphrates to the Amuq Plain (Phase B) and to Mersin, with offshoots southwards into Syria and Palestine. This culture was first recognized at Tell Hassuna, where the primitive and temporary camping sites of Level ia were overlaid by a succession of building levels (ib-vi) of a village with houses of rectangular plan and pottery of distinctive decoration.

In the Konya Plain there is a lacuna in the known archaeological record immediately following the desertion of Çatal Hüyük East, the Early Neolithic town. The unexcavated deeper levels of the adjoining mound of Çatal Hüyük West will eventually yield the evidence to fill this gap. Two trial trenches at Çatal Hüyük West have revealed two successive styles of painted pottery, described as Early Chalcolithic i (Çatal Hüyük West) ware and Early Chalcolithic ii (Can Hasan 2b) ware respectively.[30] These two phases correspond to Mersin xxiv-xxii and xxi-xx. At Çatal Hüyük West, however, there was a general cultural continuity apart from this ceramic change.

Fifty miles to the south-east lies the site of Can Hasan, near Karaman, where excavations have been in progress since 1961.[31] Figurines and other works of art suggest survival of some of the skills manifest at Çatal Hüyük, though with stylistic changes. Level 3 at Can Hasan, with its red-on-brown ware, can be equated chronologically with Çatal Hüyük West and with the earlier part of the time-span of Hacilar i. The pottery characteristic of Can Hasan 2b, the ensuing period, is red-on-cream ware, shown by radio-carbon dates averaging c. 5,000 BC to be contemporary with the later phases of Hacilar i. Architectural similarities to that site are discernible; and there are wall paintings with purely geometric patterns, resembling the meander motif and thus comparable with some of the painted pottery from the same level. Gone altogether and for good are the representational themes of the Çatal Hüyük wall paintings. The carving of personal ornaments of stone was well developed; but more important is the evidence for advances in metal-working, attested by a copper macehead and bracelet from Can Hasan 2b.

Hacilar represents a separate and distinctive Early Chalcolithic cultural province, not directly related to that of the Konya Plain. The boundary between these two provinces, probably running through the Anatolian lake district, is not yet known. In terms of the sequence in the Konya

Plain, Hacilar v-ii may be more or less equated with Early Chalcolithic i and Hacilar i with Early Chalcolithic ii, together covering the centuries *c.* 5,600–5,000 BC. The village of Hacilar had a chequered history, punctuated by several destructions by fire, until a rebuilding on largely new lines in Hacilar i. The painted pottery is the most distinctive feature of Hacilar, without which it would never have attracted the excavator's attention.[32] Here is a style of ceramic painting unrivalled anywhere in the ancient Near East for its bold patterns and fine finish: the Halaf pottery may be technically its equal, but hardly aesthetically. Wide bowls in Hacilar v-iii were largely succeeded in Hacilar ii by the most typical form, an oval cup with pinched in mouth. A taste for oval vessels, with some sub-rectangular shapes, was a feature of the pottery of Hacilar throughout the Early Chalcolithic period. In Hacilar v-iv decoration was mainly geometric; in contrast that of Hacilar iii-ii was altogether bolder and more curvilinear. This was the produce of professional potters, as indicated by the discovery in the centre of the village of Hacilar iia of three adjacent buildings evidently serving as potters' workshops, with stocks of cups, bowls and jars.

In Hacilar i came a change in the pottery, with larger vessels and less imaginative decoration, patterns being more strictly linear and largely derived from basketry. The appearance of white paint for decoration on a dark surface is an innovation pointing forward to a tradition destined to have a very long life in western Anatolia and to appear elsewhere, as in Mersin xiia. The people of Hacilar i may have included some newcomers, but they had probably not come from very far away, were not too distantly related to the earlier inhabitants and intermingled with them. In their turn they were to be overwhelmed by a disaster at once final and wide-spread, the downfall of the Early Chalcolithic cultures of which Hacilar had been the brightest jewel.

On the Anatolian plateau and eastward to the Caucasus and Lake Urmia the fifth and fourth millennia BC may fairly be termed a dark age, only partially known but certainly marked by a decline in the general level of material culture in Anatolia. Such a decline is not, however, apparent in the regions to the east, for in Trans-Caucasia and the Urmia basin the available evidence suggests no early flowering comparable with that exemplified by Çatal Hüyük, Hacilar and Can Hasan, but rather a steady if unspectacular progression from the relatively few known settlements dating back into the sixth millennium BC. Throughout all these regions there ensued, from the second half of the fourth millennium BC, a cultural advance marking an awakening in the east and a revival in the west.

The inadequate and unbalanced nature of the archaeological record may well give the cultures of the Late Chalcolithic period in Anatolia, the term used for this long time-span, the appearance of being more backward than they really were. Reliance on pottery for the interpretation of these cultures and of their interrelations is inevitably very heavy indeed. Metal must have been far more plentiful than finds might suggest, for it was hoarded and melted down for re-use. There are many sites of Late Chalcolithic date in parts of southern and western Anatolia, few known in central and none in northern Anatolia. But of these sites few have been excavated, and fewer still have provided an uninterrupted, stratified sequence of building levels. Indeed only Mersin with its neighbour Tarsus and Beycesultan, in the upper Meander valley in south-western Anatolia, have so far yielded such a long sequence throughout the whole period.

Can Hasan may to some degree be taken as the type site in the Konya Plain, with the Early Chalcolithic II of Level 2b being followed by the Middle Chalcolithic of Level 2a and of the subsequent phase during which this site was deserted: Can Hasan 2a comprised five layers and ended c. 4,500 BC or slightly later. Then ensued the Late Chalcolithic culture, distinguished by its pottery, heavy and dark in colour, found over most of the Konya Plain: its introduction marks the real break with the traditions of the earlier periods. Fresh sites were chosen by the newcomers; and present evidence suggests that these sites were abandoned in their turn at the end of this period, dated at Can Hasan, where Level I has six building levels, to c. 4,000–3,600 BC. A northern homeland for this culture and likewise for the Late Chalcolithic of south-western Anatolia seems probable. White-painted bowls and triangular arrowheads rather like those from the Konya Plain occur at Yazir, an excavated site near Sivrihisar, in the bend of the upper Sakarya (Sangarius) River.[33]

Beycesultan is the principal site of the south-west Anatolian Late Chalcolithic cultural province. A long succession of twenty-one levels with a depth of deposit of ten metres has made this the best documented site on the whole Anatolian plateau for this long dark age of retrogression and subsequent resistance to change. A time-span of c. 4,750–3,200 BC has been suggested for this sequence, divided into four phases (Late Chalcolithic 1–4) by ceramic changes, though with more continuity than innovations throughout these many centuries.[34] Metal-working is well attested, especially by a hoard of copper implements from Beycesultan XXXIV, including awls, needles, a chisel and a fragment of a dagger blade, the earliest known anywhere.[35] There is no reason to doubt the existence of a flourishing metal-working craft in Anatolia in the fifth millennium BC and thereafter, especially in the light of the earlier evidence from Çatal Hüyük; but hammering rather than casting remained the usual technique.

The impression conveyed by the known evidence from two sites in central Anatolia is that the region within the great bend of the Halys was then inhabited by people of little artistic or technical skill, content to live as villagers dependent on farming and stock-breeding. At Büyük Güllücek, in the forests near Alaca, was a tiny hamlet of three or four houses, a short-lived settlement of two levels, certainly of the later fourth millennium BC. Six levels including this period have been distinguished at Alaca Hüyük.[36] The burials at these two sites were intramural, in accord with the tradition which in the third millennium BC continued to mark off this region from the southern and western parts of the Anatolian plateau. If burial customs are a guide to ethnic affinities, it is just possible that already in the fourth millennium BC in central Anatolia the population was of similar stock to that of the Early Bronze Age. They would thus have been Hattians, who inhabited these lands till the arrival of the Hittites from *c*. 2,000 BC, and thereafter survived as the predominant element. Extramural burials suggest a different origin for the more advanced people of Late Chalcolithic Beycesultan and surrounding areas.

In eastern Anatolia, including districts within the Turkish administrative provinces of Malatya and Sivas, the sequence of prehistoric cultures differs markedly from that obtaining in regions west of the upper Euphrates. Present evidence for any period before the third millennium BC is very patchy and still largely limited to surface finds. An aceramic neolithic site in the Elazığ region, one of many sites threatened by the construction of the Keban dam, suggests the existence of settled communities there not later than *c*. 6,000 BC. This region was particularly open to influences from Syria and upper Mesopotamia, and thus cannot be considered typical of eastern Anatolia as a whole in the earliest periods. But southern influences should not be exaggerated, even though a few clear hints of contacts with the Hassuna and Halaf traditions of painted pottery were found in the writer's survey carried out in 1956 and now rendered largely obsolete by the intensive work of the teams collaborating in the rescue operations in the basin of the Keban dam. The general pattern of settlement, with periods of very thin population, had, however, been made apparent by this earlier survey.[37] When the excavations at Arslantepe (Malatya) are completed, it may be possible to add to the scanty data now available for the period *c*. 5,500–*c*. 3,000 BC in the fertile region of Malatya, just west of the upper Euphrates. Evidence for this period from the Keban dam basin is already forthcoming from Pulur and Korucutepe, the latter having several levels with mud-brick houses, though the precise area of this settlement in the fourth millennium BC is not yet certain. The pottery is buff to grey burnished, with straight rims and often decorated with applied finger-impressed rope ornament. Obsidian arrowheads are narrow, unlike the wide type found at this site in the levels of the third millennium BC. The crops cultivated included emmer wheat and six-row barley. A radio-carbon date of *c.* 3,000 BC has been obtained for the great burning which marks the violent end of this cultural period and almost certainly also the arrival of newcomers, probably from the north-east. Korucutepe stands out among the excavated sites of the Keban dam basin: comparable results are awaited elsewhere.[38]

Further to the east Tilkitepe, a very small mound close to Van, has produced a sequence of three main levels of which the earliest, Tilkitepe III, yielded Halaf pottery, painted and burnished, of the very finest quality. This was associated with evidence of the obsidian trade, including some of the biggest cores found anywhere.[39] The exports of obsidian to northern Mesopotamia have been long known from many early village sites, including Tell Arpachiyah. Exactly where this obsidian was obtained cannot be said with precision, although Nemrut Dağ, the extinct volcano at the west end of Lake Van, has a good claim to have been the source of the Tilkitepe material, unless any closer source as yet unknown was exploited. The obsidian from the Van region is often visibly distinguishable by its flecks of brown; and now spectographic analyses have brought proof of the general region of origin of many occurrences of obsidian in the Near East.[40] With the development of metallurgy, first clearly apparent in the Halaf culture, the Mesopotamian communities had less need of obsidian. This will explain why the penetration of the region of Lake Van from northern Mesopotamia at a period not later than *c.* 5,000 BC was not followed by continuing contact and influence from the southern plains. The fifth and fourth millennia BC in these remote highlands remain impenetrably obscure; but too little field work has been carried out to make any conclusion that these regions were devoid of settled population at all valid. Certainly at Karaz, close to Erzurum, there seems to have been occupation dating back into the fourth millennium BC, in an area naturally open to influences from Trans-Caucasia.[41]

The Urmia region and Trans-Caucasia, especially the valleys of the Araxes and the Kura, can be considered as one great zone sharing certain features in their general cultural development from the sixth till the fourth millennium BC, though with local differences. Although the Zagros range forms as much of a natural barrier as the Taurus and Anti-Taurus and their eastward continuation south of Lake Van, the tide of cultural influences from the Mesopotamian plain ran from the first far more strongly up on to the plateau of Iran than into Anatolia, either east or west of the upper Euphrates. This was partly the result of geographical proximity; but equally important was the fact that in the Zagros region, extending along both sides of the mountain divide, there originated one of the separate centres of the Neolithic Revolution. [42] This was not entirely unconnected with the other centres in the Levant and in southern Anatolia; but, whereas those two regions were in many respects one, the cultures which developed in the Zagros region had a character essentially their own, only later subordinated to successive Mesopotamian influences. Not until the late sixth millennium BC, at the earliest, did the indigenous cultures begin to be seriously affected by these external elements: before then the cultural influence had rather flowed from the highlands down into the Mesopotamian plain. Even thereafter the local cultures were strong enough to adapt to their own uses rather than slavishly to imitate Halaf, Ubaid and later Mesopotamian cultures.

The final Upper Palaeolithic (or Mesolithic) period and the subsequent Proto-Neolithic period in the Zagros region have been alluded to above in connection with the transition from a pattern of living mainly in caves and rock shelters to the occupation, seasonally or permanently, of open-air sites. While Jarmo and the Kermanshah district both lie beyond the geographical scope of this book, it is in these areas that any understanding of the earliest settlements around Lake Urmia must be sought.

The expedition of the University Museum of Philadelphia has for some years been endeavouring to reconstruct the pattern of life in the Solduz plain immediately south of Lake Urmia, through excavations at the great mound of Hasanlu and at smaller sites of different periods in the same plain. [43] In this valley lying athwart an important route up from northern Mesopotamia, later Assyria, the number of ancient mounds in the Solduz plain was found to equal the number of modern villages therein, affording a striking example of continuity in pattern of settlement in an area where dry farming was and still is possible. Hasanlu itself is much too large and high a mound for the occupation levels of the fourth and fifth millennia BC, let alone any even earlier levels that may lie hidden, to be accessible. Such occupation has, however, been found at the mound of Hajji Firuz, a site of modest area, where excavations have revealed a succession of six levels. A radio-carbon date of $5,152 \pm 85$ BC for the second level from the top (Hajji Firuz v) and a date of $5,537 \pm 89$ BC for an earlier level are consistent with the affinities of the pottery of Hajji Firuz, soft-baked and with chevron and other simple linear patterns in red paint, with what may be broadly termed the Hassuna tradition; but at the same time Hajji Firuz shows links with Tepe Sarab, near Kermanshah, for which radio-carbon dates indicate a time-span within the upper and lower limits of $c.$ 6,250–$c.$ 5,850 BC. Tepe Sarab itself is in many respects closely comparable with Jarmo, and the excavator of both sites hesitates to say which is the earlier.[44] The importance, or at least the chronological priority, of both sites has now been overshadowed by the results obtained from the excavations at another site in the district of Kermanshah, Ganj Dareh Tepe.[45] A radio-carbon date of 8,450 ±150 BC has been obtained from the bottom metre of this seven-metre high mound, where there are occupation layers probably of temporary encampments, since there is no trace of permanent buildings; then these layers were succeeded by four or five levels with mud brick architecture, the lowermost of these levels being preserved by the effects of a fierce burning, some of the buildings being constructed of large plano-convex bricks faced with thick mud plaster. A very interesting feature of this burnt village is the occurrence of pottery of very primitive type, heavily tempered with straw and evidently fired only during the burning of the settlement, originally being merely sun-dried. Such evidence suggests the very beginnings of this craft in the Kermanshah district, more clearly than at almost any other site in the Near East, and dating back to the eighth millennium BC. Some walls in the next two levels were faced with white plaster. In the upper part of the mound of Ganj Dareh Tepe was a level with buildings of smaller mud bricks, no longer plano-convex, with plastered floors. A second date of 6,960 ±170 BC suggests a total lifetime for this site of c. 8,500–c. 6,500 BC, though it need not have lasted more than 1,500 years. The discoveries at Ganj Dareh Tepe suggest *prima facie* that the significance of Tepe Asiab, Tepe Sarab and even of Jarmo must not be overestimated. Nothing of comparable antiquity has yet been found in the Urmia basin or further north.

At a small mound some four hundred metres from the main mound of Yanik Tepe, twenty miles south-west of Tabriz towards Lake Urmia, a succession of up to nine phases, not all distinct building levels, has been found in a sondage of 15 × 5 metres. Two radio-carbon dates of 5,184 ±82 BC and 5,297 ±71 BC indicate a general contemporaneity with Hajji Firuz to the south.[46] The total depth of deposit is 5·50 metres, mostly belonging to this early period, which, though by absolute date classifiable as 'Early Chalcolithic', is typologically comparable with Tepe Sarab and even Jarmo, and therefore could with some justice be termed 'Late Neolithic'. In the context of the northern part of the Urmia basin the latter seems the more appropriate term. Present evidence suggests that this is the earliest cultural phase in this region. The pottery is scarce, poor in texture and firing and limited in forms: heavy bowls and short-necked, straight-sided jars with hole mouth preponderate; there are also flat-bottomed dishes; some bowls are carinated; sections are thick and the fabric is heavily tempered with straw. Such is the preponderant plain ware, mostly light buff or greenish in colour; but in the upper levels there is a proportion of painted pottery. While the

D

chevron decoration at once suggested a date contemporary with Hajji Firuz, other features seemed at the time of discovery to indicate an even earlier dating: first, some of the painted ware has a chalky paint applied over a red burnished ground, a parallel with Braidwood's 'slip-paint', a feature of Tepe Sarab though not of Jarmo; the ground stone industry of Yanik Tepe is comparable with that of Tepe Sarab, described by the excavator as of Jarmoan type. This similarity is especially discernible in the bracelets and bowl from Yanik Tepe, all of alabaster, perhaps from the same source as that used in the fifteenth century AD for the dado of the Blue Mosque in Tabriz. Figurines are numerous at Jarmo, are a feature of Tepe Sarab and occur at Yanik Tepe, where there is also a skilled bone industry, for personal ornaments as well as the common awls and needles. Well constructed houses of mud brick with rectangular plan and hard lime plaster floors suggest a relatively sophisticated village, its architecture of the same standard as that recently uncovered at Hajji Firuz. No such neat buildings have been found at Tepe Sarab or Jarmo, though Ganj Dareh Tepe seems to have been ahead of all these sites. There is thus good evidence to support the argument that the first settled communities did not appear till the mid-sixth millennium BC in the northern Urmia basin, an argument not inconsistent with the known evidence from Trans-Caucasia.

A slight hint of ethnic continuity between this Zagros zone and the centres of the Neolithic Revolution west of the Euphrates may possibly be discernible in the burnt Level v at Hajji Firuz, where a massacre seems to have occurred, the victims being buried on the site in three graves for the twenty-eight bodies. The interesting feature is the use of red ochre, sprinkled over the bodies.

The Araxes valley is not at present known for certain to have sites as early as the sixth millennium BC; but further excavations are likely to yield early radio-carbon dates, if not from mounds in the Ararat plain then from earlier sites in the hills nearby. The plain around Erevan is the likeliest area for the oldest settlements in the Armenian SSR. Professor Sardarian believes that the deepest levels of sites in the plain are neolithic and date from c. 6,000 BC, a belief based partly on comparisons with material from caves and particularly from open-air settlements and an obsidian workshop at the foot of Mount Artin. An outcome of this interpretation is the opinion that the neolithic culture of the Ararat plain was of indigenous origin, derived from the surrounding hills.[47]

A transitional aceramic neolithic phase is attested in the Armenian SSR by the Artin sites: large cores were found at the workshop, at which obsidian scrapers, borers, awls and other tools were fashioned. Hunting remained the mainstay of the economy, there was no ground stone industry and there is no proof of food production, whether agriculture or stock-breeding, at the principal sites of Barozh and Zagha. Yet there are remains of stone walls, indicating that here were no merely ephemeral camping sites. On the south-west side of Mount Aragats have been found settlements with deposits at their base ascribed to a mesolithic phase and thus immediately antedating the introduction of a food-producing economy: there are traces of dependence on hunting, but in the overlying level of the domestication of animals and of a typical early farming economy. It is these indications of a transition from food-gathering to food-production which suggest an indigenous origin for the following neolithic culture of the Ararat plain. In other parts of Trans-Caucasia no such stratified remains preceding the advent of villages dependent on agriculture and livestock have yet been found to provide evidence of the transition from the earlier hunting economy. A chronological priority for sites in the Armenian SSR would hardly be unexpected, though this might imply some still undetected influence from the south.

It may well have been from the early sixth millennium BC that settled life in the Ararat plain became firmly rooted. So high a dating must indicate no priority for the earliest known settlements around Lake Urmia. The special fertility of the middle Araxes valley, or Ararat plain, could itself account for early advances. This period is exemplified by the deepest levels of two mounds, Mashtots-Blur I and Keghzyak-Blur I, the latter situated not far north of Echmiadzin. The introduction of pottery and the foundation for the first time of villages in the plain mark this period off from the preceding one. No firm chronology, however, will be possible for Armenian sites until radio-carbon dates become available for these early periods. There seems to be a rather meagre number of levels at the earliest sites to extend till the establishment of the Early Trans-Caucasian culture in the late fourth millennium BC, discussed below. Therefore either the dating proposed by Sardarian has to be lowered or a lacuna in the occupation of these villages has to be postulated.

Radio-carbon dates suggest that some of the earliest known permanent settlements in Trans-Caucasia lie in the middle reaches of the Kura valley, at Şomu Tepe and Töire Tepe, in north-western Azerbaijan SSR, and at Shulaveri, south of Tbilisi, the capital of the Georgian SSR. Owing to modern political geography, this cultural province extending along the Kura basin is divided between the spheres of archaeologists working from Tbilisi and from Baku, the sites being far closer to the former. At Şomu Tepe a date of 5,560 ±70 BC was obtained, which could provide support for Sardarian's high dating of the earliest villages in the Ararat plain. But the dates from Shulaveri I (4,659 ±210 BC and 3,954 ±300 BC, from depths of 4·4 m. and 2·2 m. respectively) point rather to the fifth millennium BC as the time of the first settlements in the Kura basin.

A priority of a few centuries for the Araxes valley might still be allowable.[48]

The general impression conveyed by the discoveries at sites attributable to the fifth and fourth millennia BC, with some dating back to c. 5,500 BC, is one of the evolution of a pattern of local cultures showing evidence of common traditions. This is particularly apparent in architecture, since round houses are found not only at Shulaveri I, not far south of Tbilisi, but also at Tegut, a small mound in the Ararat plain close to Echmiadzin. These houses are very small, only three metres in diameter at Tegut and from barely two metres to 4·5 metres at Shulaveri. Whether or not the round houses of the third millennium BC owed their origins to the period of Shulaveri, there at least three building phases have been found to have this type of house. Round houses of 8–9 m. diameter are claimed by Sardarian to have been found in the Armenian SSR.

In the Ararat plain the earliest settlements yielded soft-baked pottery tempered with sand and straw, the forms including a variety of round-bottomed vessels, bowls, jars and cups, these last having decoration of incised sprig motifs, some pots being handled. In Mashtots-Blur I and Keghzyak-Blur I the microlithic obsidian industry typical of the preceding period gradually disappeared, being replaced by large flakes and by a ground stone industry including polished stone axes and hammers, types destined to have a long history in Trans-Caucasia. Small quernstones and mortars, the remains of wheat and barley recovered from storage jars and the numerous denticulated sickle-blades all add up to evidence of thriving agriculture. Cattle, sheep, goats and dogs are said to have been domesticated and are in evidence in the rock carvings so widely distributed in Trans-Caucasia. Whatever the precise dating of these earliest villages in Armenia, there appear to have been rectangular buildings of up to 13 × 10 m. in area as well as the above-mentioned round houses.

It is at Tegut, near Echmiadzin, that pottery gives a hint of southern influences or at least contacts: here, besides the plain straw-tempered wares, there is some highly fired pottery, of which a proportion is painted and of Halaf type; this is thin in section, light reddish or orange-buff in colour and painted in red with burnish applied to the painted areas. Jars have flaring or convex neck and globular body.[49] Imports of Halaf pottery also occur in north-west Azerbaijan, in the form of a jar now in the Baku Museum, and at Kültepe (Nakhichevan) in the Araxes valley. Penetration of Trans-Caucasia by traders from the homeland of the Halaf culture in upper Mesopotamia would be less remarkable if there were evidence of their presence in the Urmia basin, but there is none yet known.

The striking designs of the Dalma painted pottery, with its bold chevrons, triangles, lozenges and sweeping bands, are altogether indigenous to the Hasanlu area and perhaps to quite a wide region round about. The paint is purplish black on a cream ground and with a maroon slip over the inside. No comparison of this ware with Halaf pottery, except for their being contemporary, can be valid: not only are forms, patterns and colours so different, but the Dalma ware is inferior in fabric, with straw temper, and is on the whole very friable. At Yanik Tepe, where a slight shift in the centre of the village between the Chalcolithic period and the Early Bronze Age (Early Trans-Caucasian II) made it possible to investigate Chalcolithic levels where they were not concealed underneath any later deposits, only a few painted sherds from the lower Chalcolithic levels represent a northward extension of Dalma cultural influence; but the Dalma impressed ware, whose decoration consists of finger-depressions, combed ornament and other impressions in the wet clay, is also represented by a few examples from Yanik Tepe.[50] The small proportion of these wares in the whole assemblage from the Chalcolithic levels at Yanik Tepe does not detract from their great importance for relative chronology based on correlations with the Hasanlu area about one hundred miles to the south, and for absolute chronology through the radio-carbon dates from Dalma Tepe and Pisdeli Tepe, in the same Solduz plain.

Whereas Dalma Tepe flourished in the second half of the fifth millennium BC, three radio-carbon dates from Pisdeli Tepe cover approximately the first half of the fourth millennium BC. Pisdeli Tepe has painted pottery with decoration in black to dark brown paint on a plain buff to cream ground, a type of pottery which falls under the rather broad classification of the Ubaid tradition. This affected the fringes of eastern Anatolia adjoining the Fertile Crescent and much of western Iran, and was remarkably persistent, just as at Mersin, long after it had died out in its original Mesopotamian homeland. Moreover it spread up into the whole Urmia basin, being first recorded in stratified context at the large site of Geoy Tepe, near Reza'iyeh, in Period M. Surface finds by the writer suggest that this Pisdeli painted pottery in the Ubaid tradition was commoner along the west than along the east side of Lake Urmia, where, as in Geoy Tepe N, the most popular type of painted pottery had simple designs in black or dark brown paint on a red burnished surface, an altogether different style from that of Pisdeli. This painted ware was characteristic of the later Chalcolithic levels at Yanik Tepe. Both this site and the stratigraphy of Geoy Tepe prove that the red burnished ware of the Urmia basin made its appearance well before the first Pisdeli ware, possibly being introduced from the east.[51]

An indigenous origin for this red burnished pottery in the Urmia basin might seem to be suggested by the succession of nine Chalcolithic levels at Yanik Tepe, some with sub-phases, with a total depth of deposit of some nine metres. A strong ceramic continuity is apparent, though in the deepest levels the pottery was on the whole thicker and less well fired than in the later levels. The few painted sherds from the deeper levels suggest a date in the fifth millennium BC. Thereafter the standard ware, with red burnished slip and light red to buff fabric, sometimes straw-tempered, became overwhelmingly dominant and thus continued till Yanik Tepe XXV, the final Chalcolithic level. There must have been a hiatus after the end of the smaller site beside Yanik Tepe, but the Chalcolithic sequence betrays great length of time and strong conservatism. A simple open shallow bowl and a short-necked jar are typical forms, others including large shallow platters, pedestalled bowls, goblets with tall slender stem and pot-stands. A rare form of decoration comprises a schematic rendering in relief of a human face, the eyes being represented by small pieces of obsidian set into the clay before firing. The normal style of decoration is more prosaic, with patterns in dark brown or black paint over the red burnished slip. A mound right by the north shore of Lake Urmia, where there are few other sites, has yielded sherds of goblets with painted decoration, not found on this form at Yanik Tepe.

Apart from the above-mentioned Halaf imports, parallels in Trans-Caucasia for the Dalma and Pisdeli material are relatively scarce, although perhaps the painted pottery found by Iessen in the Mil steppe of Soviet Azerbaijan, just north of the Araxes, may have affinities with Dalma ware: the decoration comprises chevrons and other simple linear patterns, and is purplish, brown or black on a buff or pinkish-buff ground.[52] No parallels can be sure until forms are recovered. A more certain link with the Dalma pottery of the Urmia basin is discernible at Ilanli Tepe, in Soviet Azerbaijan, where in a small settlement of 50 × 50 metres have been found remains of rectangular and curvilinear buildings constructed of 'hog-backed' mud bricks. The inhabitants used the sling, said to be unique for this period in Trans-Caucasia. The normal pottery includes large jars up to one metre high, rather poorly made; a better class of pottery has a dark red to reddish brown burnished slip, some of it with 'jabbed' decoration consisting of very small triangles in a rather random scatter, applied to the wet clay with the end of a stick.[53] This decorative technique is clearly comparable with some of the Dalma pottery. The suggestion that this decoration manifests the extension into north-western Iran of a ceramic style at home over a wide zone from the Balkans across south Russia to Trans-Caucasia, and thus a northern cultural influence, seems on present evidence improbable. A cultural connection simply from the south part of the Urmia basin northward into Soviet Azerbaijan seems far more plausible. At Ilanli Tepe another style of decoration, combing of the surface, is dated to the early fourth millennium BC: this occurs at the same time at Yanik Tepe, but there it was concealed, being applied to the clay for the better adherence of the slip. No links with the south in this period of lingering, if indirect, Ubaid influence on the pottery of the Urmia basin are clearly discernible in Trans-Caucasia, by which time the local cultures had probably become firmly enough rooted to develop along their own lines.

It is in the middle Kura valley that the largest concentration of settlement sites attributable to the period of *c.* 5,500–*c.* 3,250 BC has been investigated by Georgian and Azerbaijani archaeologists. The above-mentioned radio-carbon dates indicate the high dating which must be given to these villages. Şomu Tepe, perhaps the earliest site, has evidence of a bone industry in the form of picks; obsidian was obtained from Mount Kelbegen, just east of Lake Sevan; impressions on some of the pottery indicate the weaving of mats and textiles. The pottery is rather uninspiring, black or drab red, only a small percentage being burnished. Flat bases, projecting out beyond the line of the vessel, may suggest parallels with the earliest period of Yanik Tepe. The lack of lugs contrasts with their occurrence on pottery at sites on the Mil steppe and at Kültepe (Nakhichevan) this difference probably being one of date.[54]

In the fifth millennium BC Shulaveri I has a range of relatively crude pottery, including hole-mouth and necked jars, some with a low pedestal base. Decoration takes the form either of incision, usually in herringbone patterns or chevrons, or of knobs or pellets and notches in a row along the rim; a snake in relief is a very early example of a motif appearing much later at different times in Trans-Caucasia. The obsidian industry of this level was highly developed and abundant; the ground stone industry was sophisticated, with serpentine and basalt used for celts and other implements. Antler sleeves exemplify the bone industry, and may have been used for digging tools. Imiris-Gora, situated near Shulaveri, has a similar material culture. In Shulaveri II the houses were no longer round but oval; and the pottery seems to display less decoration but more use of burnishing.[55]

Some of the pottery collected by T. Chubinishvili and dated by him to the fifth and fourth millennia BC is tempered with straw and some with chips of basalt. Tsopi, Aruchlo and Sadachlo are all sites in the same part of eastern Georgia as Shulaveri, each with its own ceramic peculiarities. Drab grey, reddish-brown and yellow-brown wares occur at Tsopi, where a model ox may illustrate the role of stock-breeding in the village economy of this period in eastern Georgia. At Aruchlo the pottery displays a profusion of knobs and semi-circular lugs, the knobs being commonly arranged in two rows, either just below the rim or vertically, as on the necks of jars; similar decoration occurs at Şomu Tepe. As at Shulaveri axeheads of serpentine and granite demonstrate an advanced ground stone industry at Aruchlo. The date of the material from this site is estimated at *c.* 4,000 BC. According to T. Chubinishvili a bulla from Aruchlo with a design of a horned animal has parallels with Geoy Tepe M and perhaps also with the Mesopotamian cylinder-seals of Jemdet Nasr style with a row of horned animals. If correct, this parallel must imply a low date, towards *c.* 3,000 BC, for the later occupation there. At Sadachlo there is occupation of the fourth and third millennia BC.

Here therefore in the middle Kura valley there flourished a culture marked by its long duration, its distinctive architecture and its relatively crude but easily recognizable pottery, with considerable skill in stone-working. Further afield, in north Ossetia, pottery similar to that from Tsopi has been found at Shau-Legat; and there are said to be later parallels in northern Caucasia. At Samele Kldé, the Fox Cave, in the Chiatura region of north-west Georgia, the pottery includes forms dating to *c.* 3,250–*c.* 3,000 BC, though earlier sherds may occur too, seeing that the chipped and ground stone industries have older affinities: this is especially true of ground axeheads of serpentine and basalt like those from Shulaveri.

The rupestrian art of Trans-Caucasia cannot be discussed here in detail, nor can it be associated with any certainty with settlement sites. The largest group of rock drawings is that of Kobistan, forty miles south of Baku and not far from the Caspian Sea.[56] On the Apsheron peninsula close to Baku and its oil fields, in the Dubende area, there is a small cave with drawings of three highly stylized human figures, a goat and an ox. Arslanov, a specialist in these rock drawings, believes that in this cave there is a chronological sequence like that based on evidence from the four thousand drawings of the rocky waste of Kobistan and by implication applicable to other drawings. The goat is attributed to the Early Bronze Age (third millennium BC), although at a Late Bronze Age site nearby goats occur carved on some of the slabs forming a stone-built enclosure, showing the survival even into the early first millennium BC of this rupestrian art. The ox in this small cave seems to have a goat's head, perhaps reflecting the survival of a tradition of many oxen in a period of abundant goats. The scenes at Kobistan are innumerable and would require long study at first hand to yield their full story. Stratified deposits up against one rock face have been connected with a vertical succession of changing rock drawings, the large oxen probably representing *bos primigenius* and being typical of the early phases. But just how early these were is an unsolved question. Strange female figures suggest a fertility cult. Long rowing boats are the subject of some of these drawings: presumably they were used on the Caspian Sea, but when and by whom cannot be guessed. The numerous drawings of horses, often overlapping those of cattle, must be much later, not before *c.* 2,000 BC. Though almost certainly dating back in part to the neolithic period or earlier, the Kobistan group is probably mostly later than many of the rock drawings of Armenia, found on Mount Aragats, in the mountains of Geghaghma-ghan and Syoonik and at Zagha and Naltepe. Emphasis on hunting and the small scale of men and beasts are noteworthy features. At Naltepe a band of hunters, accompanied by a woman and child, are shown armed with bows and arrows, spears and harpoons; they have dogs with them, and are hunting what appear to be wild sheep, chamois and deer.[57] As in the hunting scenes at Çatal Hüyük, which could be more or less contemporary, so here too in the rock drawings of Armenia there is often conveyed a sense of swift movement. This art is nothing if not spontaneous, even if its significance must ever remain largely obscured from modern eyes. Generally the stiffer and more stereotyped the drawing the later it seems likely to be. Failing a discovery similar to that of the paintings of Çatal Hüyük, it may continue to prove impossible to link the rupestrian art to precise periods in the occupation of village sites.

The fourth millennium BC might be thought to merit especially detailed discussion, in that it was the prelude to the great Early Trans-Caucasian culture which was to dawn in the last quarter of that millennium. Unfortunately, however, the available evidence is still very meagre, only relatively few sites having levels definitely attributable to the period c. 4,000–c. 3,250 BC. Such sites are mostly those which continued into the following millennium, when they were to enjoy their greatest prosperity. Kültepe IA, in the Nakhichevan region of the Araxes valley, is the best known site of this period, there represented by 8·30 m. depth of deposit, from virgin soil at 21·10 m. up to 12·80 m., when the sequence of levels is interrupted by a sterile layer one foot thick. The plain pottery is rather crude, and includes hole-mouth jars and others with a short neck; there is also a proportion of painted ware, the paint being carelessly applied. Spindle-whorls point to the practice of weaving. Some metal objects from these early levels (Kültepe IA) are of pure copper, others containing from 0·4 per cent to 0·7 per cent arsenic; only hammering and annealing seem to have been known. Some flint blades occur, but more important was the obsidian industry, the raw material coming from the same source east of Lake Sevan as was used by the inhabitants of Şomutepe. Stone hammers and adzes attest a developed ground stone industry. Bone was worked into picks, awls and sickle-handles, these set with small flint or obsidian blades. Kültepe is not unique in this part of Trans-Caucasia in having occupation attributable to the fourth millennium BC, for at the base of the high mound of Karaköpektepe, downstream from Nakhichevan, Chalcolithic remains seem to have been reached. Kültepe, however, is especially important for its very long succession of occupation levels and for the two radio-carbon dates which help to provide a bare chronological outline for Trans-Caucasia before the Early Trans-Caucasian culture: one date is from a sample obtained from a depth of 18·20 m., not far above virgin soil, and is of 3,807 ±90 BC; the other is from a depth of 15·35 m., and is of 2,908 ± 150 BC. This second date is surely too low, the more so in the light of a third radio-carbon date from this site, from a depth of only 8·50 m., of 2,920 ±90 BC.[58]

In and about the Ararat plain are several sites with occupation probably immediately preceding the change to the Early Trans-Caucasian culture. Such as Shengavit I, Shresh-Blur I, Mokhra-Blur I and Sev-Blur I; Keghzyak I is described as transitional to the following cultural period. Kültepe IB (Nakhichevan) is of the same period. A light yellow burnished slip over a fabric fired at a modest temperature, with sand mixed with the clay, is characteristic of the pottery of these fourth millennium BC villages, of the period termed Late Neolithic by Sardarian. Geometric and representational patterns, such as sprigs, appear incised on some of this pottery; there is also punctated ornament. From Kültepe (Nakhichevan) come cups with ledge-handles, with light yellow slip or painted in red, grey or dark brown. The agricultural economy evolved along lines already laid down in the fifth millennium BC, with an improved ground stone industry exemplified by axes, hammers and hoes. Hunting seems, however, to have remained a significant source of food.

With the close of this cultural period in Armenia and of its equivalent in Georgia a new era was about to be born. Its advent is shrouded in obscurity, the threads of such evidence as there is being discussed below. The old simple order of village life was to give way to a culture not perhaps at first much more advanced, but with greater potentialities and altogether wider ramifications. The geographical scope of this book can henceforth be limited to the wide highland zone, now that Trans-Caucasia, north-western Iran and eastern Anatolia were to become one.

CHAPTER 3

FROM CAUCASUS TO EUPHRATES – THE EARLY TRANS-CAUCASIAN CULTURE

During the last quarter of the fourth millennium BC the whole vast zone from the Caucasus to beyond the upper Euphrates and to Lake Urmia began to manifest a general uniformity of material culture which was to continue for over one thousand years. This suggests an ethnic unity, which, in the nature of purely prehistoric evidence, can hardly be proved. One day, however, it may become more acceptable through data from physical anthropology. Such data are at present lacking, so that for any theory concerning the population of this highland zone in the third millennium BC recourse to other territories and later periods is unavoidable. The one conceivable alternative source of evidence is that put forward by proponents of glotto-chronology, those philologists who purport to be able to reconstruct by means of statistics the sounds of a spoken language of many centuries before the earliest surviving written records from the region.[1] The present writer believes that, while linguistic development is an invaluable source of information on the origins of an ethnic group, often the only such source, it cannot be made to yield reliable evidence beyond the limits of common prudence. Mathematical skill may lead far from historical probability. Some conclusions on ethnic affinities are given below. Some preliminary warnings are appropriate: of the uneven knowledge of the different regions of the immense zone occupied by this culture; of problems of terminology; of the meagre framework of a detailed chronology.

Much more is now known of this culture than was so in the first decade after the Second World War. This knowledge is mainly the outcome of the work of numerous Soviet archaeologists in the three Trans-Caucasian republics of Armenia, Georgia and Azerbaijan, where it has become a point of honour to investigate this culture, there termed Kura-Araxes, where a great quantity of material has been excavated and where many specialists are at work on it. This body of material is supplemented by that from a few widely scattered excavations in Turkey and Iran and from surveys largely conducted by the writer.[2] The rescue operations in

43

the areas around Elazığ due to be submerged by the waters of the Keban dam will add considerably to knowledge of the south-western region of this far-flung culture, for the first time producing a stratified sequence from that province;[3] and this will no doubt be closely comparable with the results of recent excavations near Malatya.[4] A much more coherent general assessment is now possible than when the writer completed his survey of eastern Anatolia, which was in any case a preliminary reconnaissance without pretence of being definitive.[5] Many questions, however, remain to be answered.

There has been no uniform terminology in the specialized publications on this culture. Most Soviet scholars use the term 'Kura-Araxes culture', though Piotrovskii and Munchaev call it the 'Eneolithic culture of Trans-Caucasia'. The term 'eneolithic' is in general used in the Soviet Union for the greater part of this period, though the third and final phase is reckoned there as the Early Bronze Age. Another term is the 'Trans-Caucasian Copper Age'.[6] Other terms reflect an approach based on part of this cultural zone situated in Turkey or Iran. Thus the writer has coined the term 'East Anatolian Early Bronze Age', while R.H.Dyson uses the term 'Yanik culture'.[7] But the latter is open to the objection that it is derived from one site which, however important, was certainly not in the original homeland of this culture. No new term which is at once brief and explicit can easily be devised. The term 'Early Hurrian culture', for reasons given below, might be defensible, but is too controversial; and it is anyhow undesirable to attach ethnic labels to prehistoric cultures. If any one site be taken as typical and thus fitted to give its name to the whole culture, it could be called the Shengavit culture; but this is unsatisfactory in its lack of any reference to the very wide zone involved. There is much to recommend the term 'East Anatolian Early Bronze Age', except that the introduction of bronze did not occur till the last three centuries of the third millennium BC. No geographical term for this culture can avoid being inadequate or anachronistic. The term here proposed, which will be used hereafter, is 'Early Trans-Caucasian culture': this at least cannot be confused with any other culture. The fuller description as the 'Early Trans-Caucasian and East Anatolian culture' is clearly far too long. The term to be used here does not conflict with the evidence on the likeliest centre or nuclear region of this culture.

The map (Map II) shows the wide extent of this culture. It shows too that certain centres of settlement may be discerned, among them the Araxes valley. By its geographical situation alone, it could be argued, this could have been the original home from which this culture subsequently expanded in all directions. Such a theory is attractive, but certainly cannot be supported simply on the distribution of sites. The

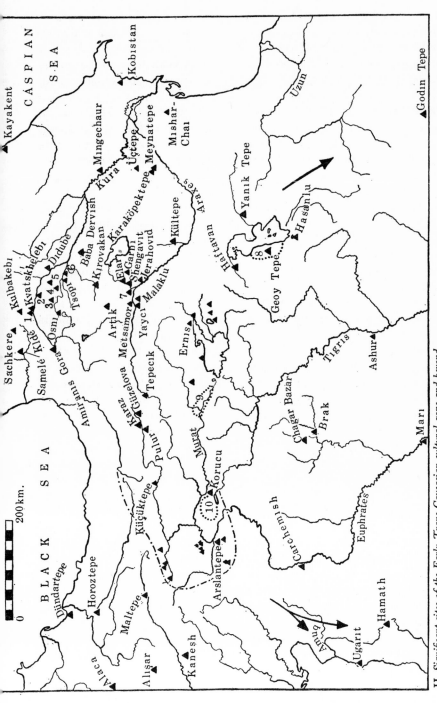

II *Significant sites of the Early Trans-Caucasian cultural zone and beyond*

Arrows show the direction of major expansions beyond the homeland of the Early Trans-Caucasian culture. The broken line indicates the approximate western limit of this cultural zone. Dotted lines enclose areas of especially dense occupation, with which should be included the Erevan plain.

Key to numbered sites: 1 Khiznaant-Gora 2 Gudabertka 3 Beshtasheni 4 Tetri-Tsqaro 5 Kiketi 6 Sadachlo 7 Sites around Echmiadzin (Shresh-Blur, Kültepe, Keghzyak-Blur, Sev-Blur) 8 Reza'iyeh area 9 Muş plain 10 Altinova (now in the Keban Dam basin) character, development and chronology of the material from each region within this cultural zone should as far as possible be assessed and compared with that from other regions before any worthwhile theory of the origins of this culture can be put forward. This is all the more necessary because of the inveterate tendency of all too many archaeologists to see their own area of work, even one site which has been the centre of their excavations, as the focus and point of origin of cultural influences extending far and wide. The physical geography of the highland zone is such that inevitably some areas are seen to have been relatively uninhabited, while in others the sites lie thick on the ground. The distribution of sites cannot in itself indicate either an external or an indigenous origin for this culture.

A tripartite division of prehistoric cultures is all too popular with archaeologists, for must not all stages of human development have a beginning, a middle and an end? Such a division into three main periods has indeed been proposed for the Early Trans-Caucasian culture by prehistorians in Armenia and Georgia;[8] for the eastern Anatolian part of the zone by the writer;[9] and for the contemporary K period of Geoy Tepe, near Reza'iyeh, by its excavator.[10] Enough is now known of the cultural sequence of the third millennium BC in Georgia and Armenia to place most of the material in one or other of these three periods; but the radio-carbon dates are too few for complete reliance to be put on them. They do, however, provide a reasonably consistent sequence of periods. These dates show, moreover, that no theory of a diffusion northwards towards the Caucasus can be accepted without close investigation, since at two sites in Georgia, Kvatskhelebi and Amiranis-Gora, occupation dated back at least as early as c. 3,000 BC. For Level CI at Kvatskhelebi a date of 2,800 ±90 BC has been obtained from an occupation level with two more stratified beneath it; and from Amiranis-Gora two dates not from the earliest level are 2,835 ±170 BC and 2,680 ±180 BC. Further south, in the Araxes valley, a date of 2,920 ±90 BC has been obtained from Level II of Kültepe (Nakhichevan). The closeness of these radiocarbon dates from three separate sites makes them the more convincing. More dates, however, are much to be desired, especially from Armenia, where none earlier than the third and final period of the Early Trans-Caucasian culture is known. For the absolute chronology of the second period there is one date from Geoy Tepe of 2,574 ±146 BC, and there are four dates from Yanik Tepe, ranging from 2,621 ±79 BC to 2,324 ±78 BC. Falling within the third period are two dates from Yanik Tepe, of 2,086 ±104 BC and 1,816 ±63 BC, and one from Shengavit IV of 2,060 ±80 BC. All these dates make it possible to fix the duration of this long-lived culture between the years c. 3,250 BC and c. 1,750 BC, with the earliest occupation in many regions much later than that opening date and with survivals continuing perhaps even as late as *c.* 1,500 BC in such conservative parts as the Van region.[11] Evidence from Haftavān, near the north-west corner of Lake Urmia, could suggest a similar conservatism there.[12]

With the increase of evidence, earlier simplifications have inevitably been to some degree invalidated: the general evolution of the Early Trans-Caucasian culture is more complex than once was supposed. One of the writer's conclusions in his original report,[13] that there was at first a remarkable uniformity of material culture, especially as displayed by the pottery, over the whole zone from Malatya to the Caucasus and from Erzincan to Lake Urmia, remains valid. Likewise does the general assertion that this uniformity tended to break down into regional variants, though not markedly so till the third period in the tripartite chronological division. Thus there may well have been a period of wide-ranging and fairly rapid settlement of this vast highland zone by newcomers; and this was then probably followed by a much longer period of cultural stability, only after several centuries breaking down gradually rather than coming to a catastrophic end.

The strong interest among prehistorians and philologists in the arrival of Indo-Europeans, particularly the Hittites, in the Near East via the Caucasus around about 2,000 BC and thereafter has tended to suggest a change in material culture in the highland zone, at least in Trans-Caucasia and eastern Anatolia. Yet no such abrupt discontinuity is apparent. The important changes appearing in the third cultural period, the outcome largely of advances in metallurgy and of more far-reaching trade, seem more probably the achievement of the indigenous population than of Indo-European invaders, of whom little archaeological trace has hitherto been detected. Moreover, the Early Trans-Caucasian culture, enduring in varying degree into the early second millennium BC, exercized a profound influence on its successor cultures.

The explanation of the long survival and apparent adaptability of the Early Trans-Caucasian culture must remain a matter for speculation. But an economic stability based on cattle and sheep-rearing and on agriculture seems to have been achieved, as Soviet authorities have emphasized.[14] Where this means of livelihood changed in the second millennium BC, there the continuity of settled life itself was broken; but where the farmers and stock-breeders maintained their ancestral way of life, the traditions of this culture continued, although increasingly modified until eventually no longer recognizable in terms of material remains.

An attempt to place the population of the Early Trans-Caucasian culture in the context of the ancient Near East, where written records were beginning to provide meagre historical data, seems here appropriate. Physical anthropology is of no help, nor are written records available from the highland zone itself till the ninth century BC, with the rise of Urartu.[15] What is known is that the Urartian language was closely related to Hurrian, so much so that, whatever the reservations of some philologists, it may legitimately be described as latter-day Hurrian.

There is thus good reason to class the Urartian people as being of Hurrian stock, a conclusion in no way undermined by the settlement of Hurrians in preponderant numbers in north Syria and north Mesopotamia during the second millennium BC. The tablets from Nuzi and Alalakh are among the sources bearing witness to the Hurrian presence in the central arc of the Fertile Crescent.[16] Mursilis I, the Hittite king who successfully carried out a lightning raid on Babylon, dated on the 'middle chronology'[17] to c. 1,595 BC, thus brought to an end the dynasty of Hammurabi and allowed the Kassites, a people of largely Indo-European ancestry who had been infiltrating into the plains of Akkad from the Zagros highlands, to take over control of Babylon, which they maintained for four centuries. On his march homeward, laden with booty, Mursilis was harrassed by Hurrians in the territory through which his army had to march.[18]

Hurrians also settled on the Mediterranean coast, where such Phoenician towns as Arvad still retained in later centuries their Hurrian name. They extended their zone of settlement westwards into Kizzuwatna (later Que and then Cilicia), where they exerted a dominant influence on the Hittite court and on the state cult of the Hittite New Kingdom in the thirteenth century BC and to a lesser extent in earlier generations. The role of the Hurrians in the Near East in the second millennium BC is now fairly clearly appreciated and known to have been geographically very wide. But it is also well understood that they had arrived as newcomers in north Syria and north Mesopotamia, where they mingled with Semites of different groups, the Amorites then being politically dominant.[19] Yet the Hurrian element in the population of Kizzuwatna entered a plain already settled by Indo-Europeans of Luvian stock, probably originating from north-west Anatolia, whose arrival (c. 2,300 BC) marks the start of the Cilician Early Bronze III period.[20] Then, some two centuries later (c. 2,100 BC), came the introduction into Kizzuwatna of a painted pottery entirely different from the products of the Early Bronze III period and with undoubted affinities with pottery found at Alalakh and elsewhere in north Syria. Some derivation of this painted pottery from that of the Early Trans-Caucasian III sub-province in the Elazığ-Malatya region seems possible, though the influence could have been in the other direction, spreading from Syria northwards into the upper Euphrates valley.[21] The Cilician Middle Bronze Age began with the arrival of this painted pottery, while the Hittite sources indicate a Hittite cultural dominance there some centuries later, in the Late Bronze Age. No intermediate date seems at all plausible for the arrival in Kizzuwatna of the Hurrians, who must surely therefore have settled there from c. 2,100 BC. They must have been present already before then in north Syria, whence they had come.

The Hurrians can therefore be reckoned as an element in the civilization of the Near East beyond the highland zone already well before 2,000 BC. Supporting this contention is the occurrence of Hurrian personal names in tablets of the Akkadian period (c. 2,340–2,180 BC) at Tell Chagar Bazar on the River Khabur.[22] Their appearance on this navigable tributary of the Euphrates means that Hurrians were even then at least beginning to gain access to the rich commerce of Mesopotamia, then first expanding through the military and trading expeditions of Sargon of Agade and his successors, particularly his grandson Naram-Sin. These expeditions, while partly to traditional objectives such as the Amanus range, opened up new markets and may well have facilitated the establishment of an Assyrian trading colony at Kanesh (Kültepe) in central Anatolia, followed later by the foundation of other such colonies.[23] They were in Hattian rather than Hurrian territory; but an important route up into central Anatolia lay through the region of Elaziğ, later known to the Hittites as Isua, whose population was, through its links with north Syria, probably Hurrian at least by the Early Trans-Caucasian III period. The growth of Mesopotamian trade, particularly in the Akkadian period and under the Third Dynasty of Ur, very probably acted as a magnet drawing Hurrians southward into Syria.

All the above evidence presupposes a homeland whence the Hurrians irrupted into surrounding regions to the south and west. This homeland can only have been in the highland zone. Who therefore but the Hurrians could have left behind them the Early Trans-Caucasian culture? No theory that they came from beyond the Caucasus and pushed through the highlands without leaving any trace of themselves will bear scrutiny, even though it is perfectly possible for nomads to leave little or no evidence of their passing. The general cultural continuity of the highland zone, emphasized above, lasted throughout the third millennium BC, and implies ethnic stability, though not proving this, the clear inference being that the population was Hurrian, and had been so since the end of the fourth millennium BC.

An objection to this theory of ethnic continuity might be lodged on the grounds that the treasures of Maikop, the great barrow in the Kuban valley, and of Alaca, the rich cemetery on the plateau of central Anatolia, indicate a cultural and even an ethnic intrusion from the northern steppes as far as Anatolia. This suggestion is perhaps based partly on the belief that the 'animal style', whose earliest manifestation (it is argued) occurs at Maikop, was an original creation of the inhabitants of the steppes, the northern nomads. One scholar has gone so far as to suggest Indo-European affinities for Maikop and for Alaca too, associating the latter with the first Hittites to settle in the bend of the River Halys.[24] This last suggestion can be dismissed as wholly unfounded. The people of Alaca were Hattian, the indigenous 'Asianic' (non-Indo-European) population who inhabited and controlled the Anatolian plateau immediately west of the Hurrian zone. The cultural influence was from Alaca and its vicinity, probably by way of Horoztepe and sites near or on the Pontic coast, to Maikop, not in the reverse direction. This can be seen as but one manifestation of the penetration of the Caucasus and the steppes just beyond by Near Eastern influences, following contacts between the highlanders and the population of the northern fringes of the Fertile Crescent. The possibility that a small warrior class of Indo-European race erected the great barrows of the Early Kuban phase and even reached as far as Alaca in no way affects the affinities of the material culture of Alaca and Maikop nor the racial composition of the majority of the population.

The burnished pottery of the Early Trans-Caucasian culture, with its bold decoration in relief and grooving, first came to the direct attention of Near Eastern archaeologists in a derivative form commonly called Khirbet Kerak ware, after a site in the Jordan valley termed in the Israeli publications Beth Yerah.[25] As so often happens, however, when a culture or type of artifact is named after one site, this is not the most important occurrence of this ware. It has been found abundantly in the plain of Antioch (the Amuq), where the American excavators have assigned it to their Amuq H and I phases. In addition to pottery vessels, a hearth of horseshoe shape, distinctive of the Early Trans-Caucasian culture and known from many sites, was found in Level 11 at Tell Judeideh.[26] Architectural parallels with the highland zone include the presence of clay benches and bins, not incomparable with those of Yanik Tepe, and more or less contemporary. In the Amuq Khirbet Kerak ware, termed 'Red-Black Burnished Ware' by R.J. Braidwood, has been found in stratified context at Tell Judeideh, the most important site, and similarly at Çatal Hüyük, Tell Ta'yinat and Tell Dhahab: it was thus very well established there. Whoever introduced this pottery evidently then made it locally, for the clay used was from local sources, an indication that people and not merely pots arrived in the Amuq plain. Braidwood seems to have missed the significance of this pottery in Amuq H-I, for he dismisses it as 'the result of some one regional ceramic variant of a general Anatolian development of the old Syro-Cilician Dark-Faced Burnished Ware'.[27] One virtue, however, of Braidwood's term for this pottery is that it emphasizes the use of more than one colour apart from black. Much of the Early Trans-Caucasian pottery proper is not black at all but light in tone. Khirbet Kerak ware was undoubtedly derived from the Hurrian homeland, but had developed along its own lines, retaining the use of incised decoration, including occasional birds, though incision occurs mostly on lids. Amuq H comprised six levels (12–7) at Tell Judeideh and four (9–6) at Tell Ta'yinat. In the following phase, Amuq I, this pottery continued side by side with other wares. Southwards through Syria into Palestine, where excavations have been relatively numerous, Khirbet Kerak ware has also been found, though less and less the further south the site. At Jericho, for example, it occurs only in tombs.[28] Its chronology first gave some evidence for the dating of the culture of the highland zone before the advent of radio-carbon dates, for it can be assigned to the Palestinian Early Bronze III period, contemporary with the Old Kingdom of Egypt (Dynasties IV–VI) and dated through secure Egyptian connections. This indicates the arrival of northerners in Palestine, who mingled with the largely Semitic population: nothing in the archaeology of Palestine contradicts their description as Hurrians.[29] They would thus have been present, if only in small numbers, when the Amorites invaded the land in the Early Bronze-Middle Bronze period,[30] an invasion resulting in a general decline of urban life and a reversion to nomadism. Hurrians certainly formed one of the elements composing the Rulers of Foreign Countries, or Hyksos, who built up the flourishing Middle Bronze Age civilization in Palestine after an influx of Canaanites from the Mediterranean littoral to the north. That these Hurrians were survivors of the original group which introduced the Khirbet Kerak ware from the north seems rather improbable: too long a time had elapsed, and they must have become absorbed in the Semitic population. Another wave of Hurrians was almost certainly caught up in the Hyksos movement. Yet in north Syria there seems to have been no discontinuity in the Hurrian presence.

Some pottery from Alaca and elsewhere in central Anatolia, dating to approximately the same period as the Khirbet Kerak ware, is to some degree comparable.[31] There is nothing to suggest direct influence from the one to the other, so that the explanation must lie in parallel development from a common cultural background in the Hurrian highlands of eastern Anatolia. Any movement of Hurrians into central Anatolia in the mid-third millennium BC must have been in very small numbers.

The evidence for the origins of the Early Trans-Caucasian culture virtually comprises pottery alone, for, as more than one Soviet archaeologist has observed, there is a singular dearth of other classes of artifact.[32] The main exceptions to this are where graves have produced metal and other artifacts seldom found in occupation levels. For the second and third periods Yanik Tepe exemplifies this dearth of non-ceramic evidence: there the cemeteries must have been extramural, no burials being found in the excavated areas of the village.

Pottery said to be of 'proto-Kura-Araxes' form (i.e. proto-Early Trans-Caucasian I in the terminology used in this book) occurs at Samele Kldé,[33] the Fox Cave, in Chiatura, situated in north-western Georgia; but the rest of the finds from this cave, the chipped and ground stone industries and the bone industry, are, as above-mentioned, more easily attributable to the fourth or fifth millennium BC. Baba-Dervish, Meynatepe and Tsopi have all yielded what appear to be prototypes of Early Trans-Caucasian I pottery, Tsopi providing evidence of the start of this culture in southern Georgia.[34] The material from the settlement, but not the cemetery, of Tetrisqaro appears likewise to date back into the late fourth millennium BC.[35] But the absence of any continuous stratified sequence of occupation levels dating back into the mid-fourth millennium BC and earlier makes it difficult to assess the place in any relative chronology to be given to this early material from sites in Georgia and in the Kura valley in north-western Azerbaijan. Even at Kültepe (Nakhichevan) evidence for the immediate antecedents of the Early Trans-Caucasian culture appears to be lacking, since a sterile layer was found between the top of Level I and the beginning of the Early Trans-Caucasian occupation in Level II; and the radio-carbon dates lend some support to the probability that this site was deserted for several centuries in the fourth millennium BC. In Georgia the round houses of Shulaveri may conceivably have provided the proto-type for those of one thousand years and more later at Shresh-Blur, Shengavit, Jerahovid, Garni, Kültepe (Nakhichevan), Yanik Tepe, Kayakent and elsewhere, as well as the modified variants at Kvatskhelebi. The excavations at Tegut lend weight to this suggestion of a very long-lasting architectural tradition of round houses in Trans-Caucasia. No proof, however, is yet available to indicate any significant influence of Shulaveri and contemporary settlements on the Early Trans-Caucasian culture.[36]

Piotrovskii's preference for an origin of this culture in the middle Araxes valley, the fertile plain now the heart of the Armenian SSR, is supported by certain aspects of the evidence, though as yet not reinforced by radio-carbon dates from levels of the Early Trans-Caucasian I period and earlier.[37] Certainly the artistry of the people of this region attained a higher level in the decoration of pottery than appears elsewhere in Trans-Caucasia, though not till the second of the three periods were the best of their products made. The limited evidence from eastern Anatolia suggests that no such high standard of pottery was normally achieved there. In the Urmia basin this culture was clearly introduced from the north, and indeed, as surveys have proved, spread as far south as the Hamadan region, where stratified material is now available from Godin Tepe IV.[38] To look to Iran for the origins of this culture would be irrelevant; and the balance of probability is against an origin in eastern Anatolia, where the richest region is that of Malatya and Elaziğ. Unless an ethnic movement thence north-eastward be postulated, this region, important as it later became in the history of conflict between the Hittite state, Mitanni and Assyria, can surely be discounted as too peripheral, situated as it is in the south-western extremity of this wide cultural zone.[39] The claims of the Erzurum plain and its environs must be judged on the evidence of the excavated sites of Karaz and Pulur, admittedly early in date:[40] though theoretically a possible centre of origin of this culture, the natural environment seems too severe, too restricted by altitude, for it to have had a surplus population to give the impetus to wide expansion in all directions. Only its geographical position, near the centre of the zone, makes it at all plausible as the original nucleus. More probably the Erzurum region was, with Georgia, the first territory in which the bearers of this culture settled in the years around 3,000 BC, after their initial expansion from their first homeland.

Other regions can be eliminated as possible nuclei of this culture. It is impossible to be sure how soon the territory of the Azerbaijan SSR, apart from the middle reaches of the Kura valley just east of Tbilisi, was settled by these people. The relative poverty of the pottery from the sites of that territory suggests that the lands just west of the Caspian Sea, though perhaps occupied as early as Georgia, were never settled by communities including the more progressive elements in the population. Perhaps more probably the indigenous population of the region around Baku and the lower Araxes valley was never overrun by the bearers of the Early Trans-Caucasian culture, but rather absorbed it at second hand, never attaining a high level. Near the Talysh region, by the south-west corner of the Caspian Sea, pottery said to be immediately preceding the Early Trans-Caucasian I period has been found; but this straw-tempered ware seems very probably earlier.[41] In eastern Anatolia the Van region seems to have been sparsely inhabited, if the small number of sites is any guide, while the Muş plain may have had a local culture, characterized by rather crude pottery of distinctive forms.[42] Further up the Murat valley, at Liz and around Bulanik, normal Early Trans-Caucasian pottery has been collected.

The arguments for the placing of the original nucleus of the Early Trans-Caucasian culture in the Araxes valley around Erevan are not based solely on the elimination of alternatives for varying reasons, nor only on the quality of the pottery nor again on the fertility of the region and its potentiality as the cradle of an expanding population finding itself in need of *Lebensraum*. There is some evidence possibly indicating continuous occupation in the Erevan plain during the period relevant to any enquiry into the origins of this culture, the late fourth millennium BC. Shengavit, now on the outskirts of Erevan, has produced results important in themselves and providing a stratified sequence of four cultural periods, of which the earliest (Shengavit I) has already been mentioned as antedating the Early Trans-Caucasian culture. There seems, however, to have been a change rather than merely a development from the culture of Shengavit I to that of Shengavit II. The most recent excavator of Shengavit is inclined to describe the latest of three successive periods at another site in the Araxes plain, Keghzyak-Blur, as transitional, that is to the Early Trans-Caucasian I culture; but at the same time he equates it with Shengavit I and Kültepe (Nakhichevan) I, neither of which seems to lead on into the subsequent period.[43] At Mashtots-Blur a sequence comparable with that of Keghzyak-Blur has been obtained, though there the lifetime of the settlement certainly lasted into the Early Trans-Caucasian I period. Other sites also have occupation before and during this same period. All these strands of evidence hardly add up to an unassailable case in favour of the theory of an original centre of this culture in the middle Araxes valley, the plain around Erevan; but they surely indicate it as the most probable centre. No objection that metal-working is attested very early in Georgia, for example at Kvatskhelebi, and that that region was more advanced in this respect than Armenia, need be taken too seriously: Metsamor, not far from Armavir-Blur, was a metallurgical workshop with its origins dating back well into the third millennium BC; and finds at Kültepe (Nakhichevan) prove that the people of the Araxes valley were not more backward in metal-working than those of regions nearer the Caucasus.[44] Nor were settlements in Armenia confined to the plain: at Garni, in the mountains above Erevan, have been excavated remains of a typical village of the third millennium BC, with the usual range of pottery and with stone-built round houses.

Several settlements have been quoted as 'type sites' of the first of the three periods of the Early Trans-Caucasian culture. Some western archaeologists have suggested Karaz;[45] Piotrovskii and Khanzadian favour Shresh-Blur;[46] Kültepe (Nakhichevan) II is recognized as an important site. No single site in Georgia seems preeminent, though Didube and Kiketi were early singled out as typical of the first phase of this culture, on which B.A. Kuftin was the pioneer authority.[47] Among the above-mentioned sites Karaz and Kültepe stand out for their material and for the extent to which it has been published. Kvatskhelebi Levels C3–C1, Amiranis-Gora and Khiznaant-Gora E are outstanding among the many Georgian sites of this culture, and are the most significant for this first period.

Armenian sites of this period include Shresh-Blur II, Shengavit II, Mashtots-Blur III, Mokhra-Blur II and Sev-Blur II, all these having earlier occupation stratified beneath these levels. Contemporary Georgian sites include Kvatskhelebi C3–C1, Amiranis-Gora, Khiznaant-Gora E, Sadakhlo, Tetri-Tsqaro, Didube, Kiketi, Zemoavchala and Sagvarjile; and a second list also probably to be included in this period are Zghuderi, Kulbakebi, Ozni, Beshtasheni (moat and hearth) and Tqviavi. These latter sites do not, however, date back as early as the others in Georgia, and perhaps a sub-division into two phases (IA and IB) would be justifiable for that region, though insufficiently documented elsewhere. This implies an end for this whole period (Early Trans-Caucasian IA and IB) in Georgia c. 2,600 BC, but probably slightly earlier in Armenia, a conclusion supported by the radio-carbon dates for the Early Trans-Caucasian II levels at Yanik Tepe, mentioned above. Apart from Kültepe in the Nakhichevan Autonomous Region in the Araxes valley, Baba-Dervish is an Azerbaijani site with occupation datable to this period. Beyond Trans-Caucasia, Hamit Koşay's site of Karaz certainly was occupied at this time, and probably Pulur likewise. Elsewhere in eastern Anatolia only scattered surface occurrences of sherds with relief decoration could point to occupation from early in the third millennium BC.[48] Current excavations in the area of the Keban dam are clearly revealing occupation of this period, which the radio-carbon date from Korucutepe suggests began by c. 3,000 BC.

The date of the beginning of the Early Trans-Caucasian I period has already been indicated as falling about or just before 3,000 BC in Georgia and perhaps also in the Araxes valley. But if the theory of an original homeland around Erevan is accepted, Shresh-Blur II, Shengavit II and the other contemporary Armenian sites must surely have to be dated back to c. 3,250–3,000 BC. This would also help to narrow the period of time in the fourth millennium BC for which there is such a paucity of evidence. An even higher date cannot be ruled out. While certain sites can be quoted as suggesting not too protracted a timespan for each of the three successive main periods of this culture, others prove that such indications can often be very misleading, the same being true elsewhere in the ancient Near East. For the Early Trans-Caucasian I period Kültepe (Nakhichevan) II can be taken as a yardstick. Here there were fourteen levels distinguished in Period II, with a total depth of deposit of eight metres (from 4·50 m. down to 12·50 m.), the radio-carbon date of 2,920 ±90 BC being from a sample obtained at a depth of 8·50 m.[49] This supports a beginning of this sequence of levels well before 3,000 BC, though too much reliance should never be placed on one radio-carbon date. In contrast to this succession of fourteen levels, there were only three at Kvatskhelebi in Period c: this suggests, in spite of the excavators' insistence that after the fire which destroyed Level c3 there was only a brief abandonment of the site, that there was in fact a long period of desertion. There are simply too few levels at Kvatskhelebi to extend over anything approaching the whole duration of the Early Trans-Caucasian culture.[50] The same can be said of many other sites, a fact suggesting that the distribution and intensity of settled life varied considerably during the third millennium BC. Over-cropping and perhaps also minor climatic fluctuations would have been among factors causing changing patterns of village economy, in turn of course affecting the life-time of settlements. Deforestation of parts of Georgia has been suggested as a factor diminishing earlier settlements of this culture in the plains.[51] Hardly any sites were occupied without any interruption. Even Shengavit has a total depth of deposit of only four metres.

It has been said that round houses were characteristic of the eastern part of the Early Trans-Caucasian cultural zone, including regions as far apart as Daghestan, in the north-east Caucasus, and the Urmia basin, near Tabriz, with all the intervening settlements and most of those in Georgia likewise having round houses.[52] Further west, however, rectangular houses occur at Amiranis-Gora and at Karaz, while the dwellings excavated at Kvatskhelebi, including nine in the most prolific level (c3), cannot be described as circular: some are square with rounded corners; others have more the plan of a squared off circle. Round houses occur at sites in Armenia including Shengavit, Shresh-Blur, Jerahovid, Kültepe (Echmiadzin) and Garni; at Ozni and Khiznaant-Gora (close to Kvatschelebi) in Georgia; at Kayakent in Daghestan; at Kültepe (Nakhichevan) in that region of Azerbaijan; and at Yanik Tepe, near Tabriz. Not all these date to this first period. A circular structure at Khirbet Kerak in Palestine cannot be classed as a house.[53] The central wooden post was a common feature already in the Early Trans-Caucasian I period, and is well exemplified at Kvatskhelebi, where there was also a hearth beside the post. The need for the central post largely depended on the diameter of the houses, those at Shengavit, not all of this first period, being of six to eight metres. At Kültepe II there was a wide divergence, from little more than a hut (3·50 m.) to as much as 13 m. in diameter: here too were the central post, hearth and ovens. Walls were never very massive, being from 20 to 70 cm. thick. At Kültepe foundations were in some buildings of stone, in others simply of mud brick or of terre pisée. Rectangular annexes, serving normally as entrance porches, occur here, at Kvatskhelebi and at Shengavit, as well as in the next period at Yanik Tepe.

The importance of the hearth has been much emphasized, especially at Kvatskhelebi, where, it has been suggested, the fire which razed the village to the ground probably happened at a time when the inhabitants were enacting an important ritual centred round each family hearth.[54] A factor supporting this suggestion is the decoration lavished on the portable hearths and stands which are so distinctive a feature of the whole Early Trans-Caucasian tradition. An altogether wider question is whether these portable hearths can in any way be compared with the 'horns of consecration' of Minoan Crete and their counterparts in the shrines excavated in the Early Bronze II levels (XVI-XIV) at Beycesultan, in south-western Anatolia.[55] At Yanik Tepe the hearths are neither portable nor centrally placed, but are put next to the doorway, suggesting that practical considerations of allowing the smoke to escape took precedence over the social attributes of the hearth, whose religious significance for this prehistoric population is understandable in the context of the long severe winters, when the family must have sat for hours in the dark, their eyes drawn to the fire.

The role of nomadism, or at least of transhumance, in the lives of the Early Trans-Caucasian people is perhaps reflected in the very form and construction of these houses, the circular plan, central post and light wattle-and-daub superstructure all recalling the Turkoman *yurt* of modern times. Yet such a plan has practical advantages, especially in the months of snow; and these houses, with their floor level often below that of the surrounding courtyard outside, must have resembled those to be seen in some villages in the highland zone today, where it is not always easy to see if one is walking beside or over the house. Kulbakebi, in the South Ossetian region of Georgia and near Tskhinvali (Staliniri), has been described as a temporary settlement, thus in seasonal use only, the houses being of wooden construction and leaving behind traces only of their foundation platforms.[56]

The permanent character of the more important settlements in the plains is clearly demonstrated by the defensive wall round the village of Shengavit, situated on a spur overlooking the high left bank of the River Hrazdan, a tributary flowing south into the Araxes. This wall was built of large blocks of stone carefully set together; on the north side was an underground passage down to the river. This invites comparison with Yanik Tepe in the second of the three periods: there a short stretch of defensive wall no less than five metres thick was uncovered together with a narrow entrance-passage running right through the wall. The stones, undressed and largely water-worn, must have been transported at least several miles to the site, presumably in carts or on sledges. Such defences indicate external danger and the communal organization needed to meet it.[57]

By far the most abundant class of material is the pottery, important not merely for its quantity but even more for its distinctive features which make it the hall-mark of this culture as a whole. Without the pottery the Early Trans-Caucasian culture would never have been recognized as a distinctive highland culture; nor would the tripartite division into three successive periods have been at all practicable. The durability and lack of intrinsic value of pottery both contribute to its overriding importance for the prehistorian. Being seldom worth the trouble of repair or rescue after accident or departure from home, pottery has greater chronological value than jewellery, metalwork, seals or other objects of economic or sentimental value, often handed down as heirlooms.

There is a considerable variety of pottery attributed by Soviet archaeologists to the Early Trans-Caucasian I period, classed by them as part of the Aeneolithic period. The ceramic tradition beginning in this period continued, with modifications, till the end of the third period: this is the main reason for the inclusion of this third period in the Early Trans-Caucasian sequence, rather than, through greater stress on metallurgy, terming it the Early Bronze Age, as the Soviet publications do. On the whole the Early Trans-Caucasian I pottery from Georgia displays a paucity of decoration, the motifs on jars from Amiranis-Gora, for example, being rather crude; Khiznaant-Gora produced its own range of pottery with yellow-brown ware. Most striking are relief spirals on jars from Kiketi, where the characteristic double spiral makes its appearance, followed a little later by similar spirals at Ozni. That site, together with Beshtasheni, shows that by the latter part of the Early Trans-Caucasian I period in Georgia there had been a considerable development of relief patterns applied to pottery.[58]

In Armenia there was a far greater development of ceramic decoration, more often in grooving than in relief, and with more sophisticated forms than those found at sites in Georgia. Dr E. Khanzadian has discussed the pottery of this period from Armenian sites, especially Shresh-Blur and Kültepe (Echmiadzin), which she believes to be decorated with motifs depicting water, earth and plants; but such interpretations appear to be rather subjective.[59]

The bold spirals and other relief ornament seen at Shresh-Blur and Karaz have an immediate impact. These first attracted the attention of archaeologists not familiar at first hand with Trans-Caucasia or eastern Anatolia; and this type of decoration was also thought by the writer to be distinctive of the first of the three periods of this culture.[60] Yet already in the first period the different decorative techniques are present, though incision was virtually confined to lids. Not for the first time typology has melted away in the light of discovery.

The Early Trans-Caucasian II period is represented by so many sites that it is hard to choose a few which might be labelled as type sites. Khanzadian suggests Shengavit III, and this site certainly deserves prominence, if only for its having a sequence extending over all three periods. Yanik Tepe is too peripheral to be considered as the most representative site, though revealing a long succession of occupation levels. Jerahovid, in the Araxes plain near Erevan, will probably prove to be of the first importance for this and the preceding period too; another Armenian site of this second period is Tagavoranast (Kirovakan). Khanzadian distinguishes two groups of Early Trans-Caucasian II pottery, one centred round Kirovakan and the other round Shengavit, approximately divided between the hill country of Armenia and onward into Georgia and, secondly, the Araxes plain.

Outside Trans-Caucasia there are sites along both the west and the east sides of Lake Urmia, Geoy Tepe K dating in part to this period but probably originating in the preceding period.[61] Apart from Geoy Tepe KI there is nothing to suggest significant settlement of the Urmia basin by the Early Trans-Caucasian people until this second period, when Yanik Tepe was reoccupied after a long interval of abandonment. At Godin Tepe, situated eight miles south-east of Kangavar on the borders of Kurdistan and Luristan, Period IV was characterized by pottery comparable with that of Yanik Tepe in the Early Trans-Caucasian II and III periods. Here there was evidence of erosion, suggesting a desertion of the site similar to that in the same period at Yanik Tepe, when at both sites in the early centuries of the third millennium BC there must have been a decline in settled life.[62] Other sites round Godin Tepe have also yielded incised ware of Early Trans-Caucasian II type. All the evidence from Godin Tepe indicates a movement from Trans-Caucasia at the beginning of the Early Trans-Caucasian II period (not before 2,700 BC) and the decline of this northern intrusive element from about the onset of the Early Trans-Caucasian III period. At Yanik Tepe, situated far to the north, this element naturally became more firmly ensconced.

The Elazığ and Malatya regions largely shared the general ceramic tradition of the rest of the cultural zone. The group of pots from Ernis, on the north-east shore of Lake Van, was dated by the writer after his survey of 1956–7 to the period now termed Early Trans-Caucasian II:[63] this dating still seems correct, though the numerous parallels at Yanik Tepe show that a more precise dating, to the closing phase of this period, is now possible.

All the above evidence of pottery attributable to this period reveals certain regional variations, such as the rather limited distribution of the incised decoration found at Yanik Tepe. It also shows that the Early Trans-Caucasian II period witnessed the expansion of this culture to its widest geographical limits.

59

Without the sequence of twelve building phases distinguished at Yanik Tepe the time-span of the Early Trans-Caucasian II period might have been judged as brief. The Armenian, Georgian and Azerbaijani sites do not seem to prove a lengthy duration, and there is still a dearth of radio-carbon dates from the Soviet Union for this period. Yanik Tepe here fills a lacuna, with its four radio-carbon dates from this period:[64] most probably this period there lasted from c. 2,650 BC till c. 2,200 BC. These chronological limits would imply the beginning of this period at Yanik Tepe only shortly after its start in Trans-Caucasia, but its continuance rather later than in the homeland to the north. This hint of conservatism is reinforced by the sudden appearance at Yanik Tepe of the third cultural period, with little evidence of transition.

Altogether fifty-seven round houses were wholly or partly excavated at Yanik Tepe. There was a progressive increase both in the diameter of these round houses and apparently also in the density of the population, the earliest levels being characterized by small houses of only about 3·50 metres in diameter and with considerable open areas in between; in the latest levels the round houses were much larger, necessitating the intro-duction of a central post, often with stones set round the post-hole. Round the circumference of the interior of the round houses was usually ranged a bench, with a series of standard fittings invariably set immediately to the right of the door as one entered; the door was often marked by a high threshold, and the floor commonly was slightly lower than the courtyard. A bin for storage was a feature of the larger round houses, while a hearth and oven were essential; another common feature was a smoothly plastered surface, sloping down a little from the wall and with a groove or runnel for carrying off liquid. This surface was presumably used for the preparation of food. Space must have been extremely cramped for the housewife, and it is hardly surprising that accidents happened: such were many of the burnings of these houses, an event found often to have its mark two or three times in one house, probably as the result of a gust of wind through the doorway causing the kitchen fire to flare up and to catch the wattle-and-daub roof alight. The door may have been the only escape for the smoke. Yet not all these destructions by fire, events which preserved in situ so much pottery at Yanik Tepe, were accidental. Attack was a constant danger to the community, demonstrated by the defences built in Level XVII and the subsequent violent destruction of the whole level.[65] Such conclusions are of course based on the limited proportion of the whole mound which could be excavated; but there is no reason for serious doubt that this was true of the site as a whole. The massive defences for a time gave Yanik Tepe almost the status of a small town, probably encompassed by marauding nomads. The continuity from one level to the next suggests local raids rather than any attack from afar, still less any occupation of the site. Yet the inhabitants of Yanik Tepe were probably themselves but one remove from nomadism, for once they had left the Araxes valley they settled only at widely separated places on their way south to the borders of Luristan. The proof of the light construction of the roofs of the round houses at Yanik Tepe, similar to those in Trans-Caucasia, was obtained from fallen fragments of burnt clay impressed with wattling.[66] In one round house at Yanik Tepe a thin screen of stakes with a low mud base was used to divide the interior into kitchen and sleeping quarters, and other houses had similar partitions. The gloom inside these houses is emphasized by the frequent occurrence of small pottery lamps. Outside the doorway there was often a rectangular porch. The beehive profile of the round houses is indicated by the way in which the mud brick walls, often surviving one metre or more in height, curve inwards, unless distorted by subsequent collapse or subsidence. One area of excavation at Yanik Tepe (Level XVII) suggests that communication from one part of the town to another may have become difficult with the growing size and density of the round houses.

The architecture of other sites shows perhaps a less complete devotion to the round house: for example, at Shengavit there are many rectangular rooms also. At other sites in Trans-Caucasia round houses were normal, as at Jerahovid, where four levels with them have been distinguished, and where borings indicate a depth of occupation of no less than ten metres, continuing down well below the modern water table. At Khiznaant-Gora D a round house has two concentric walls, stake impressions and a portable hearth in the centre.

Such was the abundance of pottery from Yanik Tepe that it could be taken as providing the best repertoire of wares, forms and decoration, this last mostly but not exclusively incised; but the quality of the decoration is not always such as to make a corpus of pottery based on this site entirely satisfactory. Undoubtedly the best products of the Yanik Tepe potters could rival those of the Armenian sites in the homeland of the whole Early Trans-Caucasian culture. Much that was made there, however, was inferior in execution. If the architectural rather than the ceramic traditions be taken as the criteria for the dividing line between the two periods (Early Trans-Caucasian II and III) represented at Yanik Tepe, then three phases of Early Trans-Caucasian II can be differentiated. It may be significant that in the first phase (Yanik Tepe XXVI-XXI), far the least well represented quantitatively, the incised lines are finer than in the rather longer phase which followed (Yanik Tepe XX-XVI), when greater boldness of design often prevailed.

Parallels with the incised ornamentation so prolific at Yanik Tepe are not easily found in lands bordering Trans-Caucasia, unless certain of the motifs carved on the dolmens of Abkhazia and further north, in the western Caucasus, be taken to show the slightest connection with Early Trans-Caucasian II motifs, a comparison which hardly seems plausible, apart from the different medium and scale. In Anatolia there is a certain amount of incised pottery at Tarsus and Zincirli, of various wares and dating to the Cilician Early Bronze II period: the parallels are not at all close, resemblances in simple geometric ornament perhaps being inevitable; but chronologically the comparison is perfectly possible, for the Cilician Early Bronze II period came to an end c. 2,300 BC.[67]

The excavators of Kvatskhelebi make it plain that, while Period B is different from Period C preceding it, the ceramic tradition throughout the third millennium BC at this site may be taken as typical of Georgia as a whole. The three levels of Kvatskhelebi B show that a uniform black surface outside, grey or pink inside and a high burnish were distinctive of the pottery of that period, contrasting with the uneven colouring of the Kvatskhelebi C pottery. Similarities with the pottery of Sachkere are stressed, though this is normally dated to the third and final period of the Early Trans-Caucasian culture. The incised decoration on pottery of Kvatskhelebi is much less ambitious than on that of Yanik Tepe, being largely limited to the simplest of chevron bands round the whole pot. The evidence from Kvatskhelebi as a whole suggests that it was by this time in a conservative area of the Early Trans-Caucasian II culture: the same seems to be true of the whole of Georgia.

At Baba-Dervish, in the Kura valley in north-western Azerbaijan SSR, there had been no decoration on pottery from the Early Trans-Caucasian I levels, while relief decoration was found 'perhaps in the middle levels'. Incised representations of birds, exemplified by a sherd from a bowl of very highly burnished black ware, could surely be of the second rather than (as suggested to the writer) of the third period of this culture. Whatever its precise dating, this provides a clear northern parallel with the ceramic tradition of Yanik Tepe.

With the advent of the Early Trans-Caucasian III period, which began in its main homeland c. 2,300 BC, the cultural stagnation which had set in over much of the highland zone, though not in the Araxes valley, seems to have come to an end in a new awakening of the Early Trans-Caucasian culture. The old homogeneity from the Caucasus to the upper Euphrates largely vanished, but in its place began to arise vigorous regional cultures, retaining much of the former traditions but evolving new forms in pottery and above all in metalwork. These changes were not the mark of a violent upheaval and the arrival of newcomers but rather of the fertilizing of the old culture through external contacts, especially with the advanced civilization of Mesopotamia, now under the Akkadian dynasty first reaching out for new commercial enterprises and markets in the highlands to the east and north of the Tigris and Euphrates valleys. A strong tradition of metal-working, based on Sumerian prototypes, arose in this period in north Syria, whence influences spread on to the Anatolian plateau.[68]

Parallels in Trans-Caucasia with Sumerian tools and weapons have long ago been noted.[69] All the available evidence goes to indicate a quickening of commercial relations, for the first time on a significant scale, with Mesopotamia. The precise routes by which this trade was conducted are uncertain. The fact that the Assyrian merchants now first established their trading colony (*karum*) at Kanesh (Kültepe) – where Level IV, the earliest, dates to *c.* 2,100–2,050 BC[70] – indicates organized contacts and the importation of tin from the east via Iran and Ashur to Anatolia. Thus eastern Anatolia appears to have been bypassed, so that Mesopotamian connections through the western part of the highland cultural zone seem less probable than through western Iran northwards to the Araxes valley. Yet there remains a dearth of supporting evidence to prove strong trading links in the period *c.* 2,300–*c.* 2,000 BC through the Urmia basin and southwards across the Zagros mountains. If the lack of contemporary burials is remembered, Yanik Tepe need not be regarded as very backward at this time, nor the absence of metalwork very significant.

Contemporary with the Early Trans-Caucasian III sites south of the Caucasus was the great burial at Maikop in the Kuban valley, long a centre of discussion.[71] It is now widely agreed to date to *c.* 2,300–*c.* 2,200 BC, and thus to be not only in certain respects comparable but also undoubtedly contemporary with at least the later of the rich burials at Alaca Hüyük, in central Anatolia, later to become the homeland of the Hittites but then occupied by the non-Indo-European Hattians.[72] Contacts between the Kuban valley and central Anatolia are thus archaeologically certain. No evidence, however, is known to indicate any continuous link of comparable burials or settlements across the highlands of eastern Anatolia, whose cultural connections with the Halys bend and with the rest of central Anatolia seem, from the pottery and other material remains, to have been rather tenuous. The central Anatolian cultural province of the Early Bronze II period, formerly known as the Copper Age, extended to the Pontic coast around Samsun, where Dündartepe and other sites show strong affinities with Alaca Hüyük and the surrounding region of the plateau.[73] Horoztepe and Mahmutlar, in the region two millennia later to be the nucleus of the kingdom of Pontus, have yielded gold and bronze objects classifiable with those from Alaca, though the Horoztepe bronzes show distinctive features.[74] Comparable figures of stags were reported some years ago on the Black Sea coast at Giresun. Maritime trade across the relatively short distance from there to the littoral north of Abkhazia seems therefore likely to have been the major factor in bringing about connections between Anatolia and the steppes north of the Caucasus. A backward flow of cultural influence from the Kaban valley into Georgia could well have affected the development of metal-working in that part of the Early Trans-Caucasian zone. Such an influence thus reaching the Georgian sites could account for the apparent advance of that region in the Early Trans-Caucasian III period, when it was no longer backward as it had been. Influence coming direct from the south through Armenia could of course have brought about this advance in Georgia, but had not done so in the preceding period.

Early Trans-Caucasian III sites are found all over the various cultural provinces now comprising the whole zone. Some regions, such as that round Lake Van, probably remained culturally stagnant, with only a weak tradition of life in permanent settlements. In Armenia, however, there seems to have been no decline in the intensity of settled communities: Khanzadian's classification of sites according to varieties of pottery is discussed below; in addition to her sites there are some others, including the settlement at Haridj (Artik), perhaps dating back earlier,[75] and also Franganots, Kiznavur, Kheznavouz, Aghtamour and the settlement and cemetery at Stepanakert. In Georgia there has to be more dependence on material from cemeteries, at Amiranis-Gora, at Sachkhere and in the mountains above the settlement of Tetri-Tsqaro. Sadakhlo and Baba-Dervish may have continued to be occupied, and there was a sanctuary at Balanta.[76] The rock drawings of horses at Kobistan, south of Baku, may date either to this period or to the early second millennium BC or even later: there can be no certainty about this. Geoy Tepe K3 and Karaz II continued to be occupied. It was in the south-western cultural province, from Elaziğ to Malatya, that the most obvious change in pottery appeared: shapes remained largely in the old tradition, but both ware and decoration altered completely. Many sites yielding pottery of this cultural province have been found, from Fero, near Divriği, to a whole group of mounds in the rich plain near Elaziğ, now called Altinova ('the golden plain').[77] Arslantepe (Malatya) has proved particularly rich in pottery of this type, originally misnamed Hittite; and recent excavations have been carried out at a contemporary site nearby at Gelinciktepe.[78] An extension of the cultural zone into the north Caucasus is suggested by the site of Zaglik; Lugovoe, Velikent, Kayakent and Mamaikutan are settlement sites in the north-east Caucasus (Daghestan and Checheno Ingushetia) yielding pottery and chipped and ground stone industries showing general affinity with the Early Trans-Caucasian tradition; and their evidence is supplemented by that from barrows (*kurgans*) at Novii Arshti and Kataragach Tapa.[79] Knobbed decoration on some of the pottery is one hint that this north-eastward extension of the cultural zone may well have occurred before the Early Trans-Caucasian III period. Pellets, relief ornament and Nakhichevan lugs are features of the pottery of these sites.

There is not so clear an indication of a long time-span for this period as there was at Yanik Tepe for the second period and at Kültepe (Nakhichevan) for the first. There is indeed a series of occupation levels (XIII-VII) at Yanik Tepe, which, with sub-phases, totals nine; but these, excavated on the summit of the site, suggest a peaceful period with spasmodic repairs and remodelling of houses, in contrast to the frequent destructions and consequent complete rebuildings of the preceding period. The three phases of Kvatskhelebi B do not suggest a very long duration. The above-mentioned radio-carbon dates for Shengavit IV (2,020 ±80 BC) and for Yanik Tepe (2,086 ±104 BC and 1,816 ±63 BC) are the sole indications of absolute chronology, apart from comparisons with sites outside the cultural zone. The most important site for such chronological parallels is Hasanlu, in the Solduz valley immediately south of Lake Urmia, for which there now exists a most useful series of radio-carbon dates,[80] including five for Hasanlu VII, the period characterized by 'painted orange ware': these five dates range from 2,280 ±140 BC to 2,121 ±138 BC. Though one date cannot be over-emphasized, the second one from Yanik Tepe lends some support to the theory that the Early Trans-Caucasian cultural traditions lingered on well into the second millennium BC in parts of the Urmia basin; and probably they did so too in the districts surrounding Lake Van. The occurrences of 'painted orange ware' east and west of Lake Urmia, the latter in Geoy Tepe K3, give indications of the chronological overlap of this class of pottery with that of the Early Trans-Caucasian III period.[81]

If the above-mentioned suggestion that the tradition of building round houses was especially characteristic of the eastern part of the Early Trans-Caucasian cultural zone is to be believed, then the change from round to rectangular buildings in the Early Trans-Caucasian III (Levels XIII-VII) at Yanik Tepe requires some explanation. T.N.Chubinishvili believes that the tradition of building rectangular houses is mainly found in eastern Georgia, represented by plans revealed by excavations at Kvatskhelebi, Gudabertka and Khiznaant-Gora.[82] Round houses or plans showing their influence, as at Kvatskhelebi, occur also at these same sites, so that there was apparently no marked division between two distinct architectural traditions. The houses at Kvatskhelebi throughout Periods C and B are essentially classifiable as rectangular: any hint of the circular plan had disappeared by the end of Period C. At Yanik Tepe, however, there was an unmistakable change. The rectangular buildings now suggest a peaceful period in which attachment to the settled life was firmly established, no hint of nomadism surviving. Even the incised and excised ornament on the pottery had vanished, leaving no trace of the imitations of woodcarving which gave a hint of nomadic origins in the preceding period. The main building found at Yanik Tepe was fairly large, and had a basement, evidently accessible only by a staircase descending from the floor above. One trace of the previous period, however, did remain: there were kitchen ranges, hearth and oven, with working surface of plaster precisely like those in the round houses. One such oven was equipped for baking *sanjak*, bread of a type still made in that area, being baked on pebbles heated in the fire, resulting in a crinkled surface, burnt where in direct contact with the stones. One site in Georgia provides an architectural contrast comparable with that of the two periods at Yanik Tepe, for rectangular houses in Khiznaant-Gora B and c succeed round houses in D.

The inherent tendency of the Early Trans-Caucasian III pottery is towards simplification of forms and decoration, towards reduced emphasis on the junction of neck with shoulder on jars and on other sharp angles of profile and towards elongation of forms.[83] Three classes of Early Trans-Caucasian III pottery have been distinguished by Khanzadian, the representative sites being Elar, Shengavit and Aragats. The relative proximity of these sites shows that they can hardly belong to three geographically distinguishable cultural sub-provinces; nor is there any clear evidence suggesting a chronological progression from one class of pottery to another. Khanzadian's first group, named after Elar, is mostly but by no means exclusively represented by sites in Armenia. The Shengavit ceramic group seems to be primarily Georgian in distribution. The Aragats group includes pottery from Armavir and some of the wares from Kültepe (Nakhichevan) II; parallels are said to be discernible at Lugovoe in the north-east Caucasus and at Yanik Tepe.

Beside the general continuity of ceramic forms at Yanik Tepe, though without any incision, there appeared one new improvement, in the guise of highly burnished jars with a silvery sheen over the black slip, probably achieved by use of graphite and very possibly representing a deliberate attempt to imitate the effect of silver.

In Georgia there are now known to be comparable products of similar date, with the same imitation of silver; and traces of metal prototypes can be discerned in the pottery from several sites. Among these is the cemetery of Tetri-Tsqaro, in the mountains above the earlier settlement: the pottery from here displays an aesthetic and technical standard unsurpassed among all the products of the Early Trans-Caucasian culture, and it dates to c. 2,000 BC. There is the same silvery graphite treatment of the surface as at Yanik Tepe, but the pottery itself is of superior quality, and there is also abundant evidence of metalworking, so conspicuously scarce at Yanik Tepe. Pottery from the contemporary cemetery at Amiranis-Gora, excavated by Chubinishvili, likewise has silvery graphite burnish:

knobs along the top of the shoulder are characteristic and seem to imitate rivets; one twin vessel takes the form of two typical jars joined together just below the widest part.[84] Rather earlier is the pottery from Sadakhlo, probably dating to c. 2,300–2,200 BC, from a site occupied since the fourth millennium BC: one jar from this site demonstrates the high artistry attained in incised patterns on pottery of this period in Georgia, being ornamented with birds, spirals and a motif to be described as a pendant axehead, the surface being black burnished. Chubinishvili believes that such signs imitate designs on stamp- and cylinder-seals of Mesopotamian origin; but there seems insufficient evidence to support such a theory, nor are the suggested connections with the Jemdet Nasr culture chronologically plausible, apart from the geographical distance involved.[85] Sadakhlo has produced a possibly anthropomorphic incised design, one of very few representations of human figures on Early Trans-Caucasian pottery, their rarity being hard to explain. Incised birds on pots from Baba-Dervish may date to about the same century (c. 2,300–2,200 BC), but there are inadequate chronological data for certainty. At Sachkhere the sequence began with the pottery of this period in the old tradition, including relief ornament. Sachkhere was contemporary with the cemetery at Tetri-Tsqaro, and was the immediate precursor of the famous Trialeti barrows.[86] The general impression from Georgian sites must surely be that this period saw a great awakening in a region hitherto relatively retrograde compared with the Araxes valley around Erevan. No longer was Georgia peripheral. New elements had appeared, and change was in the air.

The pottery from Armenian sites must seem slightly less interesting, because its innovations are less indicative of the advancing role of metallurgy. Yet here too fine wares were produced, and the first manifestations of painting began to appear, intrusive from the south as they must have been, for painting was totally alien to the Early Trans-Caucasian ceramic traditions of Georgia, and appeared only in the Malatya-Elaziğ region, too far to the west to be relevant. Recent excavations by Telemak Khachatrian of an Early Trans-Caucasian settlement at Haridj, near Artik, have been supplemented by the discovery of a cemetery, near this same site, with pottery of the Early Trans-Caucasian III period and also of the first half of the second millennium BC.[87] In spite of Khanzadian's inclusion of Yanik Tepe pottery in the Aragats group, it seems to the writer that it is in the Elar group that vessels with decoration confined to finger-depressions and thus comparable with Yanik Tepe are especially to be found. The differences between classes of pottery within this period, apart from the painted ware of the Malatya-Elaziğ cultural province, are outweighed by their common tradition.

Hitherto the discussion of the Early Trans-Caucasian culture has been based principally on the pottery, the most abundant, ubiquitous and securely classifiable artifact. Without the ceramic evidence it would indeed be difficult if not quite impossible to distinguish the three periods of this long-lasting culture. Two periods only could be differentiated, in the light of the evidence of great improvements and diversification in metal-working in the last two or three centuries of the third millennium BC. Before that time metal-working had a long prehistory in Trans-Caucasia, but it was a copper industry. The copper was often alloyed, usually unintentionally, with arsenic and other elements; but the tools and weapons were produced by hammering rather than casting, an adequate method for many purposes, but with serious limitations both in the variety of its products and in the speed of their manufacture.

A recent discovery at Metsamor, a large, low outcrop of rock in the Araxes plain upstream of Erevan, has revealed one of the factors behind the prosperity of Armenia in the third millennium BC, for here E. Khanzadian has found a centre of metal-working indeed unique in its complexity and its long life.[88] Most of the remains at this remarkable site date to the second and first millennia BC, with even later traces of use. But the earliest phase, in areas of the site where a stratified sequence was obtained by the excavators, yielded, in association with Early Trans-Caucasian pottery, a variety of metallurgical material. The most important is bronze slag, with cassiterite, the ore from which tin is smelted. This is not found anywhere in the Araxes valley, and must have been imported crude for smelting at Metsamor. Clay pipes inserted in the furnaces for use with bellows were also found. Likewise of this first phase at Metsamor are phosphorus brickettes: these were apparently made from the bones and brains of animals, ground up with clay; the mixture of phosphorus, barium and strontium is said to indicate the age of these products, being found at Metsamor not later than c. 1,000 BC. Phosphorus was used in the smelting of cassiterite to obtain tin. Here then is evidence of an Armenian centre of bronze-working in the Early Trans-Caucasian III period. The monopoly perhaps enjoyed by the Sumerians in this branch of metallurgy, best displayed in the Royal Cemetery at Ur but also in the early imports of tools and weapons from the south into Trans-Caucasia and beyond, seems thus to have been relatively short-lived.[89] The barbarians of the north, as they must have seemed to the city merchants of Sumer and Akkad, had quickly mastered the alloying of copper with tin to make bronze, enabling them to turn out mass-produced tools and weapons as well as elaborate castings by the lost wax (cire perdue) process. This last was either copied at Maikop, or, more probably, imported thither from central Anatolia or some other unknown place of origin south of the Caucasus. Sumerian metal imports into Trans-

Caucasia may have begun earlier than surviving specimens might suggest; but this trade did not flourish for long. Local initiative saw to that.

According to statistics of 1917, no fewer than 418 sources of copper were known in the Caucasus. This fact alone, rather than proximity to the Near East, could account for the advance of metal-working in Trans-Caucasia and in the north Caucasus earlier than in the steppes.[90] Early theories of a birthplace of all metallurgy in the Caucasus can, however, be discounted. But particularly rich in copper ore were western Georgia (the upper Rioni valley and the south-eastern shore of the Black Sea), much of central Trans-Caucasia and the Belokan-Kakhetia region in the eastern Caucasus. Extensive research has been carried out, largely in the State Museum at Tbilisi and by I.R.Selimkhanov at Baku, in analysing samples thought to be of native copper and also alloys: laboratories in both cities are well staffed and equipped to produce numerous results, which it is difficult to interpret concisely.[91] It seems that it is still hard to be sure in every case whether native copper has been used. One series of copper samples from Azerbaijan showed no traces of arsenic or antimony, nor were lead, bismuth or cobalt present; but silver, though like gold of irregular occurrence in native copper, was present in all but one sample.[92] Thus a high silver content generally suggests native copper, which of course could be used by simple annealing and hammering. The first major advance was the invention of smelting, without which no true metallurgy can be said to exist: the removal of impurities from natural ores vastly widened the number of sources available for exploitation. A high percentage of arsenic or of iron in a sample thought to be of native copper must indicate that in fact it is of chalcopyrites, an ore from which copper can be extracted by smelting alone. The Kedabek region of Azerbaijan has yielded chalcopyrites with high copper and iron content but with no other element except for a trace of silver. Samples from the Armenian SSR show insignificant impurities. Selimkhanov has found that arsenic and antimony rarely occur in native copper from Georgia and the Artvin region: he asserts that in Georgia in the 'aeneolithic epoch' (i.e. Early Trans-Caucasian I and II and rather earlier) native copper was not used but only copper alloys. His conclusions do not, however, agree with those of the Georgian scientists, who at least have the advantage of access to their own territory: this difference seems to arise from Selimkhanov's scepticism concerning spectographic analyses; he evidently regards quantitative analyses as alone being reliable.

From the chemical laboratory of the Georgian State Museum in Tbilisi have come numerous analyses of metal artifacts, quite sufficient to provide a full understanding of the different copper ores used and of the subsequent introduction of bronzes produced by alloying copper either with tin or with antimony.[93] The Early Trans-Caucasian I and II periods were technologically 'aeneolithic', in a primitive phase of copper metal-lurgy. A bead from Kvatskhelebi (Urbnisi) is among artifacts of this phase analysed and found to contain slightly over one per cent of arsenic, which is known to be present in Georgian copper ores. The proportion of arsenic was higher in contemporary artifacts from Kültepe (Nakhichevan), up to 4·06 per cent. The Tbilisi analyses demonstrated the great leap for-ward which occurred during the Early Trans-Caucasian III period in Georgia, in many respects the formative period for successive centuries thereafter. The content of arsenic in copper artifacts of this period natur-ally varied from one area to another, being higher in objects from the dolmens of Abkhazia (2·5 to 3·3 per cent) than in those from the earliest Trialeti barrows (1·48 to 1·97 per cent); antimony always occurs in Abkhazian specimens. Some of the axes from Sachkhere contain up to 6 per cent of arsenic, antimony being in some examples present up to 2·6 per cent. Many axes were not hammered but cast, containing a high percentage of arsenic and traces of iron. The arsenic came not by deliberate alloying but through the ore. The advantages of using copper ores containing a significant proportion of arsenic or antimony was apparently becoming understood in this period (c. 2,300–2,000 BC). Arsenical copper with antimony added has aesthetic advantages, giving a high lustre and silvery colour. Yet had there been any full awareness of the effect of the inclusion of arsenic on copper the chemical composition of weapons and personal ornaments from the Sachkhere district would not have been so similar. Artifacts from the north Caucasus contain much less arsenic (0·44 to 0·94 per cent), while those from Maikop contain 1 per cent of tin, a natural occurrence. Analyses of copper of different periods from the third millennium BC onward at Metsamor showed fourteen alloys, including tin, lead, antimony and zinc.

The range of copper artifacts of the Early Trans-Caucasian I and II periods is fairly easily summarized. Kvatskhelebi yielded a number of objects from burials, metal being so valuable that it is rarely found in occupation levels within a settlement. From a burial contemporary with the earliest level (c3) and thus datable to c. 3,000 BC, came a copper biconical bead and a double spiral pin, which, if correctly attributed to that period, must be the earliest example of a type whose widespread distribution in the closing centuries of the third millennium BC has attracted much attention.[94] Other grave-goods were found in burials contemporary with Kvatskhelebi c2 and in the cemetery at Tvlepias Tsqaro, contemporary with c1 or later levels: a spearhead with bent tang could have Anatolian affinities; other finds include a knife-blade, beads and a double-coil bracelet or torque, all characteristic of an early copper industry as yet without benefit of the technical knowledge necessary for the production of bronze and for casting. The most interesting of all the metal-work from Kvatskhelebi, and also contemporary with CI or later levels, is a copper head-band or diadem, decorated with a chevron band applied by means of punching dots in the soft metal, a horned animal and a bird being similarly rendered.[95] These creatures are comparable with some of those appearing in the incised ceramic repertoire at Yanik Tepe, possibly suggesting therefore a subordination at this stage, the Early Trans-Caucasian I period in Georgia, of the inspiration of the coppersmith to that of the potter. The taste for the double spiral, as with the above-mentioned pin, was also rooted in the ceramic traditions of the Early Trans-Caucasian culture. The metal artifacts from Kültepe II probably largely date to the Early Trans-Caucasian III period: they include an arsenical bronze tanged blade of a knife or dagger, pins and three moulds, one for casting a socketed form of axe; there was also a fragment of a crucible. Among other finds from Kültepe II were a spear-head and a sickle-blade. Khiznaant-Gora has yielded copper daggers from Level D, the one but earliest stratum, and a long copper sickle-blade from Level C. Daggers from Elar, an axe from Leninakan, a hammer-axe from Alaverdi and a socketed axe from the Ararat area are among metal artifacts from sites in Armenia.[96]

In the Early Trans-Caucasian III period, with the general and growing introduction of bronze, metalwork of all kinds shows great development, with the grave-goods from Tetri-Tsqaro and Sachkhere pointing the way to those from the barrows of Trialeti. A very fine double-spiral gold pin was found at Tetri-Tsqaro in a barrow (*kurgan*) lined with thin oak tree-trunks and containing a cart:[97] this pin, said to be paralleled only at Trialeti, could have been used to hold a cloak in position; on one side it is decorated with a meander pattern and on the other side with circles and herringbone motif. Among other metalwork from Tetri-Tsqaro are a chisel and adze of copper and a socketed axe of arsenical bronze. Sachkhere has proved to be the richest source of metalwork of the Early Trans-Caucasian III period in Georgia and indeed perhaps in the whole zone:[98] apart from simple types such as flat adze-blades, there are socketed axes betraying ultimately Mesopotamian inspiration in their forms. Pins of the 'racquet' form occur, and hammer-headed bronze pins, a type with a wide distribution, like those with double spiral head. Among other types, parallels for pins with rolled head have been discerned in Middle Ugarit 2 (c. 1,900–1,750 BC); and other Caucasian types have provided comparative material indicating trade over great distances. In his discussion of these parallels Schaeffer recognized the slight priority of the Sachkhere metalwork, though current opinion among Soviet archaeologists assigns this material to the very end of the third millennium BC, a slightly higher dating. Schaeffer alludes also to parallels in Bohemia.[99]

The distribution of hammer-headed pins seems strongly to suggest an origin in the western Caucasus, since there a concentration occurs, with the remainder extending across the Ukraine to the north German plain; this type occurs also at Alaca Hüyük in central Anatolia and at Lerna in Greece. Imitations are found at Bleckendorf in east Germany.[100] Here then there appears to be a classic example of diffusion of a metal type from its Caucasian homeland into Europe. But gone are the days when any simple theory attributing the seat of metallurgy to a single region, whether in the Near East or beyond, can be countenanced. Just as diffusionist theories concerning the Neolithic Revolution have been discredited, so likewise new evidence has complicated the interpretation of early advances and trade in metalwork. As in Caucasia so in Hungary, Rumania and Slovakia individual centres of copper-working were functioning in the first half of the third millennium BC, with sources in the Carpathians and in the lower Danube basin.[101] Some types were traded as far as Denmark, among these being spiral torques comparable with that found at Kvatskhelebi, where it is not necessarily too early to have been introduced from Europe. Pins with double-spiral head add more evidence for a European influence on the metal-workers of the Early Trans-Caucasian III period and later, since they seem to have been at home on the lower Danube as well as in Anatolia; they are found also as far east as the Indus valley. The utilitarian shaft-hole axes and axe-adzes, perhaps to be associated with extensive tree-felling, have a similarly wide distribution, even to Turkestan.[102]

The effect of metallurgy in promoting distant contacts between regions which, but for the demand for metals, would have remained entirely apart has been long understood. Stone and timber are locally available in regions of settlement in the Near East except for the alluvial plains of Egypt and Mesopotamia. Their absence in Mesopotamia, together with the lack of metals, has been interpreted along the general lines of Arnold Toynbee's theory of challenge and response as the stimulus to Sumerian industrial and commercial primacy. Sumerian achievements as pioneers in copper and bronze metallurgy must not be underestimated: the copper-smiths of central Europe and the Balkans could hardly have attained the same level of skill quite independently of the Sumerians. Yet Sumerian primacy was short-lived, and was very soon being rivalled, and equalled in their own evolving tradition, by coppersmiths of Europe.[103] The Early Trans-Caucasian cultural zone, though geographically within the Near East, was divided only by the high but narrow Caucasus from the northern steppes; and, once there, nothing could prevent the traders reaching the central European copper-working centres. Thus Georgia, with its neighbouring regions, was perhaps open as much to influences from Europe as to those from the Near East. Trans-Caucasia may have been not so much an original centre as a region into which metal-working arrived from two different directions, and where, though present in earlier periods in a modest way, it took root and from the late third millennium BC began to develop along distinctive lines, no longer owing its forms to external inspiration. Against this suggestion is the early evidence of bronze-working at Metsamor. Indubitably the great wealth of the Caucasus in copper, tin, antimony and other metals played a crucial role in its metallurgical history. Metsamor gives a hint that, just as earlier in Europe, once foreign merchants had arrived seeking sources of metals, bringing their copper and later their bronze products with them, and explaining, by choice or otherwise, their techniques to the local population, it was no time before a local industry began to arise. If present evidence indeed points to Armenia as the oldest centre of metallurgy in Trans-Caucasia, it points also to a Near Eastern inspiration. Future discoveries, though they may reveal a similar antiquity for metallurgy in Georgia, seem more likely to indicate that it was not till the conjunction there in the Early Trans-Caucasian III period of Near Eastern influences, ultimately Sumerian, with western influences, ultimately Transylvanian or Slovak, that a rapid advance and diversification in the metal industry occurred, manifest at Sachkhere and at Tetri-Tsqaro. The influence of Alaca Hüyük on Maikop emphasizes the undeniable role of Anatolia in any assessment of the factors behind the emergence of Caucasian metallurgy in the late third millennium BC. This Anatolian influence, exemplified by the spearhead with bent tang, could have come direct across the Black Sea to the Kuban valley or by the circuitous route of the lower Danube and the north Pontic steppes.

The skills of the Early Trans-Caucasian people were displayed in traditional as well as inventive ways, in a wide range of stone artifacts extending from massive quernstones, pestles and pounders, the usual equipment of the early farmers, to a variety of different stones used for jewellery. Vitreous paste and metal slag were used for beads, as well as carnelian, rock crystal and local agate; jasper is also mentioned in connection with the burials at Shengavit. It is in the obsidian arrowheads of the Tetri-Tsqaro cemetery that the finest products in that stone are to be seen, unexpectedly at a time when metal-working was making such strides. At Garni about 170 obsidian pieces were found in one building, perhaps a shop. Obsidian artifacts were also made on the site at Jerahovid in the Araxes plain.[104] Sources of obsidian in Armenia are abundant, and include Mount Aragats. Among obsidian types were arrowheads of triangular and 'mitre' form, as well as roughly chipped scrapers. The ground stone industry included maceheads and a variety of hammeraxes and polished axes. Shengavit and Kültepe (Nakhichevan) have each produced a representative range of the stone artifacts of this culture; less varied were the stone industries of Kvatskhelebi and Yanik Tepe, local flint and chert being used for sickles, of two to four blades at the former site.

The bone industry was mostly confined to small awls and borers. Small hemispherical pieces cut from the articular end of a limb bone and then polished were used possibly as spindle-whorls: these occur at Yanik Tepe and at Kara-Köpektepe, in the Araxes valley. Bone hammers from Yanik Tepe may have been used in leather-working.

Other crafts have left their mark in the excavated sites of this culture. Spindle-whorls of stone, baked clay and bone and impressions of textiles on pottery are found at many sites, including Kvatskhelebi and Yanik Tepe, with the former also yielding linen fragments, showing the cultivation of flax. Spindle-whorls are indeed commonplace at ancient sites all over the Near East; and one common type is shaped like a miniature wheel and made of pottery. Such are frequently found at Early Trans-Caucasian sites.

The function of these small wheels is not always certain: they have bilateral hubs, giving them the appearance of belonging to model carts. Such carts are known from a number of sites in or near the Early Trans-Caucasian zone, and discs of hubbed form are even more widespread, occurring at sites in Georgia, Armenia, the Nakhichevan region, Azerbaijan and eastern Anatolia.[105] Earlier Near Eastern models of carts, together with later examples from Mingechaur in Soviet Azerbaijan (late second millennium BC) and from Kerch in Scythian context have been described as having pottery wheels of the same size and shape as those found so widely in Early Trans-Caucasian settlements. Yet at Yanik Tepe there is some variation in size if not in form of these discs. Wooden wheels, detached from the cart, were often buried in a barrow. An outstanding example is one of the Tri Brata barrows, in the steppes east of the lower Kuban River, in which wheels belonging to three carts were found.[106] Models of carts are numerous in Transylvania and the Hungarian plain; but, though some are contemporary with the Tri Brata barrows and the Early Trans-Caucasian III period, most are dated by Piggott to c. 1,500 BC.[107] The very number of the discs, however, militates against their invariable interpretation as parts of model carts or wagons. Nor, as at Yanik Tepe, can it be overlooked that by no means normally do they occur in pairs. It seems improbable that these people spent so much of their time making toys. Though some of these discs belong to model vehicles, most of them could perfectly well have served as one type, though not the only one, of spindle-whorl.

There is no real necessity to see these carts, represented by models or by whole vehicles, as more than heavy ox-drawn wagons for use in the fields, as illustrated by occurrences of model oxen with yoke, for example at Kültepe near Echmiadzin. There is nothing of the swift-moving horse-drawn chariot, the mobile weapon of war, in these ponderous vehicles, whose clearest parallel is with the solid-wheeled wooden carts of the Anatolian plateau, with their creaking wooden wheels and axles. For chariots there must be horses, but these had not yet appeared as broken in for riding or for use as draught animals. Horse bones occur at Early Trans-Caucasian sites, but they may have been kept only for their meat and milk.[108] Yet by the end of the third millennium BC the horse must surely have been beginning to be domesticated in the Caucasus, for Przewalski's horse, a variety of the steppe pony, appears on a silver vessel from the Maikop barrow.[109] Bones of the steppe horse occur in south Russian sites of the third millennium BC. But full domestication of the horse seems to have come as one of the changes at the end of the Early Trans-Caucasian culture, apart from its survivals in conservative areas.

Soviet archaeologists have commendably devoted much attention not only to analyses of metal artifacts but also to classification of animal bones from numerous excavations. From these a general theory of the way of life in the third millennium BC and of changes in the patterns of settlement has emerged. Some interpretation of the necessarily indirect evidence for religion has also been attempted; and there is enough evidence for some comprehension of burial customs in part, if only part, of this wide cultural zone.

O. M. Japaridze, T. N. Chubinishvili and B. Piotrovskii are among those who have put forward explanations for the changes in the ratio of the bones of cattle to those of sheep and goats.[110] The earlier settlements, before the rise of the Early Trans-Caucasian culture, had been mostly situated in the plains, and had depended primarily on agriculture. This seems to have continued in the early third millennium BC, but thereafter to have begun to change. Earlier sites on the whole suggest a preponderance of cattle, at Kulbakebi these being 80 per cent of the total, against only 16 per cent for sheep or goats; but the 1927–8 excavations at the Early Trans-Caucasian site of Elar produced a majority of sheep or goat over cattle bones.[111] One explanation of such a change is that growing population caused pressure on the hill country above the plains: thus forests were largely cleared, and upland pastures more suitable for sheep or goats than for cattle were opened up. Deforestation may in turn have brought about a climatic deterioration in the form of lower rainfall; and the mostly small but closely neighbouring villages of the plains, with their crowded houses, became impoverished. Sites in the plains were deserted, and the population, especially in Georgia, moved more into the well watered hill country. Transhumance became increasingly significant in the economy, and is exemplified by the remains of a summer encampment in the Ossetian mountain pastures, the region of the passes north from Georgia over the main range of the Caucasus. Here, in the cave of Shau-Leget, 1,500 metres above sea level, quernstones, pottery and baked clay pot stands were found, evidently buried at the end of one summer season and never reclaimed.[112] No longer was the tightly knit village on a mound in the middle of the plain the only typical habitation site. Although plentiful evidence is being found to demonstrate continuity of occupation at settlements such as the Armenian site of Haridj, near Artik, and at industrial sites such as Metsamor, nevertheless the general pattern apparent from surveys, excavations and study of animal bones supports this theory of a shift from arable farming to animal husbandry. The numerous miniature animal figurines from Early Trans-Caucasian sites need not have the slightest religious or ritual significance; they need only be toys. But whatever the purpose of those who fashioned these models, they suggest the importance in their lives of stock-breeding. Continuity of settlement into the second millennium BC was everywhere uneven; and in eastern Anatolia the number of Early Trans-Caucasian settlements still occupied throughout the second millennium BC was very small indeed outside the region of Malatya and Elaziğ, astride the upper Euphrates. Yanik Tepe too was deserted after the Early Trans-Caucasian III period, but the presence of several occupation levels badly damaged by later pits and walls and overlying the better preserved levels of that period suggests that there this culture lasted almost till the mid-second millennium BC. Population, if not declining, was on the move. Whatever the most important factors causing this change, whether economic or political, change there undeniably was. Self-sufficient village communities were anyhow less attuned to the spirit of the age of widening commercial contacts which brought about the advances in metallurgy in the third period as discussed above. On the whole such economic factors, even though their causes remain uncertain, seem more plausible as the explanation of these changes rather than migrations or violent upheaval caused by conquering newcomers.

That the Early Trans-Caucasian people believed in some sort of after-life, a belief held in common with all prehistoric peoples, perhaps needs no emphasis, though the number of burials is not everywhere large. None was found at Yanik Tepe, where the cemetery must have been extra-mural, outside the village limits. Kvatskhelebi and Shengavit are among sites yielding evidence of burial customs through graves found within and near the settlement. At Kvatskhelebi three burials, two single and one double, were found under the floor of one house; but they antedated its construction.[113] Collective burials are reported at Shengavit, the tombs being rectangular, 'with tens of people buried in each'. The excavator claims that no differences of social class or wealth can be detected in these burials of the Early Trans-Caucasian I and II periods. Among the grave-goods are mentioned pottery, copper and stone artifacts, comprising weapons and personal ornaments. By the time of Shengavit IV, however, some evidence of distinctions in class and wealth becomes apparent.[114] At Elar cist-graves and simple pits in the soil were found.[115] The pottery from Ernis, on Lake Van, is said to have come from stone-lined graves, presumably pits, evidently a characteristic method of burial in this cultural zone. Recently (1966–7) Early Trans-Caucasian material has been found in burials near Lchashen, on Lake Sevan.

Towards the end of the third millennium BC there appeared in Georgia a new burial custom typified by the barrow (kurgan), already traditional in the northern steppes but totally alien to the Early Trans-Caucasian cultural zone and indeed to the rest of the Near East at that time. A northern origin for these barrows is all the more certain from their design and contents. One barrow at Tetri-Tsqaro was in fact in the Timber-Grave tradition of south Russia, being lined with thin oak tree-trunks and containing a wheeled vehicle. The date of the Maikop barrow (c. 2,300–2,200 BC) indicates that the tradition of building a tomb chamber, either of timber or of stones, and then heaping a mound of stones and earth on top of it had arrived at the northern flanks of the Caucasus by the opening of the Early Trans-Caucasian III period. During that period the custom of building barrows was diffused through eastern Georgia, where the earliest of the many Trialeti barrows can fairly con-fidently be dated to c. 2,300/2,200–2,000 BC, into the Dashkesen region of western Azerbaijan, where barrows of this cultural period have been excavated. Unlike the later ones in the same region, these barrows are stone-built rather than simply of earth; one is situated at an altitude of 2,000 metres in the Little Caucasus range. A reported Early Trans-Caucasian barrow near Astara and Lenkoran, containing a copper spearhead, armour scales and a whetstone carved with the head of a pig or horse, suggests penetration by barrow-builders as far south-east as the Talysh; and these contents give a hint of less peaceful conditions than in Trialeti, where the absence of weapons is a noteworthy, if negative, feature. The Trialeti barrows mostly post-date the Early Trans-Caucasian culture, and can anyhow only be discussed after examination of their antecedents.

Interpretation of the Early Trans-Caucasian style of pottery as having its origins based in religion is inadequately supported, for most of the ceramic ornament is simply decorative. Hearths undoubtedly did have some significance beyond their practical function, and have attracted attention as a feature of this culture with possible Near Eastern parallels elsewhere.[116] Hearths made in the form of a ram have been found at Haridj (Artik), Shengavit, and elsewhere. The excavators of Kvatskhelebi believe that at the very moment of the fire which destroyed the village of Level CI a fertility ritual was being enacted, illustrated by the arrangement of objects in most of the houses. Miniature models of the central hearth add to the evidence of its significance: perhaps, as the excavators suggest, they were used for burning incense. Sickles, spindle-whorls, stone points and pestles also occur. Beside one hearth in this level lay the skeleton of a deer, with the arrow still imbedded; on the other side of the same hearth were animal and human baked clay figurines, pottery, sickle-blades and querns. Thus perhaps hunting and farming were combined in one domestic cult. The anthropomorphic figurines are male, perhaps a significant difference from the normal Near Eastern emphasis on the female; here were also two stone phalli. It has been suggested, though surely too speculatively for much assurance, that the later deity Tulepia is represented by some of the figurines which are stylistically paralleled on the silver goblet from Trialeti.[117] The fact that an alternative name for Kvatskhelebi is Tulepia Kokhi is indeed very suggestive. As late as the nineteenth century AD the cult of this deity survived among the tribes of Georgia. The name Tulepia is not unlike that of the Hittite god Telepinu, nor is some connection between central Anatolia in the early days of Hittite power and Georgia in the period of the Trialeti barrows inherently improbable, slight as the evidence of Anatolian influence in this connection must be reckoned. Piotrovskii's opinion that differences discernible between female figurines and those of animals in the Early Trans-Caucasian culture are explicable by Neolithic survivals in religious outlook, accounting for the crude stylization of women, while the animals represent stock-breeding, a new and expanding economic activity, could possibly be sound.[118] A simpler explanation would be that while the figurines of women were indeed associated with the fertility cult those of animals were simply children's toys.

No assessment of the great changes taking place in Trans-Caucasia in the last two or three centuries of the third millennium BC is possible without reference to the cultural sequence of the steppes north of the Caucasus and of the plains of south Russia, including the Ukraine.

During the third millennium BC a wide cultural zone extended from the lower Dniepr through the eastern Ukraine to the lower Don and eastward to the middle reaches of the Volga. This was the North Pontic culture, to which the Neolithic culture of the north Caucasus was related till the beginning of the 'Copper Age' with the appearance of barrows of the Early Kuban culture. At least one authority believes that the North Pontic population was indigenous in its homeland since Upper Palaeolithic times, a conclusion based on the evidence of physical anthropology; yet the same writer elsewhere states that these people were of 'Proto-European Cromagnon type', and different from the inhabitants of the region in Mesolithic times, who were more akin to the Mediterranean type. It is suggested that the North Pontic people, if not indigenous, arrived from Europe via Poland and the western Ukraine. This occurred perhaps in the late fifth millennium BC, with an early and middle period lasting till the late fourth millennium BC[119]. Thereafter the late period of the North Pontic culture, otherwise termed Late Dniepr-Donets, lasted probably till c. 2,400 BC or slightly later, though a later date would fit less well with the dating of Trialeti and other Trans-Caucasian sites.[120]

The North Pontic culture, at least in its late period, was firmly based on stock-breeding, for which there is ample evidence from animal bones from settlements; and agriculture, though grain itself seems lacking, is attested by the normal ground stone industry including querns and pounders. In the Kabardino-Balkaria region of the north Caucasus, in the upper Terek valley, a Neolithic village has been excavated at Agubekovo, close to Nal'chik.[121]

The burial customs of the North Pontic culture in its final phase, probably contemporary with Agubekovo, are best illustrated by the cemetery at Mariupol near the Sea of Azov.[122] Here there is an example, paralleled elsewhere in the North Pontic zone, of collective burial on the grand scale: altogether 124 graves were found, arranged in three rows, each a long trench. The bodies were in rows beside one another and one above the other. The cemetery was very probably in use for several centuries.

A tradition altogether different from the North Pontic culture is represented by the Kurgan culture, otherwise known as the Pit-Grave culture. The Kurgan people are so named from their custom of single burials, in ochre with the body lying with legs contracted and with a barrow of stones or earth heaped over it; the body is not in the usual Near Eastern position, lying on its side, but is lying on its back with knees up. Merpert has classified the Kurgan material into four periods (I–IV), but Gimbutas believes these should be reduced to three. These are the Early Kurgan period (Kurgan I), the Middle Kurgan period (Kurgan II–III) and the Late Kurgan period (Kurgan IV).[123]

All the evidence suggests that the Kurgan culture from the first belonged to a people who had adapted themselves to the steppes by specializing in stock-breeding and thus allowing themselves the mobility which the typical steppe-dweller has sought throughout subsequent history. They favoured high river banks. In their way of life, if not by blood, the Kurgan people were the forerunners of the Cimmerians, Scyths and Sarmatians. The vast expanse of their homeland even in the early third millennium BC (Kurgan I) is indicated not only by connections with the Urals but also by close parallels in the pottery of the Dzhanbas-4 site situated south of the Aral Sea and belonging to the Kel'teminar culture; comparable pottery was also found in the Dzhebel cave near the Gurgan, south-east of the Caspian Sea.[124]

The connections of the Kurgan I people with Soviet Turkestan and beyond have contributed to the opinion of Gimbutas that their original homeland lay north and east of the Caspian Sea. Certainly there seems no reason to dispute that the later expansion of the Kurgan people into the North Pontic region was from east to west. The existence of two groups, Kurgan and North Pontic, living side by side in one village is strongly suggested by the occurrence of burials of two types comparable with other Kurgan sites and with cemeteries such as Mariupol respectively, at Aleksandriya near Kharkov in the Kurgan II period.

If its parallels with Alaca Hüyük point to a date of c. 2,300 BC for Maikop, then the Kurgan III people were at least beginning to infiltrate into the north Caucasus by c. 2,400 BC, for the cemetery excavated in the town of Nal'chik and the contemporary settlement of Dolinskoe in the same district both represent a phase early in the Kurgan III period and immediately preceding that of Maikop, usually termed the Early Kuban Copper Age.[125] At Dolinskoe were two phases of occupation. Sickle-blades attest agriculture. Arrowheads, javelin-points, scrapers and burins are common, but nearly all of flint. The great rarity of obsidian is in contrast with the earlier settlement of Agubekovo, and is a feature in common with the cemetery of Kabardino Park, near Nal'chik: this in itself suggests newcomers, since obsidian was obtainable locally. Clay pot stands of horned form, very poorly fired, are characteristic. The pottery includes large jars apparently with lugs of the Nakhichevan type, hinting at some contact with the Early Trans-Caucasian zone to the south.[126] The variety of positions of the bodies in the cemetery at Nal'chik could indicate a mixed population, presumably comprising the older inhabitants and the Kurgan III newcomers: the cemetery had two phases. Some burials were typical of Kurgan II-III (Middle Kurgan), on the back with knees bent and covered with ochre. Graves of this same type have also been found in the eastern Caucasus in the Kurgan cemetery at Novy Arshti, without any metal artifacts and stratified beneath the burials of the Maikop period, the majority in this cemetery.[127] At Nal'chik the bodies were not consistently orientated: most were contracted on the right or left side, a few were extended and five were laid face down. Little pottery or metal was found, the stone and bone industries being most prominent. Long T-shaped or 'crutch-headed' copper pins from the earliest graves at Nal'chik are clearly comparable with those from Sachkhere and also have parallels at Alaca Hüyük.[128] Thus already just before the Maikop period trade was bringing the northern steppes into contact with the Early Trans-Caucasian III culture, to the advantage of both. A maritime route across the Black Sea seems the likeliest explanation of links with central Anatolia, especially in the light of the occurrence of bronze figurines of stags of the Alaca and Horoztepe class at or near Giresun.

The famous Maikop barrow has been frequently discussed, and is one of a small group datable to the Early Kuban period, the majority of barrows in the Kuban valley being much later, of the Late Bronze Age and thereafter. It has been pointed out that the Kuban valley has long served as a granary for the highlands of the central Caucasus, rich in fruit but poor in cereals.[129] It is therefore not surprising that contacts between the steppe people of the Kurgan culture and the older population of the northern Caucasus, now just beginning to benefit from the advances being made in metallurgy and other crafts in Trans-Caucasia at this time, should bear their richest fruit in the fertile Kuban valley. The local rulers at this time may themselves have been backward in technology; but they had the keen eye of the barbarian for the gold and silver and the fine workmanship of a higher civilization. This was undoubtedly a royal burial, prepared by building a circle of undressed limestone slabs inside which a trench was dug (1·42 m. deep and 5·33 m. × 3·73 m. in area) into virgin soil to form the burial chamber. This was lined with wood and paved with a flooring of pebbles. The corner posts supporting the roof were slender, and like the rest of the timber had rotted away by the time of discovery. In the main chamber of the Maikop barrow were no less than seventeen vessels of gold, silver and stone, including the two famous engraved silver jars; there were also copper and pottery vessels. The shapes of these and of some of the other vessels could perhaps betray a connection with both the ceramic and the metal-working traditions of the Early Trans-Caucasian cultural zone. Tools and weapons include a copper transverse axe and a straight axe, both socketed and imported from Mesopotamia or else from Georgia or Armenia, where their Mesopotamian prototypes may well have been locally reproduced.[130] The wide-ranging expanse of the Kurgan III culture to which Maikop belongs, in the form of the tomb if not in its contents, is suggested by objects indicating contacts with Iran and Afghanistan: among these are a few beads of turquoise and lapis lazuli. The two smaller compartments in the Maikop barrow contained a single skeleton each, one male and the other female, with more modest grave-goods. All three bodies were painted with red ochre. Over the whole burial pit was erected a wooden roof, covered with a thin layer of earth and supported by the four corner-posts;

then above this was built a second roof, spanning more than the bare width of the grave. Over this timber roof was piled the great mound making the barrow, containing a single ochre burial accompanied by copper spearheads of leaf form and silver spiral rings. This lay 3·20 m. from the summit of the mound, which was covered with a top layer of black earth, the barrow rising to a height of at least 10·65 m. from its surroundings. It must indeed have been an impressive sight.

Comparisons with the rich burials in the central and Pontic regions of Anatolia, especially at Alaca Hüyük and Horoztepe, raise as many questions as they solve. Maikop demonstrates the mingling of Kurgan with Near Eastern cultures, represented by the design of the barrow and its contents respectively. Likewise the Alaca Hüyük graves, though Anatolian in their equipment, betray the influence of the northern steppes in the design of the tombs, with their timber roofing, and in the provision of hides of cattle, with heads and horns still attached after the funerary feast. Here surely must be the cemetery of a local dynasty of princes who, it seems, had arrived from the steppes either across the Black Sea or through the Early Trans-Caucasian cultural zone, and who had succeeded in imposing their rule, though little else, on the indigenous Hattian population.[131] The suggestion that the rulers of Alaca Hüyük had come as aliens merely from the neighbouring Pontic cultural province, centred in the administrative areas of Tokat and Amasya, is undermined by the later date generally assigned to the Horoztepe material compared with that from Alaca.[132] Another fact to be remembered is that the Pontic region essentially forms a northern extension of the central Anatolian cultural province of the Early Bronze II period. The apparent disappearance of the stone lining and wooden roof in the graves at Horoztepe, which thus no longer carry that resemblance to a house discernible in the Alaca burials and characteristic of the Kurgan culture, must surely also be reckoned as an indication that Horoztepe was later than Alaca. The pastoralism of the steppes is illustrated by the animals and landscape on the silver vases from Maikop, Przewalski's horse being among the species depicted.[133]

A little later than the Maikop barrow are the two graves at Tsarskaya (Novosvobodnaya) ; and roughly contemporary are the silver ox, diadem and jewellery found in a silver vase of Maikop form at Staromyshastovskaya. Gimbutas assigns the Tsarskaya graves, whose contents are comparable with the Maikop material though typologically slightly later, to the beginning of the Kurgan IV period (c. 2,100 BC), not more than a century later than Maikop on the chronology here proposed. Tanged daggers and spearheads, flat axes with shaft-hole and spiral rings are among the grave-goods in the Tsarskaya burials. There are indications of wide-reaching contacts, perhaps even with Hissar IIIC in north-eastern

Iran.[134] The pottery of this Kurgan IV period shows evolution of forms, though still with round bases; the most characteristic decoration comprises cord-impressed triangles along the horizontal cord impressions and the jabbed decoration made with a sharp implement. Kurgan IV influence in Trans-Caucasia may be seen in cord-impressed hanging triangles on pottery, as for example in Barrow no. 6 at Lchashen on Lake Sevan.[135] The ceramic style associated with the Kurgan IV culture was indeed to reflect its influence as far afield as Scandinavia and the upper Rhine as well as Greece. Parallels between the stone cist graves of central Europe with their so-called globular amphorae and those of the Tsarskaya phase with their pottery suggest connections between central Europe and the Caucasus at this time. Demand for such commodities as tin and amber may well have stimulated trade to flow from Europe eastward.

However acceptable or otherwise this comparison between two such widely separated regions as central Europe, including north Germany, and the Caucasus, it could be that here lies an explanation for the appearance at about this time of the dolmens so thickly distributed in Abkhazia and along the slopes of the western end of the Caucasus range. This type of tomb seems at first sight to have no parallels except perhaps in Europe. Megalithic structures of slabs set on edge were, with one or two exceptions, quite alien to the Near East.[136] They would appear to represent an intrusive element in the western Caucasus. The tomb chambers of the two barrows at Tsarskaya, thirty-seven miles south-east of Maikop, suggest in their construction the influence of the dolmens now beginning to appear immediately to the west. These chambers, unlike the timber construction of the Maikop burial pit, are built of stone orthostats with similar slabs for roofing; one of these two tombs has a gabled and the other a flat roof.[137] Thus the former echoes the house design of the timber-framed burial chambers, while both recall the dolmens, as likewise the portholes, one square and the other round, through the central partition dividing the two compartments of the Tsarskaya tombs. Yet these are stone cist-graves rather than dolmens, with single burial as the custom. Collective burial was characteristic of the dolmens, with from four to twenty burials in each: they may therefore possibly have had some affinities with the North Pontic culture.

In his classic report on the dolmens Tallgren stated that fifteen hundred were known in the western Caucasus since when Soviet archaeologists have added to their number.[138] Their distribution is thus fairly compact. The lack of dolmens in the steppes could surely be simply the outcome of the absence of suitable stone. The identity and origin of the dolmen-builders is not apparent from their distribution: either they arrived by sea and expanded from the coast inland or they came over the steppes and arrived on the coast after building the first dolmen around Tsarskaya. This latter explanation is far the more probable.

Both the design and the contents of the dolmens of the western Caucasus can be employed as dating evidence. One theory is that they were essentially stone cists, and that they signified an adaptation to rocky conditions, where no depth of easily excavated soil was everywhere available, by a group of the same people who dug the so-called catacombs, or pit-graves, north of the Black Sea.[139] Yet if the date of *c.* 2,000 BC for the appearance of this Catacomb culture is accepted, it must indicate an earlier origin for the dolmens, though undoubtedly they continued well into the second millennium BC. Such grave-goods as the axe, chisel, borer and knife-blade found in a dolmen at Abadzekhskaya have the appearance of a date no later than the Tsarskaya barrows; but much depends on whether they are of copper or, as described in the report, of bronze. If the former, they could add weight to a high dating. The material from Eshery, however, is certainly later.[140]

Of recent years Georgian archaeologists, among them Otar Japaridze, have been reappraising the discoveries made by the great pioneer B.A. Kuftin in the area of Trialeti which was then, just before the Second World War, about to be submerged by a reservoir for hydro-electricity. The chronological sequence suggested by the writer has naturally proved largely unacceptable.[141] At that time the degree of continuity of the old 'Kura-Araxes' traditions till the end of the third millennium BC and their adaptation to the advances made in the period known as the Early Bronze Age (approximately 2,300–2,000 BC), the Early Trans-Caucasian III period of this book, were not fully understood by Soviet archaeologists. Now it can be seen that the changes manifest in the 'Middle Bronze Age' of Trans-Caucasia (approximately 2,000–1,300/1,200 BC) had their roots in the preceding two or three centuries. It is to this, the Early Trans-Caucasian III period, that the consensus of opinion among Georgian scholars has assigned the earliest of three groups into which the barrows of Trialeti, numbering over forty in all, have been classified. Of these Barrow IV seems the earliest of all. Other tombs included in the first group according to the classification adopted by Professor Japaridze and other Georgian archaeologists are Kurgans XI (showing strong affinities with the Early Trans-Caucasian tradition), XIX, XXII, XXIV and XLVI. Obsidian rather than copper or bronze was used for arrowheads, as at the cemetery of Tetri-Tsqaro: the metalwork found there suggests that the absence of similar material from the Trialeti tombs of this period may be fortuitous, and is no reflection of backwardness. The pottery from this first group of barrows at Trialeti includes cups and handled jars with bulging waist, tapering base and finely incised chevron ornament on a black burnished surface, the final products of the Early Trans-Caucasian potters.

With the next group of barrows at Trialeti, including the very rich Kurgan XVII, the long continuity of the third millennium BC had at last vanished. Though the population had not radically changed, new elements were making their appearance. New forces were at work throughout Trans-Caucasia and in most of the Urmia basin too, leaving only the remoter uplands of eastern Anatolia and a few conservative communities to cling to the old ways. With changes in patterns of settlement and lack of stability it becomes much harder to synthesize the known material into a comprehensible whole. Never again was there to be a culture in the highland zone both so far-flung and so long-lived.

CHAPTER 4

NEW PEOPLES IN AN OLD WORLD –
INDO-EUROPEANS AND INDIGENOUS
POPULATIONS IN THE HIGHLAND ZONE

The period from *c*. 2,000 BC until *c*. 800 BC, covered by this chapter, cannot easily be described in one title, for a very complex pattern of material cultures emerged in the north Caucasus, Trans-Caucasia and the Urmia basin; most of eastern Anatolia remains in obscurity until the ninth century BC, with the exception of the area around Elaziğ. The old cultural uniformity of the third millennium BC continued to disintegrate, yet its traditions survived to mingle with and thus to influence the succeeding cultures. The decline in settled life, alluded to in the preceding chapter, had begun by the Early Trans-Caucasian III period and continued through the second millennium BC. This decline was particularly marked in the bleaker highlands, such as the regions of Erzurum and Van, where the Early Trans-Caucasian culture lingered on, to be followed by a long dark age when nomadism may have predominated. There seems to have been an abandonment of sites in the plains and elsewhere, most clearly illustrated by the hiatus at such sites as Armavir and Garni between the Early Trans-Caucasian occupation and that of the Iron Age or of the classical period.[1] The recent discoveries in the Keban basin near Elaziğ suggest that there too, in a fertile area of eastern Anatolia, pressure of population grew to a maximum during the third millennium BC and then declined.[2] Against this, however, it must be pointed out that many sites, such as Haridj near Artik, not far from Erevan, show no discontinuity in occupation from the late third through the second millennium BC.

This was an age when Indo-Europeans, the Hittites and slightly later the Kassites, burst in upon the world of the Near East, bringing in their wake a new social structure, new attitudes in religion and new techniques in war. Dramatic as the effects of the arrival of these newcomers may have been, however, they must not be exaggerated. For a fuller understanding of the material culture of these early Indo-Europeans a study of ethnic and cultural movements from south Russia westward into

86

central and northern Europe is necessary. There, in purely prehistoric contexts, archaeology alone can provide the information required; but in the Near East the existence of long established civilizations meant, in terms of material culture, the gradual absorption of the northerners into their unfamiliar new surroundings. Only in the surviving and contemporary written sources of the Hittite kingdom and of Mitanni can the presence and influence of these newcomers be clearly detected.

The presence of Indo-Europeans in south Russia in the late third millennium BC has been alluded to above. Philology suggests an original Indo-European homeland which at least included the Ukraine, with a probable extension towards north Germany.[3] Archaeology seems to reinforce the case in favour of a south Russian homeland. Neither branch of learning can reveal the factors causing the expansion of these peoples in all directions over the plains of Russia and ultimately, by the end of the third millennium BC, through the Caucasus and then westwards into central Anatolia. This last migrating group was that of the Hittite people, the best known of the earliest Indo-Europeans. The explanation most often given for such migrations is the pressure of growing population on the limited area of land available, resulting in the search for new pastures. It has rightly been observed that, whereas farmers expand their territory only gradually, spreading out slowly by stages from their homeland, pastoralists are more likely to advance in rapid movements.[4] Whatever the cause of this Hittite migration into that part of the Anatolian plateau which was to become their homeland, within the great bend of the River Halys, it may be guessed from traces of destruction at such sites along the natural route of the migration as Karaz, near Erzurum, that this was a rapid movement. A slow movement or series of movements would have been more likely to have brought about the disappearance of the existing cultures in the territories through which the Hittites passed; and moreover there would have been a mingling of the races, the new with the old. For such a mingling there seems to be no evidence. The Hittites apparently passed through the Hurrian lands of the highland zone, as the Kassites probably did through the eastern sector of this zone, the Urmia basin, at a similar or slightly later date. The absence of traces of their passage is hardly remarkable, for they were in truth barbarian peoples, not less capable of achieving the maturity of civilization in their own way, but hitherto deprived of the benefit of a long tradition behind them of urban life, such as had flourished for over a thousand years in Mesopotamia. It had, as discussed above, been the expansion of trade from the centres in and around Mesopotamia, the search for sources of metal and the arrival of sophisticated metal products from at least ultimately Sumerian antecedents which had stimulated the envy and no doubt the imagination of the tribal chieftains of the Kuban basin and beyond. While their cousins were moving towards Europe, some of them preferred to aim for a place in the sun, a new home in the Near East. Land must indeed have been obtainable in the vast expanses of the northern plains; but the stimuli of gold and silver, already evident in the treasures of Maikop and contemporary barrows, made the hazards of a southward venture, with the abandonment of the way of life adapted to the steppes, worthwhile. Thus came the Hittites, destined to play a role for centuries to come in the history of much of the Near Eastern world, though not in the highlands through which their migration had led them.

Attempts to restrict the original Indo-European homeland to northern Europe on the basis of cognates of the German word *Lachs*, 'salmon', or of shared vocabulary for certain animals and trees appear to be founded on unsound premises. Stock-breeding was probably more prominent in the primitive Indo-European economy before the migrations into the Near East than there or among the neolithic population of the Balkans. Copper was known; and so too were wheeled vehicles, though not exclusively or necessarily chariots; and the horse had been domesticated. The use of similar words in widely separate Indo-European languages and territories can be shown to illustrate the above-mentioned features. In addition to this evidence from comparative philology there are certain archaeological elements which have been suggested as hallmarks of the earliest Indo-European movements in and near the homeland north of the Black Sea. Here these can merely be listed: they include ochre burials, usually under a kurgan, domesticated horses, stone battle-axes imitating metal shaft-hole axes and corded ware, pottery decorated with impressions of plaited cords.[5]

The Hittites arrived in Anatolia almost certainly via the Caucasus, thus coming face to face with the Hurrians in their homeland. Through them they probably derived their brand of Old Akkadian cuneiform writing, which differed considerably from that found in the tablets unearthed in the trading colony (*karum*) of the Assyrian merchants established at the Anatolian town of Kanesh, marked by the mound now called Kültepe, some ten miles north-east of Kayseri. The same is true of the records discovered at other Assyrian colonies in central Anatolia. Their early introduction of literacy seems to have perished with their trade in the eighteenth century BC.[6] Privileges retained by chieftains in the eastern marches of the Hittite state in the later second millennium BC could either simply indicate the difficulty of defending that frontier zone or could suggest the direction whence the Hittites arrived in their new homeland in central Anatolia.

It was not in their religion or art, both Anatolian and thus of pre-Indo-European affinities, that the Hittites showed their original ancestry but in their political and legal institutions. A patriarchal bias in their laws affecting the family and the foundation of their kingship on the consent of the nobility and people expressed through their respective assemblies are both survivals from the period before their occupation of their Anatolian homeland.[7] Later, after the collapse of the Hittite Old Kingdom through the inherent vulnerability of the monarchy to internal dissensions, there began to enter those Near Eastern influences which, by the fourteenth century BC, were to transform the Hittite kingship into one of purely oriental character, despotic and theocratic, in which the king became 'the Sun' and more concerned with his role as high priest than as secular ruler. More and more the distinctively Indo-European characteristics of the Hittite people and state were to be submerged, the usual fate of a small conquering minority finding itself in a more civilized environment than its former home. In the last years of the Hittite state Hurrian influence seems to have won a dominant place at the court, and is manifested in the famous rock reliefs of the Hurrian pantheon at Yazilikaya, one mile from the city of Hattusas (Boğazköy).[8] The story of Hittite civilization and relations with neighbouring kingdoms belongs therefore more with the history of Syria and of western Anatolia than with that of the eastern highland zone from the Caucasus to the upper Euphrates, and cannot be further pursued here.

The indigenous cultures of Trans-Caucasia in the early second millennium BC can be better understood if strong continuity from the Early Trans-Caucasian III period is accepted. Changes in pottery and other artifacts can then be seen in perspective, without any necessity to assume violent or complete cultural or political upheavals. Though the larger proportion of material comes from tombs and is thus often without secure context as provided by stratified occupation levels, at least the general ceramic sequence now seems discernible in several areas.

In the vicinity of Lchashen beside Lake Sevan there had been a long history of settled life, with an Early Trans-Caucasian settlement on a hill overlooking the later cemetery: this settlement is said to comprise a village defended by a large fortress with cyclopean perimeter wall. This suggests that such fortifications had a history in this area of over one thousand years, till the time of Urartu. The wavy lines of punctated ornament so distinctive of pottery from the Lchashen tombs appear even in one burial with Early Trans-Caucasian III pottery, so that there seems to have been an uninterrupted sequence from the one to the other. At the village of Karmir, also near Sevan, was found a pottery jar painted in the style of the early second millennium BC, commonly called the Middle Bronze Age, on which a bold design of chevrons was surmounted by birds.[9] These may well recall the Early Trans-Caucasian predilection for birds and animals in the repertoire of incised decoration. This jar was painted in very dark blackish-brown on a darkish red burnished slip. Some pottery of *c.* 2,000 BC has attenuated incised patterns, a simple band of criss-cross ornament just beneath the rim and a thin chevron band round the upper body.

The cemetery at Tazekend, near the road north from Erevan to Lake Sevan, has given its name to the class of painted pottery found there and elsewhere throughout Armenia. This is the earliest of four styles of painted pottery distinguished by Kuftin, the excavator of the famous Trialeti barrows, in his endeavour to find all the then known comparative material relevant to Trialeti. His scheme seems on the whole to remain valid, largely supported by more recent discoveries both within the Soviet Union and in north-western Iran, where the polychrome pottery long associated with Kizil-Vank has been found to continue later than the limited evidence from Geoy Tepe, near Reza'iyeh, had suggested. In these successive styles of painted pottery may be discerned a continuing influence from Iran, doubtless not unconnected with the demand for tin and copper in Assyria and Babylonia.[10]

Tin-working continued at Metsamor, near Erevan, where two levels described as Middle Bronze Age are characterized by painted pottery of Tazekend style and dated to *c.* 2,000–1,900 BC and *c.* 1,700–1,500 BC, suggesting a period of desertion. Polychrome pottery and black wares occur at Metsamor in the next level, dated *c.* 1,500–1,200 BC. Thus this site too demonstrates the long duration of polychrome pottery in Trans-Caucasia. At Jerahovid, also in the Araxes plain, black-on-red painted pottery of Tazekend style occurs together with arrowheads of translucent obsidian. At Artik, near Aragats not far west of Erevan, is a site which does not support the theory of an abandonment of settled life in the second millennium BC, for here is a settlement with unbroken occupation from the late third millennium BC till *c.* 1,000 BC, with abundant pottery mostly dated to the earlier centuries of this time-span, until *c.* 1,500 BC. Here were found twenty catacomb graves comparable with the great period of Lchashen in the thirteenth century BC: their contents included a bronze standard in the form of a goat and a horse-bit with wheel cheek-pieces.[11] Garni, in the hills not far from Erevan, is another settlement where Middle Bronze Age pottery, including black-on-red jars, occurs overlying the Early Trans-Caucasian levels.

At Ouzerlik Tepe, in the Azerbaijan SSR, a site with three levels was excavated by the Azerbaijan Archaeological Expedition. Two other sites, at Khodjali and Karatepe near Oren-Kala, yielded material of the first millennium BC, Ouzerlik Tepe being dated by the excavator to *c.* 2,000–*c.* 1,400 BC.[12] The animal bones included horse as well as the usual cattle, sheep and goat. The lowest level yielded incised ware probably

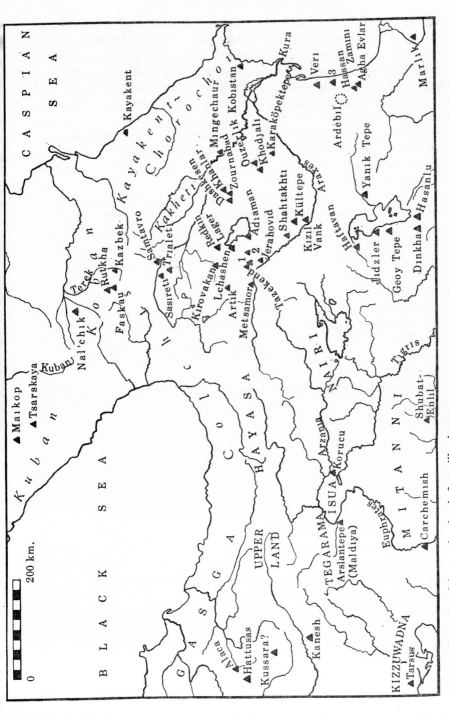

III *Significant sites of the second and early first millennium BC.*

Cultural provinces are shown in italics; Hittite, Assyrian etc., geographical names are in Roman capitals.

Key to numbered sites: 1 Mukhana Tepe (Erevan). 2 Garni 3 Khodja Davud Köprü

Map labels:

C A S P I A N   S E A

B L A C K   S E A

Kuban

▲Maikop
▲Tsarskaya
Kuban
Nal'chik▲

Terek
▲Rutkha
Faskau▲
▲Kazbek
Kayakent▲

Kayaken

Chorocho

Kakheti
Samtavro▲
Sasireti▲ ▲Trialeti
Kirovakan▲ ▲Redkin
Lchashen▲ ▲Lager
Artik▲
Metsamor▲ 1 ▲Adiaman
          2
          Verahovid▲
Tazebend

Dashkesen
Mingechaur▲
Zournabad▲
Ouzerlik Kobistan
Khodjali▲
Karaköpektepe▲
Kura

▲Veri
▲3 Hassan
Ardebil○ ▲Zamini
       Agha Evlar▲

Marlik▲

Shahtakhti▲
Kizil ▲Kültepe
Vank▲ *Araxes*

Arax

Yanik Tepe▲
Haftavan▲
Jldzler▲
Geoy Tepe▲
Dinkha▲ ▲Hasanlu

C O L C H I S

H A Y A S A

G A S G A

UPPER
LAND

TEGARAMA
Arslantepe▲
(Maldiya)

ISUA *Azania*
Korucu▲

N A I R I

Tigris

Euphrates

M I T A N N I
Carchemish▲ Shubat-
            ▲Enlil

KIZZUWADNA
▲Tarsus

▲Alaca
▲Hattusas
Kussara?▲
Kanesh▲

0   200 km.

attributable to the very close of the third millennium BC (Early Trans-Caucasian III). The richest was the second level, yielding stone mace-heads and a variety of pottery, comprising coarse cooking ware, black burnished ware in the Early Trans-Caucasian III tradition and painted pottery with trichrome decoration: this last has a light buff surface and red paint overlaid with dark brown linear patterns such as bands of wavy lines and cross-hatched diamonds. This second level and the uppermost level both yielded, in addition to painted pottery, a ware with pointillé decoration paralleled at Lchashen in the period dated by Armenian archaeologists to *c.* 1,900–*c.* 1,700 BC. There this decoration occurs on fine black burnished ware; and white-encrusted ware appears at the end of this phase. The hanging or 'pot-hook' spiral is a motif linking Ouzerlik Tepe and Lchashen. Perhaps indicating a solar cult is the swastika on the base of some Lchashen pots of this phase. In the next phase at Lchashen the relationship to Ouzerlik Tepe continues. In the Araxes valley at Karaköpektepe and at the second site of Kültepe (Nakhichevan) grey ware and painted pottery respectively demonstrate parallels with Ouzerlik Tepe, situated as it is between the lower reaches of the Kura and Araxes rivers. The excavators quote parallels with Trialeti, Kirovakan and Zournabad, this last yielding Middle Bronze Age painted pottery from the only known kurgan of this period in the Dashkesen area. Ouzerlik Tepe II was defended by a mud brick perimeter wall and a gateway with a tower.

It is in the Sevan basin at Lchashen that a fairly continuous succession of cultural periods has apparently now been obtained from the late third millennium BC until *c.* 1,200 BC. There is, however, no full certainty whether different types are in series or contemporary, since the material is for the most part from burials. Perhaps nearly all but the rich tombs of the local chieftains date to the earlier second millennium BC, the Middle Bronze Age. In this region this period has been subdivided into four phases, the first (*c.* 1,900–1,700 BC) above-mentioned with parallels with Ouzerlik Tepe. The second phase (*c.* 1,700–1,500 BC) is characterized by black ware with white paint encrusted in wavy bands round bowl necks: similar pottery occurs elsewhere in the Sevan region at Dilijan and also near Erevan, at Tazekend and Mukhana Tepe. Survivals of this phase continue into the fifteenth century BC, when the Lchashen material of the third phase includes painted pottery of the style found in the last period of the Trialeti barrows and at Kirovakan. Thus a wide distribution of this painted ware at that time is indicated. Then the fourth phase (*c.* 1,400–1,100 BC) is distinguished by small jars of black ware with decoration of panels or bands in red, white and black paint. Black ware with mauve and white encrustation is also typical of Lchashen at this time. The burials of all these phases of the Middle and Late Bronze Age at Lchashen take the form of simple pit graves, unlike the grandiose tombs of the chieftains.[13]

The Colchidic culture, extending over western Georgia and Abkhazia, has been dated over a very long period, from the eighteenth until the seventh century BC.[14] It greatly influenced the beginnings of the Koban culture, with which it used to be identified. But although there are bronze artifacts which the Colchidic and Koban cultures had in common, there are differences between them. Flat adzes, hoes and sickles occurring in the Colchidic culture do not appear in the Koban industry. It seems that Colchidic metal-working was of local origin; and the distinction from the Koban culture is emphasized by differences in pottery and burial customs. Typical Colchidic and Koban shaft-hole axes have parallels in the Kuban valley and much further north, in the Don basin and in the Ukraine. So formidable is the quantity of metalwork that any evidence helping to produce a relative chronology and typological development is welcome. The Kuban bronzes include shaft-hole axes, often associated with sickles, mainly of the type called 'Upper Kuban' and of several varieties, partly derived from forms of the second millennium BC in the Kuban basin and the north Caucasus.[15] The shape of the shaft-hole seems to be a dating criterion, some being oval of typical Koban shape and others being round and certainly earlier. Indeed it seems that both the Koban metal industry and that of the Kuban basin owed their inspiration largely to the Colchidic culture to the south-west. This influence reached the Kuban basin, however, only through the Koban region, not directly.

In spite of the general continuity from the Early Trans-Caucasian culture, already in the Early Trans-Caucasian III period an intrusive element has been discerned in the earliest barrows (kurgans) of Trialeti, a name conjured up as soon as this period is mentioned. Unfortunately the original report on Trialeti concentrates on comparative material for dating purposes more than on a detailed record of discoveries in this area before its inundation by a hydro-electric scheme, the same factor which brought about the re-emergence of the Lchashen cemetery.[16] No thorough description of the Trialeti material is here possible: the questions provoked by these burials are of two types, the first concerned with the design of the tombs and the funerary customs and the second with the goods buried with the owners. More recent excavations in Trialeti by O.M.Japaridze, have provided invaluable additional evidence clarifying the work of B.A.Kuftin.[17]

Trialeti is a district of Georgia forty miles south-west of Tiflis, part of it being called Tsalka, in the Khram valley. The excavations were carried out in 1936–40. Most of the barrows found by the expedition had their burial chamber in the form of a pit cut down into the ground; but at least eight of the barrows had no pit, the burial being on the old surface.[18]

Forty-two barrows altogether were opened by the expedition under B.A.Kuftin and six by O.M.Japaridze. The smallest of those excavated by the later expedition (Barrow no. 5) is 32 m. in diameter; Barrows 3 and 4 are much larger, being 100 m. in diameter. The burial chambers at least of Barrows 1–4 were lined with stones rather roughly dressed but carefully fitted together; and in more than one barrow the walls were carved with crudely scratched graffiti of which it is very hard to make much sense, such as a very roughly rendered horned animal in Barrow 3. Elsewhere herringbone patterns are frequent. Barrow 3 has a *dromos* or entrance passage leading to the burial chamber. Barrow 5 has a log roof over the pit grave. The historical setting of these barrows as those of Indo-European rulers of a peaceful population seems to be upheld by the absence of weapons in the tombs, by the fact that they cover only single inhumation burials and by the very wealth of their contents, displaying the eclecticism expected of barbarians recently come into contact with a higher civilization which they envy and wish to emulate in their own ebullient manner. The tradition of building barrows was certainly imported from north of the Caucasus; and the association with many of the burials of a wooden wagon drawn by oxen is another northern feature, for there are parallels at Tri Brata and elsewhere in the steppes.[19] The reason for the absence of horses from these burials is uncertain: a taboo has been suggested.[20] This tradition was derived from the Pit-Grave (Kurgan) culture of the Russian steppes, and dates back in Trans-Caucasia earlier than the final phase (Kurgan IV), seeing that the great barrow of Uch-Tepe in the Mil steppe in the Azerbaijan SSR is dated by radio-carbon samples not later than *c.* 2,500 BC.[21] The Trialeti sequence, however, represents a larger and more permanent incursion from the north, whatever the precise chronology.

Only a small part of the contents of the Trialeti barrows can be even mentioned. The first group has been alluded to in the last chapter. Barrow 17 stands out in the second group, both for its strange painted pottery and for its rich metalwork: the pottery includes jars of red ware with boldly painted spirals and swirling snake pattern in dark brown on a cream slip, without any obvious parallels.[22] Perhaps these vessels represent the *joie de vivre* of an exceptionally inventive court potter: the role of the individual craftsman even in prehistoric societies is sometimes underestimated. A silver situla decorated with naturalistic scenes in repoussé of animals in woodland and open country, perhaps to be interpreted as a development of the style of the Maikop silver vase, is mounted in gold; a gold cup is set with carnelians and turquoise in filigree; silver pins have spherical heads of gold, decorated with carnelians and granulation. Such are the treasures found in this one barrow. A silver goblet from Barrow 5 shows a procession of offering-bearers coming before a seated figure, with a row of animals in the lower register. It has been rather boldly suggested that this scene represents a Hittite fertility cult, with men wearing animal masks, largely because of the similarity of Telepinu to the folk god Tulepia of the Svans in the Georgian highlands.[23] This unique vessel somehow is echoed in the later gold bowl from Hasanlu, discussed below. These vessels were still being produced in or just before the final phase of the Trialeti tombs, exemplified by one from Barrow 15. Among the jewellery from the second group at Trialeti is a necklace of large spherical gold beads, 3·3 cm. in diameter and decorated with granulation: its centrepiece is a slider of agate with gold and carnelian mounting. These rich products in gold and silver indicate wealth and flamboyant taste but not necessarily any great technical skill.

The pottery from those barrows in Trialeti opened in 1959–62 includes jars with incised decoration probably equivalent in date to the earliest group opened by Kuftin, c. 2,300–2,000 BC. The occurrence in Barrow 5, together with a four-wheeled wagon, of a bronze dagger with reeded midrib paralleled at Ur in the Third Dynasty (c. 2,125–2,016 BC) adds weight to the dating of these barrows to the first of the three groups into which the Georgian archaeologists now classify Kuftin's material, per-haps near the end of this period, towards 2,000 BC. The writer once attempted a chronological arrangement of the Trialeti barrows mainly on the evidence of the pottery: like other schemes based on only indirect acquaintance with the material, it has had to be abandoned.[24] The first group of the Georgian classification is distinguished by the absence of painted pottery and by conformity to the Early Trans-Caucasian III cultural tradition. The second group, comprising the majority of the important barrows, is dated c. 2,000–1,600 BC. The third group of barrows is dated c. 1,600–1,400 BC, largely on the evidence of the painted pottery comparable with examples from Kizil-Vank to the south; in Barrow 15 was found a bronze socketed spearhead with a silver ferrule, which has parallels at Ugarit (c. 1,550–1,400 BC) and near Mycenae. On present evidence the sequence for Trialeti now adhered to by the Georgian archaeologists seems irrefutable.[25]

The Trialeti barrows have a parallel at Kirovakan in the Armenian SSR. The burial pit is over three metres deep, with an area of thirty square metres. In this pit were found, in addition to the body in the middle lying on a wooden bed with silver-plated ends, and bedecked with a necklace of gold and carnelian beads, both pots and bronze weapons. The pottery includes jars with geometric decoration paralleled at Trialeti, but there is none of the pottery distinctive of Barrow 17. The weapons comprise a spearhead with reeded midrib, an axehead of asymmetric form within the general tradition of Armenia and its environs at this time and three daggers. A flat axe and chisel suggest more peaceful activities. The chief treasure of this barrow at Kirovakan, however, comprises silver cups and a gold bowl with three pairs of lions rather crudely rendered in repoussé with the details engraved. This last suggests a wealth comparable with that of the chieftains buried at Trialeti. Here may be an imitation of their style with slightly less accomplishment. The burial customs suggest that here too an intrusive Indo-European element had been content to stay in Trans-Caucasia.[26]

There can be little doubt that by the end of the Middle Bronze Age, in the fourteenth century BC, there was in certain respects a unified material culture in Trans-Caucasia, the Talysh and the Urmia basin. This unity is suggested to some extent by the distribution of painted pottery but even more so by the metalwork, such as the bronze axes.[27] Bronze of the standard alloy of copper with tin had been produced in the Urmia basin since the early second millennium BC, exemplified by artifacts from Geoy Tepe D near Reza'iyeh:[28] parts of Trans-Caucasia were perhaps more precocious. The homogeneity of metalwork in much of Syria, Assyria and the Zagros region in the early second millennium BC may reflect the Hurrian expansion at that time, or it may simply have been an outcome of movement, voluntary or involuntary, of smiths from one region to another.[29]

To understand the affinities of the Trialeti barrows and contemporary material from elsewhere in Trans-Caucasia it is essential to look not only to the northern steppes but also southward to the Urmia basin. For it was here that some of the elements making up the material culture of Armenia and Georgia in the early second millennium BC originated, particularly the painted pottery. Why there now developed these strong influences from south to north, replacing those previously in the other direction, is not entirely certain. One possible factor could have been the copper trade, since it was in the later years of the First Dynasty of Babylon in Mesopotamia that, in the reign of Hammurabi's son Shamshi-iluna, the so-called Dynasty of the Sea Lands seized control of the marshes around the mouth of the Tigris and Euphrates. Thus the traditional Sumero-Akkadian sources of copper ores in Magan, possibly to be equated with Oman, imported via the entrepot of Dilmun, probably Bahrein, to Ur and thence upstream to Babylon and to many other cities, were cut off. New sources had to be found. Analyses of copper of this period compared with those of earlier samples have given clear indications of a radical change in the origin of the copper, all of which of course had to be imported into the Mesopotamian cities, situated as they were in an alluvial plain entirely devoid of minerals, apart from bitumen. The telltale trace element in the copper ores from Oman is nickel, present up to

3 per cent, whereas in Caucasian copper ores it occurs never more than about 1 per cent. In the later Old Babylonian period there is precisely this lack of nickel in copper, so that there is a strong probability of a Caucasian origin for the copper imports to Babylon and other Mesopotamian cities from c. 1,750/1,700 BC onwards.[30]

It may be objected that the cultural influences from the south spread into Trans-Caucasia well before the eighteenth century BC, even though the absolute chronology of Trialeti is still far from sure. This copper trade must have been but one of several factors, though it could have begun before the closure of the Persian Gulf trade: against this suggestion, however, is the truism that water-borne transport of bulky commodities always has the economic edge on overland transport. For this reason the copper imported by the Assyrian merchants to Ashur from the *karum* of Kanesh (Kültepe) and from their other trading colonies on the Anatolian plateau could not compete in price, reckoned in terms of the rate against silver, with the copper brought to the Mesopotamian cities and upstream to Babylon by ship from the Persian Gulf.[31] Copper from Caucasian sources would certainly have been no less expensive than Anatolian copper once it had arrived in Mesopotamia.

Could this Caucasian copper not have been transported overland through eastern Anatolia and thence into north Syria and Assyria rather than through the Urmia basin and across the Zagros passes? Theoretically such a route would have been perfectly possible: there are no insurmountable physical barriers to make it unlikely. Yet the negative evidence of the absence of known traces of occupation of the early second millennium BC in the highlands of eastern Anatolia militates in favour of a route for the copper trade past Lake Urmia. The general decline of settled life in the highland zone at this time, discussed above, makes traces of any trade during the second millennium BC admittedly very difficult to detect.

Only in the more fertile regions of Elaziğ and Malatya is there clearer evidence of continuity of settled life, though even there the Late Bronze Age appears more easily recognizable than the Middle Bronze Age. The incorporation of Isua, as the Elaziğ region was known in the fourteenth century BC and later, into the Hittite state by Suppiluliumas brought it into close cultural relationship with the Hittite homeland, if the evidence of pottery of central Anatolian type from sites in Altinova is to be believed.[32] The orientation of trade through Isua was thus from Syria northwest into the heart of Hittite territory rather than north-east. The excavations carried out in the area to be submerged by the Keban dam include those at Korucu Tepe, a mound at the east end of Altinova, where remains of significance for the fourth and third millennia BC have been uncovered, and where the levels of the second millennium BC indicate a continuity in the general economy from the Early Trans-Caucasian period of dense settlement. The first of these levels yielded grey ware with clear traces of the potter's wheel, cream slipped and red burnished wares. The next level yielded pottery similar to that of central Anatolia in the time of the Hittite Old Kingdom *c.* 1,600–1,375 BC), perhaps suggesting a relationship with the Hittite state dating back even to the raid by Mursilis I on Babylon (*c.* 1,595 BC), on the return from which the Hittite army clashed with Hurrians, possibly in or near the Elazığ region.[33] The excavator has suggested that Korucu Tepe probably then belonged to a small but thriving buffer state, its houses of mud brick with wooden reinforcement in their stone foundations being defended by a wall 5·30 m. thick. This town was violently destroyed, presumably at the time of the Hittite conquest; and in the burning was found a faience cylinder-seal of Mitannian style and attributable to the period *c*, 1,500–1,350 BC. The next period (*c.* 1,375–1,200 BC) seems to have been one of economic decline, with remains of unpretentious occupation levels: the connection with the Hittite lands of central Anatolia is emphasized by the many plates familiar in those regions, wheel-made and mass-produced for utility only; these are described as being of coarse orange ware, though in central Anatolia more often of buff ware, and a hallmark of the Late Bronze Age. An axe or chisel bit and an armour scale show that iron was being worked, if only in a limited amount. Twelve hieroglyphic seal impressions were found in the first season (1968) of excavations at Korucu Tepe. After the fall of the Hittite state there seems to have been a hiatus in the occupation of Korucu Tepe, a period corresponding to the settlement of the Mushki in Isua, Tiglath-Pileser I of Assyria stating that they had been in possession of the land for fifty years before he met and defeated them in battle.[34] The next level at Korucu Tepe is marked by retrogression, most clearly defined by crude pottery, red burnished and straw-tempered buff burnished wares, all turned on a slow wheel. The excavator ascribes this period to the tenth and ninth centuries BC or to a phase within those dates, citing the evidence of an iron fibula and beads and pendants of faience and greenstone. This means that Korucu Tepe provides an outline of the cultural history of the Elazığ region, or at least of Altinova, until the annexation of the territory by Urartu, and may give invaluable material relevant to the obscure period immediately preceding the rise of that kingdom.[35] Some light might also be cast on the Mushki, presumably still in or near this region, since they were responsible for the sack of Carchemish, subsequently being defeated by Katuwas, king of that city, who recorded his victory in the Long Wall of sculptured orthostats: this event may be attributable to the opening years of the ninth century BC.[36]

A route for the copper trade from Trans-Caucasia past Lake Urmia is made the more probable by indications of close cultural links between the southern part of the Urmia basin and the Fertile Crescent from north Syria across to Assyria. These indications were first hinted at by the work of the great traveller Sir Aurel Stein;[37] and they have recently been fully recognized by the excavations at Dinkha Tepe near Ushnu, some twenty miles west of Hasanlu and not far from the Iraqi frontier. Dinkha Tepe was first occupied early in the second millennium BC and was defended by a massive mud brick wall, later burnt and abandoned, probably by c. 1,650 BC, on the evidence of a radio-carbon date of 1,612 ±61 BC from the level immediately overlying it.[38] By the time of this later level the town had grown in area and population. The following level, Dinkha Tepe IV, was that of the Dinkha culture: as such it is the most significant period in the occupation of this site. The richest finds came from three tombs cut down into the level beneath, lined with rough stone walls and roofed with flat slabs. These all contained multiple burials with a quantity of gold jewellery and toggle-pins of silver and bronze: for gold strip-twisted earrings there may be parallels in Cyprus and connected with the international gold trade as far west as Ireland; gold pendants, one round with incised and embossed star pattern and another of crescent form, came from the same tomb as the earrings, are paralleled together at Tell el-Ajjul in southern Palestine and occur too at Nuzi and elsewhere. The suggested date of c. 1,500 BC for the earrings is reinforced by a radio-carbon date of 1,555 ±52 BC for the violent end of this period, which was followed by a reoccupation of only rather brief duration, with a radio-carbon date of 1,434 ±52 BC.[39] Whether this occupation ended c. 1,400 BC or as much as 150 years earlier, a rather improbably high date, depends on corrections which may be necessary to the radio-carbon dates or determinations. Above this occupation at Dinkha Tepe came rubbish levels of the culture now termed Iron I and discussed below.

Dinkha Tepe IV is thus dated by at least three radio-carbon dates from the site itself, and can therefore be related to the chronology independently established for Hasanlu. The Dinkha culture is associated with Hasanlu VI (c. 1,900–1,350 BC). There remains, however, a real possibility that not even Hasanlu and Dinkha Tepe together give the whole record of material civilization in the southern Urmia basin during the second millennium BC: much depends on the 'correction factors' for the radio-carbon dates, which must decide the length of the interval between Dinkha Tepe IV and Hasanlu V. The most significant feature of the Dinkha culture is the pottery, of which the finer wares are wheel-made and of red to greenish-yellow colour, with simple painting in the form of bands, sometimes with cross-hatched triangles; on some pots these alternate with double-axe motifs, birds, dots or circles with spokes, perhaps representing wheels. There can also be stylized trees comparable with those on earlier and later Khabur ware at Tell Billa, Tell Brak, Tell Chagar Bazar and Ashur in upper Mesopotamia, as well as at Kültepe (Kanesh).[40] Storage jars often display applied horizontal bands with diagonal or criss-cross incised patterns or finger impressions; combed decoration also occurs, sometimes mistakenly identified on archaeological surveys as Islamic. A light grey burnished ware seems to have been imported, possibly being comparable with the fine grey ware of Tepe Hissar far to the east, though other distant parallels are improbable.[41] Seals supplement the ceramic evidence of undoubted affinities with the Khabur ware of Syria and upper Mesopotamia, to indicate a deep penetration at least of this south-west part of the Urmia basin by Mesopotamian civilization.

Though less obvious further north, this Mesopotamian influence must have permeated the whole Urmia basin. Until more of the mid-second millennium BC levels at Haftavān Tepe have been excavated, reliance must continue to be placed on the important but rather restricted results of the excavations at Geoy Tepe, where Periods D and C are most relevant to the time of Hasanlu VI and the Dinkha culture.[42] The building discovered near the west end of the mound of Haftavān, built of stones set in mud in the manner still to be seen in neighbouring villages, seems to have been a house of some importance, only its basement surviving, filled with straw; outside were houses of altogether humbler size and construction. At least six successive building levels discovered at the east end of the site and dating to the centuries preceding the arrival of the grey ware of Hasanlu V (Iron I) type indicate continuity of occupation and considerable prosperity in a town undoubtedly of large area and population, one of the five or six largest prehistoric settlements in the Urmia basin, not excluding Hasanlu and Geoy Tepe. When the planned campaign of excavations at Haftavān Tepe has been completed, one of its achievements should be the uncovering of a wide area of the town of the second millennium BC: this town reached its greatest extent either then or in the tenth and ninth centuries BC. A small proportion of the pottery from the building levels at the east end of Haftavān Tepe is painted, with a wide variety of styles not yet entirely identifiable, the most obvious parallels being with Geoy Tepe, seventy miles to the south: a common colour scheme is red and black or brown on buff. Similar painted pottery occurs on the west side of Haftavān Tepe, designs including birds. From the arrival of the grey ware of Hasanlu V type, possibly dating from as early as c. 1,350 BC, the sequence at Hasanlu becomes largely valid for the whole Urmia basin: earlier in the second millennium BC this is less obviously so. Haftavān Tepe will assuredly in due course fill this lacuna, as well as indicating local peculiarities not found in the Solduz plain.[43]

The evidence from Geoy Tepe alone has hitherto elucidated the first half of the second millennium BC in the northern Urmia basin, except in so far as Yanik Tepe continued to be occupied till about the nineteenth century BC, perhaps representing a conservative survival. It has been observed that Geoy Tepe D and C form one cultural period divisible into two phases, the first being early D and the second late D and C.[44] Deep, straight-sided carinated bowls with slightly everted rim are characteristic of the early D polychrome pottery, the ware being red burnished and the decoration of loops and wavy lines in matt black and white paint; matt black paint on red-brown burnished slip also occurs. Zig-zags, pendant triangles and loops are used as motifs. Other varieties of polychromy comprise black and white paint on a red surface, black and red paint on a red ground and white paint on a red ground. Some contact with the Dinkha culture to the south is evident. The pottery of the later phase usually has a red or red-brown slip and includes carinated bowls with rolled rim, globular jars with tall neck and others with thickened rim. Triangles, lozenges and other geometric motifs make up the normal patterns on this later polychrome pottery, in black and red paint and with a cream-white band along the rim or the shoulder of the pot.[45]

The origin and expansion of this polychrome pottery requires some discussion, if only because of suggestions of a derivation from the Alişar III (Cappadocian) painted pottery of central Anatolia and from some of the Trialeti pottery.[46] There seems, however, little justification for the former comparison and none for the latter, even if, by rejecting the low dating of Trialeti to c. 1,550–1,450 BC, this group can be adjudged partly contemporary with Geoy Tepe D–C, though beginning earlier.[47] Why cannot an indigenous origin for the early polychrome pottery of the western Urmia basin be postulated? There seems no necessity to seek an outside origin. The main argument in favour of such could lie in the extension of the Khabur ware cultural province into the Ushnu valley, which thus came indirectly into contact with those parts of the Anatolian plateau penetrated by the Assyrian merchants. The distribution of the Cappadocian painted pottery was, however, relatively limited, being confined to the south central Anatolian region and not reaching even as far south-east as Malatya.[48] Any influence of this on the Urmia region seems therefore improbable, nor is the comparison typologically incontrovertible. Firm ground is reached in tracing the expansion of this polychrome pottery east towards Kazvin and in observing the manner in which the forms of the later phase (Geoy Tepe late D and C) were reproduced in the Iron I pottery of Hasanlu V and Dinkha Tepe, in plain grey and red burnished wares.[49]

Painted pottery was alien to Georgia in the third millennium BC and was undoubtedly introduced from outside, though Trialeti shows that there was more than one source. The painted pottery of the early second millennium BC in Armenia has been discussed above: it is unlikely to have appeared spontaneously within the Early Trans-Caucasian cultural zone; far more probably it developed on the south-eastern fringes of that zone, where traditions of producing painted pottery in varying styles, including the painted orange ware of Hasanlu VII (c. 2,500–1,900 BC), had never wholly died out. Through trade and perhaps also migrations the culture originally centred along the west shore of Lake Urmia became so diffused that the use of its painted pottery extended not only through Armenia but also well into Georgia.

Another factor was the bringing of the horse into ever greater use, though at first mainly as a draught animal. At Mari the prefect of the palace, Bahdi-Lim, urged his master Zimri-Lim to remember that he was ruler of the Akkadians (townspeople) as well as of the Hanaeans (country dwellers) and that he should not ride on horseback but only be seen in public in a horsedrawn chariot.[50] The domestication of the horse must have brought about a greater mobility, and was soon to have a lasting effect on methods of warfare, though evidence for the highland zone in the second millennium BC, in the absence of written records, is all too elusive. The rock drawings of horses at Kobistan, south of Baku, unfortunately cannot be dated closely enough to be of great significance. Horses may have been imported into Mesopotamia during the second millennium BC from the breeding grounds in the Urmia basin, though cavalry was not introduced into the Assyrian army until the reign of Tukulti-Ninurta II (890–884 BC).[51] The role of the Kassite invaders from the Zagros highlands into Akkad in the late Old Babylonian period, from the seventeenth century BC onward, is not at all clear in terms of the archaeological record, although perhaps the spread of Khabur ware into the Ushnu valley may in part be attributed to them. Or did they simply pass through, leaving no mark on the lands round Lake Urmia?

One luxury whose import involved very distant trade was amber, said to have been quite extensively used in western Iran in or about the fourteenth century BC. Nearly all amber comes from the Baltic, but it also occurs in the Ukraine. It is tempting to speculate that, along with Baltic amber, tin may possibly have been brought to Iran all the way from Bohemia. The significance of the amber trade is, however, beyond question.[52]

Although the story of Trans-Caucasia in the centuries following the period of Trialeti and contemporary monuments can be interpreted as largely continuing the cultural developments of the early second millennium BC, there were undoubted advances. These are discernible in the appearance of new metal types, which according to one chronology were first being made in about the fourteenth century BC.[53] The beginnings of a great increase in the output of bronzesmiths can be discerned from the fourteenth and thirteenth centuries BC onwards, together with the evolution of two distinct cultural provinces, one in western and the other in central and eastern Trans-Caucasia. The Koban-Colchidic culture, initially two separate groups as above-mentioned, is further discussed below. In central and eastern Trans-Caucasia, or at least in eastern Georgia, north-east Armenia and the western parts of the Azerbaijan SSR, a tradition of metal-working developed as one of the features of the Ganja-Karabagh culture. The discovery in Level II at Khodjali of a bead inscribed with the name of Adad-nirari is one of the few correlations in support of an absolute chronology, for this must be Adad-nirari I of Assyria (c. 1,304–1,267 BC).[54] Thus a date not before the thirteenth century BC for the early phase of the long-lived Ganja-Karabagh culture is indicated. It is reinforced by the parallel between an 'Amazon's axe' with the serrated butt so typical of Caucasian metallurgy at this time, found in kurgan no. 2 at Helenendorf, and the well known axe depicted as held by the god carved on the side of the so-called King's Gate at the Hittite capital of Boğazköy (Hattusas): this dates either to the fourteenth century BC, when the fortifications of the outer town were built against the threat of attack by the Gasga tribes living in the region to the north later to become Pontus, and always a threat to the Hittite capital, or to the thirteenth century BC.[55] Comparisons with axes from Beth-Shan in Palestine and from Ugarit, both firmly dated to c. 1,400–1,350 BC, add to the chronological evidence.[56] The suggestion of an ultimate origin for this type of axe in Luristan is a plausible one, reinforced by the written evidence that sculptors from Kassite Babylonia, a region open to close contacts with Luristan, were specially imported by Hattusilis III (c. 1,275–1,250 BC); but perhaps it is more to connections with Elam that one should look, as the region most influential over the metallurgy both of Luristan and of Babylonia in the period of Kassite rule (c. 1,595–1,170 BC).[57] The attribution of this type of axe to Luristan must be assessed, however, in the light of Deshayes' predilection for an Iranian origin for nearly all developments of any significance in metal-working in the Near East, including his theory of movements radiating out from Iran to Alaca Hüyük and elsewhere in Anatolia in the later third millennium BC.[58] The bronze axes of the Ganja-Karabagh cultural province and its environs are characterized by a very wide and curving cutting edge, a biconvex shaft-hole, a blade with hexagonal section and a serrated butt. These axes – Type M in the classification of Deshayes – have been nicknamed 'Amazon's axes'. The cutting edge became more exaggerated, with a curve making an arc of more than 180 degrees: this exaggeration produced a similarity to the so-called fenestrated axeheads or halberds. The occurrence of large numbers of these in Gilan, part of the south Caspian littoral of Iran, has suggested a movement of this type from there north-west into the Ganja-Karabagh cultural province; but there is not enough chronological evidence, in the absence of sufficient material from securely stratified contexts, to determine for certain the direction of this influence on the bronze industry.[59]

Discoveries by Soviet archaeologists since the Second World War have made it possible to discern the general development of material civilization in the period from the fourteenth till the ninth century BC. This is the Late Bronze Age of Trans-Caucasia, limited by one authority to the period c. 1,300–900 BC and divided into three phases.[60] Certainly this Late Bronze Age culture in Armenia did not reach full maturity before the thirteenth century BC, being most sensationally demonstrated by the discoveries made after 1950 after a fall in the level of Lake Sevan, the result of a hydro-electric scheme on the River Hrazdan, affecting its outfall. Here, on the flat, bleak marshes now revealed beside the cold lake, were uncovered many tomb chambers, lined and roofed with massive slabs. This was the cemetery of Lchashen, where, in addition to the more remarkable finds, there was gathered evidence from the whole area indicating a succession of not less than five phases extending in time from the late third until the late second millennium BC (c. 1,100 BC).[61] On higher ground beside Lake Sevan about one thousand graves, mostly of the Middle and Late Bronze Age, were excavated in 1904–8 by Lalayan, but were never adequately published.

The pottery from Lchashen of Late Bronze Age date includes small jars with black surface, decorated in red, white and black painted panels or bands. One particularly distinctive form is a bifoliate bowl, resembling two vessels joined into one: this is found widely at sites in the Azerbaijan SSR, including the highland Dashkesen area, Djulfa and Kizil-Vank, the example from this last being unpainted. Lchashen can be classed as to some degree within the Ganja-Karabagh province, alternatively called Khodjali-Kederbey. The great tombs excavated by Mnatsakanian, however, appear to represent an essentially Sevan culture, its artifacts predominantly of local manufacture. The gold work has been analysed and found to be from local sources.

The treasures from Lchashen now form one of the proudest possessions of the Erevan Museum. Such were the ecological conditions that wood was preserved, enabling a remarkable group of wheeled vehicles to survive, not unique in Trans-Caucasia but the largest and latest group. These comprised five open carts, one wagon with wickerwork sides, four with arched tilt and two chariots with spoked wheels; there were also fragments of spoked wheels from another of the Lchashen barrows, as well as a toy cart. The more meagre evidence from Trialeti is yet enough to prove that Lchashen was in the same tradition, lasting through from the Trans-Caucasian Middle Bronze Age. There were, however, developments in design of these vehicles, of which the appearance of the spoked wheel is the most important. The two-wheeled vehicles from Lchashen, the chariots or carts with spoked wheels and the toy chariot, have their axle set in the centre of the body instead of at the rear, the position adopted in the fourteenth century BC in the Near East proper.[62] The introduction of these sophisticated vehicles from the kingdom of Mitanni in north Syria, with its chariotry and its warrior caste of *maryannu* or knights, is not at all impossible; but the Mitannian seal found in Barrow 97 and dating to the fifteenth or fourteenth century BC in its style cannot be given too much significance. There is no archaeological evidence to make such an influence indisputable. If, however, the cultural infiltration from north Syria into the southern Urmia basin is recalled, it becomes not at all impossible that Mitanni was in direct contact with Armenia in the period immediately preceding the richest burials at Lchashen. By this time Mitanni had been extinguished as an independent state, under Hittite pressure but chiefly by the rise of Assyria.[63] It is perhaps not too bold to imagine a possible exodus northwards of refugees, taking with them their skills in the arts of peace and war. Yet the cultural influence on Lchashen was as much indigenous within Trans-Caucasia and more especially its own environs as from any outside region; and the design of the stone-built tombs, with their circular kerbs of large stones, is comparable with the so-called dolmens of the Persian Talysh and also with the pit graves of the northern steppes. As at Trialeti before so also at Lchashen the influence of the steppes, though muted, is still discernible, not least in the very use of this design of tomb and in the wooden vehicles.

The context of the earlier burials of Lchashen, such as Barrow 6 with its painted pottery, its cord-impressed jar of Kurgan IV type and its food offerings for the owner, has been discussed above.[64] Altogether on a grander scale are the tombs containing wooden vehicles, dated by the excavator to the thirteenth and twelfth centuries BC and later, Martirosian assigning them to the first of his three phases of the Late Bronze Age of Armenia (c. 1,300–1,150 BC), with the comparable burial at Adiaman (Getashen) at the south-west corner of Lake Sevan assigned to his third phase, in the tenth century BC.[65] The similarities of this burial to those of Mnatsakanian's fourth group at Lchashen must, however, be remembered. Over the dating of the Redkin Lager cemetery opinions vary from c. 1,300–1,100 BC to a period several centuries later, when iron was in extensive use.[66] At Lchashen the earliest burials of carts, the two-wheeled vehicles of A-frame type, have been mentioned above. The four-wheeled vehicles, or wagons, represent the later full flowering of the Sevan culture (*c.* 1,300–1,150 BC). In Barrow 9, for example, was found a wagon with basketwork covering forming an arched roof, found likewise on wagons in Barrows 1, 2 and 10. The construction of the body of these vehicles was fairly standardized: the axles were fixed to the body; the turning circle must have been very wide. Typical dimensions are given as 1·08 m. for the width, 1·80 m. for the height to the top of the basketwork sides and 5·6 m. for the length with the A-frame poles. Wear on some wheels shows that at least some of the Lchashen vehicles must have been in use before being buried, possibly for transportation of goods rather than in war: in Barrow 9 one wheel had been replaced by a new one. Wheels were of the disc type made out of three pieces, except for the wagons with spoked wheels.

The Lchashen wagons and carts give proof of the skill in woodworking of the craftsmen of this region. Oak and elm were the woods most used for the wheels, axles and draught-poles, the yokes being of oak and the framework of the arched roof of the pliable yew; beech and pine were also used. The wagon with wickerwork sides from Barrow 11 at Lchashen is typical in its dimensions, and demonstrates the immense labour which went into the manufacture of these vehicles: mortice-and-tenon or dowelled joints were used exclusively, with pegs and treenails; this wagon was made out of seventy pieces with twelve thousand mortices of varying size, round and square. A chisel or a red-hot metal implement was used for gouging out or burning the hole, but precisely for which parts of the vehicles is no longer ascertainable. Chisels and gouges were used for axle-holes and for decorative carving, as of two deer with antlers on one seat; and there is also carving on the Adiaman chariot. The skill of these woodworkers is as apparent as the wealth of their masters, who were able to command the manpower required to tap the resources of the local forests, now vanished.

The design of the Lchashen tombs and the evidence of the funerary customs have considerable significance beyond the shores of Lake Sevan, remote and ice-bound for much of the year. The entrance passages (*dromoi*) of the Lchashen tombs of the fourth group are lined, unlike those at Trialeti, with massive orthostats. Animals were buried with the owner of the tomb, but only the hide with the head and hoofs, not the whole carcase. Oxen and horses occur, perhaps indiscriminately, and the presence in Barrow 2 at Lchashen of the skulls of two oxen and one horse, surprisingly accompanied by six of the bronze bits then made in Trans-Caucasia, with cheekpieces in the form of wheels, may enjoin caution in any claim that these were the animals which drew the wagons.

Any very precise dating either of the material from Lchashen or of that from elsewhere in Trans-Caucasia in the period from the fourteenth to the tenth century BC or even later is still often impossible. At Lchashen the most distinctive pottery is a black ware with mauve or red and white encrustation, and the most easily recognizable form is the twin bowl, each part oval within an ovoid whole. These are attributed by Mnatsakanian and Martirossian also to the third of four groups at Lchashen, excluding the Early Trans-Caucasian material, and dated to the fourteenth century BC, just preceding the richest burials with the wagons.[67] Possibly, however, some of this material may belong to humbler graves chronologically overlapping, if not entirely contemporary with, the chieftains' tombs. If the latter represent burials of a local dynasty, presumably they must span several generations: they may therefore begin earlier than suggested, or, perhaps less probably, continue later.

It is the encrusted pottery which strikes the visitor to the Erevan Museum as the hallmark of the finds from Lchashen, if only by its quantity. The metalwork is diversified, with dating evidence provided by tridents which presumably served as goads for the draught animals, and which are paralleled at Ugarit in the Late Ugarit 3 period.[68] There is no known geographically intermediate example to elucidate this distant connection, probably an outcome of trade continuing after the end of Mitanni. Bidents also occur. Artik and Tazekend are among sites producing daggers comparable with those from Lchashen, with square shoulder and open-work sheath.[69] Kvemo-Sasireti, Redkin Lager and Samtavro have likewise yielded bronzes paralleled at Lchashen, including the birds, openwork bells and stags, the last surely traceable back, though not directly, through a long tradition first manifested at Alaca Hüyük. The bronze axes called 'Amazon axes' occur in Lchashen tombs of the third and fourth groups, at the cemetery of Samtavro (Mtskheta), in the hoard from Kvemo-Sasireti between Tbilisi and Gori and at Helenendorf.[70] Such is the evidence at present available to put Lchashen in its cultural context in relation to other parts of Trans-Caucasia: hardly any more far-flung parallels are yet known.

Other sites besides Lchashen have provided much evidence of the Late Bronze Age cultures, of which one of the best known is Kizil-Vank with its polychrome pottery: here new excavations should clarify the results of much earlier work.[71] This pottery seems to belong to a period (c. 1,500–1,200 BC) spanning the transition from Middle to Late Bronze Age. At Kültepe (Nakhichevan) such pottery is classed as Late Bronze Age. This represents the late stage of that tradition of polychrome pottery associated with north-west Iran and discussed above. Elsewhere plain wares predominate: grey, black and red wares continue at Kültepe (Nakhichevan) from the Middle Bronze Age. Grey wares are indeed widespread, being found, for example, in a kurgan containing five pattern-burnished pots of transitional date from the Middle Bronze Age, from Melighele and now in the Gurjaani Museum. Possible implications of these for the antecedents of the grey wares of the Iron I period in Iran could only be pursued with the help of certain evidence to fix the date of this material. In this region of Kakheti there flourished a local Late Bronze Age culture, distinguishable by its bronze daggers, miniature bronze figurines, stamp-seals whose motifs include a catherine wheel and a swastika and miniature obsidian arrowheads, whose occurrence may be compared with that of flint arrowheads at Lchashen; but data for the absolute chronology of this Kakhetian culture, whose continuation at least till the ninth century BC is mentioned below, are limited.[72] At Samtavro, the major cemetery near Mtskheta, upstream from Tbilisi on the River Kura, no less than five phases have been distinguished, extending over a very long time. Open bowls of grey ware are typical of the earliest phase, variously dated as high as the fifteenth century BC and as low as c. 1,300–1,100 BC. By this latter chronology the second phase is dated c. 1,100–900 BC and the fifth and final phase c. 600–500 BC. Once again the dearth of stratified material from occupation levels reduces the value of objects from a cemetery.[73]

The Dashkesen area, a mountainous tract in the west of the Azerbaijan SSR, was investigated in excavations conducted in 1960–5, in which considerable results were obtained. Five fortresses with cyclopean walls were found, dated to the Late Bronze Age. One remarkable barrow of this period covered no fewer than thirty-seven burials in stone-lined graves, and yielded much painted pottery, obsidian arrowheads and metalwork including bronze birds of the type found at Lchashen but more numerous in the Azerbaijan SSR than in Armenia, being characteristic of this Late Bronze Age cultural province. Another barrow in the Dashkesen area contained one cist grave, two earth graves and one empty grave with pots. The bronze industry is very diversified, including cauldrons, the typical Late Bronze Age daggers with broad shoulder and the axeheads found at Lchashen, Artik and elsewhere; personal ornaments include a belt buckle, bracelets, many types of finger-ring and large earrings too heavy to be worn directly from the ear and therefore attached to a plain bronze head-band. There is thus a general parallel, though not in design, with the contemporary tassels so characteristic of burials at Haftavān Tepe, dating to c. 1,000–800 BC.[74] The barrows of the Dashkesen region were themselves built up of earth in the Late Bronze Age, although previously in the Early Trans-Caucasian culture the mound was constructed of stones. Where stones were used in the later barrows, as for the lining of the graves, incised ornamentation including goats was frequent and comparable with ceramic decoration on some jars: these incised drawings on stones are rather more sophisticated than the scribblings in the earlier barrows of Trialeti.[75]

Of all the sites in the Armenian SSR which may help to clarify the cultural succession of the Late Bronze Age, Artik stands out, potentially as significant as Lchashen. Artik has yielded an earring of the large type above-mentioned as found in the Dashkesen area; but more important are parallels with Lchashen. Bronze tools and weapons include the familiar daggers with open-work hilts, some with decoration of a snake inlaid in copper; open-work bronze belts, birds and stags reveal close affinities with Lchashen, while the similar cheek-pieces, first appearing in about the fourteenth century BC, bear witness to the growing importance of the horse in Trans-Caucasia, a development with which the lighter vehicles with spoked wheels at Lchashen can surely be associated.[76]

In the Araxes valley in Armenia the Late Bronze II period began c. 1,150 BC, following the last phase at Lchashen. The Late Bronze III period ensued from c. 1,000 BC and the Early Iron Age a century or more thereafter, by which time the introduction of iron-working on a wide scale, discussed below, had begun to have far-reaching effects on the material culture. At first iron had been used on a limited scale, as for pins found in a pre-Urartian level at Karmir-Blur, which may date as early as c. 1,100 BC. Meanwhile traditional metallurgy, that of the bronze-smith, continued to flourish, being demonstrated by the discoveries at Metsamor. There, after the above-mentioned final level of the Middle Bronze Age, with its polychrome and black wares and dated c. 1,500–1,300 BC, activity continued in the Late Bronze Age, although on a rather reduced scale. A building level with houses cut into the hillside is dated c. 1,100–900 BC; and of the same period are remains of smelting furnaces, with slag thrown out over the houses from later furnaces further up the hillside. A whole factory for the production of the phosphorus brickettes used in smelting tin, with twenty-three furnaces, is thought on grounds of technology to date before c. 1,000 BC. It was presumably the development of iron-working which brought about the eventual eclipse of Metsamor, although east of the main site there is a large cemetery of the Late Bronze Age and Early Iron Age, suggesting some continuity of occupation in the vicinity. This is hardly remarkable, since the situation in the fertile plain, with abundant water from a spring, was sure to attract settlers. Cyclopean walls near the water are said to be pre-Urartian, though the evidence for this early dating is not entirely clear. In one area of the rock of Metsamor, above a level containing stippled pottery dated before the great period of Lchashen, was found a shrine centred on an anthropomorphic double stele made of clay, with a hearth filled with pottery in front and a lower, smaller hearth filled with ash further in front; at the rear the natural rock was cut smooth and plastered with clay, with a rough masonry wall above. In the immediate vicinity are various small hearths, perhaps for sacrifices. This shrine faces due west; and an astral significance has been suggested. It is quite plausible that this was a cult hearth or domestic altar, dated by the excavators to the end of the second millennium BC, but too fragile to have stood for long without repair. Glass making also flourished at Metsamor, as indicated by six types of metallurgical material, including zinc and manganese, alloyed in different ways to make different colours. Metsamor continued as a metallurgical site even in mediaeval times, but all the evidence of greatest activity is dated before c. 1,000 BC.[77] Further down the Araxes valley, material of the Late Bronze Age includes painted pottery with animals from the second site called Kültepe (Nakhichevan) and characteristic rough stone axes from Karaköpektepe, hardly suggesting an advanced technology there. The snake motif occurs on pottery from Kizil-Vank, Shah-Tahti and elsewhere. The latter site, together with Shah-Tepe, has yielded pottery with parallels in Iran mentioned below.

These were the centuries preceding the establishment of Urartian rule in the Araxes valley around Erevan, beginning not later than the foundation of that city as Erebuni in the early eighth century BC.

The sequence of cultures in the regions of the north Caucasus from the Kuban basin in the west to the shores of the Caspian in the east and the relations of the different cultural provinces to one another throughout the second millennium BC and in the early first millennium BC has long seemed a baffling and complex subject of enquiry, only fairly recently simplified.[78] According to this reconstruction of the evidence, there was one unified North Caucasian Bronze Age culture, spanning the whole second millennium BC, with geographical sub-provinces: there were three of these, the north-western, the central and the north-eastern. The north-western has hitherto been termed the Kuban culture; the central comprised two sections, the highland and that in the area of Piatigorsk and Nal'chik; the north-eastern is otherwise termed the Kayakent-Khorochoi culture. There were three periods of the North Caucasian Bronze Age, the extent of whose cultural zone diminished during the second period; in the third the process of regional diversification continued, especially in the highlands of the central north Caucasus.

The least known till recent years, the most backward and probably the least influential on Trans-Caucasia was the Kayakent-Khorochoi cultural province in the north-east Caucasus. The occurrence of representations of goats carved on stones of some circular enclosures apparently of this cultural period suggests that at least some of the rock drawings of Kobistan date as late as the early first millennium BC: though this cannot be proved, the presence of a circular enclosure immediately at the foot of the great boulder field of Kobistan, similar to those on the Apsheron peninsula near Baku attributed to this period, amounts to circumstantial evidence in favour of this dating. These enclosures may have served as animal pens; the carvings themselves suggest the importance of livestock to the Kayakent-Khorochoi people, who may indeed have been only partly settled in permanent communities. Such are indicated by the excavations of settlement sites at Kayakent, Dzhemikent and Aslanbek-Sheripovo. A cemetery of barrows at Gamut in the steppes has been investigated; more typical are the small cist graves in the district of Tarki, each side being normally of one slab and the lid likewise of a single slab. The burials were usually in a sitting posture in the south-west corner of the cist grave. These burials are characteristic of the eastern part of this cultural province, near the Caspian Sea. In the western part of this province burials were usually contracted rather than sitting, often with joints of sheep or cow left as food for the dead. The cultural province as a whole was relatively isolated, its origins still obscure and its late continuation necessitating its mention in the next chapter.[79]

In the west the Middle Kuban culture, spanning the first and second of the three periods of the North Caucasian Bronze Age as above-mentioned, seems to have continued until *c.* 1,200 BC, when it was succeeded by the Late Kuban culture, lasting five or six centuries and thus being partly contemporary with Urartu to the south and with the Colchidic and Koban cultures of western Georgia and Ossetia respectively. The importance of arable farming on the rich soil of the Kuban basin and the northern steppes is emphasized by an increase in the number of sickles in the Late Bronze Age, a feature also of the plains of Trans-Caucasia at this time. In the hilly, wooded environment of Colchis, however, viticulture and orchard husbandry are suggested by the common occurrence of pruning-knives.[80] Metal-working, evident from graves, hoards and stray finds, especially distinguishes this Kuban culture, even if its exact chronological limits remain hard to determine in the absence of material from occupation levels. A.A.Iessen was able to distinguish the metalwork of the Kuban basin from that of the Koban highland region of the central north Caucasus, to show that the Middle Kuban culture may have overlapped in time the Koban culture and to record numerous sources of metalwork and also of mining and smelting on either side of the western Caucasus.[81] Difficulties arising from attempts to correlate material now in museums are aggravated by the fact that much of it was found before the Revolution. In a few places in the upper Kuban basin traces of ancient mining and smelting were found. At Bagyrkulak there was extensive mining of copper: there were two veins, the more important one being mined open cast in its upper reaches and by means of a gallery 6 m. long and 1·60 m. high. Elsewhere silver-lead ores were exploited. On the River Afips workshops for casting in copper have been located. There are considerable sources of ores on the Black Sea littoral, in the Kuban basin and on the neighbouring steppe; but many of the traces of their exploitation belong to centuries well after even the Late Kuban culture. The influences affecting the metal industry of the Kuban basin came indirectly from the Colchidic culture to the south, by way of the Koban region.

From some time in the mid-second millennium BC or rather later, perhaps not till the third period of the North Caucasian Bronze Age, there evolved the Digorian culture in the highlands of Ossetia in the central Caucasus; in the fringes of the steppes to the north was the province of the North Ossetian cultures. The Digorian culture flourished in a land whose wealth undoubtedly depended on its metal-working and the far-flung trading connections which arose therefrom: the area was too mountainous for arable farming, a pastoral economy being more probable. Whether the negative evidence of the apparent absence of agricultural implements such as sickles or hoes can, however, be taken to support the theory of a pastoral economy is another matter.[82] Bronze axes, daggers, knives, spearheads and arrowheads are among finds from the cemeteries of Faskau and Verkhniaia Rutkha, both situated in the upper Terek basin, the latter in the district of Digora, home of the Digorian culture. These weapons are paralleled in the Late Talysh 2 culture, for which Schaeffer's dates of c. 1,450–1,350 BC may need little if any lowering.[83] The precise significance of this connection, probably through trade across the steppes immediately north of the Caucasus, remains to be investigated: it gave easy contact between the Kuban-Terek region and the western shores of the Caspian Sea. Bronze arrowheads from Agha-Evlar in the Talysh include a winged type not altogether unlike examples in flint from Verkhniaia Rutkha. The axes from the cemetery of Faskau have long sockets and blades; and there are serpentine maceheads of spherical, ovoid or pyriform shape, many having hemispherical knobs, a type occurring as early and as far north as the cemetery of Mariupol, near the Sea of Azov.[84] A taste for knobs was also displayed in attachment to the butt of some axes from Faskau and elsewhere. At both Faskau and Verkhniaia Rutkha occur elongated triangular flint arrowheads, suggesting that metal was still thought too valuable to be expended on missiles unlikely to be recoverable. These two cemeteries have also yielded brooches with parallels in Italy and daggers with parallels in Hungary dated c. 1,200–1,100 BC.

The Digorian culture was the direct precursor of the Koban culture, which itself owed much also to the long established Colchidic culture, so much so that it has often been termed the Koban-Colchidic culture. The above-mentioned parallels with Europe make a beginning in the eleventh century BC for the Koban culture quite possible. Decorated bronze axes from Faskau could be prototypes of the Koban industry, with its bold animal designs. An axe from Pitsunda, if correctly attributed to the fourteenth century BC, could be a very early prototype of the unified style of bronze axes associated with the Koban culture and found also in Colchis.[85] But it is hardly sufficient evidence in itself of the antecedents of this abundant industry. The people who left their clearest mark in the cultural record of the Caucasus in their distinctive bronze axes buried their dead in catacomb graves, a shaft with niches in its sides, the type of grave likewise characteristic of the Kuban basin in the latter half of the second millennium BC. This similarity could indicate an ethnic connection between the two regions, archaeologically not at all impossible, for the Koban culture was in some ways a means of communication between Colchis and other regions south of the Caucasus and the northern steppes. In its flamboyant patterns this bronze industry suggests an important influence on later manifestations of the so-called 'animal style', whatever the relations between this settled people and the Scythian or Cimmerian nomads may have been. The Koban axes are more elongated than their precursors and display a rounded and often asymmetric cutting edge, a blade with concave sides and hexagonal section, a biconvex shaft-hole and a spiked butt. These axes and so the culture which they represent have been dated from the period between the thirteenth and the eleventh century BC, on the evidence of the Digorian cemeteries more probably the later date, until an uncertain date early in the first millennium BC. The widening contacts of the Caucasus in the first millennium BC are exemplified by daggers of Assyrian and Luristan types found with Koban material, perhaps brought there by Urartian intermediaries.[86]

The terminology set out by R.H.Dyson for the successive periods of the Iron Age in north-western Iran, with Iron I beginning on the evidence of radio-carbon dates perhaps as early as *c.* 1,350 BC, will be followed here, even though it cannot be synthesized in one system applicable to the whole highland zone from the Caucasus to the upper Euphrates.[87] This terminology is based primarily on ceramic evidence, although the reference to iron prompts some discussion at this point of the early history of iron working in the Near East.

The occurrence of iron in the last centuries of the second millennium BC favours scepticism concerning the alleged monopoly of iron by the Hittites in this period. Mitanni is known to have been a pioneer in iron working. An understanding of the technical processes involved and of how these are likely to have been discovered is essential to any valid interpretation of the available data.[88] One theory is that the introduction of iron was through itinerant smiths such as the Chalybes and other groups plying their craft from one town to the next. Yet it must be remembered that there were numerous bronzesmiths, with many centuries of tradition behind them: the first attempts to use the new metal may well therefore have been by using the methods long proven for bronze. The practical advantages of iron would certainly not have been obvious for a long time, and indeed iron would have been of little use except for ornaments. Forms made in bronze continued at first to be used for the new iron products. An outstanding product of early iron working is the dagger with an iron blade from the tomb of Tutankhamun, commonly supposed though not proved to have been a gift from Suppiluliumas, the Hittite king.[89] The true Iron Age only began with the introduction of tools and weapons on a large scale and of a superior quality to those hitherto made of copper or bronze, a change which in most of the Near East may not have come before the tenth and ninth centuries BC, although the Sea Peoples who attacked Egypt in the reign of Rameses III had iron swords. Moreover, the Philistines formed the largest contingent of the Sea Peoples and, on the evidence of the Old Testament, possessed considerable skill in the working of iron.[90] This skill must have been brought with them from their earlier homeland. As long as iron was used by employing the crucibles appropriate to bronze-working no worthwhile advantage was gained from the new metal; the introduction of bloomeries and shaft furnaces made possible the manufacture of steel by reduction of iron ores. Thus came the true Iron Age, which arrived peacefully in the wake of long and widespread acquaintance with a limited working of iron by the old methods.

The highland zone of eastern Anatolia and north-western Iran is rich in sources of iron. The undoubted importance of the lands later under Urartian rule for the earliest history of iron-working, though not in itself any adequate explanation of the rise of Urartu, should enjoin caution in deducing from the dearth of material remains a relapse into barbarism.[91] Another region perhaps crucial for the development of iron-working is that extending from the Taurus mountains into north Syria, including Kizzuwatna, a major source of iron for the Hittites of the imperial period. If one derivation of the Greek word *khalyps* ('steel') from Halab/Aleppo is followed, the significance of this region must be reinforced.[92] Yet the relative backwardness of Egypt must be remembered in any consideration of the role of iron in the second millennium BC. The earliest beginnings of iron-working in Trans-Caucasia are regrettably obscure, though a few iron ornaments occur in the Ganja-Karabagh cultural province from about the thirteenth century BC onwards. Iron was slower to come into general use in the northern steppes and the Kuban basin, in the great period of the Scyths. Iron daggers are characteristic of the latest period of the Koban and Colchidic cultures. The relevance of later evidence of iron-working, such as that of the third century BC in the *Argonautica* describing the encounter of the Argonauts with the iron-working Chalybes on the

Black Sea coast between Sinope and Trebizond, should perhaps not be over-emphasized, whether or not this term was applied to a distinct tribe. In all the uncertainties concerning the early use of iron, one fact is beyond dispute, that by the time of the great Urartian sites iron tools and weapons were being made in enormous quantities, attested especially at Toprak-kale and at Karmir-Blur. At Kayalidere numerous iron arrowheads were found but only one of bronze, and that of a different design; comparable are the arrowheads from the Urartian citadel at Haftavān Tepe.[93]

The introduction of grey ware into north-western Iran marks the beginning of the Iron I period, once thought to date to *c.* 1,200 BC but now tentatively put back as early as *c.* 1,350 BC. Whichever the date preferred, it depends primarily on the series of radio-carbon dates from Hasanlu, where Period V is coterminous with Iron I and Period IV with Iron II. There are ample radio-carbon dates to indicate that the buildings of the most prosperous period of the citadel, Hasanlu IV, were erected *c.* 1,000 BC and were destroyed by fire in or just after an enemy attack *c.* 800 BC. After that there was apparently a hiatus in the occupation of the citadel, contemporary with the period of the maximum extent and power of Urartu. Strictly defined the great period of the citadel was Hasanlu IVB, with squatters occupying the ruins in IVA; then the site was completely deserted. The squatters' phase and the subsequent desertion may have lasted about a century altogether, within the Iron IIIA period in the terminology of Dyson and Young. The reoccupation of Hasanlu (IIIB) belongs to the Iron IIIB period (*c.* 700/650–550 BC). This was followed by Hasanlu IIIA, approximately contemporary with the Achaemenid empire, though exhibiting no features plainly distinguishable as Achaemenid.[94]

The question of the earliest Iranian penetration of western Iran, including the Urmia basin, has been dealt with in detail by T.C. Young in a discussion which has raised as many problems as it has solved, like all worthwhile studies of such aspects of protohistoric cultures and ethnic movements.[95] It is admitted that many matters remain very obscure, and that only the pottery has so far been studied in any detail. This is not unexpected, since pottery is the only ubiquitous surface material collected on surveys, in which Young has been especially active.[96] Surveys, however, have their limitations, conclusions of a negative character based on their results being particularly unreliable. Thus distribution maps emerging from surveys are apt to give only the minimum extent of a cultural province as determined by a class of pottery; nor are they always sufficiently informative to take into account chronological differences between separate regions, often wide apart. The real possibility of a north-eastern derivation of the Iron I pottery, which indeed is most probably the hallmark of the earliest Iranians, is largely based on parallels with Tepe Hissar IIIC, for there is found a grey ware not unlike that of Iron I and II in western Iran, with a similar taste for pattern-burnishing as a technique for decorative effect.[97] Serious problems of chronology are, however, involved; and any suggestion that the same movement of Indo-European peoples from the Russian steppes which brought the Luvians into western Anatolia via the Balkans and the Hittites into central Anatolia via the Caucasus also brought the Hissar IIIC people into north-east Iran can surely be put aside until there are many more data to support such a far-reaching conclusion.

The question of the sources of Iron I and II pottery, especially the former, naturally raises the problem of the direction from which the Iranian newcomers first entered western Iran. The evidence is partly linguistic but for the most part archaeological; and it remains tantalizingly inconclusive. Sources for Iron I and II pottery in Anatolia and the Caucasus have been mentioned by Young as possibilities. The former can in the writer's opinion be entirely ruled out, for there is hardly any pottery known from sites in Turkey comparable with Iron I or II wares in western Iran. A few sherds from mounds in the Muş plain, an area in the subsequent Urartian period less heavily populated than before, must represent penetration by a small group from the east rather than the home of any ancestors of the Iranian tribes.[98] Although the evidence from eastern Anatolia as a whole, except for the Elazığ and Malatya regions, is negative and as such unreliable, no western affinities for either Iron I or Iron II pottery can be substantiated. Caucasian derivation, however, is a possibility requiring close investigation.

The Hamadan plain may have been the centre from which the Iranians spread out north-westwards into the Urmia basin and beyond.[99] They may indeed have arrived gradually from the lands south-east of the Caspian Sea, including the area of Tepe Hissar and the Gurgan. Such a movement must have been very gradual at first, for otherwise there is a long chronological hiatus between the pottery of Hissar IIIC (c. 2,000–1,850 BC) and the earliest date (c. 1,350 BC) for the appearance of the Iron I culture in western Iran. An argument in support of this supposed immigration route is the linguistic affinity between Old Persian, in south-west Iran, and Sogdian, to the east. Undoubtedly the people speaking these dialects shared a common heritage and homeland at an earlier time, but quite where and when is a problem awaiting more data before solution.[100]

The evidence suggesting, though certainly not proving, that some other solution to the question of the direction from which the Iranians entered Iran in the late second millennium BC than the theory of a migration from north-east Iran may be possible is here set out briefly. A northern approach of the Iranian newcomers, perhaps down the west side of the Caspian Sea, cannot be ruled out simply for lack of evidence, seems chronologically more plausible than any link with Hissar IIIC and moreover is not inconsistent with the dating of the Talysh material proposed by Schaeffer for his Late Talysh 2 period (c. 1,450–1,350 BC).[101] Though this dating is based on the far from irrefutable evidence of seals paralleled at Ugarit and Beth-Shan, the connections with the Iron I culture of north-western Iran, referred to below, provide good evidence for relative chronology, with Marlik as a further link between the Talysh and Azerbaijan. Here therefore is a faint hint that already by c. 1,400 BC pottery of Iron I type had appeared in the Talysh, though not yet arrived in the Urmia basin. As Dyson observes, the date of c. 1,350 ±50 BC 'would place the Hasanlu and Marlik occupations at the end of the range formerly proposed for the Talysh area tombs'.[102] A radio-carbon date of 986 ±61 BC from Yarim Tepe in the Gurgan and dates by the old solid carbon method of 1,105 ±278 BC, 1,085 ±237 BC and 1,023 ±381 BC for the reoccupation of Hotu Cave suggest that the arrival of grey ware in north-east Iran may date as late as c. 1,000 BC.[103] Such a date would undermine an eastern origin for the Iranian migrations into the Hamadan plain, the Urmia basin and other parts of western Iran.

The distribution of Iron I pottery was very wide in western Iran, but even more so than suggested by Young. The most representative sites of this period indeed include Hasanlu V, Dinkha Tepe, Geoy Tepe, Sialk V and Tepe Giyan I⁴–I³. But the northern part of the Urmia basin is now known to be within the bounds of this cultural province, through the discovery of Iron I pottery at Yanik Tepe and at Haftavān Tepe.[104] In the Araxes valley the occurrence at Shah-tahti of a button-base goblet of grey ware and of spouted jars, these found also at Shah-Tepe, indicates either a northward extension from the Urmia basin or a westward one from the Talysh. Thus the argument for a movement from the east, by-passing Trans-Caucasia, appears to be weakened. By the reconstruction of the evidence here suggested, the Urmia region would have been the first in Iran to be settled by Iranians, by the fourteenth or thirteenth century BC. This does not preclude an ultimate origin in the culture of Hissar IIIC, but this would have lain through some undocumented migration round the north end of the Caspian Sea into the steppes north of the Caucasus and thence southward across the lower Araxes into the Talysh.

It was the pottery which most clearly manifested this new cultural tradition of the Iron I period, with a sharp break in continuity from the earlier sequence of cultures distinguished largely by varieties of painted pottery. This break is discernible throughout the greater part of Iran,

from Azerbaijan southwards to Fars and east to the Gurgan: the date of
arrival of this pottery in each region is clearly crucial to the solution of the
question discussed above of the route of the Iranian immigrations.
Ceramic continuity from Iron I to Iron II in some regions is such that
surface finds can often not be differentiated with assurance between the
two periods, though in other regions there were considerable changes.
Not by pottery alone, however, is the Iron I culture known, though its
grey ware, taste for pattern burnishing, goblets with button base and
jars with free-standing horizontal spout are sufficiently distinctive. A
paucity of iron and an absence of any large fortified settlements are also
characteristic of the period, together with the use of extramural cemeteries, at Hasanlu in the lower parts of the mound immediately beneath
the citadel. At many sites, including Hasanlu, Yanik Tepe, Tepe Giyan,
Tepe Sialk and Khorvin-Chandar these burials are simple inhumations.
But large cemeteries with tombs built of walls of undressed stones roofed
with large slabs also occur, comparable with Tomb K at Geoy Tepe,
with the Talysh tombs including those at Agha-Evlar and with the tombs
at Marlik. Thus burial customs help to demonstrate the links between the
Talysh and Iran in the Iron I period.[105]

It is in the context of the Iron I culture that the royal tombs of Marlik,
certainly from their riches those of a powerful dynasty, belong. The
inspiration of much of their contents was pre-Iranian: like the Trialeti
barrows they could well represent a dynasty of steppe dwellers who had
won control, with the help of a small band of compatriots, of the indigenous, more numerous and more civilized population. Where such rulers
came into contact with the more advanced cultures of the Near East,
conditions came into being for the production of works of art by gold-
smiths, silversmiths, jewellers and bronzesmiths blending their own traditions and tastes with those of their new masters. Such a symbiosis had
first been manifest at Maikop, later at Trialeti and still later at Marlik.[106]

The great warriors buried at Marlik had interred with them enough
datable objects to indicate contemporaneity with the Middle Assyrian
period, the fourteenth and thirteenth centuries BC, although other objects
point to a date in the Iron II period and thus to a long life for this cemetery,
perhaps as long as six centuries (c. 1,400–800 BC). Marlik Tepe was never
a settlement but a natural hill used as a cemetery, where the excavator
Dr Negahban found fifty-three tombs.[107] These are dug into the rock and
only very roughly shaped. An interesting feature is the arrangement of
the grave goods by class, comprising vessels for cooking, food and drink,
weapons and ritual vessels. In some tombs the body had been laid out on
a slab; but the skeletons were always found crushed, owing to the custom
of filling the burial chamber with earth and stones after the funeral. A
layer of brownish soil not from the hill itself, about 25 cm. thick, was

scattered over the body and over all the funerary provisions: this gives a hint of a survival of the tradition of ochre burials brought from the northern steppes. An irregular group of stones usually marked the top and position of a tomb. One class of burial comprises those of men, probably kings and leading warriors; another of women and children, probably royal; another of later date, in the early first millennium BC; a fourth class comprises not human burials but those of horses, paralleled in Luristan at a rather later date.[108] The rulers buried at Marlik were therefore presumably mounted nomads, very probably Iranian and from the steppes north of the Caucasus.

Unlike some of the stone-built tombs of the Talysh, such as those at Agha-Evlar, these burials at Marlik were in tombs not reused in the early first millennium BC but each containing only the original interment. Two cemeteries in the Persian Talysh, among the many cleared by the de Morgan brothers and summarized by Schaeffer, were at Hassan-Zamini and Agha-Evlar: there were found the cylinder-seals on which Schaeffer largely bases the dating of his Late Talysh 2 period to c.1,450–1,350 BC, contemporary with Late Ugarit 2, the years of Egyptian ascendancy in Palestine and Syria.[109] A bronze figurine of a stag from Agha-Evlar of this period is comparable with examples from Marlik, where animals are also found rendered on pottery. A bronze model from Marlik of a pair of oxen with yoke and plough faintly recalls the pottery figurines of draught animals from Kültepe (Echmiadzin) and other Early Trans-Caucasian sites. A triple vase of grey ware from Marlik, each goblet having a delicate stem rising from the apex of a conical base, is faintly comparable with an alabaster vessel from the tomb of Tutankhamun: the shape of each goblet comprising this unusual vessel is similar to the button-based type of the Iron I culture in Iran.

Among the weapons buried at Marlik were swords often deliberately bent or broken at the time of the funeral and winged arrowheads paralleled in the Late Talysh 2–3 periods.[110] Similar but not identical arrowheads have been found at Tsalka (Trialeti) and at Beshtasheni. These occurrences are dated by Schaeffer to c. 1,200–1,000 BC and attributed to an origin in the Talysh or elsewhere in Iran. But the absence of such winged arrowheads from Hasanlu and their occurrence in a grave near Kermanshah with daggers dated to c. 1,200–1,000 BC (Iron I) hardly suggests that they reached the Caucasus from that direction. Rather is a northern origin indicated.[111]

It is of course the ritual vessels which have the most attention of all the riches of the Marlik cemetery. Of these the most outstanding is the gold beaker, now in the Teheran Museum, with a design in repoussé of two winged bulls each on their hind legs and flanking a stylized palm tree: the heads of these bulls are in the round. Somehow their posture, though strained, is convincing and forceful. This design of bulls with a tree and their naturalism indicate a connection with Middle rather than Late Assyrian art; some Middle Elamite parallels for the outward-facing heads of these bulls are discernible.[112] The lions or lionesses on a gold bowl from Kalardasht, in Mazanderan, have their heads crudely riveted to the body of the vessel and details in simplified linear style, the whole effect being that of provincial work, either of different origin or later date than the gold beaker from Marlik, which could be as early as fourteenth century BC. A rich cemetery at Kalardasht yielded many theriomorphic pots of the class now commonly named after the town of Amlash, apparently because it was there that they first began to come on to the market. Now Amlash rivals Luristan in output of antiquities, of gold and bronze as well as pottery. A gold dagger found with the gold bowl at Kalardasht resembles one from Marlik; and it has a ring joining the pommel and blade in a manner paralleled in a rendering of one of a group of three daggers depicted on the gold bowl found in 1958 at Hasanlu. Thus may be detected a link between Marlik, Kalardasht and Hasanlu.[113] The writer agrees with Porada's insistence on the role of individual artists of outstanding talent and imagination, whose masterpieces were seldom successfully copied but often formed the model for long fashionable but inferior imitations. The second of Porada's three styles of the gold vessels of Marlik is exemplified by a beaker with slightly concave sides and two registers of bulls walking in opposite directions, rendered in repoussé.

The third style of gold vessel at Marlik is in fact best represented by the bowl unearthed by R.H.Dyson himself at Hasanlu.[114] Nothing can detract from the excitement of such a discovery, however much modern archaeology strives to concern itself exclusively with the evidence pertaining more closely to the everyday life of ancient man. To find such a bowl not in a tomb but in the burnt debris of a pillaged building is indeed a rare event; and it is fortunate that the detailed context of the bowl was faithfully recorded. The gold bowl of Hasanlu has a great variety of scenes and motifs which at first sight seem bewildering in their enigmatic character and in their apparent lack of any single unifying theme, even though each scene is meticulously rendered, down to the hairs on the hides of bulls, feathers of an eagle's wings and scales on a monster's neck. A double guilloche band runs round the top, just below the rim, and a single one round the bottom. There are no formal registers dividing the scenes, and there is a *horror vacui* which has led to the filling of intervening spaces with such motifs as a stool and a trio of daggers. The top is occupied by a row of three beings, clearly divine, one having a winged sun on his head and thus perhaps being the sun god, another riding a chariot drawn by a bull from whose mouth flows a mighty stream of water, surrounded either by bubbles or by a field of pebbles. The general association of a bull with the weather-god makes the identification of this figure as such fully acceptable. The two other gods have their chariots, both with six-spoked wheels, drawn by mules. A short-cropped, badly shaven man holding a tall beaker, similar in form to the silver beaker also found at Hasanlu, stands facing the weather-god and is presumably a priest, the only man not shown with long hair and beard. He has been compared with a figure on one of the reliefs from Malatya, which could be closely contemporary.[115] Behind this priest advance two men each bringing a sheep, clearly as offerings. Below the weather-god is the scene which may well be the most significant on the bowl, though nothing marks it off as such apart from its subject: a man wearing small shields or perhaps knuckle-dusters on his fists is boxing with a multi-formed monster, head and arms and upper body a man, the rest being part rocky mountain, part three-headed scaly dragon, the heads being of dogs or wolves. Below this again lies a long-backed couchant lion. To the right a female standing on two rams pulls back her robe to display her nude body. On a larger scale stands an archer with his back to this female. Above right an eagle or falcon carries a woman. To the right another woman rides a lion with a swastika on its rear haunch, recalling the Kalardasht bowl: she is looking at her face in a mirror. Beyond to the right are three daggers, then the upper half only of a man holding a beaker and then a stool. Below these is an antithetical group in traditional Mesopotamian style of two men slaying a bearded man facing front: this motif may have been introduced into north-west Iran through the medium of Mitannian seals.[116] To the right of this group a woman, apparently kneeling, is in the act of offering an infant to a man seated on a stool, holding out his right hand to take the baby while grasping a mallet in his left. Such are the themes of this bowl, whose interpretation may be open to debate but whose manufacture at a date considerably earlier than that of the destruction of Hasanlu IV in which it was unearthed is beyond dispute.

The degree to which archaeological material from the Urmia basin, including the Hasanlu gold bowl, can be correlated with the historical data, and whether a distinctively Mannaean, Median or Persian art can be distinguished are problems which the evidence discussed above cannot conclusively solve. From the fourteenth till the seventh century BC, intrusive elements are recognizable as Mesopotamian, Middle or Late Assyrian, Urartian or even Scythian. But the indigenous peoples, varied as their origins were, cannot have their material cultures artificially dissected. Since the Mannaeans were a non-Indo-European people, very probably of Hurrian affinities, it is reasonable to look on them as the oldest established ethnic group. The description of the Hasanlu bowl as Mannaean work is chronologically acceptable and not inconsistent with

its similarities to the other gold vessels from Marlik, Kalardasht and elsewhere to the north: although the rulers of Marlik were newcomers,
the craftsmen whom they employed would have belonged to the older
population of the days before the arrival of the Iron I culture with its
Iranian bearers. The interpretation of the Hasanlu bowl as being based
on a version of the epic of the Hurrian god Kummarbi seems to fit the
evidence: this god tried to regain the control of heaven, which he had
lost to Teshub, the storm god, by procreation of a stone child; ultimately
Teshub triumphed.[117] The later survival of the Mannaean people, even
if by the eighth century BC their territory had become restricted, suggests
that a living artistic tradition may have continued almost till the last days
of the two great powers, Assyria and Urartu. This was no cultural
bequest left over from a long dead past.

The pattern of settlement in north-western Iran seems to have changed
from Iron I to Iron II (c. 1,000–800 BC), with a concentration in larger
sites often fortified and displaying a regional diversity on material culture not apparent in Iron I, when sites were more numerous but smaller
and not normally fortified.[118] Hasanlu IVB, the greatest period of that
city, is especially significant and is the most fully documented; but half
the area of the citadel remains unexcavated, and thus perhaps still con-
ceals an archive of tablets which would change the present indications
that, in spite of its proximity to Assyria, even in the ninth century BC the
civilization of Hasanlu was preliterate. This seems almost inconceivable.
The historical geography of the Urmia basin is discussed below, in the
next chapter. Assyrian and Urartian inscriptions from outside the lands
surrounding Lake Urmia remain the essential data for any historical
approach, are confined to the Iron II period and later and cannot be
carried back before the reign of Shalmaneser III (859–824 BC). He was the
first of the Assyrian kings to campaign in the region, though by then
Urartu was rising as the leading opponent of Assyria. Evidence discussed
below indicates that any Assyrian control had vanished by the end of the
ninth century BC. Yet the surviving annals of Shalmaneser III mention
the Mannaeans, the Medes and the land of Parsua: the Medes are first
mentioned in his twenty-fourth year (836 BC) and Parsua in his sixteenth
year (844 BC), the first appearance of these two peoples in historical
records.[119] The Mannaean kingdom included the southern Urmia basin
immediately east of the Solduz plain: very probably the Tatau valley,
from Miyandoab southwards, may have been the heart of this kingdom,
with Medes already pressing on its borders to east and north-east by the
late ninth century BC. While the Mannaean territories may have extended as far south as Sakkiz, its centre, at least in the ninth century BC,

was probably close to the south and east shores of Lake Urmia. For reasons which space does not allow to amplify, the writer has for some time favoured the placing of the land of Parsua in the Solduz plain, thus putting Hasanlu at its very centre. Though one theory would place Parsua far to the south, the arguments from the Urartian records seem to support such a location. If Hasanlu was in Parsua in the ninth century BC, there is no *a priori* reason why it should not have been so at the time of the building of the citadel (*c.* 1,000 BC), if the association of the Iron I culture with the earliest Iranian immigrants is accepted. Like Marlik it would have enjoyed a civilization resulting from the fusion of the old Mannaean traditions with the achievements in war and peace of the newcomers.[120]

The power of the Medes was destined to grow throughout the period of Urartian and Assyrian involvement in the lands round Lake Urmia. It was but briefly curbed by the defeat of Metatti of Zikirtu by Sargon II (714 BC). A generation later Esarhaddon, seeking to avoid a repetition of his own experience when would-be usurpers strove to deprive him of his assassinated father's throne, imposed treaties of vassalage on Ramataia and other Median rulers.[121] The deliberate destruction of these treaty tablets in the sack of Nimrud (614 BC) suggests that resentment at this Assyrian tutelage was strongly imprinted in the minds of the Medes. From soon after the accession of Assurbanipal the disappearance of various frontier posts in Mannaean lands from the Assyrian records tells a story of preoccupation with Egypt, Elam and Babylon and a failure to retain control of a frontier vital to the defence of the Assyrian homeland. The threat of Assyrian expansion into the highlands of Iran by way of Mannaean territory had provided the spur which in due course brought about the political unity of the Medes, a people whose numbers and wide domains were sure to make them a major power in the Near East.

The lands between the Mannaeans in the north and the Elamites in the south, occupied by the Medes by the eighth century BC, could have easily been crossed by that other Iranian group, the Persians, or at least by some of those bearing that name. Tribal movements can often be swift, far-reaching and leaving little or no mark in the archaeological record: such movements can be stimulated by war, drought or the prospect of loot; or service as mercenaries in a neighbouring state can be followed by immigration or invasion. The appearance of the name Parsua in or near the Solduz plain from the mid-ninth century BC onwards and of the same name just north of Elam from the time of Sennacherib (705–681 BC), together with the Achaemenid Parsa (Fars), shows the problems created by any insistence on an ethnic movement from one region to another. One explanation of this phenomenon could be the arrival of separate groups once closely related from a common homeland: this is much more probable than any migration from the

Urmia basin to Fars. [122] Excavations in the Hamadan region are certainly going to illuminate the early civilization of the Medes: whether that of the Persians will likewise be elucidated remains to be seen. Attempts to isolate a distinctively Median art have not met with much success, however, if only because by the seventh century BC, the period of the treasure of Ziwiye referred to below, the different strands making up the artistic heritage of north-western Iran had become inextricably intertwined. [123]

The fortifications of Hasanlu IV have a layout and approach revealed by the excavations. The walls are carefully built of large, rather thin slabs, of stone locally available, with large towers and buttresses between them. The type of stone may explain a certain fortuitous resemblance to the gateway of the Phrygian city of Gordion and the difference from the Urartian masonry, with its preference for basalt blocks, with courses up to one metre high. At Hasanlu IV two protected roads led up from the outer town below, where most of the people probably lived, and where, as in the time of Hasanlu V, they still buried their dead in cemeteries which can just be termed extramural. An attack on the gateway is the likeliest explanation of the destruction of that part of the defences of Hasanlu IV, restored in the seventh century BC. After this attack the public buildings within the citadel were rapidly looted and set alight, so rapidly that forty young women in the main hall of Burnt Building II were unable to escape the holocaust; and caught red-handed, as it were, all those who were in the act of removing the gold bowl sadly perished as the roof fell in on them. The plans of the major buildings of Hasanlu IV show a general uniformity, comprising an entrance porch, an antechamber flanked by a small room and a staircase to the upper storey and a main columned hall. Any similarity to the *bit hilâni*, the characteristic porticoed building of north Syria, must be fortuitous, for this plan is simple enough for parallels of independent origin to arise. Whether the columned hall may be interpreted as a prototype of the Achaemenid *apadana* is again doubtful, as are comparisons with Anatolian architecture. [124] Burnt Building II has a stone platform or dais in the middle of the entrance to the porch: this is one of the features suggesting that this may have been a temple. Possibly militating against this description is the very similar occurrence, mentioned below, of skeletons of young women at Giriktepe (Patnos), where the Urartian building is reckoned to have been a palace rather than a temple. There is a blend of sophistication and crudity marking off the architecture of Hasanlu as independent of any Mesopotamian prototype, in spite of the many Assyrian objects either imported or copied by local craftsmen. Massive paving stones form the floor of the areas outside the main buildings of the citadel: these, with the thick deposit of burnt debris overlying, have made the excavation of Hasanlu IV laborious but not technically difficult. Tall thin stones were set up in several places as stelae, but no great effort was made to dress them smooth. In their total lack of carving or inscription they may be compared with the Urartian stelae at Altintepe, perhaps three centuries later. The original design of the public building of Hasanlu IV, erected c. 1,000 BC, was enlarged by the addition of store-rooms as required alongside the columned hall. These buildings attest a developed urban life well before the advent of either Assyrian or Urartian influence.[125]

The art and artifacts of Hasanlu IV can hardly be thought typical of the whole Urmia basin in the Iron II period, for its proximity to Assyria must have made it closely subject to influences from there. Weapons including daggers and axeheads, metal vessels, ivory plaques and pottery were all or mostly locally made. Among Assyrian imports are cylinder-seals of ninth century BC design, particularly with an archer and a stag, copper animal furniture feet, a gold winged figure performing a lustration and glazed wall tiles of white, black, yellow and blue paralleled in the reign of Shalmaneser III. Of less certain origin are cast handles for bronze cauldrons: though found at Nimrud and at Gordion, these could be of Urartian manufacture, though earlier than any surviving elsewhere and thus attributable. Proof of the effects of tribute and trade over long distances is afforded by the occurrence of ivories comparable with those of the group found at Nimrud by Loftus and so perhaps originating from Hamath in Syria: it is worth noting that here are more examples of this class which can confidently be ascribed to the ninth century BC.[126]

The pottery of the Iron II period, exemplified by that of Hasanlu IV, Dinkha Tepe and many other sites, is naturally the most ubiquitous class of material and therefore the most significant for any assessment of the whole cultural province of Iron II in the Urmia basin and beyond, including the Ardebil plain and the south-west Caspian littoral. Parallels occur between Hasanlu IV and Sialk VI in central Iran. The diversity and complexity of the ceramic forms appearing in Hasanlu IV has been emphasized.[127] Among characteristic Hasanlu IV ceramic forms are jars with horizontally bridged spout, two-handled bowls with tabs attached and goblets with pedestal base and one handle with a knob at the top; on the spouted jars diagonal grooving round the shoulder is common, a feature found also at other sites. The use of gadrooning on the 'palace ware' of Hasanlu IV, often more black than grey, is one of the traces of the strong influence of metal vessels on pottery, in a period when bronze-smiths were very active and when iron was first coming into wide use in north-west Iran. Tripods with bull's hooves in grey ware were used as stands for spouted jars, and were also probably inspired by metal proto-types. The variety of pottery at minor Iron II sites is likely to have been much less than at Hasanlu, just as at Gordion in the eighth century BC the pottery of the chief Phrygian city was far more diversified than in the many contemporary Phrygian sites both near and afar off.[128]

A wealth of beads and other personal ornaments has been found at Hasanlu and in burials at Haftavān attributable to the Iron II period. At Haftavān young girls were buried wearing an elaborate headdress of coiled bronze tassels, a skull-cap adorned with bronze discs and a bronze headband, the details varying with individual burials; bracelets of bronze or of iron, figure-of-eight shaped bronze earrings and massive bronze anklets were also worn. Two burials featured a long bronze chain round the neck. Beads of carnelian, glazed frit and pierced shells were popular.[129]

Although the chronological priority of the citadel of Hasanlu IV is not in itself any proof of its influence on the civilization of Urartu, if any source of inspiration of that civilization is to be sought, except for Assyria, it must be in the Urmia basin. Here was the first region of Urartian aggrandisement and of contact between the newly risen kingdom of Van and the older material culture of the Mannaean population intermingled with the Iranians, by that time well established. Just as Urartian inspiration for the architecture of the Medes and of Achaemenid Persia has been suggested, if on rather flimsy evidence, so an equally good case, if not a stronger one, may be made for a contribution by the art and architecture of Hasanlu IV to that of the kingdom which rose to power round the shores of Lake Van in the ninth century BC and which was soon to unite all the lands from the Little Caucasus to the upper Euphrates, from the Pontic ranges in the north-west to the Mannaean lands in the south-east.

CHAPTER 5

FROM THE RISE OF URARTU
TO THE BIRTH OF ARMENIA

The kingdom of Van, better known by its Assyrian name of Urartu (Ararat), expanded over the whole of the later Armenian homeland and embraced the three lakes of Van, Urmia and Sevan. Political unity thus came for the first time to the whole highland zone from the upper reaches of the Euphrates (Kara Su) in the west to the eastern borders of Iranian Azerbaijan in the east. The Little Caucasus, now the frontier of the Armenian SSR, provided a natural frontier along the north-east, while the high, forest-clad ranges above Trebizond and Çoruh formed both a deterrent to expansion to the Pontic littoral and a defence against attack. The southern frontier of Urartu bordered on the Assyrian empire, and thus provided continual sources of friction, even at times when open conflict was in the interests of neither state. Even at its greatest extent, however, Urartu did not for certain control any access to the sea: she was essentially a land-locked power, dependent on commercial links with her neighbours for more distant trade.[1]

This was Urartu at the zenith of its power, in the first half of the eighth century BC. Yet this kingdom may well have had relatively humble origins in a confederacy of petty principalities around and to the north of Lake Van. Attractive as it may be to seek earlier origins, with the support of a reference to the land of Uruadri by Shalmaneser I of Assyria in the early thirteenth century BC, there is at present no sound evidence attesting the existence of the kingdom before the ninth century BC.[2] As discussed above, there seems to have been a lacuna in the occupation of permanent settlements in the Van region and its surroundings during the second millennium BC, from whatever the date of abandonment of the sites using pottery of Early Trans-Caucasian type. Indeed most Urartian sites appear, as far as the evidence of surface exploration reveals, to have no earlier occupation. Whether this period of abandonment of settled life in the Van region lasted ten centuries or less, possibly as little as six, the antecedents of Urartu must remain obscure, unless excavations at hitherto undiscovered sites can elucidate them. This is one of the challenges to the archaeologist allowed to work in eastern Anatolia today. The probability is that in twenty years' time this problem will still be unsolved; and Urartu will still appear suddenly from the murky prehistory of a backward region, so close, as the crow flies, to the centres of the ancient Near East and so little influenced by them.

One school of thought would have it that Urartu was culturally but a pale reflection of Assyria, a typical product of the peripheral regions, with little or nothing original to contribute to its contemporaries.[3] There is much to support this opinion, though it underrates certain aspects and relies on negative evidence in dismissing the Urartians as a people backward and illiterate until the introduction in the reign of Sarduri I of the Assyrian cuneiform script. Certainly it was not till then that this script was first used in Urartu, the inscriptions of Sarduri I being written not in the Urartian language, as all those of his successors, but in Assyrian.[4] But Urartian hieroglyphs are known in the eighth and seventh centuries BC from several sites, and could perhaps represent more than the system of commercial shorthand that they may at first sight appear to form.[5] It is known that the Luvians of southern and western Anatolia wrote on wood. It is also apparent from excavations at Urartian and other contemporary sites that mud brick, unless burnt by fire, is usually poorly preserved, probably as a result of climatic and soil conditions. But if unburnt mud brick can suffer so badly, what is remarkable in the failure to discover more tablets? If unfired, they too would undoubtedly have perished. Like the Assyrians, the Urartian scribes may well have used wooden writing boards and thus have written on a wax surface. Such factors may account for the limitations of Urartian literature, represented as it is almost exclusively by the formal, rather lifeless royal inscriptions, whether recording campaigns in the barest lists of towns and districts captured or devastated or providing foundation inscriptions for palaces, temples or canals. On these written records, on the results of excavations mostly conducted in the last decades and on surveys preceding those excavations, rests the evidence for any reconstruction of Urartian history and civilization.

The very nature of their homeland must have determined much of their destiny, the people of Urartu being highlanders well adapted to the extremes of the climate and able to retreat into their mountain strongholds rather than risk rash confrontations with the enemy in open battle. When they did engage in open conflict in a set battle, the natural indiscipline of a highland race tended to show itself, if the evidence for the engagement between Rusa I and Sargon II near Mount Uaush, now called Sahend, is correctly understood.[6] The mountains which divided district from district, and which made close-knit centralized government hard enough to enforce at any time and impossible in the winter, at the same time made sustained control by an enemy, whether the organized Assyrians or the swift moving Cimmerians, impossible. As in a later period Xenophon found the Carduchoi, presumably the ancestors of the Kurds, and the Chaldians, almost certainly the descendants or remnants of the Urartians, the toughest opponents of the Ten Thousand, so the garrisons of the Urartian fortresses were able to make the best use of the mountainous terrain. However often settlements were 'destroyed' by fire, they were usually resurrected in time for the next Assyrian expedition. More serious was the cutting down of trees and orchards, comparable with the devastation wrought in the Peloponnesian War by the Spartans when they cut down the olive groves of Attica. But like the Armenians after them, as described by Herodotus, the Urartians were primarily dependent on their sheep, cattle, and horses. They were small and wiry, though capable of jumping a length of eleven metres, as an inscription of the Urartian king Menua, naming his favourite horse, records.[7] Natural defences protected the heart of Urartu, the region north and east of Lake Van, the Sea of Nairi of the Assyrian texts, from permanent danger of Assyrian attacks. There was, however, no such protection to the north, from where the Cimmerians seem to have been able to attack with impunity in the reigns of Rusa I and of his son and successor Argishti II. Urartu was safe in that quarter only so long as the north-eastern frontier past Lake Sevan was securely held: once an enemy invaded the prosperous Araxes valley the best line of defence was lost.

It is very much to be wished that the archaeological record of Urartian civilization were sufficiently detailed and authenticated to provide stylistic distinctions for pottery and other artifacts from one reign to the next. For the time being, however, all that can be said of Urartian pottery is that the characteristic red polished ware, at its best a product associated mainly with the more important sites, seems not to have come into use before about the mid-eighth century BC; and that there is a rare Urartian painted pottery which dates back rather earlier.[8] The red polished ware is particularly abundant at Toprakkale, the royal residence founded by Rusa II near Tushpa (Van Kale), though now its distribution is too wide in Urartu to permit its description by the name of this or of any other one site. Urartian pottery in general is characterized by slight burnish and by a limited range of forms, though future study may modify this assessment. Hand-made wares were still in common use. Though perhaps not obviously so at first sight, the pottery found in most of Urartu is one of the hall-marks of its material culture. In the Muş plain a few mounds have yielded surface sherds of grey ware comparable with the pottery of Hasanlu IV (c. 1,000–c. 800 BC) in the Urmia region, and perhaps likewise with that of Hasanlu V (c. 1,200–c. 1,000 BC);[9] but this is an isolated pheno- menon, on which it would be rash to base any speculation concerning ethnic movements. There remains the enigma of the formative period of Urartu and the impossibility on present evidence of assigning any Urartian pottery to the ninth century BC, let alone earlier. This problem makes the recognition of any very early Urartian sites from surface material collected on surveys virtually impossible.

Shalmaneser III recorded in his annals of his third year the sack of Arzashkun, then the capital of Aramé, king of Urartu. Where Arzashkun was situated cannot be stated with any precision, even its general location being in doubt: the present writer still adheres to his original suggestion that it lay somewhere in or near the upper valley of the Murat River (the classical Arsanias), or eastern Euphrates, between Malazgirt and Liz, near Bulanik. It may have been relatively unprotected. A location within that region, north or north-west of Lake Van, seems more probable than an alternative theory that it was very near the later capital of Van, established in the reign of Aramé's successor, Sarduri I. A pictorial record of Arzashkun, the earliest known representation of an Urartian fortress, is among the many scenes of warfare from the earlier years of his reign portrayed in bronze repoussé bands nailed to the wooden doors of Shalmaneser III's small palace at Imgur-Bel (Balawat) near Nimrud (Kalhu); this palace had been founded by Assurnasirpal II.[10] It seems likely that in an earlier period the capital or centre of the confederation of Nairi, of which at least twenty-three rulers were defeated by Tiglath-Pileser I of Assyria (c. 1,114–1,077 BC) in his third year, lay in or near the Bulanik area, since it was here in the Murat valley that this king set up a victory stele at Yoncalu. If Arzashkun had originally been the main town of Nairi, this stele could well have been set up nearby, for what more suitable place than near the enemy's capital? Against this suggestion is the strong possibility that Nairi was much too loosely knit to have been dignified with a capital city.[11] More probably the most important of its constituent principalities was centred on the area of Bulanik.

The city of Tushpa (Turushpa), whose name survived in the Greek Tospitis and the Armenian Tosp, is first mentioned in a poetical account of Shalmaneser III's third campaign, as Turushpa.[12] Not more than about twenty years later Sarduri I constructed a massive building at the foot of the west end of the citadel of Van, certainly to be identified with Tushpa. The citadel is a high precipitous outcrop of crystalline limestone which rises abruptly out of the plain and extends for a mile from east to west, though only two hundred yards wide at the most. The lake, at present about a mile from the west end of Van citadel rock, may well have lapped this end in Urartian times.[13] The building below the west end of Van citadel is securely dated by the repetition on several different blocks of an inscription of Sarduri I in Assyrian referring to the transportation of the blocks from the town of Alniu. It is on these inscriptions

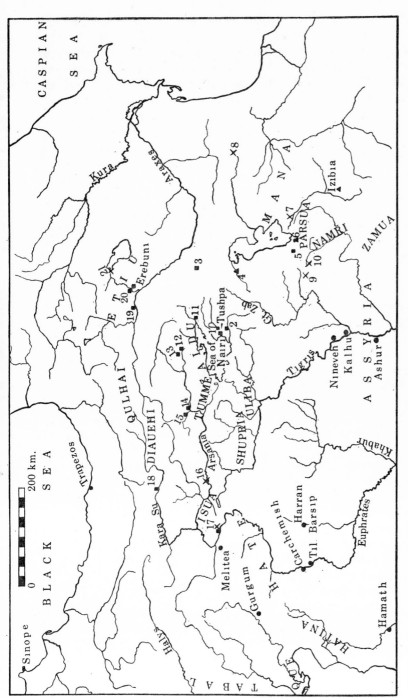

IV *Major fortresses and towns of Urartu and its neighbours*

Squares indicate fortresses; dots indicate towns; crosses indicate cuneiform inscriptions *in situ*; triangles indicate mounds.

Key to numbered sites: 1 Anzaf 2 Çavuştepe 3 Bastam 4 Haftavān Tepe 5 Qalatgar 6 Hasanlu 7 Taştepe inscription 8 Sarab inscriptions 9 Topzaua bilingual stele 10 Kel-i-shin bilingual stele 11 Körzüt 12 Kancikli 13 Aznavur (Patnos) 14 Kayalidere 15 Hirsiz Kale (Varto) 16 Palu rock inscription 17 Izolu (Komurhan) citadel and rock inscription 18 Altintepe 19 Armavir-Blur (Argishtihinili) 20 Karmir-Blur (Teishebaina) 21 Sevan rock inscription that Sarduri I is credited with the foundation of Tushpa as the new capital: this seems a reasonable assumption, though unproven. The location of Alniu near Erciş, on the north-east shore of Lake Van, seems certain, owing to the geological variety around the lake and to the absence of such limestone elsewhere near the shore, except at Van citadel itself. Clearly such heavy blocks, weighing up to thirty or forty tons each and with a bulk of over five cubic metres, cannot have come from any quarry too distant from water transport. A natural anchorage in the estuary of a large stream, now called the Deli Çay, some distance east of Erciş lies in the shadow of a minor Urartian site enclosed by a wall of unusually crude construction: this could possibly have provided the wharf from which these blocks were shipped to Tushpa. Sarduri I's building is of uncertain function, most probably a barbican or fortified gate-tower protecting the water supply from some of the numerous springs welling out from the base of the rock and also defending the approach up into the citadel. This approach is still partly discernible from steps cut into the rock. A rock inscription of Sarduri I has, like others carved on the cliffs of Van citadel, escaped mutilation by its inaccessibility, doubtless deliberate. There are many such inscriptions of the Urartian dynasty, together with one of Xerxes. The reason for the foundation of Tushpa may have been strategic, in the hope of remoteness from Assyrian attacks: a campaign against 'Seduri' is mentioned in the twenty-seventh year of Shalmaneser III. Under the old Turkish town of Van Tushpa lay hidden.

The closing years of Shalmaneser III's reign saw civil strife within Assyria, the beginning of a long decline, at first slow to gather momentum. But at once, it seems, Urartu saw its chance. The expansion of Urartu can to some extent be documented by the location of inscriptions: not all of these are in their original settings, many having been removed and incorporated in Armenian churches, after which in recent years they have again been removed to the Van museum or in some cases have perished or disappeared; but enough of them remain *in situ* to provide indications of the minimum territorial extent of the kingdom in any given reign.[14] Clearly no precise frontiers can thus be determined. The main direction of early expansion seems to have been south-east from Tushpa into the region of Lake Urmia and even beyond, the bilingual (Assyrian and Urartian) stele of Kel-i-shin, on a high pass on the Iraq–Iran frontier near Ushnu, being set up by Ishpuini, son and successor of Sarduri I. This stele suggests, if not proves, that Urartian control had even then been extended over the whole region between the west shore of Lake Urmia and the mountains now forming the frontier of Iran. Here the Urartian frontier may well have marched with that of the Assyrian territories, and it was near here that Menua built a fortress, Kalatgar, commanding the Ushnu valley, attributable to his reign by a recently discovered inscription found at the foot of the hill on which the fortress stood. The settlements in the valley below, including Dinkha, were destroyed c. 800 BC, that is during the reign of Menua, possibly as a reprisal for support of Assyria.[15] Such support would not have been unreasonable, in the light of the reference by Shamshi-Adad v, successor of Shalmaneser III, to the plundering and burning by an Assyrian force of 'eleven strong cities and two hundred small cities' of Ushpina (822 BC), these being situated in or near this region. The context makes it clear that this must be Ishpuini the Urartian king: this is one of the rather few chronological links with the firmly dated Assyrian kings, and gives the latest possible year for the accession of Ishpuini. Evidently at that time the Assyrians were still disputing Urartian claims to hegemony in the Urmia region, for only a year later (821 BC) Shamshi-Adad v levied a tribute of horses on several tribes, including the Manai and the Parsai.[16] Neither expedition has left traces which can yet be recognized in the archaeological record of any site. The motives for Assyrian interference in the Urmia region were strong: perhaps uppermost was the fear of a strong enemy in control of the passes through the Zagros mountains; but the region was important also as a source of horses, required for the army since the introduction of cavalry by Tukulti-Ninurta II (890–84 BC), and because it lay across trade routes further eastward. Urartu had enough horses, but must have been equally aware of the strategic importance of the districts surrounding Lake Urmia. By the end of the reign of Ishpuini, if not earlier, these were for the most part under Urartian rule, not only the north and west sides of Lake Urmia but the south and east also. An inscription at Karagündüz by Lake Erçek, on the road east from Tushpa, dates towards the end of the reign, since in it Menua is associated with his father Ishpuini: the land of Barsua and the town of Meishta are mentioned. Barsua has already been tentatively located in the Solduz district, while Meishta is mentioned in a rock inscription of Menua at Tashtepe, near Miyandoab, just south-east of Lake Urmia.[17] Plainly Urartian forces had already penetrated a short distance south-east of the lake in the reign of Ishpuini: equally plainly neither his son Menua nor his grandson Argishti I, who so often refer in their annals to campaigns against Mana, the homeland of the Mannaeans, could claim to have subjugated that territory. Much depends on the eastward geographical limits attributed to Mana. Later Urartian inscriptions from the region of Mount Savalan, north-east of Tabriz, suggest that the eastern littoral of Lake Urmia was not accepted by the Urartian kings as their permanent eastern frontier.[18] In other directions the territorial extent of Urartu under Ishpuini is not much clarified by the distribution of inscriptions: one at Toprakkale near

Aleşkirt indicates that the plain of Ağri (Karaköse) must have been incorporated in the kingdom. There is no proof of expansion further to the north or north-west. Whether the name of Ishpuini is indeed recalled in the Phineas of the Greek legend of the harpies is a question which perhaps can never be finally answered.[19] But if it is, it would suggest that already in the late ninth century BC Urartu was making commercial contacts with the Aegean world by one or more of the possible routes.

Such is the number of inscriptions surviving from the reign of Menua, son of Ishpuini, that he is assured of recognition as the greatest architect and greatest irrigation engineer of all the Urartian kings. It was in his reign that the frontiers were extended to include by far the greater part of the territory ever ruled from Van, though some further expansion occurred later. In the Urmia region he may not have added much to his father's conquests: the town of Meishta can hardly be equated with the insignificant remains at Tashtepe, first recorded by Henry Rawlinson.[20] The destruction of Hasanlu IV, mentioned above as dated by radiocarbon samples to c. 800 BC, may be attributed to Menua, or alternatively to his son Argishti I. Whatever the precise circumstances of that destruction, it seems that Menua consolidated the Urartian frontier south of Lake Urmia, including within it the plains of Solduz and of Ushnu. Yet Urartian rule can hardly have been altogether secure, for Mana is prominent in the annals of this reign discovered in 1961 in the temple on the summit of Aznavur, near Patnos, on the road from Lake Van north to Karaköse.[21] It is unlikely that these expeditions were limited to defensive purposes. Nevertheless two main directions of expansion are discernible in this reign, westward and north-eastward. In the absence of maps major rivers alone were likely to be recognized as natural frontiers.

If ever there was such a frontier for Urartu it lay in the west, along the upper reaches of the Kara Su, the western branch of the Euphrates. Across the river lay the town and kingdom of Malatya, one of the chief opponents of Urartu in the west, with a history extending back well before that of the Urartian state. Its situation on a route north-west from Syria into central Anatolia assured it of long-standing importance. Sculptured orthostats reused in the city gate of the eighth century BC were carved four centuries earlier showing stylistic similarities to the Hittite reliefs of the thirteenth century BC.[22] Ancient Malatya, now marked by the mound of Arslantepe, has retained its name – Milidia, Milid, Meliteia in the Assyrian and Urartian records – moving later to a new site nearby as Melitene. The Assyrian annals provide the only documentary evidence for the history of Malatya before the end of the ninth century BC.[23] The account of the third campaign of Tiglath-Pileser I (c. 1,112 BC) refers to the city of Milidia in the land of Hanigalbat, a region already penetrated by an Assyrian army in the reign of Shalmaneser I in the early thirteenth century BC, when its king Shattuara was defeated. This is a Hurrian name, and these sources suggest that Malatya was already an important city and that its population was predominantly Hurrian: so it probably remained, as suggested by the name of Arhi-Teshub, king of Malatya, mentioned in a hieroglyphic inscription from Karahüyük, near Elbistan. Assyrian power in Hanigalbat vanished after the death of Tiglath-Pileser I; it was evidently one of the chief aims of Adad-Nirari II (911–891 BC), initiator of the recovery of Assyria, to restore it, for he conducted no fewer than six successive campaigns there. Assurnasirpal II received tribute from these (882 BC), and summoned envoys from Malatya to the re-foundation ceremonies at Nimrud (Kalhu) (879 BC). Shalmaneser III in his sixth campaign received tribute from Sangara of Carchemish and from Lalli king of Malatya (853 BC). Malatya was also among the objectives of his fifteenth and twenty-third campaigns.

Malatya was apparently considered necessary as a tributary state by the Assyrian kings: it was the decline of Assyria in the last years of the ninth century BC which left the way open to Urartian expansion westwards under Menua. The next recorded king of Malatya was Sulehauali, mentioned in a rock inscription of Menua carved on the summit of a natural stronghold at Palu, near the Murat River. Apart from this inscription and a stele from an Urartian fortress at Bağin, situated near Mazgirt in the remote Dersim region, no archaeological evidence has yet been found of the conquests of Menua in the west. At Komurhan stands the westernmost Urartian fortress, with a rock inscription of Sarduri II. This was a frontier post, little now remains of the walls; significantly the pottery there, though far from the finest quality, is of Urartian type. Such pottery has not, to the writer's knowledge, been found anywhere west of the Euphrates, the distinctive Iron Age ware round Malatya being the painted pottery of Alişar IV type originating in central Anatolia and often misleadingly called Phrygian.[24] It is surely not stretching the evidence too far to suggest that the western frontier of Urartu lay along the Euphrates, that it was established there already by Menua, maintained by his successors and extended only temporarily further west. The Urartian references to Malatya do not necessarily imply annexation of that territory: the archaeological evidence is against such a suggestion. Yet comparison with the Urmia region must enjoin caution over this question, for there Urartu undoubtedly exercized political control without much affecting the material culture; and

Malatya likewise possessed an advanced and vigorous cultural tradition capable of surviving short-lived conquest.

References to Hatina, without serious doubt identifiable with the Amuq (Antioch) plain, make it clear that Malatya was by no means the most westerly point reached by Menua in extending Urartian territory and influence into the zone of Syro-Hittite civilization. He must have campaigned almost if not quite to the north-east corner of the Mediterranean. Hatina is mentioned in the Palu inscription, in connection with a campaign begun by annexing the district of Sebeteria, possibly too far west to be located at Palu itself. The name of Hatina provides one of the all too rare correlations of Urartian geographical names with those in the Assyrian annals and other texts, where it occurs as Hattina.[25] This land was ruled in the early ninth century BC by a prince with the unmistakably Hittite name of Lubarna, and was reached by Assurnasirpal II after first crossing the Euphrates and receiving tribute from Sangara, king of the land of Hatte, known at this period to have been centred round Carchemish. Then, before arriving in Hattina, Assurnasirpal had to cross the River Apre and the River Arantu, the modern Afrin and Orontes. This fixes the territory of Hattina as at least including part of the valleys of these two rivers. Halparunda, prince of Hattina in the days of Shalmaneser III, is recorded and depicted on reliefs as bringing tribute, including bronze vessels, to Assyria.[26] The Urartian expansion westward to Hatina may date to the later years of Menua's reign, after the campaigns of Adad-nirari III of Assyria against Damascus (802 BC) and against Mansuate, a city in the Orontes valley (796 BC). Thereafter Assyrian interference in the city-states of Syria was brief and ineffective for half a century; attacks in 773 and 772 BC seem to have brought no response from Argishti I, who had marched as far as Hatina in his third campaign. Probably Assyrian forces made no serious threat to Urartian influence in north Syria in the fifty years preceding the seizure of the Assyrian throne by Tiglath-Pileser III (745 BC). Yet the impact of Urartu on the material civilization of north Syria remains elusive, if not necessarily insignificant.

The historical geography of the northern campaigns of the Urartian kings remains particularly obscure owing to the remoteness of these regions from any reached by Assyrian expeditions. In the north-west zone of Urartu, from the plain of Erzurum to that of Erzincan and northward to the Pontic ranges, the kingdom of Diauehi appears to have been the chief obstacle to the advance of the Urartian army to an area described by Menua and his son Argishti I as the Pass Lands. The location of these is uncertain, but the alternatives are limited, the most probable area being between Aşkale and Tercan. The kingdom of Diauehi must have included the plain of Hasankale, immediately east of Erzurum. If it is objected that this is too close to the central homeland of Urartu to have remained so long unconquered, a comparison with the constant threat to the Hittite kingdom in the second millennium BC from the uncomfortably neighbouring Gasga tribes may seem apt. Any attempt to bring the route of Shalmaneser III's third campaign as far north as the Erzurum plain, on grounds of the philological affinity of the names Diauehi and Daiaeni, seems quite unrealistic: the Assyrian march was long enough without supposing it reached the northern frontiers, as they later became, of Urartu.[27] Nor is Diauehi likely to have extended quite as far as the territory now occupied by the Georgian SSR, though the tribute imposed by Menua after his defeat of Utupurshi, king of Diauehi, comprised gold and silver. This hardly suggests an impoverished minor tribe. It was not, however, till about the second year of Argishti I (c. 786–764 BC) that Diauehi seems finally to have been subdued, a tribute of 20·5 kilogrammes of gold, 18·5 kilogrammes of silver and over five tons of copper being exacted as a first instalment. After Argishti I there is no reference to Diauehi in Urartian royal inscriptions, a silence which can be interpreted as the result of the replacement of the local dynasty by governors appointed by the Urartian kings. Sasilu and Zua are mentioned as royal towns of Diauehi. Tiglath-Pileser I and Shalmaneser III both mention the land of Daiaeni, situated in the Murat valley probably in or near the Muş plain or perhaps further downstream near Palu. A connection between the names of Daiaeni and Diauehi, respectively 'land of the people (or sons) of Daia and Dia', and the Armenian name of Tayk (Taochi) associated with the plateau of Oltu some way northeast of Erzurum is said to be philologically plausible. One explanation of such onomastic parallels would be flight or migration of a tribe northward from the Murat valley: any such movement would have had to occur before the arrival of the Armenians, in the ninth century BC, but after Shalmaneser III's third campaign (857 BC).[28]

Even if the decisive phase of the north-eastward expansion of Urartu to the shore of Lake Sevan did not occur till the following reign, the discovery at Karmir-Blur of bronze cups bearing the name of Menua cannot be entirely ignored. They could have come from Van itself, and they formed part of the contents of Arinberd (Erebuni), the royal foundation of Argishti I, whence they were removed to the later fortress in the seventh century BC.[29] Although very probably the Araxes valley had been subjugated by some date in Menua's reign, it is to his son Argishti I that the foundation of the first fortresses in this region may be ascribed. Etiu was the term applied to much of this region, including the high, bleak shores of Lake Sevan, icebound even in April; but whether the Araxes plain itself was part of the Etiu lands is less certain, for these seem to have continued as the objective of military expeditions long after the

Erevan plain had been finally subjugated. An early advance into this plain seems likely, for once the highland region from Karaköse to Mount Ararat had been incorporated into Urartu there was no obstacle to such an expansion. The full exploitation of its economic benefits was left to Argishti I and his successors.

To Menua must go the credit for being the greatest architect of Urartu, to whom may be ascribed many of the fortresses recorded in recent years, especially in the central homeland of the kingdom. Only the small lower fort at Anzaf and that at Zivistan, both within ten miles of Tushpa, can be attributed on the evidence of inscriptions to Ishpuini. Menua clearly thought it necessary to improve on his father's efforts, for at Anzaf, a few hundred yards above the lower fort, he built a much larger fortress. This has not been excavated, but enough is visible above ground to show the use of buttresses at regular intervals along the walls, in accordance with the usual Urartian practice. Since Ishpuini's two forts lack such buttresses, it seems likely that it was in Menua's reign that this standard plan first appeared, remaining in use throughout the subsequent history of Urartu. Sargon II's famous account of his eighth campaign against Urartu (714 BC) includes details of the dimensions of fortress walls, their thickness (8 cubits, approximately 4 metres) and their height (120 courses of brick, with a stone footing beneath giving additional height, totalling 13–15 metres), corresponding remarkably with the measurements of remains found on the ground at Urartian sites round Lake Van. The upper fortress at Anzaf, with the main defensive wall visible along one side and with terraces on the other, may be considered typical of the fortresses of the Urartian homeland, whose pattern was introduced into the conquered territories and whose siting was usually comparable. This fortress of Anzaf was no mere refuge, but was built to command an important route, the road from Tushpa eastward to the north end of Lake Urmia: along this road Ishpuini, Menua and Argishti I must have marched against Mana, and Rusa I against Sargon II of Assyria (714 BC). The site chosen was typical, being on a spur standing out from a higher range of hills; steep slopes afforded protection on three sides, the fourth having a saddle connecting the spur with the higher ground. This saddle, the weakest point, was chosen as the site of an outer complex of buildings, perhaps a lower town.[30]

The outer, lower town has been found to be a characteristic element in the layout of many Urartian sites. Tushpa itself is an example of this, for there the town was situated immediately beneath the precipitous south side of the long citadel rock, whose silhouette is compared by the local inhabitants today to a camel's back. Later its site was occupied by the now ruined remains of the Turkish city of Van, destroyed by the Russians in 1916.[31] Excavations here might prove rewarding; but the

138

chances are that little has survived of Urartian Tushpa. More normally only an easily ascended slope separated the lower town from the fortress above. A later example of the relationship of the lower town to the citadel above it is afforded by the site of Kayalidere, near Varto, mentioned below. On the evidence of inscriptions Menua was probably responsible for the fortifications of Van citadel, which survive to this day as the most impressive stretch of Urartian masonry to be seen anywhere, though rivalled by other sites, including Erebuni (Arinberd), near Erevan. The smaller blocks at the top of the walls of Van citadel are of course of much later date.

The historical geography of the homeland of Urartu is much less well illuminated by the inscriptions than is that of the outlying regions. Building inscriptions are more characteristic of the central districts, except for the annals of Menua at Patnos and of Argishti I and Sarduri II at Van. It is nevertheless clear that, though some major sites were not founded till later, Menua took care to construct fortresses to defend all the main approaches to Tushpa, particularly those from the north and east. Perhaps this was a precaution against the risk of a surprise attack at a time when the king was campaigning far away from his capital. There are also many minor fortified sites along the north side of Lake Van, probably identifiable with the land of Aiadi, mentioned in the account of Sargon II's eighth campaign. Perhaps the Urartian inscriptions, even those from the heyday of the kingdom, give only a biassed and incomplete record, omitting periodic enemy incursions or civil unrest. In addition to Tushpa and the upper fortress at Anzaf, Menua built the strongholds at Körzüt and Muradiye (formerly Berkri) guarding the approach to Lake Van from the north-east through the plain of Çaldiran; at Kancikli and at Aznavur (Patnos) defending the easy road to Lake Van from the north via Karaköse, the latter standing at the east end of the route through Malazgirt and Bulanik onward to the Murat valley, on which route Menua also built the small citadel of Bostankaya. Other fortresses in the central region of Urartu could have been his work too, but are as yet undatable owing to lack of inscriptions. Menua also built strongholds further afield, such as those at Bağin, near Mazgirt in the Dersim region in western Urartu, and probably that at Palu, as well as Qalatgar, commanding the Ushnu plain and helping to secure the south-eastern frontier.

A small Urartian fortress at Old Tatvan defended the point of arrival on Lake Van from the Muş plain immediately to the west. The absence of any larger fortifications may perhaps be explicable by the difficulty of a direct advance on the lake from that direction, because of an extensive area of swamp at the source of the Kara Su, a tributary of the Murat River. Relevant to this suggestion are the absence of any but minor traces of

Urartian occupation in the Muş plain, though an inscription has been found, and the route taken by Tiglath-Pileser I and Shalmaneser III, each of whom avoided this shorter approach and chose instead to march further up the Murat valley. There are at least twenty-five artificial mounds in the Muş plain, but surface indications suggest almost entirely pre-Urartian remains; and there is a surprising absence of fortified sites. The explanation is probably that the Muş plain was not at all attractive to the Urartians.

The full purposes served by the typical large Urartian fortress can only be surmised. Presumably they formed governmental centres in times of peace, in addition to their military function. The regular discovery at excavated sites of store-rooms, usually distinguished as such by rows of enormous storage jars six feet tall and five feet in girth, suggests the collection and safeguarding of tribute and goods levied on the local population as taxes in kind in an official customs house or depot. Sargon II describes his seizure of Ulhu, situated probably near the north shores of Lake Urmia, and called by him a store city: he specifically mentions the full granaries and the wine cellars of which his troops made best use.[32] Such stores must have existed already in the time of Menua. Plainly some sites were more exclusively military while others included a town or residential quarter.

At Aznavur, close to Patnos, there is the rather unexpected combination within one large fortified enclosure of a military camp and a temple. On the very summit of a conical hill, with a magnificent view of Mount Süphan and overlooking the enclosure extending down one thousand feet below, stands a building whose surface indications and position suggested a citadel, but which on excavation turned out beyond question to be a temple.[33] Such a position, on the highest point of the site, is now known to be usual for Urartian temples: this one had its doorway facing Mount Süphan, 14,000 feet high and the second highest peak in all Turkey. Any religious significance of this can only be guessed. The square plan, with walls of massive thickness faced with beautifully dressed basalt ashlar and with shallow corner buttresses, was seen to resemble that of the temple at Toprakkale uncovered by Lehmann-Haupt and subsequently mutilated, and likewise that of the temple at Altıntepe, near Erzincan. Since then similar temples have been excavated at Kayalıdere and at Çavuştepe, and there is a comparable building at Erebuni (Arinberd) outside Erevan.[34] The special significance of the Aznavur temple is that it is the earliest. Such is the uniformity of the plan of these temples, except that the temple named Susi at Erebuni is rectangular rather than square, that it is clear that this was the standard design and that it probably originated in the reign of Menua, in the absence of any earlier example. The holy city of Musasir, probably situated somewhere in the Zagros highlands south-west of Lake Urmia, might yield relevant evidence of the origins of the Urartian temple; but its site has yet to be found.

The fine quality of the masonry of the temple at Aznavur indicates that the skill of the Urartian craftsmen had been fully developed by the end of the ninth century BC. The outer defences of the fortresses are naturally of much less smoothly dressed masonry. Mural decorations were found in the Aznavur temple, but have not yet been restored. Very probably the district of Patnos was of special significance during Menua's reign, for here stood a temple, a fortress and a palace. The fortified enclosure of Aznavur is unique in the regularity of its towers, each built as a unit and then joined by the screen wall, not bonded into the masonry of the towers: only the stone footings survive, but nothing of the mud brick superstructure. The chief purpose of this enclosure may have been to provide a base for the army at the beginning of campaigns against Diauehi and Etiu in this and later reigns; but it must have been defensive also. A long narrow mound within the lowest part of the fortress perhaps represents the spoil heap from excavations of a pool to provide water for the army's horses and for livestock in time of danger.

Little more than two miles away stood a small palace whose remains, covering earlier occupation levels, form the mound now called Giriktepe.[35] This building, of mud brick hardened in the fire of its destruction, has niches and buttresses and bears comparison with the rather earlier buildings of the citadel of Hasanlu iv discussed above. The probability that Menua brought home architectural ideas from the conquered Mannaean territory, whatever the ethnic affinities of the inhabitants of ninth century Hasanlu, is reinforced by the striking parallel with Hasanlu iv in the discovery of a minor holocaust, its victims a group of young women whose skeletons were found together in a room of the palace, each holding in one hand a small bronze lion. Here, as at Hasanlu, may have been priestesses attached to the palace, unable or unwilling to flee from the enemy who burnt the building. This suggests a sudden attack, whose date cannot be fixed on present evidence; but the occurrence of a fine red polished ware goblet of distinctive form, found also at Kayalidere and at Haftavān in late eighth century context, seems to point to one of the Cimmerian attacks on Urartu (714 and 707 BC) as the likeliest date. The palace at Giriktepe would thus have lasted not more than a century. There is, however, no proof that Menua built this palace: only the temple is firmly attributable to him by the two copies of his annals, inscribed on four blocks placed at random round the interior. The important fact is that this inscription is *in situ*. Not even at Van have any other annals of Menua been found, so that Patnos seems to have had a special significance in his reign.

Supply and storage of water, presumably mainly for irrigation, was a constant concern of successive Urartian kings. At the present time climatic conditions in the Urartian homeland are such as to make it difficult to understand the necessity for such elaborate engineering works: either a lower annual precipitation or a very large population must be postulated. It seems possible that at about the time of Menua the pastures of the warlike Hiung-Nu tribesmen, perhaps the ancestors of the Huns, became desiccated, causing them to press against the north-west borders of China, whence they were repulsed by the emperor Suan (827–781 BC). Thus was set in motion a shifting of tribal groups from east to west across the steppes of central Asia and south Russia. If drought did indeed occur at that period in Mongolia and Turkestan, as the areas are now called, it may well have affected Urartu also.[36] If this theory is thought far-fetched, an alternative explanation of the prominence of irrigation works is that the establishment of the kingdom brought for the first time stability and peace to a land of warring clans, and with it a sudden rise in population and pressure on the limited areas of cultivable soil. The greatest work was the Menua Canal (Shamiram Su), bringing water 47 miles to Tushpa from a spring on the south side of the Hoşap valley, following first a westerly and then a northerly course to Van. This canal is in use today, with its characteristically Urartian stone revetment visible in places, particularly near Edremit, five miles south of Van. Fourteen inscriptions recording the construction of this canal occur along its course, which included aqueducts across valleys; at one place another inscription refers to the planting of a vineyard, apparently still discernible in the remains of terracing, for Tariria, daughter of Menua. Perhaps it was the memory of this princess which led to the later belief that the Assyrian queen Shammuramat (Semiramis) had built this canal, whence its name today of Shamiram Su. In fact the historical Shammuramat had nothing to do with Urartu.[37]

Six miles north of Erciş, near the north-east shore of Lake Van, Menua left an inscription recording his digging of a canal to the town of Alia and to the town of the god Quera, ending in the River Dainali, probably the modern Zilan Dere, just west of modern Erciş. The canal which has been traced along the south edge of the Murat valley just west of Bulanik can be attributed to the same reign, if Malazgirt (Manzikert) can be equated through the variant form of Manazgirt with the 'City of Menua': this canal is associated with several separate sites, one a considerable town. Not far the other side of Malazgirt, towards Patnos, stands Bostankaya, whose Turkish name means 'garden rock', from the parallel ledges cut out of the now almost totally denuded rock: these were the essential keying on the the bedrock of the foundation courses of masonry, and are a diagnostic feature of Urartian fortresses. Here Menua recorded the building of a cistern with a capacity of 900 *aqarqi*, a unit of liquid measure possibly roughly equivalent to 100 litres; but evidence from Karmir-Blur, probably less conjectural, indicates that it was closer to 250 litres, or more than fifty gallons. Sargon II's reference to Rusa I's digging of an irrigation canal from a spring to water the fields around the town of Ulhu is one indication that the successors of Menua followed his example in this respect. The Menua Canal contributed a major part of the water supply for the environs of Van, supplemented by such minor works as a small dam of rough boulders just beneath a spring near the road from Van to Anzaf and eastwards.[38]

Cavalry and chariotry must from the first have played a leading part in the tactics of the Urartian army. The arts of horsemanship came naturally to the Urartian people and were especially esteemed. Menua took pride in recording in an inscription near Toprakkale that from that very spot his horse Arsibi, with himself as mount, had jumped a length of 22 cubits, about 11·44 metres. Two bronze bits from Karmir-Blur bear the name of Menua. Horses must have been readily obtainable in the Urartian homeland, without the necessity of recourse to the Urmia region, whence the Assyrians had to acquire many mounts for their cavalry, first introduced into their army by Tukulti-Ninurta II (890–84 BC). Horses were levied as tribute by Shamashi-Adad V, contemporary of Ishpuini, in a campaign against the south Urmia basin, then falling under Urartian hegemony, Horsemen were to become a recurrent theme of Urartian art.[39] To this day possession of a horse in those parts is a mark of wealth and social standing. Yet most of these are by European standards scarcely broken in.

By the end of his reign (*c.* 810–786 BC) Menua had extended the territory of Urartu to the west and north, had consolidated its hold on the Urmia basin and had begun the subjugation of the Araxes valley around Erevan. He had set an example of energetic public building of fortresses and canals, emulated but never surpassed by his successors. At his death the formative phase of Urartu had come to an end.

Argishti I has left the longest surviving Urartian inscription, the annals of his campaigns, carved just outside his tomb on the south side of the citadel rock of Tushpa. These annals were unfortunately never completed, for one frame on the rock was prepared but left blank. Not all the conquests of this reign (*c.* 786–64 BC), militarily the most brilliant in the history of Urartu, are described.[40] One section deals with campaigns in the west, mentioning Malatya, with its king Hilaruada, and Hatina; another, the longest, summarizes campaigns in the Urmia region, with frequent references to Mana; a short section mentions the land of Urme . . . ,

the name being damaged, possibly in the Muş plain. It is indeed frustra-
ting to find the Urartian annals so bald and brief, often little better than a
catalogue of towns and districts burnt or destroyed or subjected to pay-
ment of tribute. The Urartian historians were either laconic to a fault, or
else they kept their full records for tablets or other forms of document
perished or still undiscovered. In the west Urartian rule had been firmly
established by Menua, and evidently did not require much reassertion
by his son. In the north-west the wars against Diauehi ended in final
victory. But how far west Urartian territory was extended, whether as
far as the plain of Erzincan or even beyond into the barren hills to the west,
remains uncertain, for the fortress and temple at Altintepe may not have
been founded till the reign of Argishti II (c. 714–685 BC), there being no
proof of earlier Urartian occupation.

The main direction of expansion under Argishti I was to the north-
east, towards Lake Sevan, where inscriptions record his conquests; elsewhere his peaceful activities are set out for posterity. On the south-west
shores of Lake Sevan stand remains of a number of fortifications, built of
rough stones quite well put together in the cyclopean style, which Soviet
scholars have tended to date to the second millennium BC: a brief visit by
the writer, however, gave him no reason to think that these could not be
Urartian forts. If so, they could have been built by Argishti I to protect
his new frontier. Meanwhile he secured control of the fertile Araxes
valley by the foundation of a regional capital at Erebuni, which may
have become a seasonal capital of the whole kingdom, a suggestion based
on the scale and splendour of this site. This foundation he carefully
recorded in an inscription set into the citadel wall next to the gateway,
for all to see.[41] The reference to the deportation of 6,600 people from
Hate and Supani, that is from north Syria including the Euphrates
valley, indicates that this Assyrian practice was similarly followed as a
deliberate policy by Urartu. There is no evidence whether or not this
was accompanied by brutalities such as those committed by Assurnasirpal
II of Assyria and his successors. Such hints as the written records provide
suggest that the Urartians were rather more humane than their Assyrian
neighbours: they could hardly have been less so. Apart from Erebuni,
two fortresses at Argishtihinili (Armavir-Blur) further up the Araxes
valley were founded by Argishti I, who dug a canal to make the surrounding plain for the first time cultivable. Urartian rule in the Araxes valley
was unchallenged until the Cimmerian attack of 714 BC.

Argishti I attacked Surhurara in the land of Bushtu, in the south of the
Urmia basin, in his fifth year (c. 782 BC), and the land of Mana is mentioned in his annals for every year from the sixth to the twelfth.[42] Thus
for eight consecutive years Argishti I waged as continuous a war as was
then possible, namely for every campaigning season, in the Urmia basin,

The Environment

1 Mount Ararat from the north

2 View of Lake Sevan showing the peninsula with ninth-century monastery

3 Eighteenth-century
palace of Ishak Pasha at
Doğubayazit, near
Mount Ararat

4 Township in Svaneti,
western Caucasus
mountains

5 View of Shio Mghvime monastery near Tbilisi, Georgia

6 Ancient bridge over the Batman Su, between Diyarbakir and Bitlis, Turkey

7 Mountain
village in
Daghestan,
eastern Caucasus

8 Georgian
mountaineer in
traditional
costume

9 Ancient crafts in Muş province (eastern Turkey)

10 Farm scene at Gevaş near Lake Van

The Earliest Settlements

11 A typical Chellean obsidian hand-axe from Satani-Dar (Lower Palaeolithic)

12 Late Acheulean hand-axes from Satani-Dar (Lower Palaeolithic)

13 Çatal Hüyük: general view of the excavations of the Neolithic town
14 Çatal Hüyük: bull's head in a shrine

15 Kobistan, south of Baku (Azerbaijan S.S.R.) : part of the extensive rocky areas containing at least 4,000 drawings ranging in date from the Mesolithic period to the Bronze Age

16 Kobistan: a woman, goats and a stag

17 Kobistan: a communal gathering or dance

18 Kobistan: a scene possibly representing a dance connected with hunting magic

The Early Trans-Caucasian Culture

19 Round houses at Shengavit near Erevan (Early Trans-Caucasian I period)

20 Amiranis-Gora: burial in a cist grave

21 Yanik Tepe: round houses of the Early Trans-Caucasian II period

22 Haftavān Tepe, near Shahpur, Iran: mud brick houses of the late Early Bronze Age (*c* 2000–1800 BC). The stone walls in the background are later. The trench is 20 x 10 metres (Early Trans-Caucasian III period)

23 Yanik Tepe: a late Early Bronze Age building level (Early Trans-Caucasian III period)

24 Mixed carbonized grain
(wheat and barley) from
Shengavit, nearly five
thousand years old

25 Metsamor (Armenian
S.S.R.): this rock is said to
be part of an ancient
observatory

26 Metsamor: depressions in the rock associated with ore smelting

27 Arrow-heads made of obsidian from Shengavit

37 Amiranis-
Gora: head of
figurine

38 Baked clay
figurines of bulls
from Mokhrablur
and Shengavit

Middle and Late Bronze Age

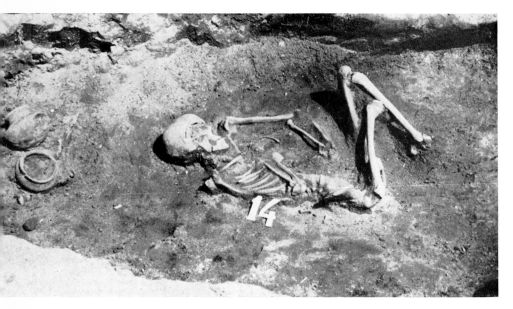

39 Lake Sevan: burial 14 (Middle Bronze Age)

40 Haftavān Tepe: a burial with a grey ware spouted jar of Hasanlu V type (c 1200–1000 BC)

41 The Kayakent-Khorochoi culture: stone lined tomb on the Apsheron peninsula near Baku
42 The Kayakent-Khorochoi culture: carvings on the Apsheron peninsula

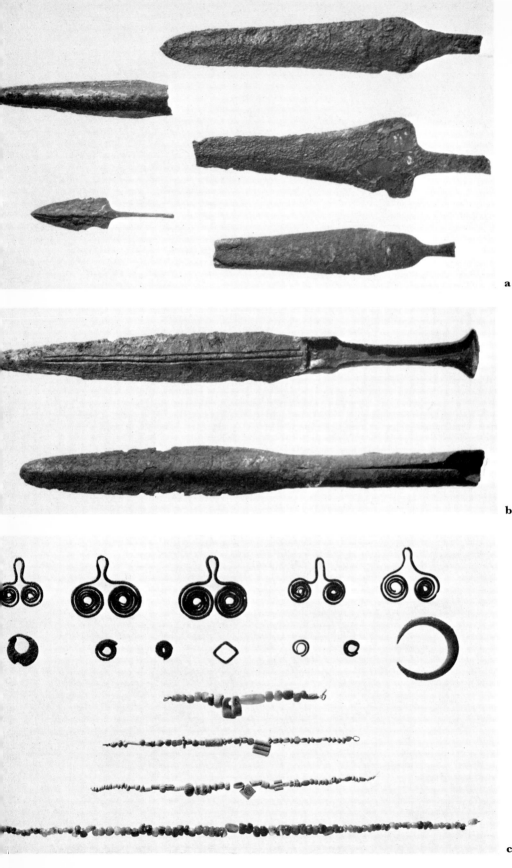

a

b

c

43 From Kizil-Vank: (a) bronze weapons (b) bronze dagger and spearhead (c) bronze pendants, cornelian and paste beads (d) painted clay figure (e) polychrome vessels

d

e

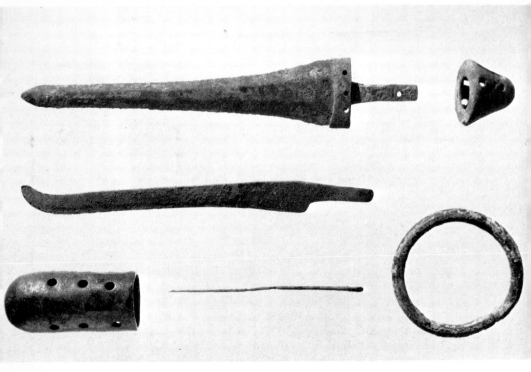

44 Bronze objects from stone sarcophagi at Gyuzaldar village near Lake Sevan, south shore

45 Haftavān Tepe: a bronze chain worn round the neck by a woman buried *c* 1000–800 BC

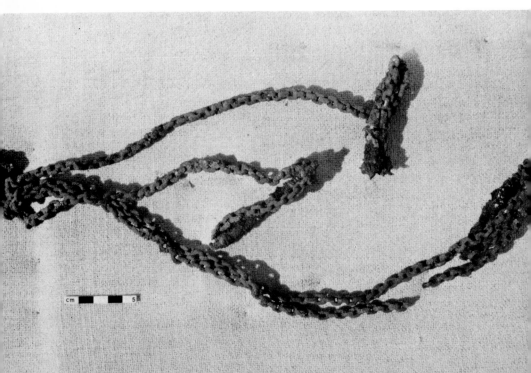

cm   5

46 Haftavān Tepe, near Shahpur, Iran: stone buildings of the late second millennium BC

47 Silver bucket from the Trialeti barrows

48 Shrine of Sarduri II, Van Citadel

49 Van Citadel: stairway down to rock-cut tomb without any inscription

50 Van Citadel: rock-cut ledges as bedding for masonry

51 Temple of Haldi, Toprakkale, Van (1965)

52 Interior of the Urartian temple at Kayalidere

53 Interior of the tomb at Kayalidere

54 Urartian tomb with eroded relief carving in the niche, near Malazgirt (Muş province of Turkey)

55 Haftavān Tepe, near Shahpur, Iran: the Urartian citadel (*c* 700 BC)

56 Urartian cyclopean wall of superior workmanship

57 Storage jars at Kayalidere

58 Rock-cut shrine at Bostankaya, near Malazgirt

59 Urartian red-polished
goblet from Kayalidere

60 A typical Urartian
cuneiform inscription

61 Bronze bull's head
protome

62 Bronze decorated
fragment from
Kayalidere with scene of
a lion hunt

63 Bronze lion from
Kayalidere

64 God standing on a bronze
bull, from Toprakkale
(damaged)

65 Fragments of bronze belts and quivers from Karmir-Blur

66 Bronze gilt bowls of King Sarduri II (Karmir-Blur)

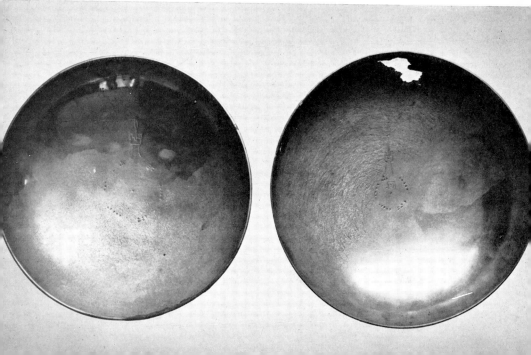

67 Kayalidere:
Urartian bronze
quivers and nails;
originally these
were fixed in a
wall (after the
Mesopotamian
style)

68 Decorated
bronze button
from Kayalidere

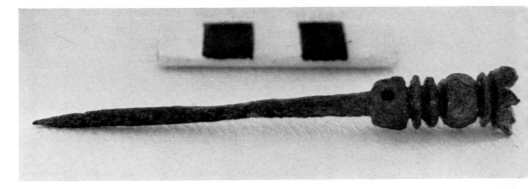

69 Bronze pin with 'pomegranate' head from Kayalidere

70 Kayalidere: Urartian bronze furniture elements

71 Bronze openwork mount, from the Caucasus, Scythian, *c* fifth century BC

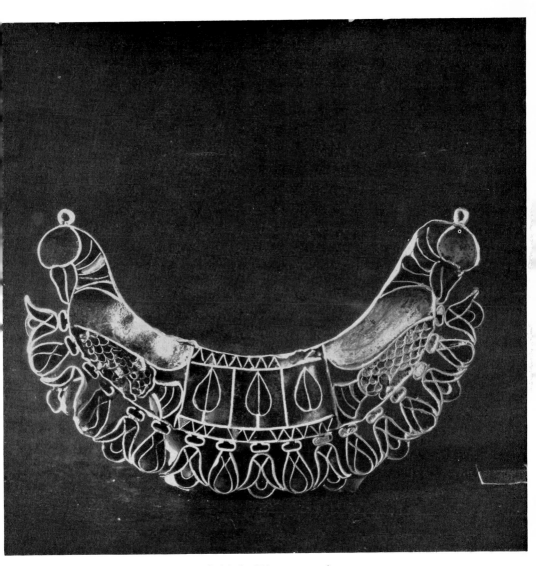

72 Gold pectoral from Armavir (sixth–fifth century BC)

73 Silver coins of Colchis 1–3; bronze coin of Dioscurias 4 (all enlarged to show detail; not to scale)

a

b

c

d

74 Nimrud Dağ: Funeral mound of Antiochus of Commagene. (a) Apollo-Mithras, west terrace (b) lion, east terrace (c) lion and eagle, west terrace (d) Heracles, west terrace

75 Garni: glass vessels of the first–second centuries AD

76 Sepulchre-crypt, Mtskheta, Georgia, end of first century AD

77 Bronze head of Anahit (Aphrodite) from Satala

Christian Architecture

78 Bolnisi Sioni, Georgia (AD 478–493). A classic example of the Caucasian basilica

79 Jvari church, near Mtskheta, Georgia, dating from about AD 600

80 Jvari church interior

81 Holy Echmiadzin (fifth-eighteenth centuries), the mother church of Armenia

82 The main church of the monastery of Haghpat, in northern Armenia, was constructed between 967 and 991. On the east wall there is a bas-relief with donor figures of the Princes Smbat and Gurgen, holding between them a model of the church

83 Ani Cathedral from the south west (built by Trdat between AD 989 and 1001)

84 Ani fortifications, completed in the eleventh century

85 Nikordsminda church, western Georgia (AD 1014)

86 Cathedral of Sveti-
Tskhoveli, Mtskheta,
built by Constantine
between AD 1010 and
1029

87 Sveti-Tskhoveli,
interior. Note the
lofty columns
anticipating the
Gothic style in
Europe

88 St Thaddeus (Karakilise) in Persian Azerbaijan (AD 1329)

Figure Sculpture and Carving

89 Aghtamar church, Lake Van. David and Goliath and other biblical figures

90 Aghtamar church:
King Gagik offers the
church to Christ

91 Aghtamar church:
Virgin and Child

92 Nikordsminda, western Georgia. The Second Coming (AD 1014)

93 & 94 Erzurum : Çifte Minare Medresesi (Seljuq school)

95 Ornamental frieze at St Thaddeus (Karakilise)

96 Figure of a bishop from St Thaddeus

97 Persian
Azerbaijan: lion
from St Thaddeus

98 Ananuri,
Georgia: carvings
on the church wall
(sixteenth
century)

99 Armenia: medieval khachkar or cross stone

100 Armenia: thirteenth-century carved folding chair

Metal Work

101 Silver gilt ikon of St George from Seti (eleventh century)

102 Berta Gospels: repoussé cover set with gems (eleventh century)

103 & 104 Mestia: staff head of ceremonial banner of clans of United Svaneti, showing patron saints of the three clans

Calligraphy and Painting

105 Ani: fresco in Tigran Honents church

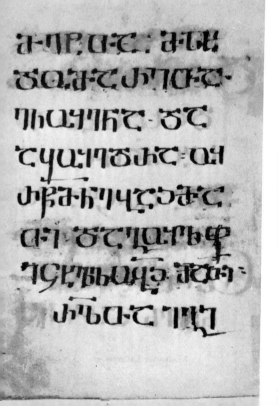

106 The most ancient Georgian inscriptions so far known date from the fifth century AD and were discovered in the ruins of a Georgian monastery at Bethlehem

107 Georgian uncial script from a tenth-century Gospel manuscript on Mount Sinai

108 Allaverdi Gospels, Georgia: St Matthew, a page of beautiful manuscript illumination, eleventh century AD

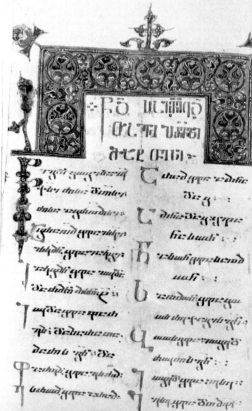

109 Works of St Gregory the Theologian: a decorated page from a codex of the Georgian version

110 Four Gospels, AD 1329, decorated at Sis by Sargis Pidsak for Leo IV (V) of Armenia (St John)

111 Four Gospels, AD 1596, copied at Constantinople by Martiros of Khizan in Armenia (baptism of Christ)

112 Shota Rustaveli, Georgia's national bard. One of the few ancient portraits of the poet, rediscovered as a section of a much faded fresco at the former Georgian monastery of the Holy Cross at Jerusalem

a

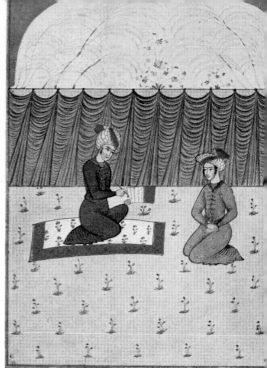

b

113 (a), (b) and (c) Shota
Rustaveli, born *c* 1166.
Illustrations from a seventeenth-
century MS in Tbilisi Institute of
Manuscripts of his poem 'The
Man in the Panther's Skin'

c

ostensibly with Mana as the chief objective. Yet it is hard to believe that so many campaigns can have been necessary for a king who could apparently dispatch Diauehi at one blow. Behind Mana stood Assyria, now in decline, but still attempting to undermine Urartian hegemony around Lake Urmia, where the power of Urartu posed a threat of which the rulers of Assyria can hardly have failed to be aware. Assyrian towns were annexed by Argishti I in his fifth year; and he claimed in his sixth year to have fought and defeated the Assyrian army. The continued resistance of the Mannaeans, however, might be explicable less as the result of Assyrian military or diplomatic activity than of interference by the Medes, already in all probability a significant element in the complex political and ethnic pattern of this region. Stirring up the tribes of the Urmia basin was a common practice of both great powers, Urartu and Assyria. The destruction of Hasanlu IV could have been the work of Argishti I rather than of Menua; the records of Argishti I refer to burning and destruction in the relevant area.

The best known monument of Argishti I is his tomb, hewn out of the crystalline limestone of Van citadel, so hard that each wedge of the long cuneiform inscription stands out in its pristine clarity. This tomb, not at first recognized as more than a funerary shrine, is approached down rock-cut steps comparable with the wider stairway down to another tomb chamber further along the same precipitous south side of Van citadel, this one having no identifying inscription.[43] This lack of any inscription suggests that, though prepared on a considerable scale, this tomb was for some reason never finished, probably owing to the sudden death of the king. The circumstances ending the reigns of Sarduri II (c. 764–35 BC) and of Rusa I (c. 735–14 BC) make either a possible owner; and the same is true of a third tomb between the two above-mentioned, this being very unfinished, with a round-topped doorway. The tomb of Argishti I has a large main chamber from which two side and two rear rooms open off: a side room to the left on entry has a pit, now filled, probably leading down to the burial chamber. The two slightly sunken areas in the floor of the main chamber would thus be for altars or offering tables but not for sarcophagi: the smaller of these two emplacements is only 1·11 by 1·11 metres. Fragments of hewn stones were found in the fill at the bottom of the two shafts cleared out in the tomb at Kayalidere, a discovery suggesting the presence of such fittings built up of masonry within the tomb. Noteworthy features of Argishti I's tomb at Van are square-topped niches, steps cut irregularly in the rock walls and decorative bronze ornaments of target form set at regular intervals round the main room and pegged into the rock. None of the bronze ornaments survives, though traces of bronze can be seen in some of the peg-holes. The stepped ledges in the walls are paralleled in the later Urartian tomb at Kayalidere,

and are probably simply cut out of faulty areas of the bedrock for insertion of masonry filling, subsequently all robbed. It is the presence of the
niches which makes this unquestionably not merely a shrine but the
tomb of Argishti I; for there is growing evidence that such niches, presumably for offerings but also perhaps for holding lamps, were a standard
feature of Urartian tombs. This is especially apparent in the tombs at
Altintepe and at Kayalidere, perhaps all to be dated *c.* 700 BC, where,
however, the niches are round-topped, unlike the square-topped niches of
the earlier tomb of Argishti I. This latter must have been sealed by stone
blocks fitted carefully to block the doorway, as was done at Kayalidere;
but of the funerary ritual at Van no evidence survives. A small sentry-
box, cut out of the solid rock, was placed by the stairway down the
side of the cliff to the tomb, and could have housed the watchman. No
other major monuments in the central homeland are attributable with
certainty to this reign.

The most important building activity of Argishti I seems to have been
in the Araxes valley. Erebuni (Arinberd) was more than a major fortress:
it was a centre of government and royal capital, with palace and temples
and with evidence of artistic attainment unparalleled elsewhere at
excavated Urartian sites.[44] The Susi temple is rectangular, not square,
but otherwise is closely comparable with the standard design of Urartian
temple, with its enormously thick walls and almost certainly very great
height. Mural decoration at Arinberd included a frieze in the formal
style adopted from Assyria, with miniature genii holding bucket and
fircone. This frieze, adorning the palace, comprised from top to bottom:
a row of palmettes and a row of parapet motifs; a band of pairs of winged
genii between a row of rosettes above and below, with each pair facing
and sprinkling a stylized tree; then on a larger scale a band of alternating
pairs of lions and of bulls, facing inward towards a target motif centred
round a large rosette; then came a second band of genii identical with
the upper band; finally, along the bottom of the whole frieze, ran a row
of pomegranates pointing down. The background was light blue, as also
in paintings decorating the walls of the temple, where horizontal bands
in red, white and dark blue occur. The general effect must have been
distinctly gaudy, and can be compared with the decoration on the walls
of Assurnasirpal II's North-West Palace at Nimrud (Kalhu).[45] A very
similar frieze was found at Altintepe. The gay colours of the Assyrian
palaces did something to counteract the gloom of their interiors; but it is
doubtful whether their Urartian counterparts were so dark within. This
formal frieze at Erebuni is typical of what has been termed the 'court
style' in Urartian art.[46] Other fragments of mural painting from Erebuni
have the characteristic light blue background, and show prancing horses
and part of a hunting scene; there is also a delightful rendering of a calf

scratching its neck. These fragments, tantalizingly incomplete, are yet enough to show that the artists of Urartu were capable of a lively natural-ism antedating by a full century the freedom in the depiction of animals displayed in the famous hunting reliefs of Assurbanipal from his palace at Nineveh, now in the British Museum.[47] Horsemanship and hunting both gave inspiration to the Urartian painter. In addition to the archi-tecture and mural painting at Arinberd were its rich contents, of which only a very small proportion has been found. By good fortune, however, many of the treasures of Arinberd were discovered in the excavations of the neighbouring fortress of Teishebaina (Karmir-Blur), built by Rusa II (c. 685–45 BC) after the destruction of Erebuni, presumably by the Cimmerians. These objects must have been recovered from the burnt ruins and removed to safety in the new governmental centre. Among these are fourteen bronze shields with dedicatory inscriptions either of Argishti I or of his son Sarduri II: the design is the same on them all, the inscription in cuneiform round the rim and three processions in con-centric rings of lions, bulls and lions, with a rosette in the centre. Among the twenty bronze helmets also found at Karmir-Blur were four with inscriptions of Argishti I and Sarduri II: their elaborate decoration has the central scene framed by two sets of four semi-circular ridges, between which are eleven groups of two figures flanking what is generally des-cribed as a sacred tree, here shown as if carved on a stele; there are also ten horsemen and eight chariots, these having eight-spoked wheels. Since this type of wheel seems not to have been brought into use for certain in Assyria before Tiglath-Pileser III (745–27 BC), who may have intro-duced it as one of his improvements of the army, it may well have been derived from Urartu, where horsemanship at least was more at home. Decorated bronze belts and quivers formed a further part of the reper-toire of the Urartian bronzesmith, and again horsemen and chariotry of the army provide the main theme. Five of the eighteen quivers found at Karmir-Blur had inscriptions of Argishti I and Sarduri II. Already in the time of Argishti I Urartian artistry in bronze had attained full maturity.[48]

Sarduri II (c. 764–35 BC) inherited a kingdom at the zenith of its power, its northern frontiers secured against attack and its great rival Assyria so humbled that it posed no threat whatsoever. Further expansion to the north is indicated by references to Qulha, an area whose identification with the later Colchis seems acceptable, and which came into direct contact with Urartu as the result of the removal of the buffer state of Diauehi.[49] There was also slight expansion around Lake Sevan. Other-wise the chief activity of Sarduri II was in the south-west, where he defeated Kushtashpili of Qumahi, a land identifiable with Kummuhi, earlier Kutmuhi, of the Assyrian annals and with Commagene of Graeco-Roman times. Urartu thus won control of north Syria by military and diplomatic successes, with considerable though short-lived effects on trade and on the balance of power in that part of the Near East.[50]

When he seized power in Kalhu from the effete Assur-Nirari v (745 BC), Tiglath-Pileser III understood that Assyria had no future unless her access to the Mediterranaean could be restored. The history of his reign shows that the strength was still there in Assyria, all that was required being a strong leader. To accomplish his objective he began by a protracted assault on Arpad, north of Aleppo. Urartu, however, was the chief enemy, and had to be defeated. Tiglath-Pileser III won a victory over Sarduri II at Halpa (Halfeti, not Aleppo) on the banks of the Euphrates (743 BC), a town described by Sarduri II as one of those of Kushtashpili, ruler of Qumaha. This prince was allied with the Urartian king against Assyria, together with Sulamal king of Malatya, who had succeeded Hilaruada at some date after the accession of Sarduri II. Quite why the Urartian army put up such a poor resistance is not at all clear: Tiglath-Pileser described how Sarduri had to flee the battlefield on a mare, and an Assyrian relief included a representation of him. This sudden collapse of the Urartian power in north Syria may have been the outcome of internal weakness in a heterogeneous coalition already weakened by Assyrian diplomacy; but the military superiority of the Assyrian army, at least outside the highland zone, seems beyond argument. Perhaps the Urartian forces were inadequately trained for an engagement in the open plains, although their cavalry should have been strong. Lack of coordination between the contingents of the various allies on the battlefield seems to be the likeliest explanation of this debacle. Whatever the reasons, the last eight years of Sarduri II's reign, which had begun so auspiciously, witnessed the ever rising power of Assyria, and culminated in the disastrous blow to the prestige of Urartu in the campaign by Tiglath-Pileser III right to the heart of the kingdom, to Van itself, where he claimed to have set up a victory stele, though he was unable to storm the citadel overlooking the town (735 BC). It is unfortunate that the annals of Tiglath-Pileser are far from complete.[51] The probability is that this further defeat brought about the fall from power of Sarduri II; but the theory that his successor Rusa I (c. 735–14 BC) was a usurper cannot be reconciled with that king's constant references to himself as son of Sarduri II. Possibly he was a younger son who usurped the throne which would normally have gone to an elder brother. The legality of many an Assyrian king's accession is similarly uncertain.

The annals of Sarduri II were carved on two basalt stelae set in tall round-topped niches hewn out of the rock at the foot of the north side of

Van citadel, at its east end. These niches, partly themselves inscribed, formed the focal element of an open-air shrine cut out of the hillside and extended out by means of a masonry platform bedded on ledges hewn out of the bedrock.[52] Such open-air shrines seem to have been typical of Urartu, smaller ones being found elsewhere on the citadel of Van and also at the foot of Bostankaya, near Malazgirt. At Altintepe smoothly dressed but totally uninscribed basalt stelae, perhaps comparable with the cruder and earlier stelae at Hasanlu, stood on a terrace built into the hillside, in a court or open space near the tombs.[53]

The architectural achievement of Sarduri II can best of all be seen at a major citadel built close to Van, for what precise reason is unknown. In such a time of power and prosperity it might seem to have served no great purpose; but it was not solely a military site but also a governmental centre, though extending along the crest of a steeply sloping limestone ridge for about 800 metres. This is Çavuştepe (Asbaşin), in the middle of the Hoşap valley south-east of Van, immediately overlooking the present road that leads from Van to Hoşap and to Hakkâri and also into Iran through Reza'iyeh.[54] The walls still visible above ground were enough to show that here was a fortress with masonry of a standard unequalled for defensive works elsewhere in Urartu: the blocks are beautifully dressed and carefully fitted together, though not of identical dimensions, so that each had to be specially shaped to fit beside its neighbours. Excavations have since revealed more walls of this fine masonry, a street partly cut out of the bedrock and a temple of the regular Urartian type, its slightly smaller dimensions being dictated by the narrowness of the ridge. An inscription by the doorway refers to dedication to the god Irmusi and dates it to Sarduri son of Argishti (Sarduri II). It is therefore a reasonable assumption that the site as a whole dates to his reign: if so, it may be that the superb masonry reflects the brief zenith of Urartian political power; there is not any evidence that masons from abroad were imported for this work. The temple was painted blue inside, as also may have been the Kayalidere temple. It is perhaps not too fanciful to speculate that with the position on the very highest point of the site this is a reflection of sky worship; but such matters are likely to remain without any authoritative answer. Two shafts hewn out of the solid rock are another feature of Çavuştepe, on the ridge beyond the temple, and are unexpectedly lined with masonry: cisterns they may have been, otherwise for storage of food; there is no evidence that they served as dungeons. At each end of the main fortress was a ditch cut through the rock for additional defence, a feature paralleled at either end of the main citadel of Van, marking the extremities of the Urartian perimeter. An ambitious plan to cut right through a saddle in the ridge was abandoned after a considerable area had been used as a quarry: a buttressed wall of rather rough masonry was then built across. Beyond this saddle the next summit was crowned by a small fort.

The fortress of Kayalidere, where only one season (1965) of excavations was allowed, yielded important, even spectacular, results, the most significant part of the site probably having been uncovered.[55] This site commands a sharp bend in the River Murat, where it turns south towards the Muş plain, about ten miles south-east of Varto; the district is hilly and subject to frequent and severe earthquakes. Although this fortress would have served well as a barrier to an Assyrian advance up the valley, there is nothing to suggest that it antedates the mid-eighth century BC. While it could have lasted into the seventh century BC, it seems likely to have had a fairly brief lifetime, its destruction possibly being attributable to one of the Cimmerian attacks, either in 714 BC or in 707 BC. Kayalidere could thus have been built either under Sarduri II or under Rusa I, the earlier reign being slightly the more probable. The general plan suggests a district administrative centre, with an upper citadel, a lower citadel and a lower town extending down part of the slope towards a branch of the River Murat below. Surface indications of a gateway show the likely line of approach from a ford. Excavations were confined to the upper citadel and to a rock-cut tomb in the cliff at its south end.

Kayalidere was important enough to have a temple, of the standard plan but using stone to a greater height and with much larger blocks than the rather small but very smoothly dressed basalt masonry of the temples of Aznavur, Çavuştepe and Altintepe. Perhaps the cruder masonry of the Kayalidere temple indicates the work of a governor imitating the fashions of the court. The double cube seems the probable reconstruction of the proportions of such a temple, as later parallels of the Achaemenid period suggest, especially the Ka'ba-i-Zardusht (the Kaba of Zoroaster) at Naqsh-i-Rustam by Persepolis. This is one of the hints of the debt to Urartu almost certainly owed by the Achaemenid architects, even though they imported their stonemasons from Greece.[56] In front of the temple at Kayalidere was a paved court with remains of a cloister along one side, distinguished by the absence of paving as having been roofed over. The most important feature of the court was a stele-base, of the same width as the door of the temple and exactly in line with it. Nothing survived of the stele itself, but the base, though broken up by the robbers who so thoroughly looted the whole site, left no doubt of its function. A small area of slabs set in the pavement nearby bore the imprint of three small hoof-marks cut in the stone, almost certainly to be interpreted as the plinth for a bronze tripod supporting a large cauldron, comparable with the cauldron and tripod found at Altintepe and with those shown on the well known relief of the great temple of Musasir from Sargon II's palace at Khorsabad.[57] When interpreting this relief in efforts to reconstruct the appearance of the typical Urartian temple, one must not overlook the fact that the Assyrian sculptors thought nothing of compressing the height of a building in relation to its length, if this was unavoidable in order to include it within the limits of the register. The temple at Kayalidere was at least thought to contain treasures, for even its paving stones were overturned in the search for plunder. Consequently none but a few fragments of the contents remained, the most interesting being part of a decorated belt or quiver, depicting soldiers in chariots hunting and being attacked by lions. For liveliness this is unrivalled in Urartian art. Probably also from the temple was a fine bronze lion, originally having a peg or nail attached to its base: there are no stylistic criteria for assigning this to any precise phase in the history of Urartu, though a late eighth century date is possible.[58]

The excavations of the upper citadel at Kayalidere outside the temple and its forecourt revealed a series of terraces, which presumably continue right down the north-east slope, the south-west side being bounded by a cliff overlooking the river below. The stone footings of the mud-brick walls were founded on the bedrock and stepped down with the gradient, there being no trace of earlier occupation and only hints of scattered squatters among the burnt ruins. Part of a long storeroom was excavated, filled by three rows of massive jars, some of the distinctively Urartian type having sunken triangles and occurring at Giriktepe (Patnos) and at Haftavān, near Shahpur. The chief interest of these jars lay in their pictographic inscriptions, the term 'hieroglyphic' being surely less applicable: the signs used include obvious representations of vessels, a goatskin and a sack, all measures either of capacity or of weight or both. Parallels for these pictographs occur at Toprakkale, Karmir-Blur and Altintepe.[59] The most comprehensible of the signs at Kayalidere are those on the rims, indicating some system of enumeration: circles, with a dot in the centre, may represent tens or even hundreds; the dots would correspondingly represent units or tens. There is, however, no proof that the Urartians used a decimal system. Most probably these numbers give the weight in each vessel of a given commodity; changes in the commodity stored in a jar over the years of its use were accompanied by the scratching on the jar's surface of a fresh number. The original number on the rim was impressed before firing. Apart from the terraces there were remains of a gateway giving access from the lower citadel: here a narrowing of the gateway and a raising of the level of the road leading up through it provided a hint of hasty efforts to reinforce the defences in face of impending attack. These efforts seem to have been wholly unavailing.

Scattered over the upper citadel were groups of bronzes, each group being found very close to the surface of the site and immediately overlying the burnt destruction debris. Therefore these groups, or hoards, comprise loot salvaged from the ruins either by the enemy or more probably by survivors of the local population returning to recover whatever they could find; they would have known best where to look. But these bronzes had to be reburied, and were never reclaimed. A collection of five quivers, one bent as if under a man's arm, was found with two pegs of iron having solid bronze knobs, the whole weight of each being 8 lb. A large undecorated shield and three furniture legs with bull's hoof feet were among many other finds. Knowledge of Urartian furniture has been augmented by the bronzes from Kayalidere, comparable in many respects with the later finds from Toprakkale (Van) and also with illustrations of thrones, chairs and footstools on the Assyrian reliefs. The clearest parallel is between the double volutes so typical of Kayalidere and those in Assurnasirpal II's relief at Nimrud. This emphasizes the cosmopolitan character of bronzework and furniture, like other crafts, in the period of Urartu, and lends weight to the belief that the Urartian borrowings from Assyrian art were essentially from that of the ninth century BC, and that afterwards Urartian art became crystallized in permanent traditional forms.[60]

The tomb at Kayalidere is not so sophisticated in appearance and finish as the masonry tombs at Altintepe; but no comparison should leave out of account the poor quality of the light volcanic tufa on which the citadel stands. The masons did their best to hew out a splendid tomb, but were hampered at every turn by the porosity of the rock and by its deep fissures. No texts survive, as do those describing Hittite royal funerals, to elucidate the funerary customs of Urartu, only archaeological evidence being available. Urartian cemeteries in the Araxes valley, at Malaklu near Iğdir and at Nor-Aresh near Erevan, show that at least there cremation was normal for private persons. Some of the grave-goods from the cemeteries at Evditepe and Alacahan, near Ernis by the north-east shore of Lake Van, may well be of Urartian date, though the mere proximity of two minor Urartian sites is no indication of the period of the burials, apparently all inhumations. Elsewhere in Urartu evidence of private burials, apart from rock tombs and those at Altintepe, is not yet available.[61] It would not be stretching the evidence too far to suggest that cremation was widespread in much of the kingdom. The discoveries so far made in the excavations at Haftavān, the large site of nearly fifty acres near Shahpur, suggest that in the Urmia region inhumation was the normal custom. Immediately after the last burial in the tomb at Kayalidere, which must have been reopened more than once for successive funerals, the doorway was carefully walled up with closely fitting basalt blocks; then a small fire was lit against the lowest block, perhaps the burning of a sacrifice; finally the entrance passage was filled up with stones and earthed over. At that time there had not been the washing down of soil from the clifftop above which has since occurred, so that the door of this tomb must then have been inaccessibly high on the cliff. There are many parallels with this, such as a small tomb near the foot of Karniyarik, a hill overlooking the plain of Shahpur and the mound of Haftavān: this tomb has a vertical shaft at the rear of the chamber. Inacessibility was an understandable consideration in the choice of a site for an Urartian rock tomb or inscription. The tomb at Kayalidere has an elaborate plan with at least seven chambers, six of which it was possible to clear. Two chambers were distinguished by their niches with round tops and by receptacles clearly intended for liquids, one being three feet deep. A rather small burial-pit, cut into the floor of a raised area in the third room, could have contained the body of someone of short stature: the conditions did not allow of the preservation of any bones. This could not have been the principal burial, and the curious shafts of bottle shape, two out of three being excavated, must surely have served as the burial chambers. Any other purpose for them it is hard to imagine: they have the form of cisterns, but these would be entirely out of place inside any tomb; nor would the porous rock here make cisterns practicable. In one room small depressions, like bowls, were cut in the rock floor, presumably for liquid offerings or libations.

Whatever the exact circumstances of the accession, reign and death of Rusa I of Urartu (c. 735–714 BC), the story told in the letter to the god Ashur from Sargon II recounting his victorious eighth campaign, of how Rusa refused meat and drink and fell into a decline leading to suicide, need not be taken at face value. This could be typical of Assyrian propaganda aimed at spreading alarm and defeatism. Rusa I had come to the throne soon after the attack on Van by Tiglath-Pileser III; but not only does he refer normally and frequently in his inscriptions to his father Sarduri, but also Sargon II mentions that in Armariali, a province evidently north-east of Van, he went to Arbu and Riar, described as the native towns of Rusa and Sarduri respectively. This suggests geographical juxtaposition, two towns in the royal domain directly administered by the crown.

The greater part of this reign passed without serious setbacks for Urartu. Twenty-three districts on either side of Lake Sevan were conquered in one day, according to an inscription on the south-west shore at Kelagran. Four of these districts or localities were on the south-west shore and the remainder on the far side, possibly even in the Kura valley, although there is no proof that the Urartian forces penetrated so far; and this would naturally mean that the claim to have subdued this territory so quickly could not be taken literally. This anyhow marks the deepest recorded Urartian advance towards the Caucasus. Otherwise the realm seems to have been at peace. Not many inscriptions are definitely attributable to this reign, but they include the Urartian-Assyrian bilingual stele at Topzaua, which, like the stele of Ishpuini at Kel-i-Shin, refers to the town of Ardini, better known by its Assyrian name of Musasir. The location and subject matter of this inscription lend point to Sargon II's fears of Urartian expansion south of Lake Urmia, leading to the Assyrian counter-attacks which culminated in 714 BC.[62] Some short inscriptions of Rusa on bronze cups from Karmir-Blur do not give any patronymic. The same is true of the Keşiş-Göl inscription recording the construction of 'Lake Rusa' not far east of Van. The architectural and engineering achievements of this reign appear considerably less than was once widely supposed, since now it seems more likely that both the royal residence at Toprakkale (Van) and the irrigation works designed to supply it, including the artificial lake, were the work not of Rusa I but of Rusa II (c. 685–c. 645 BC), whose reign was longer and more peaceful than that of his namesake.[63] The description of the irrigation works round Ulhu, however, makes it quite clear that Rusa I maintained the enlightened tradition, dating back at least to Menua, of enriching the kingdom by digging canals and making once barren land yield rich harvests and provide pasture for horses and cattle, though hardly all through the winter months, as Sargon suggested. Ulhu may be located either at Marand or further west at Ula near Shahpur.[64]

Sargon II was faced quite early in his reign with a potential danger to Assyria on that frontier which was the most decisive of all for the security of the homeland. This was the rising power of the Medes, already in the ninth century BC a people to be reckoned with in the politics of north-western Iran. By the third year of Sargon's reign (719 BC) a revolt among Mannaean tributary cities against their puppet ruler in favour of a Median prince, Metatti of Zikirtu, had to be suppressed, while other towns turned to Rusa I of Urartu for help. Deportation to north Syria was inflicted on their inhabitants. Three years later (716 BC) the serious attack on Urartian power in the southern half of the Urmia basin was begun; in the northern half it was never long challenged.[65] Sargon was opposed by a coalition of Rusa of Urartu, Metatti of Zikirtu and Bagdattu, a Mannaean ruler. There can be little doubt that Urartu was the leader of this alliance, and that its destruction was a considered objective of Assyrian policy. Ullusunu, the Mannaean puppet appointed by Sargon, soon sided with Rusa, a fact suggesting that Urartu was still regarded as the chief power in the Mannaean lands south and east of Lake Urmia. Izirtu, termed the royal city of the Mannaeans, was probably situated somewhere not far south of the lake, since directly after its burning mention is made of the city of Zibia, probably Ziwiye, close to Sakkiz. The 'mighty Medes', referred to at the end of the annals for Sargon's sixth year, were perhaps the leading clan in the confederation of Median tribes. The centre of Mannaean population may have shifted southwards as the outcome of Urartian expansion a century earlier; but more probably this territory had long been largely in Mannaean hands, and had by Sargon's time become the one surviving independent Mannaean principality or tribal domain. The role of Parsua and the Parsai may have diminished by this period. It was in the next year (715 BC) that Sargon struck another blow against the Medes by defeating and capturing Daiaukku, who was deported with his family to Hamath in Syria. This event provides a link with the Greek sources, for he is the Deioces of Herodotus. It was his son Khshathrita, the Phraortes of Herodotus, who was the first leader known to have welded the Medes into a political unity.[66] It is by no means unlikely that this was hastened by the Assyrian attacks and by the decline of Urartu in the southern Urmia basin. The Assyrian attacks on Median strongholds are depicted in reliefs from the palace of Sargon at Khorsabad: these perished when the boat carrying them down the Tigris from the French excavations sank, leaving only the drawings made of them.[67]

While the earlier campaigns of Sargon II might suggest that suppression of the Medes was his primary objective, it would be mistaken to suppose that as early as 714 BC the Medes were the chief adversary of Assyria. Urartu still filled this role, for in spite of the setbacks which the kingdom had suffered in the last years of Sarduri II these had not much affected the Urmia basin, where Assyrian penetration was much more difficult than into north Syria. The evidence provided by the highly detailed and colourful account of the eighth campaign has been much discussed since its original publication.[68] Military tactics, fortifications, irrigation, agriculture and historical geography are all elucidated, and there is a long list of the treasures looted from the great temple at Musasir. This raid came as an epilogue to the main campaign. The Akkadian words for many of these items still elude translation. It is historical geography which perhaps raises as many problems as are solved, for there is still no agreement on the route taken by Sargon's army. The present writer adheres to his conviction that Thureau-Dangin, in his commentary which he published with the text, rightly asserted that the Assyrian line of march came round the south, east and north sides of Lake Urmia and from there westwards, avoiding Van itself, to the north shore of Lake Van, continuing round its west end. The admitted weakness of this reconstruction of the route is that it presupposes either a very long march at the end across extremely difficult mountains south of Lake

Van to reach Musasir or else a position further west or north-west for that city than the two bilingual inscriptions mentioning it might indicate. This second possibility can by no means be ignored, for there is no proof that Musasir was situated anywhere near Kelishin or Topzaua, in the Zagros highlands south-west of Lake Urmia. The route of Sargon's army seems to have led him through the heart of Urartu, with descriptions of fortresses which fit more closely the known sites around Lake Van than those in the Urmia basin:

> From Armariali I departed. Mount Uizuku, the pine mountain, whose core is breccia, I crossed; to the land of Aiadi I drew near .... Thirty of its strong cities, which line the shore of the terrible sea, at the foot of great mountains, and all stand out like boundary stones: Argishtiuna, Kallania, its strong fortresses, erected among them, shining above Mount Arsidu and Mount Mahunnia, like stars, their foundation walls were visible to a height of 240 cubits; his warriors, his picked troops, powerful in battle, bearing shield and lance, the defence of his land, were stationed therein; they saw the overthrow of Armariali, their neighbouring province, and their legs trembled. They abandoned their cities with their possessions and fled like birds into the midst of these fortresses. I sent up large numbers of troops against their cities and they carried off large quantities of their property, their goods. Their strong walls, together with eighty-seven cities of their neighbourhood, I destroyed, I levelled to the ground ....[69]

Sargon goes on to describe his pillaging of granaries and cutting down of orchards and forests, these being naturally impossible to replace quickly. This must have been the most telling blow to the prosperity of Urartu, for houses and even fortresses could soon be rebuilt. From Aiadi the army continued its march across three rivers to the district of Uaiais, here described as being on the lower border of Urartu and on the frontier of Nairi: a location at or near Bitlis seems plausible.

The battle fought on Mount Uaush, evidently Mount Sahend, seems to have been decisive. Districts mentioned by Sargon before the account of this engagement may all have lain within five or six days' travelling distance from the south end of Lake Urmia.[70] Sargon's account of the battle is not corroborated by any Urartian text, so that it is difficult to distinguish fact from conceit, propaganda and the necessary verbal genuflections to Ashur and the other gods. The Assyrian army apparently gained its victory by a sudden assault, mounted before the full Assyrian forces could be deployed; but the Urartian king and his Median ally seem to have been even more unprepared. Perhaps their position in a defile of Mount Uaush gave them an unjustified confidence in their defensive strength; by implication the initiative was left to Sargon. One incident, the sending of a messenger by Metatti to Sargon, suggests a certain bravado or even recklessness on the part of the Median leader.

Coordination between the Urartian army and the allied forces was probably inadequate; and discipline seems likely to have been inferior to that of the Assyrian army, at least among the allies of Urartu. Sargon may have had reason to believe that a quick assault would catch his enemy unprepared, before the two armies of Rusa and Metatti had had time to join together effectively. The Urartian cavalry would have been of little use in the steep mountain defiles; and the reference to the shutting up of Rusa in his crowded camp is another hint that the Urartian king was defeated by a surprise attack.

The weakness of Urartu and the total inability of its army to stand up to the Assyrian troops, particularly the crack cavalry under the command of the king's brother and vizier Sinahiusur is apparent in the account of Sargon's eighth campaign. In spite of the frequent indiscipline of high-landers in battle, it is still hard to believe that the Urartian forces were ineffectual against the Assyrians, apart from the period of Assyrian weakness in the time of Menua and Argishti I. But Urartu had just been devastated, in its northern provinces, by an apparently overwhelming attack by a group of northerners from the steppes beyond the Caucasus, the Cimmerians. This attack was the beginning of a movement whose origins and ramifications are briefly alluded to below; it was recorded in correspondence from the crown prince Sennacherib to his father, who had sent him to obtain intelligence from Assyrian spies of affairs within Urartu. From these letters it appears that Rusa I's army marched against the Cimmerian lands, but that three commanders were killed, their regiments annihilated and the king forced to flee back to Urartu.[71] Thus the ground was prepared for the Assyrian victory at Mount Uaush, followed by a collapse of Urartian resistance possibly indicating internal political disintegration. The Urartian army cannot have been helped by Sargon's capture of the horse-breeding territory of Zaranda, perhaps near Tabriz. Yet the Assyrians, though able to march through and live off the land, were evidently quite incapable of enforcing permanent control over the territories of Urartu. Climate and geography made any such control impossible; and when supplies of corn and fodder for the army had been exhausted it had to move on. Sargon's whole success depended on continued speed. The distances and the nature of the ter-rain are by no means such as to make his route improbable: only the final raid on Musasir is harder to explain.

This last raid marked the culmination of the destruction wrought against Urartu by Assyrian arms. Thenceforward the two states seem to have evolved a *modus vivendi*, presumably dictated by Urartian acceptance of Assyrian superiority in the territories on the north-eastern and north-western frontiers of the Assyrian empire. A common opposition to the Cimmerian intruders was another factor determining the diplomacy of

Van and of Khorsabad and then Nineveh. Sennacherib gained invaluable experience during the years following his father's eighth campaign of the northern marches and of the Assyrian network of agents providing intelligence of events within Urartu.

It was during the reign of Argishti II (714–c. 685 BC) that Assyria kept an especially watchful eye on Urartu, at a time when the kingdom was preoccupied with marauding nomads from the steppes beyond the Caucasus, now perhaps raiding throughout the Urartian domains and later to strike at the heart of the Phrygian kingdom, with the destruction of its capital of Gordion (perhaps c. 685 BC). Argishti II met a Cimmerian force on an unknown battlefield, but like his father seven or eight years earlier he was defeated (707 BC).[72] Whether this was by superior skills or simply by overwhelming numbers will probably never be known. Clearly, however, it was not decisive, for Argishti II was to reign for some twenty-two years more. The number of inscriptions of this reign is limited: the name of Erciş on Lake Van may echo that of this king. The one inscribed object from Altintepe dates to this reign, suggesting the foundation of this site on the north-west frontier of the kingdom at this time. If so, it may have been established to give some protection against a return of Cimmerian nomads from central Anatolia. There is nothing at Altintepe proving a date before the seventh century BC. On another frontier there was military activity and perhaps even expansion, recorded in inscriptions near Sarab, at the foot of the south side of Mount Savalan, east of Tabriz near the road to Ardebil and the Caspian Sea.[73]

The site now called Altintepe, 'the hill of gold', stands some twelve miles east of Erzincan, a high hill rising out of the stony plain hemmed in by high mountains; it is now easily accessible from the modern road. Not far away is another hill with traces of Iron Age occupation but evidently less important. Altintepe is an outcrop with steep slopes but a wide flat summit, of which the Urartian builders took full advantage. Unlike many Urartian sites this one imposed no tight limits of space. In 1938 villagers found here a large bronze cauldron with tripod, but it was twenty-one years before excavations were begun.[74] The writer visited the site in 1955, and collected from the surface some distinctive painted pottery which seems likely, from its absence from the Urartian levels, to represent a later phase, possibly of the Achaemenid period. Altintepe has a temple, store-rooms, a palace or reception hall and a shrine with tombs. The excavator dates these to c. 725–c. 650 BC, but a slightly later dating seems possible, in the absence of any inscription or other indication of a date before the reign of Argishti II.[75] If the lack of traces of any violent destruction suggests continuity of occupation into the Achaemenid period, a date before *c.* 700 BC is even less probable, because of the evidently quick succession from the earlier level, with the temple, to the later level with the palace, when the temple continued in use.

On the whole, however, it seems unlikely that the palace at Altintepe was in use in the sixth century BC. Here was a building comparable in rank if not in magnificence with the palace of Argishti I at Erebuni. Yet the surviving wall paintings are exclusively of the stereotyped court style, including the familiar Assyrian theme of the divine figure holding a bucket and sprinkling water with a fircone, presumably a sacred lustration. As at Erebuni the background is in blue, with red ochre, black and white also being used. Such paintings, probably widespread in Urartu, betray the adaptation of Assyrian themes, at Altintepe executed with varying skill: an outstanding example is of two rows of genii with sacred trees and with rosettes above, between and below. The paintings on the palace walls were 2·35 m. high, of modest scale by Assyrian standards but large for Urartu.[76] Six rows of three stone column-bases indicate the design of this hall, with internal dimensions of no less than 44 by 25·30 m., sited south of the temple and on slightly higher ground. It has been suggested though not proved that this is the earliest example of an apadana, a hall with many columns, here so massive that they may have been of mud brick rather than wood, as at Karmir-Blur. The clearest parallel is with a columned hall excavated at Arinberd and dated by its contents to the Achaemenid period, thus reinforcing the description of the palace at Altintepe as an apadana inspiring the later Persian halls. The massive foundations and the girth of the columns at Altintepe indicate a building of considerable height. But if the temple next to it was of the proportions most probable according to the available evidence, a double cube, it would not have been overshadowed by the palace or reception hall.[77]

The temple at Altintepe is of the standard plan, with the interesting detail of slots on either side of the doorway. It is tempting to interpret these as intended for spears or lances, on the evidence of the relief of the temple at Musasir and of the finds from the temple at Altintepe: in the sanctuary were found many spearheads and arrowheads of iron, maceheads of iron and bronze and six bronze spearheads, as well as a carved wooden plaque and three pedestalled goblets of typically Urartian fine red polished ware. This form of goblet appears to be a degenerate version of the goblets above-mentioned from Giriktepe, Kayalidere and Haftavān: a date in the middle or later seventh century BC would thus be reinforced. All the pottery is likely to belong to the final phase of the temple. The reason for the presence of the spears is not entirely certain: like many of these objects they lay before the base on which the god's statue stood. No attribution exclusively to Haldi can any longer hold.[78] The spear may be interpreted as an emblem common to all the gods of

Urartu; but such spears offered to a temple may be trophies in thanksgiving for victory. Comparison can be made with the iron lance which Tiglath-Pileser III ordered to be inscribed with the news of his victories and set up in a public place.[79] Other objects were found by the door in the south portico of the Altintepe temple, including bronze helmets and shields, spearheads, arrowheads, ivories evidently from a throne and a magnificent and unique bronze door chain, with twenty-nine links, of which five are tubular and decorated with open-work lattice pattern. The treasures here found are the clearest proof that Altintepe escaped the ruthless plundering suffered by many other Urartian sites.

Among other finds from Altintepe an ivory lion deserves special mention, both for its intrinsic merit and for its evidence of a distinctive style in ivory-carving, very possibly native to Urartu, even though the raw material had to be imported. A fine open-work ivory plaque was also found at Altintepe, portraying a stag against a sacred tree on a hill. Carving in bone is evident at Karmir-Blur, at Çavuştepe and at Murji near Akhalkalaki in Georgia, at this last female heads and handles being found. Wood-carving is exemplified at Karmir-Blur and at Altintepe, where two fragments of model buildings were found. These can be compared in architectural interest with the bronze model from Toprakkale and with a baked clay model from Idjevan in the Armenian SSR, of a structure with two storeys said to be a temple.[80]

Altintepe was the first site to reveal indisputable evidence of major Urartian tombs, one being cut out of the rock on the hillside and the others near it built of well dressed masonry and having round-topped niches for lamps or offerings; the ceiling takes the form of a false vault. Two of the tombs had three rooms. In the tomb excavated in 1959 the burial chamber housed plain stone sarcophagi with convex lids; the outer room yielded a bronze cauldron, horse trappings, a dismantled chariot and silver-plated stools; from the burial chamber led off a smaller room with a bed, table and several vessels. Outside the tombs an open-air shrine occupied a platform built into the hillside and centred on four tall, beautifully dressed basalt stelae, devoid of any inscription: in front was a small basin, presumably for libations or incense. This shrine was in the same tradition as those on Van citadel.

The history of Urartu in the reign of Rusa II (c. 685–c. 645 BC) is the story of a revival both cultural and economic, with some evidence of military successes too. Peaceful relations with Assyria were based on mutual self-interest, fears of a renewed Cimmerian danger and preoccupation with other frontiers. Sennacherib and Esarhaddon were more concerned with events in Babylon, Judah and Egypt than with Urartu, which they must have come to regard as a useful buffer against the Cimmerians; and Assurbanipal was likewise engaged first in Egypt and later in Babylonia and Elam, where Assyria slowly bled to death in a series of costly campaigns which disastrously reduced its small reserve of native manpower. Rusa II of Urartu appears to have consolidated his north-east frontier by administrative reorganization. It is very possible that the great fortress of Bastam, not far north of Khoi, betokens a similar concern for the north Urmia basin, for the finds from the excavations there seem to belong to a late period in the history of Urartu.[81] Campaigns to the west are suggested by references to Mushki and Hate (Hatti), though location of these in Phrygia and Cappadocia seems highly improbable. Rusa II was not content with solely peaceful achievements during his long and successful reign; but there is little reason to think that Urartian power was at this time pushed far further west into Anatolia than ever before. Nor is it probable that the Black Sea coast around Trebizond, the Greek colony of Trapezos, was brought under Urartian control or reached by Urartian forces.[82]

The whereabouts of Mushki is a complicated problem, comparable with that of the location of Parsua. Even if Mushki could refer to Phrygia, it clearly had not always done so. The association with Phrygia rests on the equation of Mita of Mushki with the legendary Midas. This equation is surely not itself well enough documented to justify reconstruction of Anatolian history at this time on the assumption that the kingdom centred round the Sangarius (Sakarya) valley of north-west Anatolia was invariably the Mushki of the Assyrian and Urartian records. The Mushki are the Meshech of Genesis 10, 2, and the Moschoi of Herodotus III, 94. Their first documented appearance is in the reign of Tiglath-Pileser I of Assyria, who, in the year of his accession (c. 1,114 BC), won what must have been a resounding victory over them. His annals tell the story:

Twenty thousand men of the land of Mushki and their five kings, who for fifty years had held the lands of Alzi and Purukuzzi, which in former times had paid tribute and tax to Assur, ... came down and seized the land of Kutmuhi ... I gathered my chariots and my troops ... Mount Kashiari, a difficult region, I traversed. With their twenty thousand warriors and their five kings I fought in the land of Kutmuhi and I defeated them. ...[83]

This text shows that the Mushki had been in occupation of the land of Alzi, alias Enzi, Enzite or Isuwa, since a date soon after the collapse of the Hittite state in Anatolia. This is now the plain around Elazığ. Their seizure of Kutmuhi, the Commagene of Graeco-Roman times, brought a threat to Assyrian power on both sides of the Euphrates, which had to be dealt with at once. The Mushki never again so seriously confronted Assyria, soon to be hard pressed by the Aramaeans. Mita of Mushku, four centuries later only too ready to make trouble for Sargon II, may have been the paramount chief of a tribal confederation of people who had once come from north-west Anatolia. The region once known as Hanigalbat, around Malatya, is not impossible as the land of Mita of Mushku in the late eighth century BC. Any more westerly location makes the reference to Mushki by Rusa II harder to explain.

Shupria, the district of Hazro north-east of Diyarbakir, was evidently a sensitive frontier area, for it is mentioned on two occasions in the time of Esarhaddon. According to one reconstruction of the events, first there was a threat to Assyria from an Urartian attack, led either by Rusa himself or by a general, perhaps with the support of Cimmerian forces (*c.* 678 BC). A few years later (*c.* 673–672 BC) Shupria was firmly in Assyrian hands, Urartian refugees were returned to Rusa for sentence and an Urartian commander seized and executed by the people of Shupria, then loyal to Assyria. These changes in the balance of power might be taken to indicate that only with Cimmerian help could Urartu gain the upper hand over Assyria in the reign of Rusa II. There is no record of her ever trying to do so again.[84]

The cultural renaissance of Urartu under Rusa II is best demonstrated by the discoveries at Karmir-Blur in the Erevan plain, at Kefkalesi above Adilcevaz on the north shore of Lake Van and at Toprakkale close to Van itself. This last citadel, whose Turkish name of 'earth castle' is derived from the remains of massive mud-brick walls which have proved to belong to store-rooms, suffered grievously in the excavations of 1879 and their sequel, when for years the site was plundered and its treasures scattered over Europe from St Petersburg to London. The only compensation for this destruction was the first awareness of the existence of a civilized kingdom in the land hitherto known only from scattered inscriptions first recorded by Schulz, who was murdered at Başkale in 1829. Otherwise Urartu was discernible only in the Assyrian records and in brief references in the Old Testament.[85]

Toprakkale was probably founded as his main residence by Rusa II, and it is not impossible that Tushpa, the city at the foot of the castle-rock of Van, had stood in ruins ever since the attack by Tiglath-Pileser III (735 BC). If so, the capital must have been moved elsewhere in the next two reigns, under Rusa I and Argishti II. Toprakkale has little left of its buildings now, but there are features worthy of note. The temple was of the standard plan, constructed on a platform of rusticated lime-stone masonry, each massive block being dressed evenly round the edges but with a rough boss in the middle. There are fragments of decorative elements employing the contrasting colours of basalt and limestone in concentric circles. The temple stood on the saddle linking the spur chosen as the site of Rusahinili to the higher ground beyond. Next to the temple were ranged the store-rooms, and beyond those must have been other buildings whose only surviving trace comprises the ledges in the rock for the foundations. Beyond is a staircase leading down to a tunnel with fifty-six steps through the rock, forming a spiral staircase lit by three windows. This in turn leads to a large subterranean cistern, only rough hewn and perhaps never completed: a channel from a spring brought water along the hillside to a very small round aperture in the rock face and thence into the cistern.[86]

The treasures of Toprakkale are too numerous to be described in any detail, and partly date later than Rusa II. The throne reconstructed from seventeen elements was presumably that of Haldi in his temple: with its footstool it has been the centre of discussion of Urartian furniture, its architectural inspiration and the extent of its debt to Assyria. The use of figures, all cast like the other elements by the *cire perdue* process, is a distinctive feature of this throne, though whether they derive from wooden columns thus carved is another matter.[87] The other more functional elements have numerous parallels in the Assyrian reliefs. A hint of decadence in the art of the final phase of Urartu is discernible in the markedly attenuated lions on the bronze shield of Rusa III (*c.* 625–609/585 BC). Similar lions occur on a badly damaged shield recently appeared from a provenance said to be in north-west Iran and beyond doubt Urartian; this is accompanied by furniture elements. There is a clear contrast between the lions of Rusa III's shield and those on Sarduri II's shield from Karmir-Blur. The objects from Toprakkale seem all to be attributable to the seventh century BC, since there there is no evidence that Rusahinili existed before the accession of Rusa II (*c.* 685 BC).

There is perhaps insufficient evidence for any conclusion on the general quality of Urartian art in each reign. The discoveries at Kefkalesi, the citadel built on a hill high above Adilcevaz and thus commanding a view right across to the south shore of Lake Van, could be made to suggest that a decline had set in as early as the reign of Rusa II. The attribution of this citadel, which with its long store-room filled with huge jars resembles the contemporary Karmir-Blur, to his reign is beyond doubt, owing to the inscription giving his name on the basalt reliefs found in the palace, the first indication of which was one block lying on the surface after rolling down from above. There can indeed be no doubt that the large relief found cut into blocks used in the mediaeval castle down by the lake was of Tesheba rather than Haldi, as the writer originally suggested.[88] The weather god and the chief god of the Urartian pantheon are clearly distinguishable only by the animal on which they stand, the bull and the lion respectively: the bull is well known as the symbol of the weather god beyond and before Urartu, as for example on one of the Late Bronze Age reliefs from Alaca Hüyük in central Anatolia.[89] The relief scene from the palace at Kefkalesi comprises a pair of figures of Haldi facing inward in front of an architectural facade crowned by elaborate parapets, comparable with the less sophisticated rendering in a bronze model from Toprakkale. The parapets have two pairs of eagles perched on them, each with a rabbit in its beak, held by the tail. This is a unique theme in Urartian art. Impressive as this relief scene is, oft repeated, it betrays a quality of carving rather inferior to that of the much larger relief found near the lake. This relief, with the problems of its precise interpretation and with the fine detail of the god's dress, appears therefore likely to be slightly earlier in date than the sculpture of Kefkalesi itself. There is no evidence that the larger relief came from Kefkalesi instead of from a shrine nearby. This relief was in its entirety very large, well over three metres high, though probably – to judge from the top block as found – carved from two pieces rather than in one monolith. The god Tesheba stands before what can only be described as a 'spear tree', probably combining the sanctity attached to a particular tree, perhaps a cypress, and the emblem of the spear or lance associated with Urartian temples such as Musasir and Altintepe, known from Sargon's account and from actual finds respectively. Below is referred to more fully the mention by Moses of Khorene of the custom of the priests of Armavir, Argishtihinili in Urartian times, of consulting as an oracle the *sos* tree, in its sound and movement in the wind. The reason for Rusa II's choice of Adilcevaz as a major centre for building activity cannot be explained without new written evidence. But there can be no question of its importance in this reign, for it is comparable with Karmir-Blur and outstanding in its use for the first and only known occasion in Urartu of relief carving as a form of architectural embellishment. Sculpture in the round hardly occurs in Urartu, the list of booty from Musasir suggesting that cast bronze was the customary Urartian method of rendering forms in three dimensions; but relief carving may have flourished, if only belatedly, being almost unknown before Rusa II.

The contents of Karmir-Blur, the citadel of Teishebaina built by Rusa II, were largely of earlier date and transferred from Arinberd when it was replaced as governmental headquarters for the north-east. They have been briefly alluded to above. The whole plan of the citadel, though not the entire outer town, has been recovered.[90] Within the roofed portion of the citadel by far the greater space is occupied by store-rooms; the living quarters must have been on the first floor above, in this respect comparable with Kefkalesi and with the Urartian citadel of Haftavān Tepe, near Shahpur.[91] This accounts for the paucity of access as shown in the published plan. The facade of the citadel building comprises towers about twelve metres wide, also flanking the main gateway on the south side, with buttresses between. There is a minor entrance on the north-west. These entrances give access directly to either extremity of an irregularly shaped parade ground or public place in front of the citadel building. It is hardly remarkable that only a sustained attack by a Scythian force brought destruction to Karmir-Blur.

For over a century, from the Cimmerian attack on Rusa I until the Scythian participation in the campaigns of the Neo-Babylonian dynasty, the nomads who had erupted into the Near East from north of the Caucasus played a major part in the fortunes of Urartu and the lands to the west as far as Lydia, as well as coming into direct conflict with Assyria. The starting point of any historical evaluation of these peoples must remain the testimony of Herodotus, who, in spite of his credulity on many questions, should not be treated without respect. Therefore any dismissal of the distinction between Cimmerians and Scyths as entirely irrelevant and unreal needs to be examined very critically. If these two groups were in fact identical, or were simply the west and east branch of the Scythian tribes, it is hard to account for the distinction made between them both by Herodotus and by the Assyrian sources. Against this it has to be admitted that the Akkadian version of the Behistun inscription has 'Cimmerians' where the Old Persian and Elamite versions have 'Saka'. But failure always to differentiate hardly eliminates the difference. The cause of the arrival of these nomads, their affinities, where they settled and what mark they left in the archaeological record are all legitimate questions which demand some consideration.[92]

Herodotus states that the Massagatae attacked the Scyths, who in their turn, being thus pressed westward, expelled the Cimmerians from their pastures along the north shore of the Black Sea. Some remained, to be encountered by Greek colonists, while others moved into Europe; but most of them were driven south across the Caucasus, probably through the Darial Pass. The Scyths took a more easterly route, 'with the Caucasus on their right', presumably either through the Derbend Pass or along the Caspian coast. The account by Herodotus has the merit of general consistency with the evidence from other sources, mainly Assyrian.[93]

The main body of Cimmerians can be discerned moving into Urartu, their arrival perhaps being the cause of subsequent military and administrative reorganization in the north-east marches of Urartu, demonstrated by the shift from Arin-berd to Karmir-Blur. Whatever their precise route through Urartu, the Cimmerians may well have reached its western frontier very quickly, the defeat of Argishti II (707 BC) apparently ocurring when the Urartian king moved beyond his acknowledged frontiers into lands by then reckoned as Cimmerian. Sargon II two years later met his death in a successful action by the Assyrian army in the Taurus mountains against a Cimmerian force, probably the main body. Herodotus mentions their attack on the Greek colony of Sinope on the Black Sea coast (perhaps *c.* 700 BC). The subsequent sack of the Phrygian city of Gordion, the capital of the kingdom situated in the upper Sangarius (Sakaraya) valley, left its mark in the record revealed by the excavations.[94] This destruction has been variously dated between *c.* 696 BC and *c.* 675 BC. This means that the great bulk of material from the Phrygian level of the city and from the tumuli must date round about the end of the eighth century BC, even if many of the unexcavated tumuli are likely to be rather earlier. The records of Esarhaddon's reign show that their repulse by Sargon II had not finally deterred the Cimmerians from seeking land and plunder in the north-west provinces of the Assyrian empire.[95] Teushpa and his followers were defeated by Esarhaddon in the land of Hubushna, probably the foothills of the Taurus immediately adjoining Hilakku, later Cilicia Aspera. Thus Kue, the plain of Adana, was secured. Further east, in the district of Shupria, they appear in association with Rusa II of Urartu: it is tempting to suggest that he had employed the Cimmerians, scattered after their defeat by the Assyrian army, as mercenaries or auxiliaries. His father's experience would have enjoined caution in the use of these nomads.

A quarter of a century later the Cimmerians reappear far to the west, where they attacked and defeated Lydia, whose king Gyges was slain. Assurbanipal gloated over his death, attributing it to his desertion of himself in favour of his rebellious brother in Babylon, Shamash-shum-ukin (652 BC). Lydia, however, proved resilient enough to recover and to counter-attack under a new and strong ruler, Alyattes, who eventually, fifteen to twenty-five years after the sack of Sardis, was able to rout the Cimmerians. Under his rule Lydia flourished.[96] This defeat proved to be the swansong of the Cimmerians as a menace to ordered life in Anatolia; they seem to have found a permanent home in the region later called Cappadocia and known to the Armenians as Gamir.

Whatever the cause of the movements of steppe peoples leading to the expulsion of the Cimmerians, they seem to have been of either Thraco-Phrygian or Iranian affinities. Linguistic evidence inclines more to the latter, with the names of Teushpa, Tugdamme and his son Sandakhsatra being Iranian.[97] The problem can be clarified if it is realized that the arrival in the Near East of these Cimmerians and Scyths has been given greater prominence than other movements in earlier centuries for two reasons: first, this occurred at a time when Assyrian historiography had been much developed, even if at the sacrifice of chronological order, and late enough to be within the ken of Greek historians; second, this movement was the first irruption through the

Caucasus since the migration of the Hittites which affected the Anatolian plateau as well as Iran. The Cimmerians and their Scythian cousins must, however, be seen as the last wave of the Iranian migrations which had begun as long ago as the fourteenth or thirteenth century BC. The Scythians did not necessarily follow the Cimmerians in hot pursuit, as Herodotus would have us believe, but perhaps after some years, though they may have been present in parts of Trans-Caucasia much earlier.[98] Not till Esarhaddon's time had they come closely within the orbit of Assyria, under their leader Partatua. Such Cimmerians as had arrived in north-west Iran probably became absorbed in the larger influx of Scyths, who were eventually powerful enough to terrorize a wide zone for twenty-eight years until suppressed by the Medes under Cyaxares. As the Umnan-Manda, a term evidently used for either group by the Assyrians, they had a chequered history, for some time the allies of Assyria in its decline, but at the end determined to share in the spoils of its destruction (612 BC).[99]

There can at present be little if any certainty concerning the material culture of these two groups in the lands on either side of the Caucasus. The theory that the Cimmerians can be associated with the Catacomb culture of the eastern Ukraine and the Don basin, distinguished by pit graves, runs up against the difficulty that these people were expelled from their homeland in the second half of the second millennium BC. If these were the Cimmerians, they must have had an intermediate home near the Caucasus until the late eighth century BC. This would not be inconsistent with a passage in one of the letters sent by an Assyrian agent home to the capital, in which the land of Guriania is referred to as lying between Urartu, to which it paid tribute at that time (c. 735 BC), and the land of the Cimmerians.[100] This indicates relative proximity of the Cimmerians; and if Guriania can be equated with the Cyrus (modern Kura) basin then a location of the Cimmerians close to the heart of Georgia can be suggested. The association of two cemeteries – Samtavro near Mtskheta and Mingechaur in the Azerbaijan SSR — with the Cimmerians and Scyths respectively is an attractive theory. But identification of any entire material culture with the Cimmerians still seems uncertain: the Koban culture of the eleventh to seventh centuries BC represents the fruition of developments in metal-working dating back well before the arrival of any Cimmerians or Scyths. This was a tradition which had its influence upon them, which they helped to disseminate but which was the work of the settled population, not of these newcomers. Very probably the Scyths in due course found a home on the Mukan steppe of Azerbaijan, a pasture for nomads of later periods.[101] The later Scythian burials, after the return north from the former Urartian and Mannaean lands, are discussed below.

No detailed discussion of the impact of these northerners on the art and material culture of Urartu and neighbouring regions can be attempted here. Much argument has ranged over the so-called animal style and on some of the items of the treasure of Ziwiye, near Sakkiz, whose very name may preserve that of the Saka (Scyths), as the Crimea or Krim does that of the Cimmerians.[102] Attempts to disentangle the various ethnic elements in the art of Ziwiye have shown the complexity of the civilization of the region just south of Lake Urmia in the seventh century BC. The recently excavated tumuli of Sé Girdan, close to Dinkha Tepe in the Ushnu valley, yielded a silver vessel, a whetstone or sceptre 37 cm. long ending in a feline head and a few other objects. These tumuli seem rather more likely to be Scythian than Median, though the good stone tomb in one tumulus may militate against this attribution. Sé Girdan cemetery seems roughly contemporary with much of the Ziwiye treasure, in the seventh century BC.[103] Many of the items from Ziwiye were made some time before the burial of the hoard. The date of the bath-tub sarcophagus could be as high as c. 730 BC, though parallels from Ur suggest at least a century later. Scythian workmanship is most discernible in a silver dish with concentric design using three motifs attributable to this origin, a hare, a crouched animal possibly a lynx and the head of a bird of prey. The theory that all the Ziwiye treasure, excepting only some obviously Assyrian work, could be described as the native art of that region and thus termed Mannaean, is no longer tenable. The famous gold pectoral displays Urartian and Scythian influences. The interlacing pattern characteristic of the gold belt pieces from Ziwiye is likewise typical of Urartian work, being found on the bronze belt from Zakim, near Kars, and on the stone relief from Adilcevaz. One piece from Ziwiye shows very clearly the combination of the Urartian setting with the Scythian couchant stags and goats. Official Urartian art, however, is lacking at Ziwiye, situated south of the Urartian territories even at their widest extent. But it is represented by the bronze fragments, probably of a belt, from Guschi, thirty miles north of Reza'iyeh.[104]

It cannot be an easy task to trace the interaction of Urartian civilization with the local cultures of Trans-Caucasia, nor necessarily a practicable one until more stratified material from settlement sites is recovered in Armenia and in those parts of Georgia open to contact with Urartu. Throughout Trans-Caucasia the cultures already established in the late second millennium BC were in the ninth century BC still largely continuing. The Koban region and Colchis, the valley of the River Rioni, were at the time of the Urartian expansion north of the River Araxes still the centre of a flourishing, skilled and prolific metal industry discussed in the last chapter and most distinguished by its bronze axes with their bold animal and geometric patterns. The Ganja-Karabagh culture, also discussed above, was to continue as late as the seventh century BC. In the Araxes valley there was general continuity in the region of Kültepe (Nakhichevan) and Kizilvank from the Late Bronze Age into the Early Iron Age: red and grey wares dated approximately to c. 1,000–c. 800 BC do not look in the least similar to known Urartian pottery. In the same region the long stratified sequence at Karaköpektepe includes Early Iron Age levels.[105]

The eastern parts of Trans-Caucasia, now within the Azerbaijan SSR, fall beyond any known trace of Urartian influence, though there must have been contacts through trade. The Kayakent-Khorochoi culture had originated late in the second millennium BC, in the Late Bronze Age, and continued at least till the end of the ninth century BC if not later. Dating evidence seems to be rather uncertain. This cultural province extended along much of the west shore of the Caspian Sea and also through Daghestan, the north-east Caucasus. If the pottery is an adequate guide to the general standard of this culture, this region remained very backward well into the first millennium BC: the wares are coarse and plain, with rough red to reddish brown surface. Nothing could be further removed from the contemporary civilizations of the Near East.

Hunting and the magic associated with it may have long remained an important element in the life of the Kayakent-Khorochoi population, if due significance is attached to scenes incised on orthostats at a Late Bronze Age settlement on the Akdas Duzu, an open area on the Apsheron peninsula close to Baku, and to other carved slabs no longer *in situ* but in the same district. Among subjects depicted are lions, goats, a man raising a club and dancers. Specialist opinion in Baku holds that at least two stones are carved with the scene of a dance over and round a corpse, one showing a priest in the group: this seems plausible in the light of Strabo's reference to this in his description of Albania.[106] Either an alligator's or a lizard's head is shown on women in scenes of copulation on some of these stones. There seems little doubt that many such carvings may date into the Hellenistic period; but the hunting magic had its roots thousands of years before.

The dating at one time proposed for the greater number of the Koban tombs, and thus for the Koban-Colchidic metal industry, was as high as c. 1,400–c. 1,200 BC, with a late group characterized by iron daggers, fibulae and bronze decorated bands or belts and dated c. 1,200–c. 1,000 BC. It can now, however, be claimed with assurance that a much lower chronology must be adhered to.[107] The presence of fibulae, or safety-pin brooches, of simple bow type in this late class of Koban tomb and in the Iron Age cemeteries of Trialeti is alone sufficient evidence that a date before the eighth century BC cannot be seriously upheld. Thus much of the Trans-Caucasian material is brought to a period contemporary with the heyday of Urartu. Cemeteries of cist graves have been found in the Trialeti district at Kuschi, Maralyn Deresi, Tak Kilisi and Tsintsqaro.[108] Apart from fibulae, the finds include swords with the double splayed pommel found in Luristan. A date as late as the time of the Median kingdom in the early sixth century BC has been ascribed to some of the graves in these cemeteries in Trialeti.

Local artistry in bronze is exemplified by miniature figurines, one with a woman's breasts and a ram's head, from Melighele: these are now in the Gurjaani museum in the east Georgian province of Kakheti, and are attributed to the ninth or eighth century BC. One class of bronze ornament, perhaps originally with a practical function, is the elaborately decorated band or belt, found in the late Koban burials. It seems possible that these were first made in the Koban area and were diffused thence throughout Trans-Caucasia, being marked by boldly mobile animals and by borders and filling designs of running spirals or other motifs. A belt from Sanahin in Armenia has running spirals on the border and centre panel and one surviving panel of four prancing horses, their bodies curiously undulating in the unmistakably Caucasian style. A similar belt was found at Dashkesen, in western Azerbaijan; and a fragment of one was among finds from the Early Iron Age graves at Akdas Duzu on the Apsheron peninsula, dated to the ninth century BC. The finest and best preserved of these bronze belts are those from the Chabarukhi hoard and from burial no. 5 at Maralyn Deresi, respectively 90 cm. and 98 cm. in length: men, stags and horses form the majority of the figures, but two antelopes, a boar, does, a fish, foals, birds, a snake and six mythical creatures also appear. Comparable fragments have been found at Akhpat and Kirovakan. The scene on the belt from Stepanovan in Armenia is quite different and includes an A-frame wagon and a chariot with spoked wheels: this bronze ornament is dated c. 1,100–c. 900 BC by Martirossian, and it must be admitted that the difference of subject-matter from the above-mentioned belts, if such they are, could justify this seemingly high dating. But if this is reckoned as one of the same class of ornament it ought perhaps to be given a lower date. Another chariot scene appears on an engraved bronze strip or belt from Akhthala in the Araxes valley: this shows a charioteer on a chariot drawn by two horses, with four-spoked wheels and a chariot-pole ending in a flower or triple bud. A parallel with this belt is discernible on an ivory from Ziwiye with a design of a chariot, and this suggests a date not earlier than the eighth century BC for the Akhthala belt.[109]

Chronologically the bronze strips or belts in the Urartian style could have derived their first inspiration, though not their subject-matter, from the Caucasian belts. In regions not very far from Van examples in Urartian style have been found at Guschi and probably at Kayalidere; in north-eastern Urartu they occur above all at Karmir-Blur but also at Zakim, near Kars, and side by side with local material in the Early Iron Age cemetery at Metsamor. This last illustrates the easy juxtaposition of Urartian and local elements in the material culture of the Araxes valley. Their distribution makes an origin for such belts towards the north-east frontier of Urartu by no means impossible.[110]

In conquering the Erevan plain and beyond to Lake Sevan, however, Urartu had penetrated a region already possessed of a strong indigenous culture, just as occurred in the Urmia basin. In both regions alike the imported Urartian elements stand out from the local culture but never destroy it. Beyond the north-east frontier only the faintest echo of Urartian civilization seems detectable. Just as there was continuity from the pre-Urartian centuries so Trans-Caucasia maintained its old ways into the Median and Achaemenid periods.

The end of Urartu as an effective force in the politics of the Near East probably came with the Scythian raid through its lands southward into Syria, when Assyrian control over territories west of the Euphrates was lost.[111] The kingdom may then have been infiltrated by Armenians, if an ingenious suggestion that Erimena means 'the Armenian' is accepted: he was either successor of Sarduri III (c. 645–c. 635 BC) or simply the father of the next king, Rusa III, who may therefore have been a usurper. Sarduri III had sent a delegation to Assurbanipal in Nineveh, humbly acclaiming him as an overlord.[112] It is difficult to believe that this acceptance of Assyrian overlordship, previously so long resisted, could imply anything but the gravest threat to Urartu, of which this is the only hint in the written sources. Whatever the course of events, it is clear that the successors of Rusa II were quite unable to maintain the revival of Urartu which in his long reign he had so brilliantly achieved.

The final end of Urartu is understandably obscure, in a period of disorder when the written sources fail and chronology becomes open to debate. Dates between c. 625 BC and c. 585 BC have been given for the fall of the kingdom, but there remains the problem of whether Urartu fell suddenly as a whole to the Medes, who seem undoubtedly to have administered the coup de grâce, or whether inroads by Scyths from their homeland in eastern Trans-Caucasia or from the steppes beyond the Caucasus had already reduced the area of Urartu to an enclave around Van. Alternatively the northern marches may have held out after the capture of Van by the Medes (perhaps c. 590 BC).[113] The Armenian advance, discussed below, may already have engulfed the western provinces. On the whole it was probably a combination of these adverse elements which brought this resilient kingdom to an end, although the people did not entirely vanish.

The Cimmerians, after their long years of ravaging Phrygia and Lydia culminating in the sack of Sardis (652 BC), had turned back east to the Taurus, where they had met their match in an encounter with an Assyrian army soon after 640 BC.[114] Yet the removal of one threat, as often elsewhere, only magnified another. Just as the campaign by Rusa I against the Cimmerian territories in Trans-Caucasia may have goaded the northerners to attack his kingdom so now the destruction of the Cimmerians as a military power in Anatolia may have opened the way immediately to the above-mentioned raid by a Scythian horde into Syria and Palestine (c. 637 BC). Babylonian chronicles refer to a march by Scyths 'as far as the district of Urartu' (609 BC) and to the subsequent annexation of Urartian lands in the upper Tigris valley (608–7 BC).[115] This annexation implies the continuance of Urartu at least till that date. It is uncertain whether this was as a shattered remnant surviving the depredations of Scythian nomads then enjoying their twenty-eight years' rule of 'Upper Asia', the highlands of Anatolia east of the River Halys, or as a tributary kingdom under the overlordship of Cyaxares, king of the Medes (633–584 BC). Herodotus states that the Scyths ruled all Asia for twenty-eight years, from the victory of Madyes, son of Partatua, over the Median ruler Khshathrita (Phraortes in Greek) until the defeat of the Scyths by stratagem by Cyaxares, son and successor of Khshathrita.[116] The most favoured dating for this period of Scythian domination is from 653 BC till 625 BC. This does not entirely rule out the first alternative, that Urartu was under the Scythian horde, for the Median kingdom was very loosely administered. Urartu, however, almost certainly had to acknowledge Median suzerainty in some form before its final absorption.

Karmir-Blur seems to have fallen to a Scythian attack, on the evidence of the distinctive arrowheads with a hook on the tang, generally agreed to be a hallmark of the Scyths.[117] One interesting suggestion is that there was a very strong garrison maintained till the last at Erebuni (Arin-berd), and that at the time of the fall of Urartu this was taken to defend Van, while at the same time all valuables were taken to Karmir-Blur. It has also been suggested, perhaps less plausibly, that the presence of Scythian arrowheads in the store-rooms of Karmir-Blur indicates the recruitment of Scythian mercenaries by Urartu.[118] The latest documented reference to Urartu is in the Old Testament: Jeremiah calls on the kingdoms of Ararat, of the Minni (Mannaeana) and Ashkanaz (Scyths) with 'the kings of the Medes' to attack Babylon, thus summarizing the political grouping soon after the disappearance of Assyria (*c.* 594 BC) and not long before the Exile from Jerusalem.[119] If indeed the Scyths remained a menace to stable government in Anatolia till 585 BC, Urartu could have survived till that date, when the war between the Median kingdom of Cyaxares and Lydia ended in an agreement making the River Halys their common frontier. By then Median power must have been secure throughout the former Urartian lands. The exact date of the final end of the kingdom of Van is of minor importance, since it had long ceased to wield any real power.

Of all the peoples involved in the troubled period of the eclipse and downfall first of the Assyrian empire and then of Urartu the Armenians were perhaps unique in being newcomers, at least in the sense that their existence had previously gone unrecorded. The Medes and Parsai have been observed since the ninth century BC in the Urmia basin; the Cimmerians, rulers of a wide territory on either side of the Sea of Azov, appear round the east end of the Black Sea from *c.* 730 BC. Their movements and those of their Scythian cousins have been traced above. The mounted Scyths and the Cimmerians also were apparently too formidable to be defeated quickly in open battle, only being worsted when their initial energy and cohesion had been diminished by many miles of wandering in Anatolia and beyond, and possibly also as a result of demoralizing contact with alien, settled cultures. The elan of the nomad had reached its natural exhaustion away from his native habitat. Many ethnic and chronological problems still await solution; the paucity of securely dated finds, apart from some imported Greek objects in some of the Scythian tombs, hinders any definitive discussion of the Cimmero-Scythian culture. One thing, however is clear: that is the common Iranian origins of Medes, Persians, Cimmerians and Scyths alike, the Phrygians probably being distantly related to the Iranian group of the Indo-Europeans. The Old Persian inscriptions of the sixth century BC refer to three groups of Saka: these are the Paradraya, Tigraxauda and Haumavarga, these doubtless forming clans or septs of the Scyths as a whole. Herodotus claims that the Persians called all Scyths Sakas.[120]

The dark age which followed the fall of Urartu is not strongly illuminated by archaeological evidence, since there seems to be a lacuna in the material civilization of the Van region, and there is the persistent paucity of material from stratified settlement sites in Trans-Caucasia. At Argishtihinili (Armavir-Blur) there appears to be an Achaemenid level overlying the main Urartian occupation; but knowledge of what pottery can be safely assigned to this period is meagre. Yet since relatively little is known of Achaemenid pottery within Iran, and since there is hardly likely to have been one uniform pottery through the whole empire, it is not remarkable that parallels in Trans-Caucasia may go un-recognized. The homelands of the Koban and Kolchidic cultures and of the Kayakent-Chorochoi culture, at the west and east ends of the Caucasus, had been ravaged by the Cimmerians and Scyths respectively; but these local cultures seem to have survived their depredations, perhaps because the nomads did not linger on their way into Anatolia and Iran.

Local wares in use in Trans-Caucasia in the Urartian period probably continued into Achaemenid times, as suggested by some pottery found near Sachkhere, in Georgia, comprising jugs and jars with dull red painted decoration in geometric patterns on a buff slip; and finds from a cemetery at Khrtanots might be of the seventh or else of the sixth century BC in date or even later. [121] At Arin-berd the Persians may have built an imitation of one of their temples in their homeland, with a fire altar for the Zoroastrian cult: pottery, necklaces and a horse-bit are dated, with Milesian coins, to the fifth century BC. A hoard of Colchian coins was found at a cemetery of Achaemenid date at Dablagomi in western Georgia. A cemetery of the early years of this period is that at Beshtasheni following the Early Iron Age cemeteries above-mentioned. These two cemeteries have yielded material comparable with the Kazbek treasure and cemetery of the mid-sixth century BC. [122] There are thus hints of a continuity in the material culture of the indigenous population, deprived of the protective power of Urartu, which might have been expected and which is suggested by the survival in the Araxes valley of the Alarodians, the remnant of the Urartian people.

North of the Caucasus, in the Kuban basin, there are several Scythian royal tombs of the sixth century BC, though some of their contents were made in the previous century. At Kostromskaya is a barrow having a chamber of wooden construction with pyramidal roof: round the chamber were twenty-two sacrificed horses. Perhaps craftsmen captured in Iran or in the Assyrian empire were brought back by the Scyths of the Royal Horde, whose return northwards through the Caucasus is recounted by Herodotus, from whom there is a full description of Scythian burial customs. [123] The owner of the tomb of Kostromskaya was buried with his scale armour, round shield of iron, leather quivers, bronze-headed arrows and other equipment of war; there was also a large whetstone and pottery, all ritually broken. Oriental influences are marked in the contents of the Kelermes barrow, also in the Kuban valley: even the design on the back of a silver and gilt mirror, showing a goddess holding two lions apart in the traditional Mesopotamian manner, betrays little Greek influence. [124] This was to become more prominent later, especially on the north coast of the Black Sea, and resulted from contacts with the Greek colonists, tolerated by the Scyths for the sake of trade. The wealth of these royal burials, both in the Kuban valley and in the lower Dnieper basin, must reflect the prosperity of the Scyths on their return north, when they found their ideal habitat in the most fertile region of the Eurasian steppes, a region which had drawn them from beyond the Caspian Sea to oust the Cimmerians in the eighth century BC and which was later to provide a similar magnet for the Sarmatians.

Nomadic art has been described as timeless, but it would be more accurate to say that its different variations could be dated if only the evidence to do so was available. Discussion of the 'animal style' ranging over two millennia can have but limited value; nor need all art based on bold representations of animals, however rendered, have any link with nomads or with the northern steppes. Moreover there is no evidence of Scythian artistic achievements before their arrival within the sphere of Near Eastern cultural influences. Among the earliest objects attributable to the Scyths are some in the mixed treasure found at Ziwiye, near Sakkiz, a treasure also displaying Urartian, Assyrian, Mannaean and possibly Median traditions.[125]

In the Azerbaijan SSR the remains attributable to the Scyths, even if dated correctly, contain objects of local origin. The burials at Mingechaur, on both banks of the River Kura, are of fourteen types covering periods from the third millennium BC onwards. One class of graves at this cemetery contains many iron weapons, red pottery, a variety of jewellery including earrings, girdles, necklaces and engraved sealstones. Here was no unsophisticated people. Some of the graves were roofed with stone slabs, the bodies being extended, as also in burials of approximately contemporary date on the citadel at Haftavān Tepe: there an agate finger-ring was the characteristic find in otherwise impoverished burials. It would be not unreasonable to describe these burials at both sites as Scythian: the wealth of the Scythian royal tombs thus found a paler reflection at Mingechaur, and can be associated with Strabo's reference to Sakasene.[126]

If the account given by Herodotus of the Cimmerian route southwards and of the more easterly route taken by the Scyths on their way into Iran is not to be discounted, the great cemetery may in its later phases be associated with the Cimmerians, though this association must raise many of the still intractable problems connected with any attempt to trace their antecedents. Homer spoke of them as inhabiting a country of mist and gloom on the edge of the world; Herodotus regarded them as the earliest inhabitants of south Russia. Strabo erroneously identified them with the Thracian Treres and thought that they entered Asia Minor through the Balkans.[127] There seems no doubt that the Cimmerians

175

can be said, on linguistic grounds, to have been an Iranian people or at least ruled by Iranians, for the names of Teushpa and of Tugdamme and his son Sandakhsatra are all Iranian. But no satisfactory equation of the Cimmerians with any of the material cultures of south Russia or the Caucasus has yet been achieved: the ousting of the Catacomb culture from the North Pontic region occurred too early, in the second half of the second millennium BC; any equation with the Late Bronze Age remains north of the Sea of Azov and on the lower Dnieper cannot be reconciled with the written sources; any identification of the Cimmerians with the Koban culture ignores its very early roots. The Cimmerians appear to have divided, after their defeat by the Scyths who then pressed upon them, into a western and an Asian branch. If their sojourn near the Caucasus was for no more than one generation, it is unreasonable to expect that any indisputable traces of their presence are likely to be identified.[128]

A reappraisal of Scythian art, best seen today in metal though originally carved out also in wood and textiles, is required in the light of the implications of all the above evidence. It goes without saying that the Scyths were steppe-dwellers, who, if circumstances encouraged or compelled them to do so, could move swiftly over vast distances. The great burial at Pazyryk, in the High Altai, is closely comparable with those of south Russia: Chinese instead of Greek influence is present, while the influence of Achaemenid Persia is predominant and gives the general date. The role of carpets in disseminating artistic motifs is made plain by those found at Pazyryk.[129] All this is beyond dispute; but perhaps less generally accepted is the probability that the Scyths developed the full repertoire of the 'animal style' only after passing the Caucasus into north-west Iran. South of Lake Urmia they came into contact with the thriving and ancient metal industry of Luristan, whose origins dated back many centuries. The Scyths were less originators than disseminators of the style which has been too easily credited to them. In fact this was a Caucasian tradition, manifested in variations determined by time and locality but thriving more or less unbroken since the period of the great Maikop barrow. This Caucasian tradition was the product of the continual interaction of influences from the Near East on those from the steppes, with the former largely predominant.

An ultimate origin in the northern steppes for works of art based on wood-carving cannot, however, be denied. This has been discussed elsewhere in relation to a group of small wooden animals from the tomb of a young princess (Tumulus P) at the Phrygian capital, Gordion.[130] These are dated to the last years of the eighth century BC, and must have been inspired by traditions brought in by the Phrygians from their Thracian homeland, together with the general custom of tumulus burials, perhaps as early as the twelfth century BC. Whatever the precise date of the arrival of the Phrygians in north-western Anatolia, their ultimate origins must have been in the Indo-European homeland in south Russia. There is no sign of similar tumuli in Urartu.

If Herodotus is to be believed, the Armenians arrived in the former Urartian kingdom not through the Caucasus but from Phrygia in the west: he described them as settlers from Phrygia. Strabo gives an account of how an eponymous hero Armenos, not mentioned elsewhere, led the Armenians into their new homeland, one group arriving by the direct route from Phrygia via Akilisene, now the province of Erzincan, while another group took a circuitous route through the very recently de-populated Assyrian territories as far as Adiabene, the Nineveh (Mosul) region.[131] The inclusion of Amida (Diyarbakir) in the thirteenth satrapy in the administrative reorganization of his empire by Darius I lends slight support to this account of the arrival of invading Armenians from the south into the heart of Urartu. The suggestion that there are tumuli strung out along the road from Malatya to Diyarbakir and that these are of 'Thracian' type, whatever that may mean, is quite unsupported by the known archaeological traces in that region.[132]

The Thraco-Phrygian origins of the Armenians are unsupported by any archaeological indications; but perhaps this can be dismissed as largely the outcome of the almost total lack of archaeological evidence in the territory formerly occupied by Urartu, with its downfall to the Armenians themselves, its conquest by the Medes and its later absorption into the Persian empire. The apparent absence in eastern Anatolia of tumuli such as characterized the Phrygian kingdom, especially Gordion itself, is indeed curious. This lack of visible traces of the Armenian new-comers, together with their difficulty in subduing the recalcitrant Alarodians or Chaldians, the remnant of the Urartian population, could suggest that they formed a small conquering group of clans rather than a migration in numbers large enough to obliterate or absorb the older inhabitants. There are many parallels for the imposition of the language of a conquering minority on a much larger indigenous people; and certainly the present-day Armenians do not have the Indo-European appearance which the affinities of their language might suggest. Contrary to the superficial conclusions from the linguistic and historical data, a strong case can be made for an ethnic affinity of the Armenians with the Hurrians and with the Hattians of central Anatolia, and thus indirectly with the Urartians whom they supplanted. The evidence is set out briefly below.

Herodotus has been proved substantially correct on other matters, and therefore it seems he should likewise be believed when he says that the Armenians were settlers from Phrygia and were armed like the Phrygians, in the great army gathered by Xerxes for the attack on Greece. Certainly nothing suggests that the Armenians could have entered Urartu from the north or east; but the evidence on the ground remains obstinately negative. The disintegration of the Phrygian kingdom of Gordios and Midas had initially been the result of the destructive Cimmerian raids; but later the rise of Lydia to become the leading power of western Anatolia sealed the fate of Phrygia as a great power. According to accepted theory, the Armenian tribes were refugees, formerly part of the Phrygian people, driven from their home in north-western Anatolia to seek new territory east of the upper Euphrates, a movement which Urartu was too harassed to resist effectively if at all.[133]

The Thracian origins of the Phrygians, if not the date of their arrival in Anatolia, seem reasonably beyond dispute, both philologically and from their burial customs. The Armenian language has certain affinities with Albanian and to a lesser degree with Greek, but also is generally to be classified with the eastern rather than the western branch of the Indo-European family of languages, this eastern branch including the Iranian group.[134] An ultimate origin with other Indo-European peoples in the steppes north of the Black Sea seems therefore probable. In fact this is true of the Phrygians and of their language; and one classical source, Eudoxos, states that the Armenians spoke a tongue very akin to Phrygian. Surely therefore there is little cause to deny the Phrygian ethnic character of the Armenians? This, however, is unsupported by any tangible proof apart from that of language.

The Phrygians themselves had occupied and come to dominate a wide zone of western Anatolia, whose indigenous population was by no means obliterated. It would fit the modern evidence of physical anthropology far better if the Armenians were to be described as of old Anatolian, very probably Hurrian, stock, who had been subjugated by the Phrygians and had adopted their language but not their tradition of burying kings and chieftains in tumuli in the manner of the northern steppes. If of Hurrian ethnic affinity, the Armenians probably came as refugees from immediately west of Urartu, perhaps from the region of the Taurus highlands formerly within Tabal. Rusa son of Erimena could have belonged to a tribe which had penetrated the western marches of Urartu in the late seventh century BC. The Armenians would thus have been much closer blood relations of the Urartians than of the Phrygians, under whose yoke they had come for perhaps five centuries.[135] The absorption of non-Indo-European elements into the Armenian language was largely responsible for its idiosyncratic character: this could well have occurred earlier in central Anatolia rather than after the occupation of Armenia.

The similarity of the name of Hayasa, of the Hittite records of the Late Bronze Age, to Haii, the name given to themselves by the Armenians, who called their new land Hayastan, has led to a theory of an origin for some of the Armenians north of the Hurrian zone where they have tentatively been placed. Hayasa was probably situated in the upper Euphrates valley between Erzincan and Erzurum.[136] Another Armenian group seems to have acquired the name of a district of Arm- or Urm-, the land of Urm- occurring in the Urartian records and possibly to be located in the Muş plain. If correctly placed, this district was closer to the Persians than Hayasa. This may therefore account for the fact that the Persian sources, and following them the Greek, use only the stem Arm-, never Hai-.[137] This discrepancy suggests the lack of unity and cultural distinction and comparative anonymity of the Armenian invaders of Urartu. If, as suggested above, the Armenians were of Hurrian not Thraco-Phrygian origins, they could have arrived and settled in large numbers without leaving trace of any abrupt change in the material culture.

The *Cyropedia* of Xenophon, a history in a romantic vein, is too late to be accepted without reservations, although it seems certain to contain a considerable kernel of historical fact concerning the early phases of Armenian settlement; and it gives invaluable information on the history of Armenia under the Medes and Cyrus the Great. From this emerges a fragmentary outline of events. The more fertile plains having been settled by the Armenians, the old Urartian population (the Alarodians) had perforce retreated to the mountains and upland pastures; there then ensued protracted guerilla fighting and pillaging of the Armenian lands by the highlanders. Then, according to Xenophon, the Median king conquered the king of Armenia: this could have been not Cyaxares (633–584 BC) but his son Astyages (584–55 BC). Cyrus the Great, again according to Xenophon, imposed with Achaemenid impartiality a peace on the Armenian king, obliging him to pay tribute and to accept co-existence with the Alarodians. They in their turn – whose name was from the same root (Arrt) as Ararat-Urartu – had to pay rent to the Armenians for use of some of the better land for agriculture, and to accept the Armenian flocks in their uplands without molesting them or demanding more than an agreed sum. Following the peace established thus by Cyrus there was an abortive rebellion, in which Armenia joined, after the deaths of Cambyses and Smerdis (521–19 BC). For this there is another source, close to the events, in the inscription of Darius I carved on the cliff face at Behistun and made deliberately inaccessible by removal of the steps on completion. Here the land and people are mentioned by Darius I as Armina and Arminiya, the earliest references to them. Darius I cannot have distrusted all Armenians, for he sent one named Dadershish against the rebels, though soon replacing him by a Persian, Vaumisa, who at length crushed the revolt by two victories.[138]

There are no major sites around Lake Van or elsewhere in Armenia which can be dated to the sixth century BC. But it is by no means impossible that some of the remoter and more crudely built strongholds, attributed to the Urartian period and classed as refuges from the Assyrians or Cimmerians, were in fact Alarodian strongholds against Armenian incursions into the mountains. Such could be the fortifications now known as Kefirkalesi, high in the foothills of Mount Suphan and with patches of snow even in August. No trace has yet been found of the fortresses which Xenophon says were built by Cyrus the Great.[139]

The reorganization of the Achaemenid empire by Darius I led to the creation of Armenia as the thirteenth satrapy and to the inclusion of the Matienians, Saspirians and Alarodians in the eighteenth satrapy. The land of Matiene is the Urmia basin, now Iranian Azerbaijan. Herodotus provides the main evidence that, by his time if not slightly earlier, the Alarodians had either abandoned or been driven from the territory which they had long held in the Armenian domains, and had sought more fertile lands in the lower Araxes valley. Though later Armenian, this valley must have been the last territory to be occupied by the newcomers. In spite of the destruction wrought by the Scyths, life may have continued relatively unbroken in much of the Araxes valley. Strabo describes the Scyths as occupying the richest district of Armenia, which retained the memory of this occupation in the name of Sakasene.[140]

One puzzle confronting historians is the early history of the Kurds. If they are to be identified with the warlike Carduchoi, highlanders who opposed the retreat of Xenophon's Ten Thousand on their long march to the Black Sea, it is apparent that by the end of the fifth century BC they were already in possession of much of the region where they live today. The best lands were in Armenian hands, and so largely remained until modern times and the catastrophes that then occurred. Therefore the Carduchoi may well have occupied the poorer lands which had been the refuge of the Alarodians at least until the reign of Cyrus. Armenia has never been exclusively the home of the Armenians.[141]

Archaeological evidence from the Urmia region is too sketchy to add flesh and bones to the tenuous historical framework for the troubled years between the fall of Urartu and the reign of Cyrus the Great; nor is the Achaemenid period, in this culturally and politically peripheral region, any clearer. Pottery almost alone comes to the aid of the enquirer.

Yanik Tepe, near Tabriz, was pock-marked with pits all over the summit of the mound: such pits are commonly found on sites in western Iran, and make the task of interpreting the plans of the levels into which they are dug very difficult. Frequently, as at Yanik Tepe, they follow a period of abandonment of the site, there lasting over a millennium. These pits at Yanik Tepe, whatever their purpose, yielded a great quantity of a distinctive pottery, wheel-made and with rather carelessly applied red painted decoration on an unburnished surface. Comparisons with the so-called Triangle ware of Hasanlu IIIA suggest a date round about 600 BC: thus it would be tempting to ascribe this pottery to the Medes. Yet their long establishment in this region means that they must have used a different pottery previously.[142]

The period of Hasanlu IIIA has yielded pottery which can form the basis for a corpus of material attributable to the Achaemenid period. To this can now be added the pottery from the later levels of the citadel at Haftavān Tepe: there the wares are largely plain yellow buff to light red, wheel-made and sometimes with the outside surface partly shaved before firing; the shapes are distinctive. It is, however, from the excavations at Hasanlu that a chronological outline of material from the Urmia region can best be obtained, even though only provisionally. After at least a partial burning of the Hasanlu IIIB citadel pottery including new forms appears in Hasanlu IIIA, post-dating the annexation of Mannai by the Medes, between c. 610 BC and 590 BC. Jars with trefoil rim may be compared with a small jug with rim of similar form from Haftavān. Some plain ware from Geoy Tepe A seems to be of Hasanlu IIIA type. Yellowish white ware with decoration in purplish paint is rather like an earlier ware found at Ziwiyeh. Much of the material originally assigned to Period IIIA is in fact Urartian: this is true of Agrab Tepe, the small fort close to Hasanlu probably built as a frontier post soon after the destruction of Hasanlu IV. More distant parallels for Hasanlu IIIA pottery are to be found at Susa, in levels dated to the sixth and fifth centuries BC by tablets. Though the range of material of this period in the Urmia basin is still limited, further discoveries at Haftavān are sure to add to those types already definitely attributable to the Achaemenid period.[143]

The eighteenth satrapy, extending from Lake Urmia towards the lower Araxes, may well have maintained a degree of independence of the central government in Persepolis, anyhow after the defeats suffered by Xerxes in Greece. Achaemenid official art and architecture seems to have left little or no imprint. When the empire fell to Alexander the Great, he had no time to come there himself; and Macedonian control lapsed very soon after 323 BC, if it ever existed. According to Strabo the local Persian commander Atropates made himself king over an independent state, which thus came to be known as Media Atropatene, and which he prevented from falling under the Macedonian yoke. Strabo also mentions salt works on Lake Urmia in his time; and he claims that this region could produce ten thousand horsemen and forty thousand footsoldiers. If so, the population must by then have been considerable.[144]

This account of the dark age of Armenian history may end with a reference to the inscription carved on the orders of Xerxes high on the precipitous south cliff of Van citadel and copied through a telescope by Layard. No other Achaemenid inscription is known in the Van region. Nor can any site be dated to the period of Persian rule, unless the enormous grid laid out on Zernaki Tepe, above Erciş, but never completed, can be reckoned as one of the fortresses with whose construction Cyrus the Great is credited by Xenophon. This was evidently a time of cultural decline, if not of a reversion to barbarism. It seems unlikely that any major Urartian sites round Lake Van continued in use. Xerxes was nevertheless able to recruit many of the hardy highlanders for his great army. Herodotus has left indications of a rough tribal society, in which no survival of the civilization of Urartu is discernible.[145]

When an awakening came, Rome was thrusting herself into the highlands of Armenia, and the long history of conflict on the eastern frontier of the Roman empire was about to begin.

CHAPTER 6

ARMENIA AND GEORGIA —
HISTORY AND INSTITUTIONS

The formation of the Armenian and Georgian nations is closely bound up with the cataclysmic events which set the Near East in turmoil throughout the middle of the first millennium BC. Among the most important of these events were the irruption of the Cimmerians and Scythians across and around the Great Caucasus range; the successive downfalls of Assyria, of Urartu and then of Babylon; the dramatic rise to power of the Medes, and then their replacement in 550 BC by the better organized Persians, headed by the conqueror Cyrus.

The Persians were inspired by the new religious teaching of Zoroaster, and by a fresh concept of imperial responsibility, which distinguished their rule from earlier oriental despotisms.

Persian rule over Asia Minor and most of Armenia lasted from 546 to 331 BC. Like the rest of the immense empire, Asia Minor was administered in provinces or satrapies. According to Herodotus, Anatolia, Armenia and regions adjoining comprised the following satrapies:[1]

1   The Ionian and other Greek coast cities from the Sea of Marmora to the Gulf of Antalya, with Caria and Lycia, and the adjacent islands, while these were under Persian control.
2   Lydia, with the interior of Anatolia from the Gulf of Adramyttium to the Cilician border.
3   Phrygia, which combined the frontage of the Marmora and Pontus with the plateau as far as the salt desert, and Cappadocia north of the Halys.
4   Cilicia including the Taurus highlands and as far as the upper Halys.
5   Syria, immediately to the south-east of Cilicia, from the Amanus to the Arabian desert and Egypt.
10 Media with Ecbatana and large tracts of Western Iran.
11 The Caspian provinces, including parts of Azerbaijan.
13 The Armenians, with the Pactyans and 'the peoples beyond as far as the Euxine Sea'; the capital of this satrapy was the city of Van.

18 The Matieni and the Saspeiri (ancestors of the Georgians), and the Alarodians (remnants of the Urartians).
19 The Moschi, Tibareni, Macrones, Mossynoeci and Mares, tribes of Caucasian and Kartvelian stock, dwelling in the mountainous regions south of the Black Sea.

This distribution was essentially geographical, but it also took account of populations and former dynasties. Each province had its satrap or viceroy, over whose activities a royal secretary kept vigilant watch. There were local military levies with various forms of equipment; but the western coastguards were a separate command. Some provincial commands were hereditary fiefs; sometimes several were assigned to a single high commissioner from the Court. During the campaigns of Xerxes, the Armenians together with the Phrygians were placed under the command of Artochmes, a son-in-law of King Darius Hystaspes. On these same campaigns, the Alarodians (Urartians) and the Caucasian tribe of the Saspeiri were commanded jointly by a certain Masistius, son of Siromitres.[2] Their weapons and armour resembled that of the Colchians, who themselves wore wooden helmets and carried little shields of raw oxhide, short spears, and knives.

The Persian empire was the greatest which the world had seen. Armenia lay on the northern borders of the empire's central heartland. The land was rapidly drawn into an immense network of international communications and trade routes. From north to south ran the highway connecting Colchis on the Black Sea with Media, via the Araxes river valley. Thanks to this, the former Urartian city of Argishtihinili in present-day Soviet Armenia attained prosperity and importance; this city, under the name of Armavir, became capital of Armenia under the dynasty of the Orontids.[3] The Armenian provinces south of Lake Van also gained strategic and commercial importance through their position on the Royal Road linking Susa with Ancyra, the modern Ankara, and with Sardis and western Asia Minor. The improved road transport and security system of the Persian empire did much to improve Armenia's commercial position. However, the Armenians and Alarodians, together with neighbouring tribes forming between them the Thirteenth and Eighteenth satrapies, had to furnish the Persian Great King with tribute totalling six hundred talents of silver, as well as horses, slaves and various military supplies in kind. This tribute certainly imposed a severe strain on the Armenian economy, and on that of the Georgian tribes.

Farming, stock raising and wine producing remained the staple occupation of the bulk of the nation. Herodotus describes Armenia as having a people 'rich in flocks',[4] and Xenophon calls it 'a large and prosperous province'.[5] Though little fresh engineering work seems to have been undertaken, the Van and Araxes regions continued to benefit from the remarkable canal systems of the old Urartian kings.

The classic account of Armenia under the Persian Achaemenid rulers is that of Xenophon, who crossed it with his Ten Thousand in 401–400 BC.[6] Xenophon unfortunately arrived on the Armenian plateau in November, with the result that his men suffered terribly from the snow and the north wind's icy blast. Many died; others were blinded by the snow, and had their toes rotted off by frostbite. The hereditary satrap of Armenia at the time was Orontes, and his deputy, the lieutenant-governor of western Armenia, was called Tiribazus. This latter was a personal friend of the Persian Great King; whenever Tiribazus was present, it was his exclusive privilege to help the supreme ruler mount his steed.

The satrap Orontes lived in a fine palace, while the ordinary houses in the surrounding township were surmounted by turrets. Elsewhere, in the more mountainous and exposed regions, houses were built largely underground:

with a mouth like that of a well, but spacious below; and while entrances were tunnelled down for the beasts of burden, the human inhabitants descended by a ladder. In the houses were goats, sheep, cattle, fowls, and their young; and all the animals were reared and took their fodder there in the houses.

Such houses exist in Armenia and parts of Georgia to this day, though they are now being replaced by more modern dwellings. Their method of construction is described by Vitruvius, and is based on the principle of the corbelled cupola, tapering towards the summit. The Georgian variant of these dwellings is known as the *darbazi* house and is often supported at its underground base by finely carved beams and pillars.

Xenophon's Greeks captured the tent and household of Governor Tiribazus of Armenia, complete with a set of silver-footed couches and drinking cups, and also took prisoner some 'people who said they were his bakers and his cup-bearers'. The common people naturally did not pretend to such luxury, but even they were not badly off. Organized in village communes, they were ruled by their own headmen, who were in turn responsible to the satrap through the local deputy governors. These villagers gladly provided Xenophon's men with plenty of 'animals for sacrifice, grain, old wines with a fine bouquet, dried grapes, and beans of all sorts'. Sometimes they drank a kind of barley wine:

Floating on the top of this drink were the barley-grains and in it were straws, some larger and others smaller, without joints; and when one was thirsty, he had to take these straws into his mouth and suck. It was an extremely strong drink unless one diluted it with water, and extremely good when one was used to it.

When Xenophon inspected his troops in bivouac:

he found them faring sumptuously and in fine spirits; there was no place from which the men would let them go until they had served them a luncheon, and no place where they did not serve on the same table lamb, kid, pork, veal and poultry, together with many loaves of bread, some of wheat and some of barley. And whenever a man wanted out of good fellowship to drink another's health, he would draw him to the bowl, and then one had to stoop over and drink from it, sucking like an ox.

In another place, Xenophon draws a pleasing picture of his troops feasting in their quarters, 'crowned with wreaths of hay and served by Armenian boys in their strange foreign dress; and they were showing the boys what to do by signs, as if they were deaf and dumb'. Thus we see that from their earliest years, the Armenian people have always been hospitable to strangers, who have not always repaid them as they deserved.

Xenophon further gives special praise to the quality of Armenian horses, which the local people used to rear specially for the Great King of Persia.

The horses of this region were smaller than the Persian horses, but very much more spirited. It was here also that the village chief instructed them about wrapping small bags around the feet of their horses and beasts of burden when they were going through the snow; for without these bags, the animals would sink in up to their bellies.

During the fraternal strife between Artaxerxes II and his brother Cyrus the Younger for the Persian throne, in which Xenophon and his Ten Thousand played a prominent role, the Armenians seized their opportunity to reassert their country's autonomy. The satrap Orontes, who figures in Xenophon's *Anabasis*, was married about 401 BC to Princess Rhodogune, daughter of Great King Artaxerxes II. Orontes took the side of his father-in-law Artaxerxes against Cyrus, who was defeated and killed.

Artaxerxes II turned out to be a feeble ruler, under whom the once mighty Persian empire fell into decay. Profiting by this, Orontes set himself up in Armenia as a virtually independent dynast, and became extremely wealthy, having a personal fortune of three thousand talents of silver. In later years, Orontes even turned against his father-in-law and overlord, Great King Artaxerxes, and led a revolt of the chief satraps which broke out in 366 BC. Eventually, Orontes submitted, was pardoned, and granted the satrapy of Mysia; he died in 344 BC.[7]

The name Orontes is of Iranian origin, deriving from Avestan *aurand* ('mighty, hero'), and closely related to Pahlevi *arvand*, with the same meaning. The Armenian forms of the name are Erwand, Arawan, and also Hrant. The Orontid dynasty is of great historical importance, since it spans much of the gap between the old Urartian kings (the First Monarchy in Armenia), and the Third Armenian Monarchy of the Artaxiads in classical times. The Orontids guaranteed the social and historical continuity of Armenia, as it evolved from its pre-Armenian phase and passed into the Hellenistic age.

Under the last Persian kings of the Achaemenid dynasty, Armenia enjoyed peace and prosperity.[8] The rulers of Iran now interfered little in Armenian internal affairs, and trade and agriculture flourished. This state of things was abruptly shattered by the invasion of Alexander the Great of Macedon. The battle of Arbela (Gaugamela) on 1 October 331 resulted in decisive victory for the Macedonians and Greeks over the last of the Achaemenids, Darius III Codomannus. Loyal to the last, the Armenians furnished 40,000 infantry and 7,000 horsemen to the Persian Great King, under the personal command of their own sovereign, King Orontes II. The Armenian cavalry made up the right flank of the Persian line of battle at Arbela.

During this catastrophic battle, Orontes II apparently lost his life. At any rate, Alexander the Great celebrated his victory by sending Mithranes, a son of Orontes II, to be satrap of Armenia in his father's stead. It is interesting to note that this Mithranes was a former Iranian governor of Sardis in western Asia Minor, who had defected to the side of the Macedonians, and thus found himself ranged at the battle of Arbela on the opposite side to his own father.[9] This is an instance of one of Armenia's perennial tragedies – of divisions of allegiance whereby father and son, brother and brother, through the ages would find themselves fighting on opposing sides, sometimes even against their own Armenian homeland.

Alexander the Great died at the zenith of his power, at the age of thirty-three. But his cultural and imperial heritage lived on. Far to the east, in Bactria, Parthia, Afghanistan, and at many sites in modern India and Pakistan, Greek or rather Hellenistic cities grew up almost overnight. Stagnant, sleepy backwaters were revitalized, and decayed trade routes brought swiftly back into operation. Greek taste in building, sculpture and the arts, and knowledge of Greek literature and philosophy spread to out of the way corners of Anatolia and Central Asia. Greek science and technology produced rapid improvements in living standards, hygiene and sanitation, and in domestic amenities, at least for the select few. Greek ingenuity in engineering and construction left its mark over many regions of the old Persian empire.

Armenia, which lay close to Alexander's expansion route towards India, could not escape the impact of the new Greco-Oriental world civilization which he helped to create. At the same time, in this new world of Hellenism, the vestiges of the earlier world of 'Iranianism' were not effaced, nor were the elements of local advanced culture inherited from Urartu. Armenia now found herself in close touch with a number of Hellenistic countries, and thus open to new economic and social influences. The exclusively agricultural economy and rural existence of Achaemenid Armenia, where the use of coined money was scarcely known, were suddenly altered. The important overland route of transit trade, connecting China, India and Central Asia with the Mediterranean world, passed through Armenia, while there was a parallel northern route through Caucasian Albania (Azerbaijan), Iberia and Colchis debouching on the Black Sea.

Great cities arose along these routes, which became homes of foreign merchants and centres of diffusion for Greek culture. The growth of a money economy and of urban life generally made for the decay of Armenia's traditional tribal-patriarchal society, and for the emergence of new patterns of urban stratification, including the growth of a town bourgeoisie and artisan class, and the commercial exploitation of slaves, though this latter institution never reached the massive proportions which it did in Greece and Rome. From the third century BC, Armenian royal authority grew more absolute, and the administrative machinery more complex, especially in regard to the royal court and the taxation and fiscal systems. The clan chiefs and rustic headmen began to turn into a more sophisticated courtier and squire class, enjoying greater luxury and ease, and demanding a higher standard of living.

A feature of this period of Armenian history is the foundation of a number of new cities, combined with the revival of towns which had flourished long before, under the Urartian kings. It is perhaps significant that Xenophon, traversing Armenia in 401–400 BC, fails to mention any cities of importance – though his route, which lay northwards from the plain of Muş, effectively passed well to the west of the Van region and the fertile Araxes valley, perhaps to avoid meeting any hostile city garrisons.

The Armenians, like the Urartians before them, used to name their main cities after the kings who founded them. This helps us to pinpoint the date of the foundation of many key Armenian towns. Now Orontes I, Xenophon's contemporary, had his capital at the ancient city of Armavir, north-west of Mount Ararat, in the fertile plain of the Araxes. From this site, King Orontes IV (212–200 BC) transferred his residence a few miles westward, to the new city of Ervandashat or Orontosata, which he named after himself, while Armavir still remained the religious centre of the Armenian kingdom. A few decades later, Artaxias I (190–159 BC) chose to reside further down the Araxes valley, at the rather malarial, marshy site of Artashat (Artaxata), also named after the reigning monarch. Artaxias is said to have built and adorned this capital with the aid and encouragement of the celebrated Hannibal of Carthage, who retired to Armenia after his defeat at the hands of Rome.[10]

Far away to the west, towards the borders of Cappadocia, King Arsames (260–228 BC) built the renowned city of Arsamosata or Arshamashat, on the bank of the Aratsani, a major tributary of the Euphrates. This town became the capital of the independent Armenian kingdom of Sophene (in Armenian, Tsophk), and an entrepot of international trade. Arsames inaugurated the regular striking of coins with Greek inscriptions, using the title of 'Basileus Arsames'.[11]

At a later period, Tigranes the Great (95–55 BC) was the architect of the city of Tigranocerta – again named after himself – on the site of the present Farkin (Mayyafariqin). To complete this short list of royal foundations, we should recall that the most holy city of Armenia, Echmiadzin, residence of the Supreme Catholicos and within sight of Ararat, was originally called Vagharshapat, after Valarsh I (AD 117–140), himself a prominent member of the Arsacid dynasty which succeeded the house of Artaxias.[12]

To appreciate Armenia's international position within the Hellenistic world, we must take stock briefly of the general situation in the Near East and Asia Minor. After Alexander the Great's sudden death in 323 BC, his generals quarrelled over the partition of his dominions. Ptolemy created a Greek kingdom in Egypt; Seleucus did the same in Syria and Mesopotamia, with his capital first at Seleucia, replacing ancient Babylon, and then at Antioch on the Orontes. Antipater conserved the old kingdom of Macedon, with its European dependencies as far as the Black Sea and also the Adriatic, with sovereignty over the city states in Greece. The attempts of Lysimachus to create a kingdom of the Bosphorus, with a capital on the Gallipoli peninsula, united his rivals against him, and ended with his death in 281 BC.

Hardly had Alexander's successors established an uneasy balance of power in the Near East and Aegean region, when new disturbances burst upon the civilized world from outside. Celtic tribes from the middle Danube shattered Macedon, devastated Thrace and Phrygia, and established themselves on the Asia Minor plateau to the west of Armenia, under the name of Galatians. Here they remained until Roman and Christian times, being the recipients of one of St Paul's epistles. Soon afterwards the Iranian speaking people of Parthia overran the Persian plateau and deprived the Seleucids of their possessions east of the Euphrates. The Parthians effectively separated the Seleucids of Syria, as well as the Armenians, from those eastern provinces of Alexander's realm which developed into the Greek kingdom of Bactria and also took in large regions of the Indus valley. These Eastern losses led the Greco-Syrian kings of the Seleucid dynasty to seek compensation at the expense

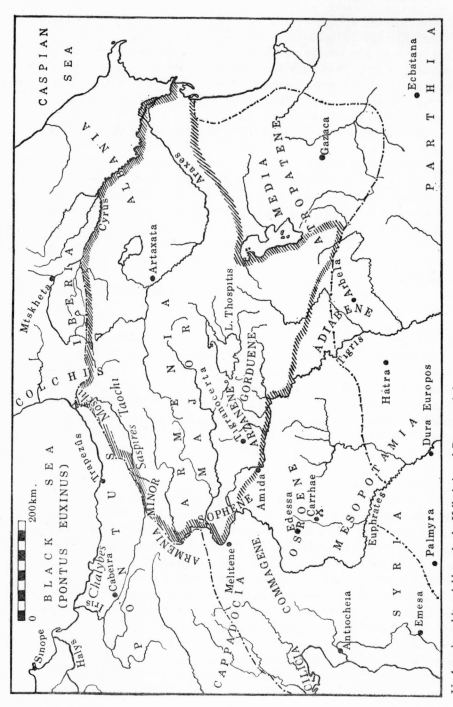

V *Armenia and its neighbours in the Hellenistic and Roman periods*
The cross-hatched band indicates the maximum limits of Armenia (AD 62–387). The broken line indicates the extent of the empire of Tigranes (c. 70 BC). Tribal names are in italics.

of Egypt to the south, and of Armenia and other independent states of Asia Minor to the north.

During the Seleucid period, Armenia became divided into several virtually independent kingdoms and principalities. The classification adopted at this epoch persisted, with certain changes, well into the Byzantine era. The most important region, of course, was Greater Armenia, situated east of the upper Euphrates, and including vast areas all round Lake Van, along the Araxes valley, and northwards to take in Lake Sevan, the Karabagh, and even the southern marches of Georgia. Lesser Armenia, on the other hand, was a smaller and less fertile kingdom, to the west of the upper Euphrates; it included the present-day districts of Sivas and Erzincan, and bordered on ancient Cappadocia. To the south-west lay the two little kingdoms of Sophene and Commagene, separated from one another by the middle Euphrates, and having the fertile and desirable Melitene (Malatya) plain running between them. Sophene and Commagene often featured as buffer states between Parthia and Armenia on the one hand, and Syria and Rome on the other. Their royal houses had strong dynastic links with the Armenian Orontid house. Through their proximity to such great cities as Antioch and Palmyra, the kingdoms of Sophene and Commagene became great centres of Hellenistic, and then of Roman art and civilization, which they in turn helped to transmit eastwards into Greater Armenia and Trans-Caucasia.

The Seleucid kings never succeeded in asserting direct rule over Armenia proper. They collected tribute from local Armenian princes, whom they used to confirm in office by granting them the title of 'strategos', corresponding to the old Persian viceregal title of satrap. This situation changed somewhat under the Seleucid king Antiochus III, known as the Great (223–187 BC), an ambitious monarch who cherished dreams of restoring the empire of Alexander the Great. The Armenian king Xerxes rashly declined to pay tribute to Antiochus, who besieged him in his capital of Arsamosata and forced him to submit. Xerxes then received the sister of Antiochus in marriage. This lady, Antiochis by name, soon had the unfortunate Xerxes, her spouse, murdered, and united the Armenian kingdom of Sophene to the dominions of Antiochus III, her brother. The ill-fated King Xerxes has left some small coins bearing his portrait. We see on them a dignified, bearded, somewhat donnish-looking figure, wearing a pointed hat or tiara of unusual shape, with a peak in front and a streamer or tassels floating down the back.[13]

Antiochus III appointed a scion of the Armenian Orontids, Zariadris (Zareh), to be strategos of Sophene in 200 BC. At this time, in Greater Armenia, the power of the main Orontid dynasty was drawing to a close. The last ruler of this line was Orontes IV (212–200 BC). Both he and his brother Mithras, High Priest of the Temple of the Sun and Moon at the city of Armavir, are mentioned in Greek inscriptions discovered there in 1927. One inscription contains an address of High Priest Mithras to his brother King Orontes; another evidently alludes to the king's tragic death.[14]

This event was the result of an uprising headed by a local dynast called Artaxias, son of Zariadris, and evidently instigated from Syria by King Antiochus III himself. Following this coup, Antiochus appointed Artaxias to be strategos of Greater Armenia in place of the dead Orontes.

Artaxias was the founder of the third and greatest Armenian monarchy, counting the Urartian kingdom founded by Aramé as the first, as does Moses of Khorene, and the Orontids as the second. The name Artaxias is the equivalent of the Persian Artaxerxes, and the Armenian Artashes.

For a decade after being installed by Antiochus III, from 200 to 190 BC, Artaxias and his junior partner, Zariadris of Sophene, bided their time. Ultimately, Antiochus overreached himself by challenging the Roman Republic to a trial of strength. No sooner had Antiochus sustained at Magnesia his great defeat at the hands of the Romans (190 BC) than Artaxias and Zariadris seceded from the Seleucid state. In the Peace of Apamea (188 BC) which sealed the Roman victory, the Senate in Rome granted them the status of independent rulers. This was Armenia's first juridical contact with the Roman Senate, which was glad to acquire two grateful allies in a strategic part of the world – pending completion of the usual preliminaries to swallow them up and annex their lands to the Roman republic.

Under this new-found Roman patronage, the two Armenian kingdoms of Greater Armenia and Sophene pursued a lively expansionist policy. From the Medes and Persians, Artaxias took Media Atropatene, the modern Azerbaijan, extending virtually to the banks of the Caspian Sea. From the Georgians he seized a broad slice of territory to the northwest of Lake Sevan. From the Chalybes, Mossynoeci and Taokhoi, the Armenians took much of the upland plateau round Erzurum, and some of the wild mountain country of the Pontic Alps. The province of Taron, round about the town of Muş, was cleared of remaining Seleucid garrisons.

One important result of this territorial growth was the cultural and linguistic consolidation of the Armenian people. Except for the Georgian marchlands, and for a few remote tribal districts, such as Sassoun, Armenian became the dominant spoken language of the peasant masses, the hunters and tribesmen, and the townspeople, except for those of Jewish and Greek birth. The Greek geographer Strabo (58 BC–AD 25) lays special stress on this result of the conquests of Artaxias and Zariadris. Thanks to their work of unification, he says, 'all the inhabitants of these various districts today speak the same language'.[15] It must be remembered, however, that prior to the invention of the Armenian national alphabet after AD 400, all works of literature, religious texts, and government decrees, were written down and transmitted in Iranian written in Aramaic characters, or else in Greek. The Armenian royal family and aristocracy were bilingual, speaking Greek or Iranian as well as Armenian – rather as the Russian Court prior to the 1917 Revolution spoke English or French in preference to Russian.

The development of political organization in Georgia presents a rather different picture from that prevailing in Armenia. Though not artistically or culturally backward, the Georgians had never known the discipline of a unified military and state power, such as the Urartians imposed upon Armenia. It is true that Greek legend has enshrined the renown of the Colchian kingdom of King Aietes, to which Jason and the Argonauts sailed in quest of the Golden Fleece. The Urartian annals record two campaigns of King Sarduri II (764–735 BC) against Colchis, which figures in the Urartian sources as 'the land of Qulha'. Sarduri claimed that he captured and burnt one of the royal cities of Colchis, Ildamusha, and led the inhabitants away captive. Memorial tablets made of iron were set up in prominent places in the Colchian towns.[16] What remained of royal state in Colchis was ruined a few years later, about 730 BC, when the irruptions of the Scythians and Cimmerians from the North Caucasian steppes overwhelmed the local Georgian communities, and spread panic and destruction throughout the Near East.

The predominant external social influence in Colchis from the seventh century BC onwards was that of Greek settlers from Miletus, who built up trading stations and important cities all round the eastern end of the Black Sea. Among these were Trapezus (Trebizond), Bathys (Batumi), Phasis (Poti), Dioscurias (Sukhumi) and Pitiunt (Pitsunda).[17] At the same time, flourishing towns grew up in the interior, upon the fertile plains and up lush river valleys: such a place is Vani, not far from Kutaisi, where the Georgian Academy has been excavating for a number of years. The archaeologists Nino Khoshtaria and Otar Lortkipanidze have made a number of exciting discoveries, which convey the impression of a flourishing hybrid Greco-Colchian town, where Milesian wares and Greek customs merged with those of the local Colchian populace.[18]

This is not to say that the Colchians at this period were successful in forging a strong and unified political organization. The classical authorities fail to mention any outstanding Colchian rulers. Attempts to prove the existence of a Colchian dynasty during the Hellenistic period rely on such evidence as local imitations of the gold staters of Lysimachus, in which the name of the Greek dynast has been abbreviated to 'Achus' (or 'Akes'). Apart from this fragmentary and dubious mention, we have no evidence that any King Akes ever existed at all.[19]

The fact that the Colchians, prosperous though they were, failed to leave much of a mark on the political history of Caucasia was partly due to the pestilential, malarial climate of the Rioni delta, with its unhealthy swamps.

Writers such as pseudo-Hippocrates allude in fact to the sallow, sickly and flaccid appearance of the Colchians and their indolent temperament. At one time, they were ruled by provincial dynasts known as *sceptukhs* or sceptre-bearers. Mithradates Eupator (120–63 BC), the great king of Pontus and Rome's formidable enemy in the East, brought Colchis under his sway and appointed his son, Prince Mithradates, to be viceroy. Soon afterwards this prince was charged with treason and put to death, following which governors were set over Colchis, one of them being Strabo's great-uncle Moaphernes. Pompey's invasion of Georgia in 66–65 BC brought both Colchis and Iberia into the Roman orbit. Pompey appointed a certain Aristarchus to be dynast of Colchis, as commemorated on silver coins struck in Aristarchus' name and depicting Pompey himself. Subsequently Colchis belonged to Polemo I, king of Pontus and then, until AD 23, to his widow Pythodoris. The Romans then divided Colchis into four small principalities and appointed rulers over them at their own discretion.[20]

In these circumstances, political hegemony in Georgia naturally passed into the hands of the better organized and less vulnerable new kingdom of the Iberians, which developed in central and eastern Georgia during the last four centuries BC. The Iberian nation, we have seen, represented a consolidation of ancient ethnic groupings of the Transcaucasian region, together with the remains of the Diauehi (Taokhoi), the Moskhoi (Meskhians) and other Anatolian elements. To judge by the abundance of warrior graves of the period the supremacy of the Iberians over the Scythians, Cimmerians and other Indo-European invaders of the Kura valley was not won without a struggle. The earliest cities of the Iberians were fortified strongholds like the troglodytic rock-town of Uplis-tsikhe near Gori. Later on, the political centre of Iberia moved eastwards down the river Kura to the vicinity of Mtskheta, a city whose name is sometimes explained as 'city of the Meskhians', though this etymology remains debatable. Situated at the confluence of the rivers Aragvi and Kura, Mtskheta-Armazi is the site of an enormous and ancient necropolis, that of Samtavro, and was defended by the two massive strongholds of Harmozika – Armaz-tsikhe, or 'castle of Ahura-Mazda' – situated on Mount Bagineti, and Sevsamora on the left bank of the Aragvi.[21]

Possession of ancient Iberia was a prize worth fighting for. Its wealth is revealed by the amazing splendour of gems and precious metals consigned to the earth together with the corpses of local princes and princesses, such as the so-called Akhalgori hoard of Achaemenid gold and precious objects discovered in 1908 in the Ksani valley.[22] The flourishing international trade connexions with Persia and central Asia apart, Strabo and other Greek and Roman authorities agree that whereas most tribes of the Caucasus occupied barren and cramped territories, the eastern Georgians as well as the Albanians in present-day Soviet Azerbaijan possessed 'territory that is fertile and capable of affording an exceedingly good livelihood' – statements which apply equally today. The lowland farmers, we are told, lived and dressed rather like the Medes and Armenians, while the fierce Georgian highlanders resembled the Scythians and Sarmatians, with whom they maintained constant relations. By the beginning of the Christian era the greater part of Iberia, as Strabo says, was well built up where cities and farmsteads were concerned, their houses, market places and public buildings being constructed with architectural skill.[23] These observations are amply borne out by excavations carried out over the past thirty years by the Georgian Academy of Sciences, and summarized in the Academy's own report on the Mtskheta expedition, the first volume of which appeared at Tbilisi in 1955.[24]

The political organization and social structure of pre-Christian Caucasian Iberia had much in common with contemporary Hellenizing kingdoms of Asia Minor and central Asia during the Seleucid period. The Georgian Annals (*Kartlis tskhovreba*, 'The Life of Georgia') give a picturesque, legendary version of the beginnings of kingship in Iberia, connecting it with the name of Alexander the Great, who never actually invaded Georgia at all, but is credited throughout the East with all manner of buildings and mighty feats. According to these annals, Alexander entrusted the administration of Georgia to a relative of his by the name of Azon (very likely a confusion with the name Jason, of Argonaut fame), who proved such a tyrant as to alienate not only the Georgians, but even the Greeks whom he had brought with him. The oppressed Georgians revolted under the lead of Parnavaz, a descendant of Kartlos, eponymous ancestor of the Kartvelian or Georgian nation, after whom Sakartvelo, land of the Georgians, is named. This Parnavaz was a nephew of Samara, patriarch of the Iberians of Mtskheta; with the help of King Kuji of Colchis, Parnavaz drove out Azon and his Greek mercenaries, and was recognized by the kings of Syria and Armenia as legitimate ruler of Iberia. He reorganized the army of the Kartlosids and appointed seven or eight *eristavis* or 'heads of the people', one of whom was made *spaspet* or commander in chief. These officers were each assigned one province of Georgia to govern, the spaspet being responsible for the central area of Inner Kartli, around Mtskheta and Uplistsikhe.

It seems that this office of spaspet was in fact occupied by the member of the Iberian royal family next in seniority to the king: Strabo states that in the royal hierarchy, 'the second in line administers justice and commands the army'. It is possible also to equate these high dignitaries with the viceroys of Iberia whose hereditary necropolis was uncovered in Mtskheta-Armazi, together with engraved gems bearing portraits of two of them, Zevakh and Asparukh. These viceroys bore the Iranian title of *pitiakhsh* or *bdeashkh*, roughly approximating to that of satrap. Other official and court titles of which we have record include those of royal architect and *epitropos* or lord chamberlain, or master of the court.[25]

There existed four main castes or classes in Iberian society during the classical period. These were the royal family; the priesthood; the free warriors and yeoman farmers; and 'the common people, who are slaves of the king and perform all the services that pertain to human livelihood'. The priests also acted as diplomats, in that they 'attended to all matters of controversy with the neighbouring peoples'.[26] The slaves, many of them prisoners of war, looked after the needs of the royal household and aristocracy, and toiled at public works such as the building of the enormous ramparts at the castles at Mtskheta-Armazi, Uplis-tsikhe and other centres. We must, however, agree with Academician Hagop Manandian that chattel slaves did not play a role in the economy of Classical Armenia and Georgia comparable to that played by slaves in Rome, Egypt or Greece, where they were organized and exploited on a broad industrial scale. Even at this early date, the trend was rather for Caucasian slaves to be kidnapped and sold into the larger markets of the Near East. The Heniochi, Strabo tells us, would raid the wooded regions around Colchis, hide their portable boats in the forests and 'wander on foot night and day for the sake of kidnapping people', whom they held to ransom or sold into slavery.[27] This trade later reached its climax in Ottoman times. We have little specific information about the existence of a Georgian merchant and artisan class in classical times, probably because this was composed, then as later, largely of Greeks, Armenians, Jews, Persians and other foreign elements.

From the standpoint of world history, the most dramatic era in the annals of Armenia and Georgia is certainly the titanic struggle waged over several decades by King Mithradates Eupator of Pontus in alliance with his son-in-law, King Tigranes the Great of Armenia (95–55 BC), against the encroachments of the Roman Republic in the East.

Mithradates the Great (120–63 BC) has good claim to feature prominently in the roll of Caucasian dynasts. His capital of Sinope was situated on the Black Sea coast, only a few score miles to the west of the country of the proto-Georgian tribes of the Mossynoeci, Macrones and Chalybes so vividly described in Xenophon's *Anabasis*. His long life formed a continuous drama of amazing feats of endurance and acts of heroism, combined with gruesome deeds of treachery and murder.

The personal outlook and political conduct of Mithradates were conditioned by the troubled times in which he lived. His father was assasinated by courtiers during a banquet in the royal palace in Sinope, and the young prince Mithradates found himself a precarious, puppet ruler at the age of eleven. His own mother began intriguing against his life, as she favoured the claims of a younger brother of Mithradates. So Mithradates fled to the mountains of Asia Minor, and was for several years a hunter.[28]

Returning to Sinope in 111 BC, Mithradates threw his mother into prison and later put her and his younger brother to death. Feeling himself now secure, he turned his attention to dreams of conquest and world dominion. In return for assistance against the Scythian nomads, the Greeks of the Cimmerian Bosphorus and the Tauric Chersonese recognized the suzerainty of Mithradates. As well as occupying Colchis, Mithradates seized Paphlagonia and part of Galatia; he set his son Ariarathes on the throne of Cappadocia and drove out Nicomedes III, the young king of Bithynia.

The Roman Republic saw this as a direct challenge to its vital interests in Asia Minor. The Romans restored the legitimate kings displaced by Mithradates. While hiding his resentment, Mithradates prepared for war. He had long hated the Romans, who had seized Phrygia during his minority, and he now aimed at driving them from Asia Minor altogether.

The immediate cause of the rupture was an attack on Pontic territory by King Nicomedes of Bithynia, at Roman instigation. Unable to obtain satisfaction, Mithradates declared war in 88 BC. He swiftly overran Galatia and Phrygia, defeated local Roman armies, and ordered a general massacre of all Romans resident in Asia Minor. Then Mithradates sent large armies into European Greece, and his generals occupied Athens. But Sulla in Greece and Fimbria in Asia defeated the armies of Mithradates in several pitched battles. The Greek cities were disgusted by his severity and soon threw off their allegiance to the Pontic crown. By 84 BC, Mithradates was obliged to abandon most of his conquests, conclude peace, surrender his fleet, and pay compensation of two thousand talents to the Romans.[29]

Soon the Second Mithradatic War broke out. The Roman commander Murena invaded Pontus in 83 BC, but was repelled in the following year. Hostilities lapsed, but constant disputes occurred, culminating in yet another general war in 74 BC. Mithradates defeated Cotta, the Roman consul, at Chalcedon. Then a new Roman commander, Lucullus, worsted Mithradates, and drove him to take refuge in Armenia with his son-in-law, King Tigranes II. After the victories of Lucullus and Pompey, Mithradates established himself in 64 BC at Panticapaeum in the Crimea. Though nearing his seventieth year, the dauntless old king was planning fresh campaigns against the Romans when his own troops revolted. After vainly trying to poison himself, he ordered a Gallic mercenary to kill him.[30]

Thus perished Rome's greatest enemy in Asia Minor. The body of Mithradates was sent to Pompey, who buried it in the royal mausoleum in Sinope. The fame of Mithradates became legendary from classical times onwards; his courage, bodily strength, shrewd intellect, sublety and guile were a byword throughout the civilized world. He spent much of his time in practising magic, and had so saturated his body with various poisons that his system had become invulnerable. His tragic end is the theme of a tragedy by Racine.

The meteoric career of Mithradates Eupator coincided with and contributed to the period of Armenia's greatest expansion, under King Tigranes II (95–55 BC). On succeeding to the throne, Tigranes began by conquering the neighbouring Armenian kingdom of Sophene, which belonged to a branch of the Orontid dynasty. Then, in 93 BC, he attacked Cappadocia, forcing Ariobarzanes I to seek asylum in Rome. This brought Armenia into conflict with the Roman Republic; the struggles, which lasted for several decades, have been described in detail by Plutarch, Appian and others, and form the subject of special studies by modern historians.[31]

After the conquest of Cappadocia and Sophene, and the subjugation of Commagene and neighbouring lands around the Upper Euphrates, Tigranes turned his attention to the east. Seventy valleys which Tigranes had once been compelled to cede to Parthia were recaptured, and the defeated Parthians were forced to give up additional territories in Mesopotamia. The Parthian monarchs ceded to Tigranes the title of 'King of Kings'. The post of governor of Nisibis was given to Guras, a brother of Tigranes. All these territorial expansions took place in the period from 89 to 85 BC.

The next step was the annexation of Syria, which had a more or less voluntary character: the population hoped that Tigranes would restore the empire of the Seleucids, and protect them from Roman tyranny. By 83 BC, Antioch was in Armenian hands, and rather later, parts of Cilicia, as well as Phoenicia. This vast realm was controlled, in a rather loose fashion, from the newly founded capital city of Tigranocerta, on the site of the modern Mayyafariqin, in southern Turkey.[32] Tigranocerta was populated largely by the enforced transfer of thousands of urban dwellers from Cappadocia, Cilicia and Syria, many of whom bitterly resented their migration and longed to return home.

Danger signals appeared in 70 BC, when Lucullus took charge of Roman forces in Asia Minor. He defeated Mithradates, who took refuge with his son-in-law, King Tigranes of Armenia. Lucullus sent to Tigranes an ambassador, named Appius Claudius, to demand the extradition of Mithradates, which Tigranes contemptuously refused. This Appius Claudius was a most ingenious man, who succeeded in organizing a regular Roman 'Fifth Column' within the empire of Tigranes, as well as leaving us the most vivid surviving account of the Armenian court at its apogee. It is from the account of Appius Claudius that we learn, for instance, that Tigranes had many vassal princes waiting upon him, including four who, when the king went for a ride, 'ran by his horse's side in ordinary under-frocks'; in the king's throne-room, these vassals would stand with their hands folded together in an attitude of abject humility. The report of Appius Claudius is reproduced in the Life of Lucullus by Plutarch, who also hands down the famous comment by Tigranes, when the Roman army finally arrived opposite Tigranocerta, that 'they were too many for ambassadors, and too few for soldiers'. Thus, the Roman writer adds, the Armenians 'continued sneering and scoffing'.[33]

In spite of their small number, the well disciplined Romans inflicted a crushing defeat on the vast but ill-ordered hosts of Tigranes (6 October 69 BC). After several months of siege, Tigranocerta itself was captured. Among the vast booty seized, Lucullus found eight thousand talents of coined silver money, of which each soldier received eight hundred drachmas. This is an impressive total for those days, and gives us some idea of the tremendous wealth and resources of the Armenian empire under King Tigranes the Great.

On the advice of King Mithradates Eupator, Tigranes carried out a radical reorganization of his army, with a view to employing a new and different strategy against the Roman invaders. From now on, the Armenians avoided pitched battles, and resorted to hit-and-run guerilla tactics. Lucullus advanced far into Greater Armenia, and marched on the ancient Armenian metropolis of Artaxata. However, the Romans met with a determined resistance. The Armenians mustered a strong force of Georgian auxiliaries, including a vanguard of Iberians with long spears, in whom Tigranes confided more than in any other of his foreign troops, as they were the most warlike of them all.[34]

Eventually, Lucullus was faced with a wholesale mutiny among the Roman legions, who found the climate and popular resistance among the Armenian highlanders too much for them. Lucullus was replaced by Pompey, who was joined by a son of Tigranes the Great, Tigranes the Younger by name. This Tigranes the Younger had the ambition of displacing his venerable father with Roman support and taking over the crown of Armenia for himself, though he was to be bitterly disappointed in his ambition, being finally disgraced and put to death.

Pompey completed the conquest of Armenia (66 BC) and marched forthwith into Caucasian Albania, Iberia and Colchis. The Georgians put up a tremendous resistance, climbing up into trees when defeated in open battle, and shooting down upon the Roman soldiers from the branches. In the end, the Georgians and Colchians were forced to submit. The king of Iberia sent Pompey a bedstead, table and a throne of state, all made of solid gold. Pompey, according to his biography written by Plutarch, handed all these into the custody of the public treasurers, for the use of the Roman commonwealth.[35] It is interesting to note that many gold ornaments and a bedstead fashioned in part from solid silver have been recovered by the Georgian Academy archaeological expeditions in the ancient capital of Armazi, showing that Plutarch's account is by no means fabulous or exaggerated.

From now on, Armenia became a buffer state between Rome and Parthia, while the Iberian kings of eastern Georgia were content to be clients and allies of the Roman Senate. Tigranes of Armenia reigned until 55 BC and was succeeded by his son Artavazd II, who played a crucial part in the disastrous campaign of Crassus against the Parthians (53 BC). Artavazd advised Crassus to avoid the plains of northern Syria, in favour of the mountainous regions of Armenia, in order to escape the swift manoeuvres of the Parthian cavalry. Crassus ignored Artavazd's advice, and this strategic error led directly to the annihilation of the Romans at Carrhae. Artavazd was obliged to seek a Parthian alliance, which he cemented by marrying his sister to a son of the Parthian ruler Orodes.

The rise to power of Mark Antony heralded fresh Roman campaigns against Parthia. Artavazd found it prudent to resume his alliance with Rome against Parthia (37 BC). Mark Antony now followed the advice which Artavazd had previously given to Crassus – namely, to advance on Persia by way of the Armenian highlands, and invade from the north-west. The movement of Mark Antony's huge army of Romans, Spaniards and Gauls, along with their cumbrous war machines, was an awe-inspiring sight. The nimble Parthians avoided pitched battle, but harried the Roman legions unceasingly; the Romans suffered terrible privations from hunger and thirst.

Roman losses were disastrous, and Mark Antony blamed these on Artavazd for his lukewarm support. Mark Antony decided to punish him and subdue Armenia, but first attempted to lure the Armenian king and his family to visit the court of Cleopatra in Egypt. In 34 BC, Mark Antony suddenly invaded Armenia, and carried off Artavazd and his family to Egypt, where Cleopatra had them murdered in 31 BC.[36]

Following the defeat of Mark Antony at Actium (31 BC), the Armenian nobles and the Parthians restored to power a son of the murdered Artavazd, who reigned from 30 to 20 BC as Artaxias II. After the death of Artaxias II, there followed a most confusing period of Armenian history, in which the kings of Media Atropatene, the modern Azerbaijan, played a leading part. The last legitimate king of Armenia of the Artaxiad line was Tigranes IV, who contracted a dynastic marriage with his own half-sister, Princess Erato. Tigranes IV and Erato reigned together from about 8 BC to AD I, when Tigranes was slain in a campaign against some northern barbarians.

Apart from the Urartian kings, the Artaxiads were the most powerful dynasty ever to rule in Armenia. They were eminent for their cultural, literary and administrative achievements. Artavazd II was celebrated as author of plays and other literary compositions in Greek. The Armenian coinage of the period is much prized by numismatists, and includes magnificent silver tetradrachms of Tigranes the Great struck at Antioch and Damascus, and also in Tigranocerta within Armenia.[37]

During the first century AD, the Romans consolidated their power to the north of Armenia, in Iberia. The excavations at Mtskheta-Armazi, in Iberia, not far from Tbilisi, combined with inscriptions, coin finds and the annals of Roman historians give ample proof of this Roman dominance. The Romans found a willing ally in the king of eastern Georgia, Farsman I, whose brother Mithradates was placed on the throne of Armenia with the help of the Emperor Tiberius (AD 35). A Roman garrison was installed at Garni to maintain the unpopular Georgian against the local nobility and the pro-Parthian party. Some sixteen years later, in AD 51, Mithradates was treacherously murdered by his own nephew, Rhadamist, son of the ambitious Farsman of Iberia, who had dreamt of uniting Armenia with his own kingdom of Georgia, and founding a pan-Caucasian empire. This blood-thirsty dynastic struggle, which is recounted in the *Annals* of Tacitus, forms the subject of a tragedy by the French dramatist Prosper Jolyot de Crébillon (1674–1762). (First performed in 1711, this play, entitled *Rhadamiste et Zénobie*, held the stage for a long period. This tragedy in turn provided a libretto for Handel's opera, *Radamisto*.)

This Georgian intervention and the resulting popular discontent and disorders led directly to the inauguration of a new and important Armenian dynasty, that of the Arsacids, who ruled from AD 53, until their extinction in AD 428. The first Arsacid king was Tiridates I, brother of the Parthian king Vologases I. The two Parthian brothers invaded Armenia, occupied Artaxata and Tigranocerta, and had little difficulty in getting rid of the Georgian Rhadamist.

This Parthian incursion was the signal for fresh Roman intervention in the war-torn land. The young emperor Nero's advisers appointed the seasoned general Corbulo to command the expedition charged with recovering Armenia. Corbulo found the eastern Roman legions in a deplorable condition, produced by decades of inactivity. He set himself to train them into a usable army, and the soldiers suffered nearly as much from his training as from the ensuing campaign. Two summers of drilling were followed by a winter under canvas in part of Armenia. In the piercing cold, frost-bite crippled the men, and sentries died from exposure at their posts. Deserters were executed.[38]

During Corbulo's campaign of AD 58, Artaxata was captured. Next year, the Romans advanced on Tigranocerta, whose citizens closed their gates against him. To discourage them from a long resistance, Corbulo executed a captive Armenian noble in his camp, and fired the head into the town. It landed right in the middle of a council of war, and the towns-people promptly surrendered. A Roman nominee was placed on the Armenian throne, but Tiridates counter-attacked and defeated a fresh Roman army at Rhandeia (AD 62).

Nero prudently decided to compromise. Tiridates was to receive the crown of Armenia, but from the hands of Nero in Rome. Though Tiridates was to be a client king of the Romans, Nero rightly judged that his investiture would satisfy the honour of the Parthians as well. Three years later, Tiridates made the journey to Rome. As a magus or priest of the Zoroastrian religion, he had to observe the rites which forbade him to defile water by travelling upon it, so he travelled all the way by land.[39] At Rome, in ceremonies of great pomp, Nero placed the Armenian crown on the head of Tiridates amid general rejoicing (AD 66). The Senate voted a special grant for the occasion, and sumptuous feasts and games took place, in which Tiridates himself excelled. The temple of Pompey was specially gilded for the occasion. Nero accorded Tiridates a subsidy of fifty million sestertii, perhaps worth two million dollars of modern money, and sent him home with a team of Roman masons and architects to re-build Artaxata after the ravages of Corbulo, who was soon afterwards disgraced and forced to commit suicide in AD 67.

The long and prosperous reign of Tiridates I marks a return to an Eastern, Parthian orientation in Armenian culture and religion. The period of his brother Vologases I, who reigned in Parthia until about AD 80, saw the rise to prominence of certain Oriental features in Parthian public life. For the first time, Aramaic lettering is used instead of Greek on the royal coinage. A fire altar now appears among the designs of the official coin issues, which had wide currency in Armenia. There is a Zoroastrian religious tradition which attributes the collection of the surviving manuscripts and traditions of the sacred book of the Avesta to

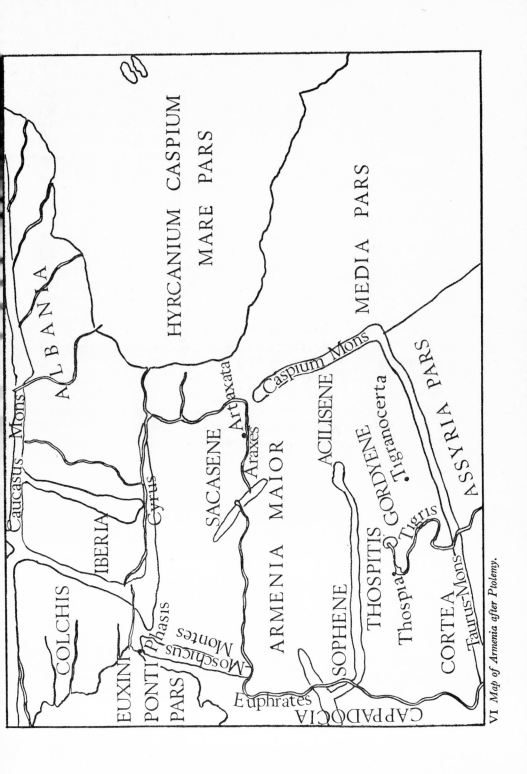

VI Map of Armenia after Ptolemy.

a Parthian king Valarsh (Vologases), who may be the same as Vologases I, brother of the founder of the Armenian Arsacid dynasty.[40]

After the Hellenistic and Romanizing phase of Armenian history, stretching from the Orontids to the advent of the Arsacids in the first century AD, a new phase of 'Iranianism' was now entered into by Armenian and Georgian society. In this new phase, the Armenian and Georgian aristocracy began to pattern itself on the Iranian, exactly as the Arsacid monarchy of Armenia tended to become institutionally a mirror of the Parthian empire.[41] Instead of the autocratic centralism characteristic of the Roman empire, the Armenians and Georgians adopted the more flexible system of feudal allegiances, which had been characteristic of Iranian state structure since Achaemenid times. Unlike the formidable army of bureaucrats, tax gatherers and provincial governors on which the Roman emperors depended, the Armenian and Georgian kings tended to rely on the loyalty of the great aristocratic houses, over whom from time to time the Armenian and Georgian kings set viceroys of their own to strengthen the wavering allegiance of their vassals. Great offices of state became hereditary in certain noble families. Thus, the Bagratids, claiming descent from Kings David and Solomon of Israel, received from King Valarsh I of Armenia (AD 117–40) the dignity of head of the royal cavalry, along with that of *tagadir* or hereditary coronant of the Armenian kings. Other noble families shared the remaining chief offices of state. These included such posts as Seneschal, Grand Chamberlain, and also High Constable. According to Moses of Khorene, King Valarsh appointed two royal secretaries, one of whom was deputed to remind him of deeds of beneficence and patronage to be fulfilled, the other of acts of vengeance to be carried out. The patronage secretary was also instructed to restrain the king from excessive severity, and to recall him whenever possible to a mood of mercy and magnanimity.

Under Tiridates I, who died about AD 100, Armenia remained a more or less docile buffer state. Nero and his immediate successors showed sense and moderation in maintaining Armenia as a neutral bastion against inroads both by nomads of the north Caucasian steppe, and by the Parthians themselves. An abrupt change in policy occurred under Trajan. Motivated, as Dio Cassius opines, by a sheer 'passion for glory', Trajan marched against Parthia in AD 113, and dethroned and killed the Armenian king, Parthamasiris. The scene is shown on an issue of Roman bronze coins, as well as on a relief reproduced on the triumphal arch of Constantine in Rome. The Armenian capital of Artashat (Artaxata) fell to the Romans soon after. The Roman occupation of Artashat was commemorated by an important inscription set up there by the Fourth Scythian Legion in AD 116, and discovered in April 1967.

(Interesting particulars of this inscription are given in the Venice journal *Pazmaveb* for 1968.) Trajan advanced into Parthia and captured Ctesiphon, while Armenia groaned for three years under the yoke of a Roman legate. After Trajan's death in AD 117, the more prudent Hadrian handed back Rome's eastern territories to their old rulers and to client kings. The throne of Armenia was now occupied by another Arsacid monarch, Valarsh I, builder of Vagharshapat, the modern Echmiadzin.

The next major event in the history of Armenia and Georgia was the conversion of both lands to Christianity early in the fourth century. The conversion of Armenia was effected in 301 by St Gregory the Illuminator, that of Iberia (eastern Georgia) by St Nino about the year 330.[42] Political conditions strongly favoured the conversion of eastern Georgia to the new official creed of the Romans, and the Iberian ruling class adopted it without a struggle. The Georgians, with the Armenians, became an outpost of Christendom in the East, their cultural and social life being henceforth deliberately orientated away from the culture of Zoroastrian Iran and later, the Islamic civilization of the Arab world, towards the great centres of Orthodox Christianity, with all that this entailed in the field of social life and material culture generally.

The structure of the Georgian monarchy necessarily underwent fundamental changes as a result of the adoption of Christianity as the state religion. The old pagan kings of Iberia, it seems, were theophanic monarchs in the Anatolian and Mesopotamian style, and their cosmocratic claims, evolved in the course of the first century of our era, manifested themselves in the title of Great King.[43] They had already advanced far since the days when the *mamasakhlisi* or father of the tribe residing at Mtskheta was revered by his peers as *primus inter pares* among the Georgian dynasts. No doubt the examples of 'Divus Augustus' and Claudius the God, whose friends and allies the Iberian kings were proud to be, encouraged them even further in their pretensions. The cosmological aspect of the Iberian political theophany appears obvious from the number – seven – of the *eristavs* or dukes subordinate to the Iberian Great King at this period, symbolizing so it seems the seven circumsolar planets. The break with the past brought about by Iberia's conversion to Christianity also coincided with the inauguration of a new dynasty in eastern Georgia. The Iberian Arsacids had recently become extinct, and Mirian (later canonized as St Mirian), the first Christian king of Georgia, was also the first ruler of the new Chosroid dynasty, who were themselves a branch of the Iranian Mihranids, one of the Seven Great Houses of the Persian Empire.

The Chosroids ruled in Iberia for over two centuries, until the institution of monarchy was abolished for the time being by the Persians in the course of the sixth century. They had a strong sense of family solidarity – the *Life of Peter the Iberian* (a Georgian saintly man prominent in the religious schisms of Byzantium) speaks of Peter's father reigning conjointly with his two uncles 'according to the custom of the Iberian royal house'.[44] However, the royal family had constant difficulty in keeping in check their own unruly vassals. The Crown, naturally enough, regarded the ducal fiefs of Iberia as non-inheritable, exactly as the office of high constable was non-inheritable; the members of the princely class, who provided the mainstay of the feudal order, tended to treat them as hereditary apanages. The Crown's attempts to control ducal succession were resented and resisted, the consequent tensions contributing to the downfall of the monarchy in the sixth century.

The Georgian feudal system took on definitive shape at this early period, and continued in being right up to the Russian annexation in 1801. It developed features similar to institutions characterizing Western Christendom in the later Middle Ages. In fact, it used to be thought that Georgia's feudal system derived from the influence of the Crusaders, remnants of whom, still clad in medieval chain armour, were mistakenly discerned in the picturesque, old-world Georgian mountain tribe of the Khevsurs.[45] But it is now clear that analogies are rather to be sought in Byzantium and Sassanian Iran, whence the Chosroid dynasty actually hailed. Here, under the Sassanian Great Kings, royal power rested on a delicate balance between feudal allegiance and bureaucratic absolutism. Under the supreme authority of the King of Kings was a motley assemblage of vassal rulers, provincial satraps and the four *bdeashkh* (or *pitiakhsh*, 'guardians of the marches' – a title often encountered in old Georgian sources), also chiefs of clans – certain of them hereditary dynasts, others being viceroys appointed by the king. Beneath these were ranged the nobles and knights, some of them vassals of the princes, others owing direct allegiance to the sovereign. At the lower end of the scale came the peasants – free yeomen and serfs, rather than chattel slaves – who followed their lords into battle, and formed the rank and file of the Persian army. It is of a similar social hierarchy on a smaller scale of which the fifth century author of the *Martyrdom of St Shushanik* gives us a glimpse when he speaks of 'the grandees and noble ladies, the gentry and common folk of the land of Georgia'.[46]

Whereas the Iberian kings, possibly for reasons of state, adopted Christianity quite readily, paganism did not give up its hold on the populace without a struggle. In some cases, it simply adopted a Christian colouring and went underground, so to speak, persisting in various guises in remote Caucasian glens right up to the present day. The *Life of St Nino* relates how King Mirian and one of his dukes summoned the mountain clans, men of wild and savage appearance, and preached the Gospel to them. But they refused to be baptized. So the royal duke turned the sword on them and cast down their idols by force. The king laid heavy taxes upon those who did not wish to receive baptism, who therefore banded together and became nomads. Some of these were converted by St Abibos of Nekresi (a holy man of the sixth century), but others have remained heathen until the present day.[47]

At a place called Kola in south-western Georgia, a group of heathen parents hurled their children, aged between seven and nine years, into a pit and stoned them to death rather than submit to their conversion to Christianity; these children are numbered among the martyrs of the Georgian Church.

In some instances, the adoption of Christianity, by imposing standards of conduct and morality higher than those socially acceptable to the people of that age, brought with it personal and domestic problems of an acute kind. An Armenian noble lady named Shushanik, for example, was married to a Georgian governor, Varsken, who abjured Christianity in favour of Mazdaism in order to curry favour with the Persians. Shushanik refused to take part in a carousal where men and women were eating and drinking together, upon which her depraved husband

> began to utter foul-mouthed insults and kicked her with his foot. Picking up a poker, he crashed it down on her head and split it open and injured one of her eyes. And he struck her face unmercifully with his fist and dragged her to and fro by her hair, bellowing like a wild beast and roaring like a madman.

After seven years of such ordeals, eaten up by ulcers and vermin and kept in close captivity, the saintly princess finally expired.[48] Her tormentor Varsken was ultimately put to death by the Georgian King Vakhtang Gorgaslan, who reigned from about 446 to 510, and features in Georgian history as a Caucasian 'King Arthur' of knightly prowess and valiant feats of arms.

In both Armenia and Georgia, the adoption of Christianity eventually contributed to the downfall of the independent monarchies there. Instead of supporting their sovereigns against the Sassanian Great Kings, the bishops aided and abetted the feudal lords in their disloyal intrigues. The patriarchs in both countries set themselves up as independent centres of authority, rivalling the royal power. The Armenian monarchy of the Arsacids was abolished in 428, at the instigation of the powerful barons; the Iberian monarchy succumbed in the following century, though that of Lazica on the Black Sea continued in vigorous existence for a considerable time.

Even without monarchs to lead them, the nobility and people of Armenia and Georgia put up a dogged fight for their land and faith, first against the Sassanians, and then against the Arabs. One famous event was the Battle of Avarayr on 2 June 451, in which sixty-six thousand Armenians under Prince Vardan Mamikonian encountered an army of two hundred and twenty thousand Persians, reinforced by squadrons of armoured elephants. Although the Persians won the day, the carnage was so great that they gave up their dream of converting Armenia to the Zoroastrian religion.

In the seventh century, Iran and Caucasia succumbed to the power of Islam. Viceroys of the caliphs of Damascus and Baghdad sat in Dvin, the administrative capital of Armenia, and in Tbilisi (Tiflis). Terrible reprisals took place against the local Christian population, though without crushing their proud spirit.[49] These patriotic wars against the Saracens find their expression in the Armenian popular epic cycle, *David of Sassoun*. Many Armenians emigrated into various parts of the Byzantine Empire, as far afield as Bulgaria and Constantinople; more than one of them occupied the Imperial throne, notably the unpopular Leo the Armenian, who reigned from 813 to 820, and was then murdered by a group of conspirators.[50]

While the Georgian monarchy was in abeyance, a new and virile ruling family was rising to prominence in the marchlands of Georgia and Armenia. This was the clan of the Bagratids, who were to unify Georgia under a single crown and reign there for a thousand years. Although the Bagratids claimed for prestige purposes to be descended from David and Solomon of Israel, they were in reality princes of Speri (Ispir), in the Upper Chorokhi valley north of Erzurum, and had a castle at the modern Bayburt. The family first attained the highest dignities of state in the Armenian kingdom, and then spread into Georgia. Towards the end of the eighth century, Ashot Bagration, 'the Great', settled at Artanuji in Tao, south-western Georgia, receiving from the Byzantine emperor the title of kuropalates or 'guardian of the palace'. As time went on, Ashot profited by the relative weakness of the emperors at Constantinople and the Arab caliphs of Baghdad, and set himself up as hereditary prince in Iberia.

In Armenia also a national revival took place, gathering momentum during the ninth century. Here, the outstanding figure was another Bagratid prince, also called Ashot the Great, but coming from a different branch of the family from that of Kuropalates Ashot of Iberia. The Armenian Ashot the Great was high constable from 856. Six years later, in 862, the caliph granted him the title of 'Prince of Princes of Armenia, of Georgia, and of the lands of the Caucasus'. Ashot the Great succeeded in winning the trust both of the Arabs and of his own compatriots. Urged by the catholicos of Armenia, the Armenian nobles ultimately sank their differences and resolved to appoint Ashot as their king. The caliph of Baghdad ratified their choice in 885, by sending Ashot a royal crown, and naming him 'King of Kings'. The Byzantine emperor soon followed suit and also sent Ashot a crown and royal gifts.[51]

Though the caliphate might show goodwill towards the new Armenian monarchy, local Muslim rulers were far from being reconciled to its existence. The Muslim dynasty of the Sajids, nominally vassals of the caliph, were building themselves a powerful state in Azerbaijan, which Armenia found to be an implacable foe. The reign of Ashot's son, King Smbat I the Martyr (890–914), was occupied with struggles against the *amirs* of Dvin and of Manzikert, as well as with dynastic quarrels with his uncle, the High Constable Abas of Siunia and Vaspurakan. Smbat was harassed by the repeated incursions of the Sajid amirs Afshin and Yusuf, treacherously egged on by the Ardsruni princes of Vaspurakan. In 908, Amir Yusuf proclaimed the Ardsruni prince Khachik-Gagik of Vaspurakan as king of Armenia, so that the country was divided into two rival monarchies. Eventually, the Amir Yusuf invaded Armenia at the head of an army, and besieged King Smbat in his fortress. In 913, King Smbat capitulated to Yusuf under promise of amnesty, but the perfidious amir cast the king into a dungeon, and crucified him the following year, after inflicting inhuman tortures upon him.

Even these tragic events could not reverse the economic and social revival of Armenia, which had gathered momentum under Ashot the Great. According to the chronicler Asoghik:

In the days of Smbat I and in those of the rule of his father, peace reigned everywhere in our land, and each one, in the words of the Prophet, dwelt safely under his vine and under his fig-tree. The fields became settlements, and the settlements cities in their population and wealth, so that even the shepherds began to appear in silk garments.[52]

Naturally the reference by Asoghik to shepherds in silk garments is pure hyperbole, but his general optimism is shared by another historian, John the Catholicos:

And in those days the Lord showed benevolence to our land of Armenia, he defended her and favoured her in all good undertakings. At that time all dwelt in their inherited possessions, and having appropriated the land, they set out vineyards and planted olive trees and gardens, they ploughed up fields among the thorns and gathered a harvest an hundred fold. The barns were filled with wheat after the harvest and the cellars were filled with wine after the gathering of the grapes. The mountains rejoiced since the herds of cattle and of sheep multiplied on them. Our chief *nakharars*, feeling themselves safe from plundering raids, built stone churches in isolated spots, villages and settlements, and covered them heavily with whitewash.[53]

The son and successor of the martyred Smbat, King of Kings Ashot the Iron (914–28) rid the country of Muslim marauders and re-established public order and security. Armenia reached the apogee of power, prosperity, and cultural achievement under his successors: Ashot's brother Abas I (928–52), who set up his capital at Kars; the son of Abas, Ashot III the Merciful (952–77) who transferred the capital to Ani; and then the sons of Ashot the Merciful, Smbat II, the Conqueror (977–89) and Gagik I (989–1020).

However, there were already signs of potential fragmentation and decay of the body politic. Ashot the Merciful split off the district of Kars-Vanand and granted it, with the title of King, to his younger brother Mushegh. In 970, Smbat of Siunia proclaimed himself king of the north-eastern marches. The kingdom of the Ardsrunis of Vaspurakan, centred on the Aghtamar and Lake Van region, was further partitioned into several apanages. The division spread into the realm of the Church, so that from 969 and 972 there were simultaneously two rival catholicos-patriarchs, each one supported by a different Armenian king.

During the eleventh century, Georgia and Armenia were overtaken by events which wiped large areas of both countries off the map, and might well have led to the extinction of the population of both countries. First, the ruthless Byzantine emperor Basil II (976–1025), known as 'the Bulgar-Slayer', stormed into Caucasia in 1021, annexed the independent Armenian kingdom of Vaspurakan (round Lake Van), and seized large areas of southern Georgia, notably Tao, Kola, Ardahan and Javakheti. Fresh trouble broke out following the accession of Emperor Constantine Monomachus (1042–54), who, with incredible folly, abolished and annexed the Bagratid kingdom of Armenia centred on Ani, and replaced the tough Armenian frontier guards with his own unreliable mercenaries.

Retribution overtook the Greeks during the 1060s, when the Seljuq Turks from Central Asia began to surge into Armenia and Anatolia from the direction of Persia, which they had occupied with comparative ease. The Turks captured Ani in 1064, Armenian resistance having been sapped by Byzantine oppression. From 1066, the Seljuqs raided deep into Georgian territory, as recorded in a notable inscription by the Georgian chronicler Leonti Mroveli, carved in the Trekhvi caves in Kartli province.[54]

The downfall of eastern Christendom in this area occurred in 1071, at the battle of Manzikert, north of Lake Van. The forces of Seljuq Sultan Alp-Arslan dealt a crushing defeat to the Byzantines, capturing Emperor Romanus IV Diogenes. The king of Georgia, Bagrat IV, died in the following year, and suzerainty over that ravaged land passed to his mediocre son, Giorgi II.

The flow of emigrants from Armenia, now overrun by the Turkish ethnic element, turned into a torrent. They went to the Crimea, Russia,

Rumania, Poland, Byzantium, and to the lands of the caliphate. But above all, they succeeded in founding in Cilicia, on the Mediterranean coast, a remarkable new kingdom, that of Cilician Armenia.[55] This realm was ruled by the Armenian Rupenid dynasty, then by the Lusignans, for Cilician Armenia owed its survival partly to the Frankish Crusaders, and derived many features of its wonderful art and culture from them. The Cilician Armenian state lasted from around 1080 right up to the final onslaught by the Mamluk Sultan of Egypt, in 1375; it figures in the travel narrative of Marco Polo, as does Greater Armenia and the Caucasus.

Within the Caucasian area, hegemony of the Christian nations passed to the Georgians, whose lands lay north of the main corridor of Turkish invasion, and were defended by high mountains and rugged terrain. King David the Builder (1089–1125) was aided by the arrival of the Crusaders in the Near East, and the consequent disarray of the Saracens. A great reformer and statesman, David was also renowned as a military leader, and routed the Seljuq Turks several times. He annexed large tracts of the former Armenian kingdom; eventually, in 1122, David succeeded in gaining possession of the ancient capital city of Georgia, Tbilisi, which had for centuries been in the hands of a dynasty of Muslim amirs, who defied the Christian kings of Georgia. A unique portrait coin of David the Builder in his royal regalia is preserved in the British Museum.[56]

The great work of David the Builder was ably continued by his grand-daughter Queen Tamar (1184–1213), who was appointed co-regnant of Georgia already in 1178 by her father Giorgi III, during his own lifetime. Tamar married first of all a dissolute scion of the Russian Bogolyubskoi family of Suzdal, whom she eventually divorced for sexual misconduct of an unnatural kind and expelled from the kingdom, though not without bloody civil strife. In 1189 Tamar married David Soslan, an Ossetian prince with Bagratid blood in his veins. She bore him the future King Giorgi Lasha (1213–23) and Queen Rusudan (1223–45). At the outset of Tamar's reign, there was a movement to limit the royal prerogative by setting up a kind of House of Lords, with authority matching that of the sovereign. Unlike the efforts of the barons under King John, Tamar's English contemporary, this Georgian constitutional movement came to naught; it seems to have been devoid of popular support, and had as its aim the substitution for the relatively popular monarchy of a system of oligarchy which would certainly have been even more oppressive for the urban proletariat and peasant classes.

Among the many political and military triumphs of Tamar's reign, special interest attaches to the foundation of the Empire of Trebizond.[57] This came about as a result of the capture and sacking of Constantinople in 1204 by an army of Frankish desperadoes and freebooters styling themselves the Fourth Crusade. The Byzantine empire being thus dismembered, Tamar and her Georgians occupied Trebizond and areas of the Black Sea coast still further westward. A scion of the imperial family of the Comneni, Alexius, who had been educated in Georgia, was placed at the head of the new and independent empire of Trebizond, which continued its existence right up to the year 1461, when the city was taken by the Ottoman Sultan Muhammad II. It is interesting to note that local imitations of the silver aspers of Trebizond, known as Kirmaneuli after Kyr or Emperor Manuel who reigned from 1238 to 1263, formed the basic coinage of western Georgia for about two centuries. In 1208, the Georgians sent an expeditionary force into Persia and occupied Ardebil; they later raided Tabriz and Kazvin. A Georgian dynasty, the Beshkenids, ruled the important town and district of Ahar in Persian Azerbaijan for several generations.

At its apogée the Georgian kingdom was a political organism of great complexity, with a large bureaucracy and sophisticated social hierarchy. The monarch ruled by the doctrine of divine right, though strong feudal institutions prevented the royal power from degenerating into sheer depotism. The central administration was headed by five senior vizirs or ministers: the high chancellor (an office long associated with the dignity of archbishop of Tchqondidi), the war minister, the lord chamberlain, the chancellor of the exchequer, and the atabag or high constable, each with a staff of subordinate officials. This administrative structure has been especially well analyzed by W.E.D.Allen in his *History of the Georgian People*, on the basis of contemporary charters and other documents. The *eristavis* or dukes who ruled the provinces were nominally subject to removal by the sovereign; when they died, their heir was supposed to submit their sword of office to the king, and await the sovereign's pleasure. In practice, it usually proved hard for any Georgian monarch to remove such vassals from their rocky castles without resorting to civil war. It is interesting to note that several official titles, through long tenure in one princely line, actually became used as regular surnames, for instance Amilakhvari, originally 'master of the royal stables', Amirejibi, 'master of the chamber', Meghvinetukhutsesi, 'chief wine steward', as well as Eristavi or 'duke', with its common Russianized form Eristov.

The Orthodox Church of Georgia bulked large in the country's life, and battling bishops led their troops into the fray alongside the armies of the king. The Church had wide powers of jurisdiction in the field of morals and private conduct, a monopoly of education, as well as enormous economic privileges, grants of land, and valuable immunities and benefactions.

In Tamar's time, the Georgian feudal system reached its high point; fiefs, and arrière fiefs, allodium and immunity, vassalage, investiture and homage – all these familiar terms of Western feudalism had their equivalents in the social system of medieval Georgia.[58] The nation was divided into the categories of *patroni* (from Latin patronus) and *qma*, which could mean alternatively vassal or serf – hence the Georgian word for feudalism, *patron-qmoba*. One of the features of the new centralized power of the Georgian state at this period was a marked deterioration in status of the free husbandmen or *mdabiuri* – a class whose importance had already been stressed by Strabo in classical times. By the reign of Tamar, the increasing power of the *aznauris* or squires, the bishops and priors, and the royal officials and tax-collectors was imposing intolerable strains on these yeomen farmers, who also bore the brunt of many expensive wars. The majority were eventually reduced to a semi-servile condition, though the highlanders of the Caucasus mountains retained their traditional liberties right up to the end of the monarchy in 1801.

Armenian and Georgian medieval law codes provide copious information on the feudal institutions and laws of both countries. Frankish influences predominated in Cilician Armenia, with its close links with the Crusaders. It is interesting that the medieval law code known as *The Assizes of Antioch* has survived only in its Armenian recension, which was made in 1265 by High Constable Smbat, brother of King Hetum I. Among local Armenian lawgivers, pride of place belongs to Mkhitar Gosh (1133–1213), whose code enjoyed such authority among the various Armenian communities abroad that it was translated into Latin, Georgian, Polish, Russian and even Qipchak.

The royal legislation of Georgia was codified by King Giorgi the Brilliant (1314–46).[59] The Georgian codes are valuable from the sociological viewpoint, since they lay down the varying amounts of blood money or wergild which were payable by the guilty party in cases where members of different ranks in the social hierarchy were killed or wounded. We also have in Georgia and Armenia the system of establishing guilt or innocence by ordeal. The principal tests applied were hot iron, boiling water, and single combat.

CHAPTER 7

PAGANISM, HELLENISM, CHRISTIANITY

The ancient cults and beliefs of Armenia and Georgia provide a fascinating theme for research. Their origins stretch back into remote prehistory. We have only to think of the zoomorphic clay hearths of Early Bronze Age Armenia, and of the forbidding clay idols of Late Bronze Age times; of the *vishaps* or dragon stones, which mark the sources of Urartian or pre-Urartian irrigation systems;[1] of the procession of hierophants portrayed on a silver goblet from Middle Bronze Age Trialeti; and above all, of the sophisticated pantheon of Urartu, headed by the supreme god Haldi.

The ascendancy of the Armenian elements over the Urartian, and then the coming of the Medes and Persians and of the Greeks, did not wipe out these age-old beliefs and rituals. They simply added a fresh dimension to native Anatolian and Caucasian traditions. Symptomatic of this is the adaptation of the Urartian Haldi temple at Arin-berd or Erebuni by the Persian Achaemenids, who converted it into an *apadana* or assembly hall, for use in connection with the religion of Zoroaster. While there was considerable change in the official religious ideology of Armenia and Georgia during the Achaemenid period, continuity with earlier periods was certainly an important factor.

The complex structure of Armenian paganism took on definite shape during the age of the Orontid dynasty and the early Artaxiads.

In addition to the famous temple of the Sun and the Moon at Armavir, the Armenians maintained a whole group of sanctuaries and shrines in the holy forest at Ashtishat (Acesilene), in the province of Taron, not far from Muş.[2] There a row of imposing temples stood, the most renowned dedicated to the goddess Anahit. A golden statue of this patron and protectress of Armenia dominated an immense hall. When the Roman armies of Mark Antony brought fire and sword to Armenia, the first soldier to lay a sacrilegious hand on the statue of the goddess was struck blind on the spot.[3]

Anahit's father was Aramazd, the Ahura-Mazda of the Iranians, corresponding in the minds of the ancient Armenians to Olympian Zeus of the Greek pantheon. From Armenia the cult of Ahura-Mazda spread northwards into Georgia, where the deity gave his name to the royal city and acropolis of Armazi, not far from Tbilisi.

The pantheon of ancient Armenia was an international, syncretic one. Native, local gods were worshipped side by side with deities imported both from Greek mythology and from the Iranian world, as well as survivals from the ancient cults which had derived from the era of Urartu. Often, there existed two or three embodiments of the same divine personage: Aramazd/Ahura-Mazda/Zeus is a case in point.

The ancient Armenians attached great significance to oracles and divination. Moses of Khorene tells how Ara, great-grandson of Arma;

adopted a boy who was of the seed of Anushavan, dedicated to the cult of the plane-tree, richly endowed and intelligent in word and deed. The child was consecrated to serve the cult of the plane-trees of Aramaneak, centred in Armavir. According to the rustling of their leaves, and their movement, men used for long ages to carry on divination in the land of the descendants of Haik.[4]

All this presents an illuminating parallel with the venerable oracle of Dodona in Epirus, seat of the most ancient of all Hellenic sanctuaries. The temple of Dodona was dedicated to Zeus. The method of gathering responses was by listening to the rustling of an old oak tree – perhaps a remnant of very primitive tree worship. Sometimes auguries were taken from doves cooing in the branches, the murmur of a fountain, or the clanging of brazen cauldrons hung – as also in the shrines of Urartu – round the tree or the temple building. It was from the oracle of Dodona that Lysander sought sanction for his ambitions, while the Athenians frequently appealed to its authority. Of additional interest is the discovery at Armavir of a Greek votive inscription mentioning a 'pinakion', which is a clay or pottery tablet on which questions to be put to the oracle were inscribed in advance. The same word exists in Armenian in the form *pnak*, meaning a saucer or dish.

Among the most universal cults of the ancient Armenians was that of Mithra, who was identified on the one hand with the sun, or Helios, on the other, with Apollo and Hermes. Mithra was originally conceived of as a kind of angel, a power of light who fights on the side of Ahura-Mazda. This warlike characteristic he seems always to have retained. Names compounded of his, for instance, Mithradates, and also Buz-Mihr ('Great Mithra'), were common in both Armenia and Georgia. Mithra's festival, the Mithrakana, was celebrated in Iranian lands on the sixteenth day of the seventh month, and survived in modified form right up to Muslim times. Through Cilicia the cult of Mithra spread to Rome, and thence as far as London and other remote areas of the Roman empire. The typical bas-relief, which is found in abundance in the museums of Europe, represents Mithra in the form of a youth with a conical cap and flying drapery, slaying the sacred bull, the scorpion attacking the animal's genitals, the serpent drinking its blood, the dog springing towards the wound in its side, and frequently in addition, the sun god, his messenger the raven, a fig-tree, a lion, an ewer, and torch bearers.[5] The head of the divine hierarchy of Mithra was Infinite Time; Heaven and Earth were his offspring, and begat Ocean. From Heaven and Earth sprang the remaining members of a circle analogous to the Olympic gods. Ahriman, embodiment of evil and darkness, was also the son of Time. Mithra was the most important member of the circle, the mediator between man and the supreme god.

The antiquity of the cult of Mithra in Armenia can be judged from the presence of a High Priest of that name, a member of the royal Orontid family, at the shrine of Armavir around 200 BC; also by the prominence accorded to the composite deity Apollo-Mithra-Helios-Hermes, portrayed in the funeral monument of King Antiochus I of Commagene at Nemrut Dağ. In the form 'Meherr', Mithra features later in the Armenian national epic *David of Sassoun* as the Great Meherr, Lion of Sassoun, who planted a splendid garden in Dzovasar and filled it with every kind of animal and fowl which God had created, and made his summer mansion there; he also founded a hermitage to which the sick, maimed and blind repaired for comfort and healing.[6]

The arrival of Hellenism in the East with Alexander the Great and his successors started off a veritable symbiosis – the wholesale syncretism of Greek with Oriental divinities – which affected both Armenia and Parthia. Henceforth Semitic, including Babylonian, also Iranian and Greek deities began to be considered identical and even interchangeable. Ahura-Mazda became the Iranian equivalent of Bel, Mithra of Shamash, and Anahit, the 'Mother of Armenia', of Ishtar or Nanai. In Armenia itself, Ishtar was worshipped in the guise of Astghik, sister of Anahit; Astghik was the Armenian Venus, a voluptuous goddess of maternity and amorous delights. Nanai reappears as the Armenian Naneh, patron saint of warriors and of virgins.

As time went on, the gods and goddesses of Hellas became hopelessly intermingled in Armenia with those of the Iranian and the Meso-potamian world. Temple prostitution was practised at the shrines of Anahit, the mother of Armenia, doubtless in imitation of Babylonian and Syrian custom.[7]

Astghik's lover was the Iranian god Verethragna, god of war and victory, known in Armenian as Vahagn. Venerated in the guise of Hercules the dragon slayer, Vahagn was also identified with Ares, the Greek god of battle, son of Zeus and Hera. Vahagn was a solar deity, in support of which one may cite an Armenian pre-Christian song which runs:

> In travail were heaven and earth,
> In travail, too, the purple sea!
> The travail held in the sea
> The small red reed.
> Through the hollow of the stalk came forth smoke,
> Through the hollow of the stalk came forth flame,
> And out of the flame the little boy ran!
> Fiery hair had he,
> Ay, too, he had a flaming beard,
> And his eyes, they were as suns![8]

Another prominent Armenian god was Tir, from whose name derives that of Tiridates given to several Armenian kings. Tir, originally Tishtrya, is another Iranian deity, leader of the Stars of Ahura-Mazda against the Planets of Angra-Mainyu, the Spirit of Evil. Tishtrya was identified with the star Sirius, and he brought rain regularly to the earth, after conquering the Demon of Drought. Among the Armenians, Tir became a God of Oracles and of Dreams, and was a defender of the arts and letters. Later on, he became associated with Apollo and Hermes of the Greek pantheon. He acted as the scribe or recording angel of Aramazd. To this day, Armenian folklore assigns to Tir the task of registering when a man is about to die.

Special herds and flocks were kept for the purpose of affording sacrifices to the gods and goddesses of the Armenian pantheon. We have an illustration of this in Plutarch's *Life of Lucullus* where we read of the crossing of the Euphrates by the Roman general and his army. Lucullus met with a lucky omen on landing on the Armenian side of the river:

> Holy heifers are pastured on purpose for Diana Persia (Anahit) whom, of all the gods, the barbarians beyond Euphrates chiefly adore. They use these heifers only for her sacrifices. At other times, they wander up and down undisturbed, with the mark of the goddess, a torch, branded on them; and it is no such light or easy thing, when occasion requires, to seize one of them. But one of these, when the army had passed the Euphrates, coming to a rock consecrated to the goddess, stood upon it, and then, laying down her neck, like others that are forced down with a rope, offered herself to Lucullus for sacrifice.[9]

We have few idols or images surviving to testify to the character of Armenian paganism of the Hellenistic type. The early Armenian Christians took the Biblical prohibition of graven images very seriously, and melted down or otherwise disposed of virtually all the statuary left over from the classical phase of Armenian civilization. All the more interest attaches to a bronze head of Aphrodite/Anahit, which has been in the British Museum Greek and Roman Gallery for nearly a century. This head, about one and half times life size, is from a colossal statue of Aphrodite/Anahit, reputedly from Satala, the modern Sadagh, in eastern Anatolia, not far from Erzincan. This place is memorable as the site of the Emperor Trajan's encampment in Armenia during his campaign of AD 113; here, Trajan deposed the Armenian king Parthamasiris, who was soon afterwards treacherously murdered by the Romans.

It might be expected that the accession of a Parthian king in the person of Tiridates I would herald a rejection of the Greco-Roman pantheon in favour of purely Iranian gods. Tiridates himself was a Magian, who indeed was prepared to ride for nine months round the Mediterranean to Nero's court at Rome, rather than pollute the elements of the sea by undertaking a voyage by boat. However, the Arsacids never adopted full Zoroastrianism. The Sassanians would not recognize either the Parthian or the Armenian Arsacids as true believers, and it was only with the persecutions of Yezdegird in the fifth century that a sustained effort was made to convert Armenia to official, state Zoroastrianism.

The Parthians were a tolerant nation. They indulged in a widespread cult of the deified monarch, who was sometimes called 'Brother of the Sun and Moon'. At the same time, the Magi were respected by the king, and each Arsacid had a royal fire burning continually for him. Parthian coins also show an abundance of Greek deities – Victory, Tyche, Zeus, Artemis, and so on. Jews were numerous in Armenia and Parthia, and proselytized without hindrance. In Bactria and the eastern provinces, Buddhism had a strong foothold.

It may be that in Armenia, as in Parthia, Greek religion and culture were largely a preserve of the upper classes and urban bourgeoisie. But worship of the Greek gods and goddesses was widespread and pervasive. Hymns to Apollo were engraved at Susa. Statuettes of Zeus, Heracles, Athena, Aphrodite and other deities have been found in many Parthian city sites. But whenever Greek cults are involved in the Parthian and Armenian context, there is always the chance that they may be Oriental deities in disguise.[10]

This rather sophisticated mythology was not entirely comprehensible to the Armenian masses, especially the peasantry. But many feasts and festivals dear to the Armenian people have their roots in these pre-Christian days. Such is the festival of Navasart, when Anahit is worshipped in song, dances, and an abundance of flowers and leafy blossoms. Again, the festival of Vardavar, 'the bearing of roses', celebrated in August, was marked by processions and dances in honour of the goddesses Astghik and Anahit. A vivid evocation of this festival occurs in the novel *Samuel* by the Armenian novelist Raffi, or Akop Melik-Akopian (1835–88).

The temples of pagan Armenia were numerous, both in the country and in the cities. There were special temple-towns, such as Ashtishat and Bagavan, containing several important sanctuaries. Christian churches and monasteries later succeeded to the wealth and the veneration belonging to those ancient sacred sites. These shrines, like Holy Echmiadzin today, were often the scenes of great concourses of people gathered for worship and religious festivities. Treasure houses were attached to each shrine, often exceedingly rich in images, gold and jewels. Hospitality was accorded to strangers, in the form of meat, flowers, fruit and even money. Agathangelos gives an account of the sacrifices offered up by one victorious monarch after a successful campaign:

He commanded to seek out the seven great altars of Armenia, and he honoured the sanctuaries of his ancestors, the Arsacids, with white bullocks, white rams, white horses and mules, with gold and silver ornaments and gold embroidered and fringed silken coverings, with golden wreaths, silver sacrificial basins, desirable vases set with precious stones, splendid garments, and beautiful ornaments. Also he gave a fifth of his booty and great presents to the priests.

The priesthood was hereditary in a well-organized caste. The high priest was sometimes of royal blood, and exercised political power as the repository of secret lore and wisdom, and of knowledge of omens and auguries. Two families, those of the Vahunis and the Spandunis, are mentioned as furnishing a cadre of qualified priests to the temples of pagan Armenia. The priests were certainly very wealthy, since we hear of the confiscation of great riches from them by St Gregory the Illuminator, after Armenia's conversion to Christianity. Priestesses were also much in evidence, especially in connection with such popular divinities as Anahit and Astghik.

Finds of ancient bronze statuettes with fantastic headdresses and mummers' costumes suggest that early pagan festivals were accompanied by elaborate mimes and dramatic spectacles. This helps to explain the hostility of the early Armenian Church to every manifestation of the drama and the theatrical arts.

Armenian popular superstitions and demonology, also cults connected with witchcraft, have their roots in the country's pagan past. The *daeva* or demon spirit of the Avesta was feared in Armenia, as also in Georgia; the Armenian form is *dev*, the Georgian, *devi*. The devs haunted stony places and ruins; they appeared as serpents and in other monstrous forms, some corporeal, other incorporeal. Then there were the *druzhes*; like their Avestan counterparts, these were lying, perjuring and harmful spirits, believed to be of female sex. The *yatus* or sorcerers of the Avesta had their Armenian counterparts, who were even able to slay men.

There were destructive female demons known as *parik*, whose husbands were called *kaj*. These *kajis* feature prominently in medieval Georgian literature, including Shota Rustaveli's romantic epic, *The Man in the Panther's Skin*.

Among ancient pagan superstitions may be mentioned fear of the evil eye. Moses of Khorene, for instance, records that King Ervand had so powerful an evil eye that he could break stones in pieces merely by gazing fixedly at them. The general belief was that people on whom the evil eye was cast pined away, without even knowing the cause of their ailment, and that nobody is safe from it. This superstition has persisted right up to modern times. It is said that the ancient Armenians had the same aversion for parings of nails and hair as was common among the Iranians, arising from the teachings of the Avesta. The sacred character of fire, of course, also had its roots in Iranian religious beliefs, as did the taboo on the defilement of water, particularly running water – a valuable sanitary precaution in the East.

Ancient Armenian literature and mythology contains frequent mention of *vishaps*. These were corporeal beings, acolytes of the huge stone dragon and fish-like monsters erected in Urartian and earlier times in connection, it seems, with ancient irrigation systems. These vishaps could appear either as men or as serpents, and could soar away into the air with the help of oxen. They were fond of carrying away grain from the threshing floor, brazenly assuming the shape of mules and camels to do this. In such cases, the fifth century Armenian writer Eznik tells us, the Armenians would call out: 'Kal, kal!' ('Stop, stop!') These vishaps would even suck the milk from cows. Some vishaps went hunting on horseback, and lived in comfortable mansions. They kept royal princes and heroes captive, among these being Alexander the Great and King Artavazd of Armenia. They sometimes appeared enormous, and compelled men to do obeisance to them. They also entered into human beings and their breath was poisonous. There was a whole colony of them at the foot of Masis (Mount Ararat), with whom Vahagn fought; later these vishaps stole the child Artavazd and left an infant dev in his stead.

Allied to the vishaps were the *nhangs*, a term borrowed from Persian *nihang*, or 'alligator, crocodile'. They lived chiefly in the rivers, such as the Aratsani or Murat-Su. They adopted the form of mermaids, used their victims for their lust, and then sucked their blood and left them dead. At other times they became seals, catching swimmers by the feet and dragging them to the bottom. On land, werewolves were also to be feared.[11]

Of a more kindly nature were the *shahapets*, or 'protectors of the homestead'. These are mentioned by the early historian Agathangelos as the protecting genii of graves. They appeared in the shape of men or of serpents, and also watched over the vineyards and olive trees.

Pagan Armenian burial customs seem to have had some resemblance to those of ancient Babylonia. The friends and relatives of the deceased came to the ceremony of wailing. At the funerals of the rich, professional mourners were employed, led by the 'mother of the dirge', who sang the story of the life and death of the deceased, while the nearest relatives tore their garments, plucked their hair and screamed. They cut their arms and faces. During the funeral they had music, produced by horns, violins and harps. Men and women danced facing each other, and clapped their hands. One ancient Armenian Christian writer went out of his way to forbid 'wailing over the dead, cutting of the hair and other evil things'. When the deceased was a king or other great personage, servants and slaves committed suicide over his grave.

Ancient gravestones are found in the shape of horses and lambs, perhaps symbolic of sacrifices for the dead. The modern custom of distributing bread and raisins and strong drink after the burial is probably a survival of an ancient sacrificial meal. Today, in Soviet Armenia, sacrifices of animals are regularly made on festival days, even in the courtyards of the cathedral of Echmiadzin. The Armenian and Georgian custom of spending Easter Monday eating and drinking in the graveyards, by the tombs of one's ancestors, clearly goes back to ancient pagan rituals.

Several Armenian legends concern the end of the world, and are entwined with ancient dragon myths. Such is the Armenian version of the Iranian legend of Thraetaona, who fought with Azhi-Dahaka, the demon-like dragon. After his defeat at the hands of Thraetaona, Azhi-Dahaka was chained up in a cave in the Elburz mountains by his victor. Thence he is to rise at the Last Day, and be slain by Sama Keresaspa.

In the Armenian recension, as recorded by Moses of Khorene, Azhi-Dahaka is transformed into a king Azhdahak of Media, who combats King Tigranes I of Armenia. In a later chapter, Moses of Khorene states that Azhdahak was fettered and imprisoned by Hruden in Mount Demavand, escaping only to be recaptured and guarded in a cave of that same mountain. Moses of Khorene likewise says that Azhdahak had once been kissed on the shoulder, and that from this kiss had sprung serpents, who were fed on human flesh. Faustus of Buzanda, another early Armenian chronicler, tells a similar tale about the ill-fated Armenian king Pap.

This interesting legend seems to have contributed to another popular Armenian tradition, about the legendary King Artavazd, son of Artaxias or Artashes. This king Artaxias was much beloved of his people, and when he died, many citizens preferred to die too rather than live on without him.

Artavazd, son of King Artaxias, seeing that many people committed suicide over his father's grave, exclaimed:

'Thou didst depart and tookest with thee the whole country. Shall I rule over ruins?'

Thereupon the shade of his father cursed him, saying:

'When thou goest a-hunting up the venerable Masis,
May the *Kajes* seize thee and take thee up the venerable Masis!
There mayest thou remain and see no light!'

Artavazd is said to have perished while on a hunting party near Masis (Ararat), by falling with his horse from a high precipice. One Armenian legend says that he is still chained in a cave of Masis, and two dogs, gnawing at his chains, try to set him free in order that he may bring the world to an end. The chains become very thin about the season of Navasart, the ancient New Year festivities in August. Therefore, in those days, the blacksmiths used to strike a few blows with their hammers on their anvils, in order to strengthen the chains that restrained Artavazd and save the world, a custom which continued into Christian times. [12]

The legend has features which recall the story of Prometheus Bound, and also closely resemble the popular Georgian cycle of folk tales about Amiran, the titan who challenged Jesus Christ to a rock hurling contest, and was also chained up in a cave for his temerity. The gnawing away of the chains by a dog, and the striking of blacksmiths' anvils as a precaution, are also paralleled in Georgia. [13]

The region immediately north-east of Armenia, known as Caucasian Albania (the modern Soviet Azerbaijan) is particularly interesting from the viewpoint of comparative religions. The Albanians were worshippers of the Sun and the Moon:

As for gods, they honour Helios, Zeus, and Selene, but especially Selene; her temple is near Iberia. The office of priest is held by the man who, after the king, is held in highest honour; he has charge of the sacred land, which is extensive and well-populated, and also of the temple slaves, many of whom are subject to religious frenzy and utter prophecies. And any one of those who becoming violently possessed, wanders alone in the forests, is by the priest arrested, bound with sacred fetters, and sumptuously maintained during that year, and then led forth to the sacrifice that is performed in honour of the goddess, and, being anointed, is sacrificed along with other victims. The sacrifice is performed as follows: Some person holding a sacred lance, with which it is the custom to sacrifice human victims, comes forward out of the crowd and strikes the victim through the side into the heart, he being not without experience in such a task; and when the victim falls, they draw auguries from his fall and declare them before the public; and when the body is carried to a certain place, they all trample upon it, thus using it as a means of purification. [14]

During the Parthian and Sassanian periods, Caucasian Albania came under the influence of the Zoroastrian religion, though local pagan cults remained strong. Caucasian Albania embraced Christianity, under Armenian influence, early in the fourth century, but even after this we hear of 'witches, sorcerers, heathen priests, finger-cutters and poisoners'. A gruesome account of this sect of 'finger-cutters' is given in the medieval *History of the Caucasian Albanians* by Movses Daskhurantsi.[15]

The official cults of pagan Georgia are described in the chronicle *Kartlis tskhovreba* or 'The Life of Georgia', and in the *Life of St Nino*, the evangelist of Georgia.

According to St Nino's biographer, the Georgian national gods were named Armazi (to be identified with Ahura-Mazda of the Zoroastrian pantheon), Zaden, Gatsi and Gaim. Armazi is depicted in the *Life of St Nino* as an idol in the form of a man made of copper, clothed in golden armour and having shoulder pieces and eyes made from emeralds and beryl stones, and holding in his hand a sword which revolved in his grasp. Gatsi was a golden idol, Gaim a silver one with a human face. These images were worshipped, says the pious hagiographer, by the royal court at Mtskheta-Armazi and all the common people. When St Nino offered up a prayer to God, the Almighty sent down hail 'in lumps as big as two fists' on to the abode of the heathen idols and smashed them into little pieces. This miracle unfortunately deprives us of the opportunity of judging for ourselves whether these Georgian sources really give a faithful account of the cults of pagan Georgia, or whether they are not somewhat embellished with reminiscences of Baal, Moloch and kindred deities of Old Testament fame. Simple folk whom St Nino encountered at the town of Urbnisi worshipped the sacred fire of the Zoroastrians, and also images of stone and wood; there was, too, a miracle-working tree to which the people attributed wondrous powers of healing. Tree worship is also attested in Georgia through the cult of the wood-goddess Dali, who corresponds to Artemis in Greek mythology. Byzantine accounts of the Emperor Justinian's Lazic wars speak of tree worship as an official cult among the Abasgians (Abkhazians) of the Black Sea up to the sixth century AD.[16]

The prevalence of Mazdaism in Georgia is confirmed by the archaeological evidence, which includes no less than five silver bowls discovered at Armazi and at a place called Bori, depicting the sacrificial figure of a horse standing before the ritual fire-altar. One of the bowls even has an inscription in Middle Persian, commemorating a dignitary named 'Buzmihr the good pitiakhsh', the name being an abbreviated form of 'Buzurg-Mihr' or Mithra the Great.

In Colchis, the gods and goddesses of the Greek pantheon were revered by members of the ruling classes who were in touch with the Hellenic cultural sphere of the Black Sea. Strabo speaks of a temple of the sun-goddess Leucothea and an oracle of Phrixus in the land of the Moskhoi – the Georgian province of Samtskhe; this temple was formerly rich but was later desecrated and robbed of its treasures. A temple of Apollo existed at Phasis (Poti) at the mouth of the Rioni as early as the fifth century BC, as is witnessed by the discovery in north Caucasia in 1901 of a silver drinking bowl of that period with the inscription: 'I belong to Apollo the Supreme of Phasis'. Later, a huge statue of the goddess Rhea also stood in a conspicuous site on the Phasis estuary.[17]

Even after sixteen centuries of Christianity, many elements of paganism live on in Georgia to this day. Hellenism and Zoroastrianism are long forgotten, but the people have gone back to far older traditions. The cult of the Moon God lives on in universal veneration of St George, who is also known as *Tetri Giorgi*, or 'White George'. The Georgian Shrovetide festival of fertility and rebirth is entirely pagan in inspiration. It is called *Berikaoba*, and involves processions and orgiastic carnivals in which the act of sexual intercourse is mimed, and ancient phallic rites are perpetuated from year to year.

The introduction of Christianity into Armenia by St Gregory the Illuminator (AD 301) and into Eastern Georgia by St Nino (AD 330) counts among the most important events in the history of these two peoples. Christianity helped to prevent the assimilation of the Trans-caucasian nations by the Persians, Arabs and Turks. The vitality of Christianity in Armenia and Georgia is amply demonstrated by the survival of the two national Churches today, after fifty years of Soviet anti-religious propaganda.

The early history of the Armenian and Georgian Churches has many features of interest. St Gregory was a Parthian, like the Arsacid royal house itself. For a century, the primacy of the Armenian Church re-mained in the family of St Gregory, passing frequently from father to son, like the rule of the Hebrew Patriarchs of the Old Testament.[18]

The Armenians refused to subscribe to the conclusions of the Council of Chalcedon (AD 451), which they justifiably saw as a political move by Emperor Marcian and his faction to impose Byzantine Caesaro-Papism on the independent, apostolic Churches of Eastern Christianity. This eventually led to a split with the Georgians, who re-entered the Byzantine Orthodox fold decisively under Archbishop Kirion, in AD 607.

Monastic life, based on both cenobitic and eremitic patterns, had been introduced into Georgia during the sixth century by monophysite refugee monks and hermits, the so-called Syrian Fathers, who founded several monastic communities on Egyptian and Syrian models. Georgian monks installed themselves at the monastery of St Saba in the Kedron gorge in Palestine, where they celebrated the liturgy in their own tongue.[19]

Not long after the schism with Armenia, Georgia attained the status of autocephaly or ecclesiastical autonomy, as a national Church within the Orthodox community. The last catholicos-patriarch of Georgia to be consecrated by the patriarch of Antioch was John III (744–60); since that time, the Georgian patriarchs have been elected and consecrated by the Georgian bishops at Mtskheta.[20]

The Armenian Gregorian Church has through the centuries suffered cruel persecution and several attempts at systematic extermination. It also had to contend with dangerous heresies, particularly that of the Paulicians, or Tondrakites. These Paulicians, who feature prominently in Gibbon's *Decline and Fall of the Roman Empire*, were medieval successors of the early Christian Gnostics, and of the Manichaeans. The Paulicians, whose teachings were much attacked and distorted by their enemies, apparently held that St Paul was the only true Apostle, rejected the Old Testament, and claimed that the world was created by a spirit at war with the God of the New Testament. They had strong iconoclastic tendencies, smashing images and even crosses whenever they could.

From AD 830, the Armenian branch of the Paulician movement was centred on a village called Tondrak, hence the name Tondrakites. They attacked the feudal privileges of the Armenian barons, who united with the clergy in persecuting and suppressing them. The Tondrakites are hailed by modern Soviet historians as ancestors of present-day Communism; a tract purporting to be their manual of doctrine was published in 1898, under the title, *The Key of Truth*.[21] The Paulicians are also important for their influence on the development of Bogomilism in the Balkans, where there were important Armenian colonies, particularly in Bulgaria.

CHAPTER 8

LITERATURE AND SCHOLARSHIP
IN ARMENIA AND GEORGIA

The distinctive Armenian and Georgian alphabets, as employed up to the present day, were both invented early in the fifth century AD, with the object of spreading the Christian faith in the vernacular tongues in both of these Caucasian lands. The older studies of the history of Armenian and Georgian literature therefore tend to begin from the time of St Mesrop-Mashtotz, inventor of the Armenian script. So much was destroyed by jealous early Christians that reconstruction of the earlier periods is a difficult matter.

Archaeological research during the past half century has materially altered our concept of the history of literature, science and learning in Transcaucasia. A key site here is the village of Metsamor, a few miles to the west of Echmiadzin, and within sight of Mounts Ararat and Alagöz.[1] Close to the village is a massive rocky hummock, perhaps half a mile in circumference, with outcrops of craggy stone. The hummock is riddled with caves, underground storage vaults, and prehistoric dwellings, and is now seen to have been a major scientific, astronomical and industrial centre, operating in the fields of metallurgy, astrology and primitive magic from a period hardly less than five thousand years ago.

The Metsamor 'observatory' is covered with mysterious, cabbalistic signs. Indeed, hieroglyphic writing in Armenia goes back to very early times, perhaps to the New Stone Age. All over Armenia, we find pictograms or petroglyphs, carved or scratched on rocks, caves and cliff faces, and showing simplified human and animal figures. There is little doubt that these served as means of communication, as well as of ritual and artistic self-expression. A modern parallel can be drawn with the Conan Doyle story of Sherlock Holmes and the Dancing Men. Other forms of hieroglyphs and codes of conventional signs developed during the Bronze Age, under the stimulus of cultural contacts with the Hittites, who used both picture-writing and cuneiform script. The Urartians, of course, were highly literate, as their numerous monumental inscriptions show, while Assyrian and later, Achaemenid Persian, systems of writing also spread into the territory of Armenia.

Enough has been said in earlier chapters to show the wealth of literary and religious texts in various languages, which existed in pagan Armenia during the Artaxiad and the Arsacid periods. An interesting passage in the History of Moses of Khorene relates how King Artashes (Artaxias I) ordered the borders of villages and farms to be marked out:

> For he multiplied the population of Armenia, introducing many immigrant tribes and settling them in the hills, valleys and plains. This is how he designed the boundary marks: he had rectangular stones carved, with a saucer shaped cavity hollowed out in the centre. These were then buried in the ground, and four-cornered turrets fixed on top, projecting a little above ground level.

Three such stones have been found at various times not far from Lake Sevan, all carved with indentations at the top, as if to resemble a turret, and having inscriptions in an unusual form of Aramaic script. Although Professor A.Dupont-Sommer once suggested that the stones commemorate a fishing expedition undertaken by King Artaxias in Lake Sevan, this explanation appears highly unlikely. There seems every reason to believe that these are three of the official boundary marks, so carefully and accurately described by the Armenian national historian, and that they embody in their Aramaic inscriptions the name of King Artaxias I along with that of the local landed proprietor.[2]

Georgia also is rich in epigraphic monuments of pre-Christian times. In 1940, two stone slabs were discovered not far from the ancient capital of Mtskheta, bearing inscriptions. One of these is the bilingual epitaph of a Georgian princess named Serapita, with closely corresponding though not identical texts in Greek and Middle Persian. The latter is written in an unusual form of Aramaic writing which is usually termed the Armazi script. First published in 1942 by Academician Giorgi Tsereteli, the epitaph of Serapita is moving in its pathos and dignity:

> I am Serapita, daughter of Zevakh the younger, *pitiakhsh* (high constable) of Farsman the King, and wife of Iodmangan the victorious, winner of many conquests, and master of the court of Ksefarnug, the great King of the Iberians, and son of Agrippa, master of the court of King Farsman. Woe, woe, for the sake of her who was not of full age, whose years were not completed, and so good and beautiful that no one was like her in excellence; and she died at the age of twenty-one.[3]

This text dates from about AD 150. Other Iranian texts written in a form of Aramaic occur on silver dishes and other products of the silversmith and goldsmith, sometimes in conjunction with engraved cult scenes. These objects often preserve the names of an owner, usually a high official or prince. Thus, a certain 'Buz-Mihr', or Great Mithra, the 'good pitiakhsh', had his name engraved on a silver bowl found in

Georgia. This is one of a group, each with an engraved medallion showing a horse standing before a Zoroastrian fire-altar.[4]

Roman occupation left its mark with several noteworthy inscriptions in Armenia and Georgia. In one, the emperor Vespasian recalls that he has sent engineers to the aid of his good friend and ally, the king of the Iberians (Georgians), to repair his walls against barbarian invasions; then again, we have Roman tombstones and other remains from the Araxes valley region of Armenia. A fine collection of these may be seen in the Historical Museum of Armenia in Erevan.

The official adoption of Christianity by King Tiridates III in AD 301 inaugurated a new phase in the intellectual and spiritual life of the Armenian people.

Like many a missionary of modern times, the founders of the Armenian Church had to set themselves the task of translating the New Testament and essential prayer books into the language of the people. Originally, prayers and chants were conducted either in Greek or in Syriac, and by foreign preachers with little or no knowledge of the Armenian tongue.

The main obstacle to the spreading of Christian knowledge in Armenia was, of course, the fact that the language had as yet no alphabet of its own. Like Georgian, Armenian has a number of consonants which cannot be expressed by a single sign in either Latin, Greek, or any Semitic alphabet. The difficult but vital task of inventing an alphabet for the Armenian language was ultimately achieved by Mesrop-Mashtotz, whom the Armenian Church reveres among its saints.

Little is known about Mesrop's early life. His main biographer is Koriun, one of Mesrop's disciples. Mesrop-Mashtotz was born in the year 361, in the province of Taron, and graduated from one of the schools established by Catholicos Nerses the Great. As a man of exceptional ability who had mastered Greek, Syriac, Persian and other languages, he was appointed royal secretary at the city of Vagharshapat or Echmiadzin, then the capital of Armenia. After a few years of government service, Mesrop resigned his post and entered the Church.

Mesrop was some forty years of age when he first began his preachings in different parts of Armenia. It was during these tours that he conceived the idea of inventing Armenian characters and translating the Bible, thus marking the beginning of the national literature. The invention of a national alphabet, he considered, would not only help to propagate the Christian Faith, but would also establish a strong tie to bind together Armenians living in Eastern and Western Armenia and elsewhere; since the Persians and Byzantines had partitioned Armenia between themselves in AD 387, this was an urgent task.

Mesrop's project was supported by Catholicos Sahak, himself an erudite scholar. The king of Eastern Armenia, Vramshapuh, also expressed interest, and told Mesrop that he had once seen in Mesopotamia a set of characters which had been devised for Armenian by a certain Bishop Daniel the Syrian. These were promptly sent for, but proved unsuitable for rendering the complicated phonetic system of Armenian. No doubt Daniel's system was based on Syriac, which is written from right to left, and has basically the same twenty-two characters as Hebrew. The Syriac alphabet fails to provide a complete system for writing the vowels. Since the Armenian alphabet as invented by Mesrop and his disciples was found to need thirty six characters, it is hardly surprising that Syriac failed to provide an adequate basis for writing Armenian.

Mesrop and his pupils now set to work to devise a fresh system for Armenian. They decided to write the characters from left to right, as in Greek. As far as possible, Mesrop retained the order of the Greek alphabet, while interpolating a number of new signs, which had to be devised to render those sounds which occur in Armenian and in Georgian, but not in Greek. The work was completed in Samosata, probably in AD 404 or 406. Later on, Mesrop and his group of disciples devised alphabets for the Georgians and for the Albanians of the Caucasus. The Armenian and Georgian alphabets have continued in use to the present day, with the original sets of characters, though nowadays written in modern, cursive script. This is a great tribute to this remarkable pioneer, who passed away at a ripe old age in the year 440.[5]

Mesrop is buried in the crypt of the church at Oshakan, not far from Echmiadzin. The shrine is guarded to this day by a lineal descendant of Mesrop's patron and protector, Vahan Amatuni, *Hazarapet* ('Lieutenant-General') and Great Prince (*ishkhan*) of the Armenians; the Amatunis were from time immemorial hereditary lords of Oshakan, which is the Auzacana of the geographer Ptolemy.

The Armenian classical language, as written down by St Mesrop and his disciples, is known as *grabar*, or 'book language'. From the fifteenth century onwards, poets and scribes began to use the popular spoken idiom of the people, known as *ashkharabar*, and to write it down. During the nineteenth century, there were developed two main spoken and literary languages, Eastern Armenian, based on the Armenian of the Ararat region, and Western Armenian, based on the idiom of the Armenians of Istanbul.

The original Armenian alphabet was written in large capital letters or uncials, of a monumental character and size. Between the tenth and eleventh century, we find a type of curved uncials, called *boloragits yerkatagir*, or 'iron capitals'. The 'middle' *yerkatagir* of the eleventh and twelfth centuries has more straight lines, and there is also a small *yerkatagir* script. Sometimes a combination of more than one style of *yerkatagir* occurs, referred to as 'mixed letters'. From the thirteenth century onwards, the predominant script is the small *bolorgir* writing, which closely resembles most Armenian printing of the present day. In the eighteenth century, a form of cursive writing was developed, under the name of *notrgir*.

Mesrop's example was followed by a brilliant school of disciples, who set out to create a new Christian literature, systematically covering all the main fields of knowledge and including theology, philosophy, history, geography and astronomy. These classic writers of the fifth century are often known as the 'interpreters', because they brought knowledge to the people.

Eminent among these pioneer writers was Eznik of Kolb, a much admired author who wrote a polemical treatise under the title, *Against the Sects*. Here he champions the Christian faith against Zoroastrianism, and also confounds Manicheeism and Gnosticism. The information conveyed by Eznik concerning the pagan beliefs of the Armenian people, and the astronomical, mythological and religious beliefs of the followers of Zoroaster is of vast interest.[6] Eznik's work is complemented by that of the distinguished Armenian Neo-Platonist of the fifth to sixth centuries, David Anhaght, or 'the Invincible', so styled because nobody could overcome him in argument. Three main philosophical works come from David the Invincible's pen, namely *A Definition of Philosophy*, *An Analysis of the Introduction by Porphyrius*, and *An Interpretation of Aristotles' Analytics*. Such was the interest aroused by David the Invincible's speculative thought that almost five hundred manuscripts containing the text of his works, as well as commentaries and interpretations, are to be found in the Matenadaran Manuscript Library in Erevan alone.[7]

Although they owed a great deal to the Armenians in these early stages of Christian literature and learning in the Caucasus area, the Georgians later caught up rapidly. Markedly inferior to the Armenians in the realm of science and philosophy, the Georgians ultimately moved ahead in the field of poetry, especially the epic, and were highly accomplished in fiction and story-telling.

Once equipped with an alphabet of their own, the Georgians set to work to adorn public buildings with carved inscriptions, and to evolve a literature both original and in translation. The monumental carved *khutsuri* inscription on Bolnisi Sioni cathedral dates from 492–3, and the mosaics from the Georgian cloister built by Peter the Iberian near Bethlehem are somewhat earlier. From Armenian, the Georgians soon translated the Four Gospels and Psalms of David, to be followed by other Biblical and liturgical texts. Many of these early redactions, which go back in some instances to lost Syriac and Greek originals, are exceptionally interesting and preserve readings not witnessed elsewhere. In the *Passion of St Eustace the Cobbler*, put to death by the Persian governor of Tbilisi in 545, we find a curious formulation of the Ten Commandments, and an account of the life of Christ which recalls Tatian's Diatessaron, a Gospel harmony of the second century, and suggests that the Georgian Church in early times possessed a Diatessaron of its own. The apologia of Archdeacon Samuel in this *Passion of St Eustace* is of great value, as showing how the Christian faith was expounded among Persian and Georgian Christians in Sassanian times.[8]

Pride of place among the first original works of Georgian literature belongs to the *Passion of St Shushanik*, composed by the martyr's father-confessor Jacob of Tsurtavi between 476 and 483. The background of the saint's life is well known from historical sources. Shushanik's father, Vardan Mamikonian, was the hero of the Armenian national rising of 451 directed against the Sassanian king Yezdegird of Iran. Shushanik married the Georgian duke Varsken, lord of Tsurtavi, a strategic castle on the frontier between Armenia and Georgia. Varsken became an apostate, abandoning Christianity for Mazdaism to ingratiate himself with the Persian court. Shushanik's refusal to follow him in this step infuriated her ambitious husband, who tortured and humiliated her for seven years, until she finally succumbed and died.

This vivid realism, combined with patriotic and religious fervour, is also in evidence in the *Passion of St Abo*, a perfumer from Baghdad, put to death by the Arab governor of Tbilisi in 786. His life was written by a Georgian contemporary, Ioane Sabanisdze, partly to inspire his own countrymen to further efforts through the heroic example of this Arab stranger who chose martyrdom for the sake of Georgia's own Christian faith. Abo's Passion is impregnated with the simple unquestioning faith of early Christianity, and contains valuable historical data, including an account of the Turkic Khazars who lived by the Volga and adopted the Jewish faith, and were visited by St Abo during his travels.[9]

A different, though equally interesting group of hagiographical documents is concerned with the lives of early Georgian hermits, monks, and anchorities. These are no dry chronicles of monastic trivialities; they breathe a warm, human spirit, and are characteristically Georgian in their sympathetic treatment of human foibles. One readable collection, known as the *Lives of the Syrian Fathers*, was compiled and revised by Catholicos Arsenius II of Georgia between 955 and 980. These Syrian Fathers, thirteen in number, arrived in the Caucasus at various times between the end of the fifth and the middle of the sixth centuries, and brought with them the rules and precepts of Syrian and Egyptian monasticism, which they helped to implant in Georgia.

Hermits though they were, the Syrian Fathers were by no means mis-anthropic in outlook. St Iese of Dsilkani, for instance, obliged his parishioners by diverting the River Ksani to flow through their town. Several of the Fathers were distinguished by love of animals. Ioane Zedazneli made friends with bears near his hermitage, while St Shio employed a tame wolf to guide the donkeys which brought supplies to his lonely grotto. St David of Garesja and his disciple Lucian in their desert abode in Outer Kakheti received milk and curds from three tame deer. The cellar of their cave was infested by a fearsome dragon with bloodshot eyes, a horn growing out of his forehead, and a great mane on his neck. Eventually God sends a thunderbolt which burns the dragon to a cinder. St David – and this is another typically Georgian touch – protests vigorously to Heaven against this violence to one of his own protégés, and has to be pacified by an angel sent especially by the Almighty Himself.[10]

Other endearing touches are found in the *Life of St Gregory of Khandzta* by Giorgi Merchule, written in 951, in which we read of a Bishop Zacharias who was annoyed by a blackbird persistently pecking at his ripe grapevine. Zacharias makes the sign of the cross over the bird, which immediately falls dead; repenting of his severity, the bishop makes the sign of the cross once more, and the blackbird revives and flies off to its nest. A discerning reader can extract from these vitae countless facts about daily life in medieval Georgia. Sometimes it is necessary to read between the lines, as in the *Life of St Serapion of Zarzma*, where the monkish biographer's criticism of a hostile peasantry discloses the existence of resentment among the poor farmers at the prosperity of the monasteries, which monopolized the best land and conveniently forgot their vow of poverty.

From the fifth century AD, both Armenia and Georgia developed an exceptionally rich tradition of historical writing. The value of Armenian and Georgian historiography lies not only in its rich and colourful accounts of local events within Caucasia, but in the light which it throws on the annals of other countries, particularly Byzantium, Sassanian Iran, the Arab caliphate, and the Seljuq and Mongol dominions.

The earliest Armenian historian is the rather mysterious figure known as Agathangelos, who purports to have been a contemporary of King Tiridates III and an eye-witness of the conversion of Armenia by St Gregory the Illuminator. In fact, he probably lived about the middle of the fifth century. His account of the evangelization of Armenia was translated into Greek, as well as Syriac, Coptic, Arabic and Georgian.[11]

The struggle of the Armenian people against the Persians and the Byzantines is narrated by such chroniclers as Faustus of Buzanda, who concentrated on the period between AD 330 and AD 387; his continuator,

Lazarus of Pharpi, who carried on the narrative up to the year 486; and Eliseus the Vardapet, whose *History of the Vardanians* is our best source for the revolt against the Great King of Iran, led by Prince Vardan Mamikonian, and culminating in the battle of Avarayr in 451. For the seventh century, a prime source is Bishop Sebeos, who wrote a history of the Byzantine emperor Heraclius and his age, covering the period from AD 590 to AD 660.

Much of the ancient, pre-Christian historical tradition of the country is contained in the work on the Armenian antiquities going by the name of *The History of Armenia*. The author of this work is known as Moses of Khorene. For many years, Moses of Khorene was regarded as an author of the fifth century AD, but there are indications that he lived somewhat later, probably in the eighth century. For this reason, he is sometimes known as the pseudo-Moses of Khorene, especially as much of his historical data has been shown to bear a legendary character. Latterly there has been a tendency to rehabilitate Moses of Khorene, especially as he undoubtedly used authentic ancient sources including Armenian pagan traditions, and Greek and Syriac authorities. Certainly he is a most delightful and imaginative writer, who made a vital contribution to ancient Armenian folklore and mythology, as well as to history in the narrower sense.[12]

The tradition of these classic Armenian historians was worthily continued by Catholicos John v of Draskhanakert, called 'Patmaban', or 'the Historian' (consecrated 898, died 929); by Thomas Ardsruni, author of the *History of the House of Ardsruni*, in which is given an account of the great house of Vaspurakan, up to the tenth century; and by Aristakes of Lastivert, the eloquent chronicler of the Seljuq invasions which overwhelmed Armenia in the eleventh century.

The Georgians also were accomplished historians. The earliest Georgian chronicle, called the *Conversion of Iberia*, dates from the seventh century, and centres on the mission of St Nino and the events attending the adoption of Christianity in Georgia during the epoch of Constantine the Great. Around 800 Juansher Juansheriani composed his history of King Vakhtang Gorgaslan, the Georgian 'King Arthur'. These ancient historical works, though influenced by the Bible and by monastic prejudice, are valuable sources for the history of the Caucasus.

Another group of Georgian histories dates from the eleventh century, when Sumbat son of David composed a history and genealogy of the Bagratid kings, in which he attempted to prove their descent from David and Solomon of Israel – a claim shared by the Bagratids of Armenia. About the same time, Leonti Mroveli, archbishop of Ruisi, composed his *History of the First Fathers and Kings* dealing with Georgian history prior to the fifth century. The era and personality of Leonti

Mroveli are established by an inscription dated AD 1066, found in the Trekhvi caves.

The chronicles of Juansher, Sumbat and Leonti Mroveli were combined with other historical works to make up the vast corpus known as *Kartlis tskhovreba*, or 'The Life of Georgia'. New works were added from time to time to keep the corpus up to date. A final revision was made by King Vakhtang VI early in the eighteenth century. Separate histories of the individual kingdoms and principalities were composed later in the same century by a natural son of Vakhtang VI, Prince Vakhusht (1695–1772).[13]

A special place in the early history of scholarship and learning in Armenia and Georgia belongs to Ananias of Shirak or Anania Shirakatsi (*c*. 600–70). Born in the Armenian province of Shirak or Siracene, Ananias travelled to Erzurum and to Trebizond in search of knowledge and information.[14] He was a kind of early Armenian Newton, combining enthusiasm for geography and astronomy with an interest in metaphysics, chronology and mathematics. He was an innovator, who refuted the ancient belief that the world was flat and surrounded by the ocean; also refused to believe that the earth was supported on the back of a large number of elephants. Rather, it was held up by the atmosphere and the winds; 'The earth is in the centre, all round the earth is the air, and the heavens surround the earth on every side'.

The world – and here Ananias was unable to free himself from conventional beliefs – was composed of four elements: fire, air, earth and water. These elements were indissolubly linked by a predestined pattern of interlocking and interaction. The world was undergoing a constant process of movement and of evolution. 'Birth is the beginning of annihilation, and annihilation in its turn is the beginning of birth. From this immortal paradox, the earth derives its eternal existence.'

One of the best Armenian treatises on geography, formerly attributed to Moses of Khorene, is now generally ascribed to Anania Shirakatsi. This work makes use of some fifteen ancient sources, including the works of Ptolemy. In the first part of his *Geography*, Shirakatsi presents general information on the roundness of the earth, its relief, climatic zones, seas and oceans. The second and more extensive portion deals with the three continents then known – Europe, Libya (Africa) and Asia. The part covering Europe is divided into twelve countries, Libya into eight, and Asia, into thirty-eight. In describing each country, Shirakatsi takes note of the boundaries, the location, the inhabitants and their customs, the names of the seas, mountains and rivers, also natural resources, flora and fauna. As might be expected, Shirakatsi is especially well informed on the countries of south-western Asia, namely Persia, Mesopotamia, Asia Minor, Georgia and the Caucasus. Such is the wealth of data provided on Armenia itself that the best ethnographic and historical atlases of ancient Armenia are based extensively on Shirakatsi's observations.[15]

The writings of Anania Shirakatsi have been cherished in Armenia throughout the centuries, and copied out by generations of scribes. This was at a time when – apart from some 'obscure minstrels' whose verses were not counted as 'literature' – the Church had a virtual monopoly in the field of letters. The tolerant attitude of the Armenian and Georgian Churches towards such intellectual manifestations in the field of experimental philosophy contrasts favourably with that of the Roman Catholic Church in respect of scientists such as Galileo, a thousand years later.

The Armenian and Georgian Churches were situated in the border-land between Byzantine Christianity on the one hand, and the Arab caliphate, Persia, and the Indian sub-continent on the other. Armenian and Georgian Church literature served as a bridge between the ancient wisdom literatures of Syria and Mesopotamia, of Iran and India, and the spiritual world of Byzantium and of Latin Christendom.

Prior to the schism of AD 607, the Armenian and Georgian Churches were in close religious communion. Armenian served as the vehicle from which many religious texts were translated into Georgian. After the schism, the Georgians re-entered the communion of Orthodox Christianity, while the Armenians went their own way, seeking allies among the Monophysite Churches, particularly the Copts and the Jacobites of Syria. Georgian monks founded cloisters and libraries in all the main centres of the Christian East, including Palestine, Mount Sinai, the Black Mountain near Antioch, Cyprus, and also, Mount Olympus, Mount Athos, and Bachkovo (Petritsoni) in Bulgaria.

The world of learning is indebted to the Armenians and Georgians for preserving and transmitting numerous ancient texts, which have perished in their original form. Among the most important of these is the lost treatise, On Nature, by Zeno of Citium (335–263 BC), the founder of the Stoic school, which is preserved in Armenian; also works of the Greek grammarian Dionysius Thrax (born 166 BC), Theon of Alexandria, the rhetorician, Hermes Trismegistus, the fictitious 'divine' author of a large collection of religious writings, and Porphyry (AD 233–305), a neo-Platonist critic of Christianity. The Georgians transmitted to the West the Buddhistic story of Barlaam and Josaphat, which reached them via the Arabic. This work contains, in modified form, an account of the conversion of Gautama Buddha, the Bodhisattva prince, his Great Renunciation, and his missionary journeys. The Georgian version was rendered into Greek by St Euthymius the Athonite (955–1028), the learned abbot of the Iviron or Georgian monastery on Mount Athos.

From Greek the tale passed into Latin, and thence into the main languages of medieval Christendom; it also became popular in Ethiopic.[16]

The tenth century, in both Georgia and Armenia, saw a wonderful flowering of spiritual literature, sacred odes and hymns. Of outstanding literary calibre is the Armenian mystical writer Gregory of Narek, author of the *Book of Lamentations*, available in French translation by Isaac Kechichian.[17] Gregory of Narek was born about 945, and was educated at the monastery of Narek, south of Lake Van. Gregory's father, Khosrow the Great, bishop of Antsevatsik, was also a well-known ecclesiastical writer, author of a Commentary on the Armenian Liturgy. At Narek, Gregory was placed under the care of his great-uncle Anania, and grew up in an atmosphere of intellectual and religious fervour, in contact with Greek and also Arabic philosophy.

Gregory of Narek is considered one of the spontaneous mystical geniuses of medieval Christendom. His writings include a Commentary on the Song of Songs; a Panegyric on the Virgin Mary; a Panegyric on the Twelve Apostles and Seventy-Two Disciples; a Panegyric on St James of Nisibis; Anthems in honour of the Holy Ghost, the Holy Church and the Holy Cross; Hymns and Sacred Odes. Gregory of Narek's hymns have been set to music by some of Armenia's best composers, and are regarded as models of their kind.

Gregory of Narek's most famous work is the *Book of Lamentations* (or: *Prayers, Elegies*). This consists of ninety-five separate Lamentations or canticles, put together rather like the Psalms of David to form a connected whole. The Lamentations are written in rhythmic prose, sometimes free verse, and are breathless and tumultuous in their passionate outpouring. Sometimes Gregory appears to be wrestling with his God, like some doughty Jacob of old; sometimes he is imploring a Deity who has left him lonely and forsaken, like Job abandoned in the land of Uz. But the final tone of the Lamentations is optimistic, even triumphant.

Following the fall of the Bagratid and Ardsruni kingdoms, the tradition of Armenian spirituality was carried on in Cilician Armenia by such remarkable figures as St Nerses Shnorhali, or 'the Gracious', and his kinsman, Archbishop Nerses of Lampron.

St Nerses Shnorhali was the younger brother of the Armenian Catholicos Gregory III Pahlavuni, who was elected to be supreme pontiff of the Armenians in 1113, at the age of twenty. For nearly fifty years, Nerses the Gracious was the right hand of Catholicos Gregory III, following him from one refuge to another to escape the raids of the Saracens. When Gregory retired from the office of Catholicos, Nerses was unanimously elected to succeed him (1166) and occupied the Catholicosate for seven years, until his death in 1173.

St Nerses Shnorhali was a prolific poet and theologian. He wrote a verse history of the Armenian nation, a long elegy on the fall of the city of Edessa to the Saracens, a Panegyric of the True Cross, and a vast poem on the Life of Christ, under the title *Jesus, Only-Begotten of the Father*. Nerses Shnorhali is the author of many commentaries on the holy scriptures, as well as on the lives of the saints; he enriched the Armenian liturgy with hymns, anthems, sacred poems and prayers, which are in use to this very day.[18]

Nerses of Lampron was born in 1153; his father was Prince Oshin of Lampron, his mother Princess Shahandukht, a niece of St Nerses Shnorhali. At the age of twenty-two, Nerses of Lampron was appointed archbishop of Tarsus. He was also the abbot of the monastery of Skevra, and is often referred to by his contemporaries as the 'Modern St Paul', or 'Doctor Universalis'. Nerses of Lampron was versed in Greek, Syriac and Latin, and was constantly employed in diplomatic missions on behalf of his sovereign lord, King Levon II. He was instrumental in securing the support of Emperor Frederick Barbarossa for the young Armenian state of Cilicia, and in preparing the way for securing a royal crown for the Rupenid dynasty. He died at the age of forty-four, in 1198, too soon to witness the fruition of his political plans.

Nerses of Lampron left behind him a wonderful literary heritage, comprising more than thirty major theological writings, including treatises, sermons, homilies, hymns, and epistles, one of these being a letter to the future King Levon on the perils of court life. His *Panegyric on the Assumption of the Virgin Mary* is much admired. Nerses of Lampron was a strong advocate of reunion with Rome, and translated into Armenian the monastic rule of St Benedict, the Catholic Mass, and various Papal Bulls addressed to the Armenian nation.[19]

It should not be thought that education in medieval Armenia was confined to theology and such traditional studies as history and mathematics. Science and especially medicine were very well developed, following the example of the seventh century experimental philosopher Anania Shirakatsi. In medicine, there are several outstanding names. The most prominent is that of Mkhitar Heratsi, author of a celebrated treatise, *Relief from Fevers* (1184).[20] Mkhitar Heratsi mastered the technique of surgical operations, and used silk thread for sewing up wounds. He employed mandragora for an anaesthetic. He carried out experiments on animals, and was aware of the value of special diets in treating disorders, and of music and psychotherapy for the relief of nervous complaints. For the first time in the history of medicine, Mkhitar Heratsi introduced the notion that typhoid, malaria and septic fevers were infectious 'mouldy fevers', as he aptly termed them. Heratsi abandoned the use of the classical *grabar* tongue, in favour of colloquial Armenian, with the result that his researches became available to the masses of the population. There are more than 850 medical manuscripts in the Erevan Matenadaran alone.

As noted earlier, Byzantine pressure followed by the Seljuq invasions of the 1060s proved fatal to the Armenian Bagratid monarchy of Ani. Situated further north, in the impregnable Caucasus mountains, the Georgians held out more successfully. Under such monarchs as King David the Builder (1089–1125) and Queen Tamar (1184–1213), Georgia entered into a Golden Age, which found worthy fulfilment in the realm of literature and learning.

The outstanding work of the Georgian Athonites, Abbots Euthymius and Giorgi, was continued by Ephrem Mtsire (1027–94), who translated into Georgian the works of St John Damascene, Ephraim the Syrian, St John Chrysostom and Dionysius the Areopagite. Ephrem Mtsire was the author of the original biography of Simon Metaphrastes, and a leader of the Georgian monastic community on the Black Mountain close to Antioch. Another outstanding figure was Arsen of Iqalto (d. 1125), the erudite rector of Iqalto Academy, near Telavi in Kakheti. In Palestine, excellent work was done at the Monastery of the Cross near Jerusalem, built about AD 1030 by St Prochorus the Georgian, a disciple of Euthymius the Athonite.[21]

During the Middle Ages, many Christian countries witnessed a struggle between the ecclesiastical power and the laity for control over poetry and literature generally. In Georgia, the Bagratid kings and queens were great champions of the Christian faith – 'Swords of the Messiah', as they proudly styled themselves. At the same time, the convivial Georgians greatly enjoyed tales of love and adventure, as well as independent philosophical speculation. They were by no means willing to endure clerical domination over their leisure time, knowing that their record in battling against the Saracens and other foes of Christendom was second to none in the medieval world.

If one asks a Georgian to name a single poet who means more to him than any other figure in the country's literary history, he will undoubtedly mention the name of Shota Rustaveli, author of the romantic epic, *Vephkhis-tqaosani*, or *The Man in the Panther's Skin*.

Reliable facts about Rustaveli's life and career are scanty. We have to rely on a small body of popular tradition, combined with what biographical data are provided, probably by a later hand, in the prologue and epilogue to the great poem. Even the dates of Rustaveli's birth and death are disputed, though the Soviet Georgian government took the decision to celebrate the eight hundredth anniversary of his birth in 1966.

It is usually assumed that Rustaveli was a contemporary of the great Georgian queen Tamar (1184–1213), perhaps a high official at her court. In the prologue, Rustaveli (or very likely a disciple) writes:

Tears of blood flow profusely as I praise our Queen Tamar whose praises I have sung. My ink is a lake of jet, and my pen a pliant reed. My words, like lacerating spears, will pierce the heart of the hearer.

I was told to compose in her honour elegant, sweet-sounding phrases, to sing of her eyebrows and lashes, of her hair, her lips and her teeth – Badakhshan ruby and cut crystal. An anvil of soft lead can break even hard stone.

In the epilogue to the poem, the author (or his imitator) explains that he was a native of the province of Samtskhe, from the little town of Rustavi – hence the surname Rustaveli. Tradition adds further that the bard was educated at Athens and at the Iqalto Academy in Kakheti province, and had travelled much in Asia. The preface to *The Man in the Panther's Skin*, if taken literally, would indicate that Rustaveli suffered from a hopeless passion for his sovereign lady, Tamar:

> She whom vast armies obey deprives me of life and of reason;
> She alone can cure me, or leave me to death and the grave.

It is said that the queen's disdain led Rustaveli to withdraw from secular life and finish his days at the Monastery of the Cross in Jerusalem, where his picture indeed appears on a coloured fresco. However, there are some who dismiss the whole corpus of tradition about Rustaveli as so much pious fiction. For instance, the late Dr Jaromír Jedlička, who translated Rustaveli into Czech, thought that 'the *Vephkhis-tqaosani* was not written in the time of Tamar, its author is not Rustaveli, and the prologue and epilogue were written much later than the poem itself'.

Whether or not the traditions about Shota Rustaveli are correct, there is no denying that we are in the presence of a poetic genius of the first order. *The Man in the Panther's Skin*, apart from the prologue and epilogue, is the creation of a single poet of great sophistication and learning. In this respect, it cannot be readily compared with the unlettered, spontaneous outpourings of folk bards of Central Asia or the Balkans. We should seek affinities rather in the circle of Dante and Ariosto in Italy, and in the wonderful Persian school of epic and romance headed by Firdawsi and Nizami of Ganja.

The fact that Rustaveli's poem is known to every peasant and humble working man throughout Georgia does not alter the fact that it is a literary, rather than a folk production. Certainly there are cycles of tales and legends deriving from *The Man in the Panther's Skin*, but these folk-tales evidently flow from the work of Rustaveli, rather than the reverse. To cite an analogy, the fact that many of Shakespeare's verses are used as familiar English proverbs does not show that Shakespeare has incorporated into his plays large numbers of already existent folk sayings. It is Shakespeare's genius which has imprinted these verses and aphorisms of his upon the consciousness of the English people and the world.

Likewise, scores of lines from Rustaveli's *Vephkhis-tqaosani* have become a part of Georgian everyday speech.

Shota Rustaveli is a poet with an elegant and accomplished technique. Metrically, *The Man in the Panther's Skin* astonishes by its virtuosity, and also by its richness of sonoric invention. Two different metres are used: the so-called 'high shairi', which creates a musical major, and the 'low shairi', which creates a musical minor. The poem is divided into quatrains. The rhyme scheme is *a:a:a:a:* Each rhyme is made up of two or three matching final syllables, thus imposing severe demands on the poet's resourcefulness.

The lofty tone of the work is set from the opening lines, in which the bard invokes the supreme, single Deity:

He who created the world, almighty, all powerful, breathed into all living creatures the breath of life from on high; gave possession of the world in all its splendour; made kings to rule over us, each in His own image.

It is noticeable that Rustaveli's God is a universal force, and that he never uses conventional Christian religious symbolism. The individual members of the Holy Trinity are never mentioned. This helps to explain the hostility of the Georgian Orthodox Church, which burnt copies of Rustaveli's poem whenever it dared.

Rustaveli goes on to make some pertinent and acute comments on the role of the poet in society:

Poetry is, first of all, a branch of divine wisdom, conceived by and known to the godly, a comfort to all who hear it. It pleases and instructs the worthy and virtuous man. The pre-eminence of poetry is that it can say things shortly....

Many poems are composed for mirth and revelry, for the lover, the joyous and the merry, for sport and amusement, and for the pleasure of companions. They may please the ear, but remember, only he who writes majestic poetry is a poet.

Rustaveli goes on to expound his idealised, Platonic concept of perfect love – a rarefied cult in whose name knights of old did battle for their beloved, and of which troubadours sang in sweet despair:

Love is sacred and gentle, undefinable, powerful. It has nothing in common with lust. It is something beyond it. Love can never mingle with lust; it is one thing, lust is another. Between them lies a broad, impregnable boundary.

He who loves should be constant, never lewd nor faithless. Separation from his beloved should wring sigh upon sigh from his heart. He must always be true to her, though she frown upon him in anger. I hate the soulless lover who only seeks hugging and noisy kissing.

While his poem is an allegory of Georgia's heroic age, Rustaveli chose an exotic setting for its narrative framework, which he claims to have found in some old Persian tale. The venerable king Rostevan of Arabia gives up his throne to his daughter Tinatin – as in fact King Giorgi III did in favour of Queen Tamar, his own daughter. A great feast is arranged at court, then a hunt during which the king and his suite encounter a knight clad in a panther's skin sitting by a river, sobbing bitterly. Rostevan gets no reply to his greeting, and orders the stranger to be seized and brought to him by force; but the knight jumps on to his steed, kills his assailants, and vanishes amid general consternation. Queen Tinatin is deeply intrigued by this mysterious episode. She summons her beloved Avtandil, commander of the royal army, and begs him to set out in quest of the stranger, promising him her hand when he returns.

After long and toilsome travels, Avtandil runs to earth the man of mystery in a desert cave. The meeting of the two heroes is very touching and they soon become intimate. The man in the panther's skin is named Tariel, and tells Avtandil his tragic life-story. He is a prince and general of India, the affianced of Nestan-Darejan, daughter of the Indian emperor. At Nestan's instigation, Tariel murdered her first betrothed, a prince of Khwarazm, to save her from a hateful match and guarantee the succession to the Indian throne from foreign usurpers. Hereupon riots broke out in the kingdom, and Nestan was secretly abducted from the palace. Since then Tariel has abandoned the world of men and roamed through the deserts of the world, looking for his beloved and bewailing his sad fate.

Avtandil comforts Tariel, and swears to remain for ever his faithful friend – indeed, the ideal of loyalty and friendship is one of the leitmotifs of Rustaveli's poem. Avtandil returns to Arabia to report to Tinatin on his discovery, and the two friends set off again to scour the world for Nestan-Darejan. After many vicissitudes, and thanks to an adventure as amorous as it is comic, Avtandil comes at last upon the princess's trail, shut up in a remote fortress in the land of the Kajis or demons, to whose ruler she is to be forcibly wed. With the help of a third hero, Pridon, the two knights raise an army, besiege the castle, and rescue the princess. Then follows feasting and merry-making, first at Pridon's palace, then in Arabia at King Rostevan's court, afterwards in India. Tariel and Nestan-Darejan ascend the throne of their ancestors in India, and Avtandil and Tinatin rule in felicity over the Arabian kingdom.

The poet's range of interest is amazingly wide; it embraces a mastery of political and judicial questions, familiarity with court life and cere-monial, and a grasp of the subtleties of the art of war. He can portray the structure and life of a great sea-power, its crowded cities and ports teeming with life and activity, and the feverish speculations and shifting fortunes of its inhabitants. Rustaveli was familiar with ancient Greek philosophy, with astronomy and astrology, and with the poetry of his Persian contemporaries, such as Nizami of Ganja (1140–1202).

A feature which Rustaveli shares with such world figures as Shakespeare is his ability to contrast scenes of high seriousness with interludes of earthy humour. In the middle of Avtandil's quest for the fair Nestan-Darejan, he arrives in the bustling port of Gulansharo. There, the mature but passionate Fatman, wife of the chief merchant, falls for the handsome knight. Under cover of giving him the information he needs, she seduces the knight, much against the latter's better judgement.

> Avtandil secretly wept. His tears flowed to mingle with oceans.
> Two vessels of shining black jet shone brightly in ebony pools.
> 'See me, O lovers', he thought, 'a nightingale far from its rose
> Now like a carrion-crow sits and sings on the dungheap!'

Always the courteous gentleman, Avtandil pretends to enjoy his hostess's frantic embrace. Fatman imagines that the knight has really fallen for her wrinkled charms. Rustaveli comments ironically:

> If a black crow finds a rose, it imagines itself a nightingale!

Romance, comedy and philosophic ideas thus occupy a prominent place in Rustaveli's *The Man in the Panther's Skin*. This fact has led some to question whether it ranks as a genuine epic at all. However, those who consider that no poem is an epic without a goodly seasoning of 'blood and thunder' and martial deeds will not be disappointed. Rustaveli is the poet of chivalry *par excellence*. He repeatedly exalts knightly prowess and the boon companionship of valiant comrades in arms. The most captious critic could scarcely desire more stirring scenes than Tariel's battle with the hosts of Khataeti (China), or the final assault on the supposedly impregnable fortress of the demon Kajis.

> Then the measureless wrath of God struck down the realm of the Kajis.
> And Saturn blotted the sun, so that darkness covered the heavens.
> The field was strewn with the wounded, corpses were heaped upon corpses.
> And ever the slaughter continued, till the dead were a mighty army.

Rustaveli's great poem, national in its inspiration, and yet infinitely polished and subtle in its execution, is the swan song of Georgia's Golden Age. In the epilogue, Rustaveli (or his later imitator) writes prophetically:

> The tale of our heroes is ended and has passed away like a dream.
> They have all gone from this world. Such is the treachery of time.
> Even for him who thinks it long it flies away in a flash.
> I, Rustaveli, a Meskhian, have written this tale of adventures ...
> Trust not the fleeting world; its smiles are delusive and false.
> It passes away and is gone like a flash before our eyes.
> Man, your endeavours are all in vain for fate will deceive you.
> Happy is he on whom fate will bestow its smiles.[22]

Between 1225 and 1240, Georgia was overwhelmed and ravaged by Khwarazmian and Mongol hordes from Central Asia. Late in the fourteenth century, fresh invasions by Leng Timur, or Tamerlane, cut short the brief national revival which had been headed by King George the Brilliant (1314–46). Constantinople, capital of Orthodox Christendom, fell in 1453 to the Ottoman Turks. The feudal nobles exploited the situation by setting themselves up as petty sovereigns on their own. Georgia was carved up by the Ottomans and the Safavi Shahs of Iran into spheres of influence – a situation which prevailed right up to the Russian annexation of 1801.

The popularity of Rustaveli's poem helped to keep the torch of nationhood alight during those dark years. A manuscript copy formed a part of every well-provided maiden's bridal trousseau. In the cave monastery of Vani, in Samtskhe province, destroyed by the Persians in 1552, there have been discovered at least two stanzas of *The Man in the Panther's Skin*, scratched upon the walls. From the seventeenth century onwards, we possess a number of richly decorated manuscripts, adorned with miniatures depicting scenes from the poem; these are mostly executed in the Persian manner characteristic of contemporary Safavid Iran. At the same time, popular cycles of prose tales about Tariel and other heroes and heroines of the poem circulated among village storytellers and bards.

Although the Armenians in medieval times produced several delightful writers of fables and lyrical verse, they did not bring forth any literary epic of the scale and sophistication of Rustaveli's *Vephkhis-tqaosani*. However, there was already taking shape among the storytellers and rustic bards of mountain Armenia the remarkable cycle of heroic tales and ballads, known variously as *David of Sassoun*, *Sassoun's Strong Men*, or *Daredevils of Sassoun*. Discovered and written down during the nineteenth century, these sagas of vanished Armenian supermen are now counted among the treasures of world folk literature, as well as commanding a strong emotive response among Armenians all over the world.

The mountain region of Sassoun is situated to the south-west of Lake Van, and is famed, like the Scottish highlands, as an outpost of rugged clansmen and warriors. In fact, the gallant Armenians of Sassoun never submitted to Turkish domination; they held on to their independence to the last breath, many being massacred by order of Sultan Abdul Hamid following the insurrection of 1894–5.

The David of Sassoun cycle has its roots in the tenth century, when Armenia was throwing off the domination of the Arab caliphs of Baghdad. At this time, Sassoun was part of the independent Armenian kingdom of Vaspurakan, ruled by the dynasty of the Ardsrunis. It was King Gagik of Vaspurakan (908–37) who built the wonderful church of Aghtamar, on an island in Lake Van; a descendant of his, Sennacherib or Senekerim (1003–21), ceded the kingdom to the Byzantine emperor. It is interesting to find the Assyrian name Sennacherib transferred to the Arab caliph of Baghdad, so that the David of Sassoun story begins with a feud of epic proportions between Sennacherib of Baghdad and Gagik of Armenia. The possible influence of biblical reminiscences of King Sennacherib of Assyria, foe of the Urartian ancestors of the Armenians, can certainly not be ruled out.

The ancestress of the mighty men of Sassoun, Lady Dzovinar, is a pious Armenian princess, who consents to wed the ninety year old caliph of Baghdad to save her people from extermination. She stipulates, how- ever, that she shall be allowed to retain the Christian religion, and that the caliph will not exercise his conjugal rights for forty days after the wedding ceremony. On Ascension Day, during the wedding festivities in Blue Castle, King Gagik lets his daughter Dzovinar go to a nearby monastery with her bridesmaids and chaperone. After praying in the monastery, and wandering along the shores of Lake Van, the princess and her attendants organize a picnic near the shore, where they eat on the grass. By God's grace, a fountain of sweet water spurts forth – a 'Milk-Fountain' in some versions. Lady Dzovinar drinks a full cup from this fountain, and miraculously conceives a son, who becomes the superman Sanasar; she then drinks another half-cup, and conceives a second, twin son, the puny, half-size Balthasar. When Lady Dzovinar arrives in Baghdad, and turns out to be pregnant, serious complications ensue. The caliph threatens at first to cut off Lady Dzovinar's head, but is dissuaded by her eloquence and charm. In this tale, perhaps, we have an echo of the Immaculate Conception of Christ by the Virgin Mary.

In spite of the caliph's threats, Dzovinar's twin sons, Sanasar and Balthasar, grow up and flourish lustily at the Arab court. Caliph Sennacherib marches on Jerusalem and besieges the Christians there. The caliph is about to win a complete victory, when God sends angels with fiery swords, who fall upon the Arab army and spread such con- fusion that the infidels finish by exterminating one another in the dark. The Caliph then vows to sacrifice to the idols his two putative sons, Sanasar and Balthasar, who flee to the Christian Armenian king Mushegh in Muş. After this the brothers accomplish sundry heroic feats of arms, and meet with many adventures. Both make successful marriages, Sanasar winning the hand of Princess Golden-Braids of the Copper City.

This section is rich in adventure stories and Armenian ethnographic lore. In addition to echoes of the times of Saladin and the Crusaders, the reader also recognizes strong Old Testament overtones. Clearly the expedition of Caliph Sennacherib against Jerusalem, and the subse- quent flight of his two putative sons to Armenia, is to be linked with the well known passage of the Second Book of Kings, Chapter XIX, when Sennacherib the Assyrian attempts to subdue King Hezekiah of Israel, and himself comes to a bad end:

And it came to pass that night, that the angel of the Lord went out, and smote in the camp of the Assyrians a hundred fourscore and five thousand: and when they arose early in the morning, behold they were all dead corpses.

So Sennacherib king of Assyria departed, and went and returned, and dwelt at Nineveh.

And it came to pass, as he was worshipping in the house of Nisroch his god, that Adrammelech and Sharezer his sons smote him with the sword: and they escaped into the land of Armenia . . .

Sanasar and the Princess Golden-Braids had three sons, of whom the eldest, Meherr or Mher, was the strongest of the three, though the youngest, Ohan-the-Thunder-Voiced, had a voice which could be heard throughout seven cities. Meherr was the kind of giant who could pull up trees by their roots, and would break a man's arm in seven places by giving him a hearty handshake. He overcomes a lion that was ravaging the countryside of Sassoun, and rides the land on his magic steed, Colt Jalali. Meherr overcomes many foes of Armenia, both natural and supernatural. He kills the White Dev, and vanquishes and then befriends the mighty Melik or Sultan of Egypt. Following the Sultan's death, his widow invites Meherr to the Egyptian court, where they have a tempestuous love affair, during which the queen conceives a son who is to be the saviour of the Egyptian state.

'Meherr' or 'Mher' is a form of the name of the god Mithra. The life-giving properties of Meherr-Mithra are underlined when, shortly before his death, he plants a splendid garden on the favourite hunting ground of the Sassoun warriors, Dzovasar, and makes it into a game preserve near which he builds a summer mansion for himself. After ruling Sassoun for forty years, Meherr dies, shortly after his true Armenian wife has given birth to a son, David, who is to be the legendary David of Sassoun.

The central section of the epic cycle, entitled 'Splendid David, Light of Sassoun', is the climax of the whole work. Meherr being dead, David's kinsmen send the baby to be suckled by the Egyptian queen, with whom Meherr has had such a passionate affair. David's half-brother, the future Misra Melik or Sultan of Egypt, is afraid and jealous of the infant, and wants him destroyed. Misra Melik ill-treats and humiliates David in every possible way, but still the lad grows up a superman like his father and grandfather.

The rivalry between David of Sassoun and his half-brother Misra Melik runs like a theme song through this central part of the cycle. They compete in various contests, such as mace-throwing, in which David easily gets the better of Misra Melik. Eventually, the embittered

Egyptian ruler decides to get rid of David altogether, under pretext of sending him home to his relatives in Sassoun. However, David has little difficulty in worsting the strong men sent to kill him on the way, and these now become his devoted bodyguard. Returning to Sassoun, David becomes a regular public benefactor, killing robber demons, rebuilding his father Meherr's monastery, and punishing the greedy tax-gatherers, like some Armenian Robin Hood. He helps the ploughmen by ploughing up vast areas of land single-handed, and then wolfs the entire pilau which the group had brought with them for several days' rations.

The exploits of David of Sassoun take on a Homeric grandeur when we come to the attack launched by Misra Melik, Sultan of Egypt, against the freedom-loving Armenians. David is mounted on the magic horse Jalali, which had belonged to his father, Great Meherr. After inflicting a signal defeat on the hordes of the Egyptians, David is lured into Misra Melik's encampment and treacherously trapped in a deep pit. The loyal citizens of Sassoun see a vision of David's plight, and hasten to rescue David from his toils. Hearing them approach, David shakes himself. Instantly, the chains and rings binding him spring apart, the millstones piled on top of the pit crack, splinter and rise sky-high, and anyone who is hit by one of the flying pieces falls dead on the spot. In the final confrontation between David and Misra Melik, it is the Egyptian ruler who is lowered into a well, which is covered with forty millstones and forty buffalo-hides, and spread over the top with carpets and quilts. But with one stroke of his sword, David slices through all this protective covering, and carves Misra Melik in half from head to loins. Modest and democratic as ever, David, his Uncle Toros and their thirty-eight warriors return to Sassoun with nothing but an ox cart, and the Egyptian monarch's ear stuck at the end of David's spear.

A veritable Hercules, as well as being something of a Till Eulenspiegel in his love of merry pranks, David is a great womanizer – unlike the stately heroes of Rustaveli's *Man in the Panther's Skin*, with its cult of chivalry and platonic love. He plans to wed the matchless beauty Khandut Khanum, princess of Tabriz, but on the way there falls for the wiles of Chimishkik Sultana, ruler of the city of Akhlat, near Lake Van.

David was an ardent young man and did not care whether she was a Turkish or Armenian lady, and Chimishkik Sultana was a sorceress. She bathed him, she wined him and dined him, she made the bed, and crawled to bed with him. They exchanged rings.

The next morning, David rides off to Tabriz, leaving his bride forlorn. (It is interesting that the name 'Chimishkik' is the same as that of John Tzimisces, a warlike Byzantine emperor of Armenian descent, who reigned from 969 to 976). From then onwards Chimishkik Sultana becomes a sworn foe of David of Sassoun, and it is an arrow from the bow of their little daughter that finally deals David a mortal blow.

Arriving at Khandut's court in Tabriz, David finds the lady importuned by forty suitors, who have been living and carousing in the palace for months and even years. Perhaps this is an echo of the passage in Homer's *Odyssey*, where Odysseus finds his wife Penelope beset by a crowd of suitors who are devouring his substance. At all events, David makes short work of these rivals, as he does of Shahpouh, king of Iran, and other mighty monarchs who are attracted by Khandut's incomparable charms.

David's son is Little Meherr, who is doomed to be childless, and also immortal, as the result of his father's curse. As Leon Surmelian observes, the second Meherr is a complex, mysterious, contradictory character – and perhaps the most fascinating one in the Sassoun cycle. There is both evil and good in Little Meherr. The strongest of all the Sassoun strong men, he is a rebel, a vagabond, the prototype of the wandering Armenian driven by the furies from place to place. He is dispossessed of the headship of the Sassoun clan because he is sterile, and cannot produce an heir.

There are few passages in Armenian literature to rival the pathetic grandeur of the passing of Little Meherr. Weary of a life of exile and privation, Little Meherr kneels before his father's grave, crying out in anguish:

> Blessed is our Lord God, great is his mercy.
> Rise up father dear from your dreamless sleep!
> I am frozen numb on this wintry peak.
> Tell me where to go, O where can I dwell
> On this ancient earth crumbling beneath me
> When I am alone and I have no share
> No part in Sassoun, and without an heir.
> Expelled from our House by mine own kin
> I wander around with no place to rest
> Longing for your words, your fatherly scent,
> Living in exile, homeless everywhere.

David's voice answers Meherr sorrowfully from the tomb, saying that he can no longer offer help now that serpents and scorpions have made his bones their nest. He bids him go to the old citadel of Van, to Raven's Rock, and enter inside for evermore.

> That's the door to knock. Wait till judgement day,
> The end of this world. It will be destroyed
> And a new world built to support the feet
> Of your fiery horse. When that happens, son,
> And you ride again, the whole world is yours.

Finally Meherr reaches Raven's Rock, swings his mace and splits the crag wide open. God takes him in, and the two halves of the rock come together. Meherr finds shelter at long last, and is freed of his misery. (The rock is still shown to visitors by local peasants and is called 'Mher-Kapisi'.) They say that the cliff opens twice a year, on the Festival of Roses, or 'Vardavar', and on Ascension Day. When the crag splits open, Meherr rides forth on his charger to see whether the world has changed, and will support him and his steed. But soon the hooves of his horse begin to sink into the crumbling soil, and Meherr hastens back to the security of his cavern. He never remains outside for more than two hours at a time.

Though *David of Sassoun* may originally have been in verse, the variants current today are in a kind of rhythmic prose, interspersed with lyric passages, songs, prayers and invocations. The cycle forms an enormous corpus, which has been edited in three volumes at Erevan, complete with variants and additions deriving from many generations of village story tellers. From this great corpus, a standard version of the epic has been compiled by leading Armenian scholars, though the authenticity of some of the episodes and connecting narrative remains a matter of discussion.[23] Since the work has been current for about a thousand years, but only written down over the last century, there is obviously room for further research and for difference of opinion on many matters of detail.

CHAPTER 9

ARMENIAN AND GEORGIAN
ARCHITECTURE AND FINE ARTS

From the architectural standpoint, Armenia and Georgia are as full of picturesque buildings, both ancient and modern, as they are of spectacular scenery.

An abundance of stone of excellent quality, combined with exposure to influences from Iran, Mesopotamia, and from the Roman and Hellenistic world, favoured the development of original forms of architecture and new structural techniques. A succession of religious creeds, from Urartian times onwards, called forth ingenuity of the highest order in building temples worthy of pagan deities and then of the God of the Christians. The twentieth-century visitor, however intent on studying the effects of modern technology on Armenian and Georgian industry, agriculture and education, can scarcely go a mile without being brought face to face with a fine church, a ruined castle, an ancient bridge, even an entire city hewn in the solid rock.

Armenian and Georgian architecture is notable for its versatility, since the people have to cope with an extremely wide range of climatic conditions, ranging from the wind-swept plateau of high Armenia, and the alpine pastures of upland Georgia, to the swampy marshlands of the Black Sea coast. We have already cited the account by Xenophon of the underground dugouts inhabited by the ancient Armenians in exposed areas. In highland Svaneti, on the other hand, village houses have always been equipped with high stone watchtowers, with a view to spotting marauders from neighbouring clans and hostile tribes. Classical writers spoke of the Mossynoeci tribe living by the Black Sea in wooden towers (*mossynes*), whence their name.[1] In Guria province, wooden houses constructed on similar lines are common even today, the living area being supported on high wooden stilts. The family have to mount a step-ladder onto a platform, which gives access to the human living quarters, while the livestock scuffle on the damp, humid earth underneath.

Georgia and Armenia are rich in remains of palaces and public

249

buildings. In the earliest times, these were quarried out of solid rock, following the example of the Urartians at the ancient citadel of Van. In Georgia, the city of Uplis-tsikhe, near Gori, was hewn out stage by stage during the Bronze Age and the Graeco-Roman period. This type of construction reached its apogeee late in the twelfth century AD, with the completion of the rock city of Vardzia, in the upper Mtkvari valley close to the modern Turkish frontier. Vardzia is made up of several storeys, being cut out of a high vertical cliff face. The city numbers at least five hundred rooms and apartments, including chapels, banqueting halls, cellars, stables, connected by a labyrinth of stairs and subterranean passages.[2] As in Cappadocia, some of the earliest Georgian churches and monasteries are carved out of solid rock, the outstanding example here being the St David of Gareja group of hermitages in Outer Kakheti.

During Hellenistic and Parthian times, Armenia was covered with splendid cities. Foremost among these was Tigranocerta (now in southern Turkey), the short-lived capital of King Tigranes the Great, which was largely razed to the ground by the Roman legions of Lucullus and Pompey. The alternative Armenian capital of Artaxata (Artashat) in the Araxes valley, which was fortified by King Artaxias the Great with the help of Hannibal of Carthage, was also several times burnt to the ground.[3]

There is however one superb site of the Arsacid period which has been systematically excavated and is now included on the regular tourist route for visitors to Soviet Armenia. This is the summer palace of the Armenian kings at Garni, eighteen miles east of Erevan. Garni is perched high up in the hills, overlooking the Azat river which flows down from the snow-covered peaks close to Lake Sevan. The village of Garni is renowned for its fruit, including grapes (from which is made the excellent Garni *vin rosé* served in Armenian restaurants), also apples, pears, apricots, and nuts.

From prehistoric times, man has made his dwelling on the Garni promontory which juts out high above the Azat river. This triangular promontory is impregnable for about four-fifths of its circuit, being joined to the upland slopes and orchards by a narrow and easily defensible causeway. Though harsh in winter, the climate is ideal in summer. Garni is well above the 5,000 ft mark, and is temperate even in July when Erevan and the Araxes plain are sweltering in temperatures around 90°.

Professor Babken Arakelian's excavations in Garni have laid bare the remains of round houses from the Early Bronze Age, about 2,500 BC. An Urartian inscription records that the Vannic kings also used Garni as an outpost and probably a summer residence. Enormous blocks of finely carved grey basalt surround the perimeter of ancient Garni, on the side which communicates with the hinterland. The lowest courses of these massive fortifications were laid down during Urartian times. No cement was used, but the blocks are fitted tightly together with consummate skill and art. Later, in the time of the Orontids and Artaxiads, the fortress walls were raised to a greater height, and the stone blocks clamped together with iron and lead braces. Fourteen massive turrets and bastions were added.

Garni became a favourite summer residence of the Artaxiad and Arsacid monarchs. When Artaxata down in the Araxes lowlands became unbearable in the heat, the Armenian kings could relax and also transact affairs of state in Garni, where such cultivated rulers as Artavazd II found time to compose plays and literary works. Garni is mentioned by Tacitus in connection with the civil wars of AD 52–3 in Armenia, involving the Georgian pretender Rhadamist. A Greek inscription found at Garni, opening with an invocation to Helios, records that King Tiridates I, founder of the Arsacid dynasty, built a palace for his queen and restored the citadel here, in the eleventh year of his reign (AD 77).

The most famous feature of Garni is the classical temple, built of grey basalt in the second half of the first century AD, and largely destroyed in an earthquake in 1679. Many European travellers visited the site during the nineteenth century, and in 1834 Dubois de Montpéreux drew an outline reconstruction of the temple, which accords in its general features with the later and more systematic re-creation by Professor N. Buniatian (1933). The temple was on a raised platform, at the highest point on the Garni promontory. A flight of nine steps led up to the front portico of the shrine, which was surmounted by an elegant triangular pediment. The rectangular inner cella or naos was surrounded by a peristyle of twenty-four Ionic columns. The dimensions of the cella, which apparently housed an image of Mithra, were modest, 5·14 by 7·92 metres. At each side of the front stairway was a massive pedestal, adorned with a bas-relief depicting the figure of Atlas holding up the pillars of the universe; evidently these pedestals once supported some kind of altar. All round the pitched roof ran a richly carved frieze, in which many specifically Armenian motifs were mingled with Hellenistic ones. Here we see carved luxuriantly in stone the conventional acanthus leaf, along with the pomegranate and the vine.[4]

Fifty metres to the north-west of the Hellenistic temple stand the remains of a remarkable Roman bath, which dates from the third century AD. This bath was built on the usual Roman plan, with cold, tepid and hot chambers. The furnace and steam heating systems were highly elaborate. The layout of the bath is similar to that in the royal city of Armazis-Khevi, close to the modern Mtskheta, in Georgia.

A particularly interesting feature of the bath at Garni is the partly destroyed mosaic floor, which adorned the vestibule of the bath. The outer pink frame encloses allegorical scenes based on marine mythology of the classical world. The blending of blues and greens gives a subtle illusion of the movement of the sea. In the centre we see a male figure, symbolizing Ocean, and a female one who is Thalassa, the Sea. On the four sides of the central area are hybrid creatures each having the torso of a fish, the front end of a horse, as well as certain human features. These marine centaurs carry Nereids on their back, including Thetis, the mother of Achilles. There are also lively representations of dolphins, fishes and fishermen. At the top of the mosaic is a Greek inscription, the sense of which is:

We worked without receiving any reward.

The significance of this remark is hard to seize, unless it is a complaint about bad conditions of work and poor pay. Perhaps it means that the work of the bath house staff resulted in nothing more tangible than water and hot air, which ran away and evaporated, leaving no durable result behind.

The adoption of Christianity in Armenia and Georgia early in the fourth century posed new problems for local architects. The earliest churches at Echmiadzin in Armenia and at Mtskheta in Georgia were evidently simple structures of wood, and perished long ago.

The first conventional stone-built churches belong to the vaulted basilica type, without a tower or dome. Though usually simple, not to say plain in design, the basilica has considerable possibilities of development, as well as making economical use of available ground space. The Transcaucasian basilica may sometimes have only a single nave, rather like a glorified barn. Usually, however, there are three naves, occasionally cut off from one another by continuous walls. The central nave is normally surmounted by a roof carried up by a short vertical stretch to a higher level than that of the two flanking ones. In most examples, there is a double row of pillars dividing the internal space longitudinally into nave and aisles, each separately vaulted.

The original patriarchal cathedral at the Armenian capital of Dvin was of the basilican type, but this is entirely ruined.[5] The most impressive Armenian basilica partially extant is that of Ereruk, situated four kilometres from the royal city of Ani. Originally a pagan temple, Ereruk was transformed into a Christian basilica in the fifth and sixth centuries AD. Even in its present ruined state, this grandiose shrine amazes the beholder by the refinement of its decorative motifs, and the technical mastery of its finely chiselled masonry.[6] Links with the classical world are affirmed in doorways flanked by Corinthian columns, and surmounted by graceful arches with elegant pediments. The barrel vaults of the naves and side aisles were fortified by salient arches forming ribs. Two towers flanked the portico or narthex at the west end. This feature, combined with the presence of a clerestory, establishes a link with Syrian architecture, where the basilica reached a high point of refinement earlier than in Armenia itself.[7]

The cathedrals of Bolnisi and Urbnisi, both in the Kartli province of Eastern Georgia, also belong to the basilica type, but do not possess the refinement of Ereruk. Bolnisi was built between 478 and 493, and contains interior brick vaulting of a much later period, probably the seventeenth century.[8] Far from being a short-lived or alien form of church architecture, the basilica continued in use long after the domed church was well known to Caucasian architects. Thus, the delightful church of Parkhal in south-western Georgia is a straightforward basilica, dating from the period of Bagratid power in the ninth and tenth centuries.[9]

Interesting though these Caucasian basilicas are, it is with the domed church that the Armenians and Georgians made the most important discoveries, and perfected the most new structural and decorative formulae.

In technical terms, the Armenians and Georgians set themselves the problem of how to site a circular or polygonal tower or dome over a space in the roof which was usually square or rectangular. The object was to achieve a harmonious exterior ensemble, a landmark for the Faithful in the country around, at the same time as creating within the structure a lofty and unified inner space, imbued with an atmosphere conducive to worship and religious awe.

There are two principal methods of siting a dome over a rectangular interior space. In one case, use is made of the architectural device known as the squinch (in French, *trompe*), which can be employed without interior columns or pillars; as an alternative, the device known as the pendentive is used, but this relies on interior columns, usually four in number. Squinches can be built in several ways: by corbelling out the courses of masonry in the upper corners of the interior room, each course projecting slightly beyond the one below; by building one or more arches diagonally across the corner; by filling in the corner with a little conical vault which has an arch on its outer diagonal face and its apex in the corner. The arched squinch is often stated to have been developed almost simultaneously by the early Sassanians in Persia, who used unfinished broken stone or coarse round cobbles set in gypsum mortar (as at Firuzabad), and by the Roman builders of the late Imperial period.[10] Muslim architecture, following Sassanian archetypes, makes great use of squinch forms, especially in the Syrian, Egyptian and Moorish phases. The distinctive stalactite work, which is so marked a feature of mature Muslim architecture, especially in Turkey, and also in many later Armenian churches, is in its essence a decorative development of blended niche squinch forms.

Closely allied to the squinch is the pendentive, which may be defined as a triangular segment of a spherical surface, filling in the upper corners of a square, rectangular or polygonal room, to form at the top a circular support for the dome. The intersections with the walls against which it abuts are semi-circular, and usually carried by arches. An early approximation to the pendentive form occurs in a domed room in one of the side buildings of the baths of Caracalla (AD 217), Rome. Here, however, the result is achieved by corbelling, whereas the true pendentive is built like a portion of a dome with radiating joints, a superb example being St Sophia in Constantinople, built in 532, and restored by the Armenian architect Trdat in AD 990. Pendentives are also frequent in Muslim architecture, often decorated with stalactite ornament, or with delicate ribbing. Sometimes the curve of the pendentive and the dome is continuous and without a break; this form is known as the pendentive dome.

The Armenians and Georgians took over these prototype forms, which in many respects look back to the Zoroastrian fire-temple and were usually made from mud brick or rubble masonry, and recreated them in perfectly chiselled and scientifically assembled stone-work, which has stood the test of centuries.

The earliest, basic type of domed church built in Armenia is the so-called 'apse-buttressed' or 'niche-buttressed' square. Cruciform within, this type has four principal axial buttresses, and often four lesser ones in the corners. A semi-circular niche opens out in the middle of each of the four sides, the eastern niche behind the altar serving as an apse. The dome, resting on squinches, covers the entire central space. This popular design of church is found almost simultaneously in Armenia at Avan (c. 600) and at St Hripsimé in Echmiadzin built by the Catholicos Komitas in 618, and in Georgia, at the Jvari monastery on a high hill above Mtskheta (c. 605).[11] A little later, need for a larger inner space dictated the introduction of four free-standing piers to support the central dome. Barrel vaults were introduced to intervene between the base of the dome, and the supporting buttresses. A good example of this development is the cathedral at Bagaran, built between 624 and 631; the groundplan of this monument resembles a Greek cross inscribed in a square.[12]

Once they had evolved the technique of domed church construction, the Armenians advanced rapidly towards complete mastery of its most advanced form – namely, the circular domed church, in which the vertical element assumes complete prominence, and the horizontal nave and aisles are relegated to insignificance. The apotheosis of round church building was attained very early, in the time of the Armenian Catholicos Nerses III of Ishkhan, 'the Builder', who was responsible for erecting the wonderful circular domed cathedral of Zvartnotz, near Echmiadzin, between 643 and 652. The monogram of Catholicos Nerses, in Greek letters, occurs at regular intervals in the stonework. The pillar capitals portray the eagle of Zvartnotz, while at intervals round the outer walls we come upon little images of the master builders carved in stone, each with his set square or similar tool of his craft.

Zvartnotz was built in three storeys of monumental proportions. The height was about 45 metres, the diameter close on 36 metres. The sanctuary within was cruciform, but only the niche of the apse had a solid wall. The other three niches were open exedrae, each with an arcade supported by six columns. There was a circular ambulatory between the inner shrine and the outer wall of the cathedral; between the facings of finely cut masonry was a core of rubble and concrete. Even in its present ruined state, the cathedral of Zvartnotz remains one of the architectural wonders of the world.[13]

The Saracen yoke, which weighed heavily on Armenia and Georgia for three centuries, effectively put a stop to any new development in religious architecture. As soon as this burden was removed, and political independence re-established, the Armenian and Georgian master-builders resumed their work where their predecessors had been forced to abandon it, and evolved fresh masterpieces in both new and traditional designs. Among the main foyers of Caucasian church architecture in the tenth and eleventh century were the southern Armenian kingdom of Vaspurakan, under the Ardsruni dynasty,[14] the Armenian Bagratid capital at Ani, and the fast-growing kingdom of the Georgian Bagratids in the north, extending from Tao-Klarjeti (in modern Turkey), right across to Kakheti in the extreme east.

The principal church buildings of the Armenian and Georgian kingdoms from the tenth century onwards were mostly of a type combining features of the basilica and of the centralized, domed church. The effect is of two basilicas, often built to different heights, intersecting, with a lofty dome crowning the junction. These edifices have a nave and choir, also transepts. The larger churches have several pairs of free-standing pillars in the nave, giving an aisle on either side. The pillars themselves often assume the form of clustered piers, so characteristic of later Gothic cathedrals in the West. In a few rare instances, as in Trdat's cathedral at Ani, the arches between the pillars are slightly pointed, again anticipating the later Gothic cathedrals of Europe.[15] Even where the arches are rounded, as in the Cathedral of Sveti-Tskhoveli at Mtskheta, the lofty columns give an impression of soaring height and

255

heaven-ward impulse which is most impressive.[16] At Ani and elsewhere, skilful use of blind arcading on the exterior, with high narrow windows, combine to give the impression of additional height.

The question of the Armenian antecedents of Western Gothic and Romanesque architecture was raised, in a somewhat dogmatic fashion, by the Viennese art historian Josef Strzygowski over half a century ago.[17] There has since been a reaction against some of his theories and assumptions. This has resulted in turn in failure to take into account Armenia's part in the transmission of certain characteristics of the Gothic style to the West, particularly at the period of the Crusades.

This is not to claim, of course, that the Armenians invented such features as the pointed arch, which was used in Syria from the eighth century, and in Egypt and North Africa from the ninth, as in the great Cairo mosque of Ibn Tulun built in 876-9. But it is significant that the actual spread of the pointed arch and related architectural features into Western Europe really got under way after the Seljuq conquest of Armenia, when Armenians fled to Cilicia and set up the Rupenid kingdom in conjunction with the Crusaders, and when the Frankish barons came into regular contact with Arab and Turkish culture. It is noteworthy that Armenia and Anatolia formed part of a single and extremely dynamic state during much of the period of the Great Seljuqs, between 1040 and 1157, and more particularly after the Seljuq victory at Manzikert (1071).[18] It was precisely this westward push by the Turks that helped to provoke the First Crusade of 1095-99.

A recent student of the problem, Mr John H. Harvey, highly sceptical of any Armenian Christian architectural influence on European Gothic, nevertheless singles out a group of Islamic buildings in or close to Armenia for mention in this particular context.[19] These buildings include the Great Mosque at Diyarbakir (the ancient Amida), a complex of buildings with a consistent use of pointed arches, including arcades of successive moulded arches, with inscriptions indicating construction dates equivalent to AD 1117-25. Then there is a pointed-arched bridge over the Tigris two miles below Diyarbakir, rebuilt in AD 1065. At Siirt, southwest of Lake Van, is a mosque begun in 1129, but altered in the thirteenth century, and sharing certain features with the mosque of Diyarbakir.

In connection with the origins of European Gothic, Mr Harvey singles out for special mention the Great Mosque at Bitlis, in the heart of southwestern Armenia. Bitlis lies to the east of the Crusader zone of influence, but the Great Mosque represents a style of early Seljuq architecture with which the Crusaders were certainly acquainted. The Seljuq state centred on Bitlis was set up in 1084, and the Great Mosque, a product very largely of Armenian architectural genius, was completed about AD 1126. The structure is in a simple pointed-arch style, with arches in square recessed orders, impost mouldings, and pointed barrel vaults supported on cross-ribs of square section. The main front has a series of tall pointed-arched recesses containing the doorways, and above the bay containing the *mihrab* is a dome carried on pendentives, and a cylindrical drum, surmounted by a conical stone roof of typical Seljuq style. 'Here at Bitlis,' our authority concludes, 'we have a building which in its architectural elements forms a perfect eastern counterpart of Cistercian Fontenay'.

Another interesting example of the unexpected diffusion of architectural forms devised wholly or partly by Armenians occurs in the case of the Anatolian *kümbet* or tomb tower, which becomes a regular feature on the landscape from the eleventh century onwards. In architectural design, and in the stone carving and blind arcading which regularly adorn these structures, these Muslim *kümbet* bear an unmistakable resemblance to the steeple dome-tower and roof-cone of Armenian churches of the same period and earlier. The geometrical and interlace stone carving parallels that of the Armenian *khachkar* or memorial stone.

These *kümbet* are found in considerable numbers in once Armenian districts such as Akhlat, near Lake Van, and Erzurum. It is now recognized by art historians that the same Armenian masons sometimes erected both Christian and Islamic buildings. Thus Caucasian church towers could well have served as prototypes for Islamic tombs, just as later Armenian churches often seem to borrow their carved doorways from those of contemporary mosques.

The interest and beauty of Armenian and Georgian church architecture is heightened by its wonderful sculpture work, in both high and low relief. Special care was lavished on such features as the tympanum and archivolt of doorways, on the surrounds of windows, and on the circular or polygonal drums of churches. Early buildings of the fifth and sixth centuries were contemporary with Sassanian Iran. A number of Persian motifs feature on column capitals of this period, including wild animals depicted in a realistic manner. The Iranian motif of the royal hunt is later transformed into the figure of St George on horseback, often accompanied by other warrior saints.

Each nation had its own special techniques and modes of expression in sculpture. The Armenians excelled with their *khachkar* or memorial cross stone, often showing such motifs as the tree of life, and whole cycles of Biblical scenes.[20] The *khachkar* is unknown in Georgia, where a splendid feature of ancient churches is the stone iconostasis or altar partition, sometimes carved with sacred scenes, including lives of local, Georgian saints.[21] The altar partition, on the other hand, does not feature in Armenian churches, where the sacred mysteries are celebrated on a raised altar platform some three feet high, in front of which a curtain is drawn at specified moments during the divine service.

Armenian taste in carving later developed close affinities with that of Islam. The Armenians were fond of angular, geometrical patterns, whereas the Georgians favoured a more sinuous, rounded interlace, in association with a leaf-like palmette motif. Indeed, much of Georgian art is affected by the cult of the vine, which also features prominently in such monuments of Armenian sculpture as the church of Gagik at Aghtamar.[22]

Many religious buildings in both Georgia and Armenia have reliefs depicting the pious founder of the church holding up a model of the edifice. Jesus Christ is frequently depicted giving His blessing to the church, and to its donor. These reliefs, such as that of Kuropalates Ashot at Opiza in Tao-Klarjeti, are of great interest, as they preserve rare or unique likenesses of ancient kings and establish the original shape and outline of the buildings themselves.[23]

British scholars have done much to make known the treasures of Armenian and Georgian sculpture to the Western world. H.F.B. Lynch's standard *Armenia: Travels and Studies* gives rich documentation on Ani and many other sites. The Edinburgh scholars David and Tamara Talbot Rice have included Caucasian sculpture in many of their publications on Byzantine and Russian art. Still more recently Mr David Winfield has undertaken a systematic survey of the Georgian churches of Tao-Klarjeti, now within the eastern vilayets of Turkey. Among other little-known examples of Georgian stone-work, Mr Winfield has published the first comprehensive reproductions of a remarkable column with figured sculpture at the cathedral church of Oshki, and representing the apotheosis either of St Simeon Stylites, or of the Bagratid dynasty.[24] This outstanding example of mid-tenth century sculpture is of cardinal importance in assessing the possible eastern origins of the Gothic and Romanesque figured sculpture of Western Europe.

Closely allied to sculpture in stone is the art of the wood carver. Here again, the Georgians and Armenians have always excelled. Several masterpieces in the form of column capitals and church doors are up to a thousand years old. Outstanding surviving examples include a group of eleven wooden doors from Svaneti, in mountain Georgia, also a wooden capital from one of the Lake Sevan churches, which is adorned with confronted peacocks and ducks. Tamara Talbot Rice makes a case for comparing the treatment of these bird figures with that on an Achaemenid gold disc from the Akhalgori hoard, found in Georgia.[25] Again, one can see in Erevan a magnificent carved wooden door from a church in Muş. This door, with its delicate ornamentation, dates from

1134; it was saved during the Ottoman pogroms of 1915 by the self-sacrifice of the local inhabitants, and brought safely to its present place of exhibition.[26]

Of related interest is the art of carving in ivory. An outstanding example of this is exhibited in the public showrooms of the Matenadaran Manuscript library in Erevan—the ivory cover of the Echmiadzin Gospels. Older than the gospel manuscript itself, the ivory cover is dated to the sixth century AD. It is fully comparable with the best examples of Byzantine ivory work, and has a series of panels showing the Virgin and Child, the Flight into Egypt, the Adoration of the Magi, the Entry into Jerusalem and other episodes from the life of Christ. Both front and back plates show a pair of angels, bearing up a wreath in which is framed a cross.[27]

A field in which the Georgians have always particularly excelled is that of metal and repoussé work, the history of which goes back to the Early Bronze Age. In some of the best examples, the craft of the goldsmith is associated with that of the artist in enamel. Perhaps the loveliest of all cloisonné enamels of the Byzantine type were produced in Georgia, to judge by the much mutilated but still superb examples which adorn the Khakhuli icon, now preserved in the State Museum of Art in Tbilisi. The central feature here is a tenth century enamel of the Virgin which, though so much damaged that only the face and hands survive, is comparable in beauty and expressiveness to the scarcely less damaged twelfth century Byzantine icon of the Virgin of Vladimir. This enamel of the Virgin forms the central feature of a splendid triptych, adorned with exquisite gold filigree work and granulations which provide settings for cabochon jewels and numerous small cloisonné enamels, depicting Christ Pantocrator, the Archangel Gabriel, Saints John and Mark, and St Gregory the Theologian. The triptych was made by three unknown masters of the Gelati school, during the reign of Dimitri I (1125–54), to enshrine the miracle-working image of Our Lady of Khakhuli, which had been brought for safety from its original home in south-western Georgia, when the area was overrun by the Seljuq Turks.[28] The Holy Virgin has always been held in special reverence at the monastery of Gelati, which is not far from the Western Georgian capital of Kutaisi. There is a fine mosaic of the Virgin in the apse of the main cathedral church at Gelati, dating from 1125–30, and probably connected with the creation and installation of the Khakhuli triptych.

Other genres of precious metal work in which the Georgians excelled include jewelled processional crosses, Gospel covers, and silver and gold plate and drinking vessels for both Court and Church use.[29] Two great masters are known to us by name – Beka and Beshken Opizari – so designated after the monastic centre of Opiza in Klarjeti, where they plied their craft with high distinction during the twelfth and early thirteenth centuries. One of Beka's masterpieces is the icon of Our Saviour of Anchi, while Beshken fashioned the remarkable silver cover of the Berta Gospels.

This is also the point to consider briefly Armenian metal and repoussé work, in particular reliquaries, triptychs and book covers with raised reliefs. The Armenians are known to this day as skilful craftsmen in silver, gold and fine jewellery. Unfortunately, the ravages of time and greedy invaders have destroyed virtually all the earliest examples of Armenian metal work, before the thirteenth century. Of what remains, the best collections are in the museum at the rear of Echmiadzin cathedral; in the State Historical Museum of Armenia, Lenin Square, Erevan; in the treasury of the Armenian patriarchate of Jerusalem; and in that of the Catholicosate of Cilicia, now established at Antelias, close to Beirut in the Lebanon.

Of the Antelias collection, we may single out the silver cover of the Gospels of Catholicos Constantine I, made in Cilicia in 1248, and showing Christ enthroned, on the front plate, and Christ crucified, on the back plate.[30] Both these compositions are surrounded by small crosses and medallions depicting the Holy Virgin, saints and also symbolic figures of winged beasts. Another book cover belonging to Catholicos Constantine I, dating from 1255 and fashioned from silver gilt, is now in Erevan. Dedicatory inscriptions frame two large compositions: the Deesis figures upon the front plate, and four standing Evangelists on the back one. As seen on some Byzantine ivories of the eleventh century, Christ stands between the Virgin and St John the Baptist, instead of being enthroned according to the more usual pattern of the Deesis.

Perhaps the finest example of Armenian metal work is the silver gilt reliquary, in the form of a triptych, presented to King Hetum II by the Catholicos Constantine II in 1293. This masterpiece, known as the Reliquary of Skevra, has been frequently illustrated. The central panel shows St Gregory the Illuminator and the Apostle Thaddeus, on either side of a large cross. The apostles Peter and Paul are shown in bust, in circular medallions, together with four saints, one of whom is St Vardan Mamikonian, the hero of the Battle of Avarayr. The wings of the triptych represent the Annunciation, while there is a medallion framing the figure of King Hetum II kneeling in the attitude of a pious suppliant.[31]

Every major Armenian and Georgian church and cathedral had a fine collection of altar furnishings in gold and silver. Jewelled tabernacles, censers, pontifical mitres adorned with precious stones, embroidered silk on cloth of gold, silver doves wherein is contained the Holy Chrism, pontifical crosses, and ornamented golden chalices are some of the articles on which the greatest skill and craftsmanship are lavished.

Among the relics of Antelias is an embossed silver chest, in which are kept the bones of the right hand of St Gregory the Illuminator. In both Echmiadzin and Antelias, we see a number of relics comprising the right hands of saints, enclosed in silver or gold cases shaped like hands, giving the appearance of gauntlets. There are several items of Armenian ecclesiastical regalia in the Victoria and Albert Museum in London, including so-called 'Tau crosses', the head being shaped like a letter 'T', often entwined with fantastic embellishments in guise of serpents and other forms.

Both the Armenians and the Georgians of medieval times excelled in the art of painting. This took on two main forms – fresco painting, and the illustration of illuminated manuscripts.

Fresco painting in Armenia has a long and distinguished tradition, going back to Urartian temples and palaces in which both sacred and secular art of a formal kind reached a high degree of perfection. The Armenian and Georgian Churches both favoured the decoration of religious buildings with sacred paintings. Around AD 610, the Armenian theologian Vrtanes Kertogh wrote that many Christian scenes were already portrayed on the walls of shrines and cathedrals, among these being the Virgin and Child, the martyrdom of St Stephen, the tortures inflicted by King Tiridates on St Gregory the Illuminator, portraits of the martyred virgins Hripsimé and Gaiané, and the miracles of Christ and scenes from His life.[32]

Vrtanes further states that 'all that the Holy Scriptures relate is painted in the churches'. The famous church of Aghtamar is rich in mural paintings dating, like the structure itself, from the tenth century, and showing a cycle of episodes from the life of Christ, from the Visitation and the Nativity to the Crucifixion and the Ascension. The historian Stephen Orbelian speaks of the rich paintings which adorned the churches of Siunia, in north-eastern Armenia, during the tenth century, while the sacred poet Gregory of Narek praised the portraits of saints in the church of the Holy Cross founded by Stephen of Mokk in 983.

The representation of the human figure is anathema to the proponents of Islam. Following the invasion of Armenia by the Seljuqs, the interior of many Armenians churches was defiled and the frescoes removed or plastered over. However, the tradition of fresco painting was worthily continued by the Georgians.

Georgians frescoes, for all their classical poise and elegance, and their expressive austerity in the portrayal of the human face and figure, are not slavish imitations of Byzantine models. In the case of such gems as Ateni, Qindsvisi, or the little church at Ubisi, the Georgian artists endow their paintings with movement and grace. Far from reproducing stereotyped Greek saints, the Georgian artists enrich their subject with naturalistic touches, often highly original and even humorous. The frescoes often include likenesses of royal personages and local grandees. Outstanding examples include the fresco of King David the Builder at Gelati, and of King Giorgi III and Queen Tamar at the rock city of Vardzia.[33] The earliest Armenian and Georgian illuminated manuscripts to survive the ravages of time date from shortly before AD 900. However, richly decorated Gospels were already in use in Armenia much earlier, to judge from the remarks of the theologian Vrtanes Kertogh, who flourished around AD 610, and refers to 'the book of the Gospels painted, and bound not only with gold and silver but with ivory and purple parchment'. The Holy Scriptures were first translated into Armenian from the Syriac, and later revised with reference to the Greek. Therefore the Armenians would have been familiar with such masterpieces of Syriac manuscript illumination as the Gospel of Rabbula, dated to AD 586. Proof of this is provided by a set of four miniatures bound in at the end of the Echmiadzin Gospels of AD 989, but themselves of a much earlier date: indeed, the miniatures have parallels with Armenian frescoes of the seventh century.[34]

The Lazarev Gospel of AD 887, preserved in the Matenadaran Library in Erevan, is the first dated Armenian manuscript to have come down to us. Some controversy attaches to the beautiful Gospels of Queen Mlke, assigned by some authorities to AD 862, but by others to AD 902.[35] The first Georgian illuminated Gospel manuscripts are those of Adishi (AD 897) and the First Jruchi Gospels (AD 936–40). These are outstanding for their decorative elements and artistic treatment of draperies. From the stylistic viewpoint, they are related to the Hellenistic tradition, while from the iconographic aspect, they recall some Syro-Palestinian compositions.[36]

Byzantine influences are seen in the decorations of initial folios, which contain the Epistle of Eusebius to Carpianus, explaining the concordance between the Four Gospels. As time went on, we find the canon tables adorned increasingly with elaborate arcades, the general effect resembling a church porch. There may be frontispieces, with a reproduction of a decorated cross on a pedestal, or portraying the Deesis, or image of Christ flanked by the Virgin and John the Baptist. The four Evangelists constantly appear at appropriate points in the manuscripts, each one painted on a separate sheet; usually, the Evangelist is shown writing assiduously at a desk, with a church and other buildings in the background.

The summit of perfection is reached in Georgia with such masterpieces as the Allaverdi Gospels of 1054, and the Vani Gospels of the twelfth century; the superb Gelati Gospels are also of this period.[37] Dignity, harmony and brilliant use of colouring are characteristic of this group.

The Georgians adhered in their Gospel illumination to hallowed Byzantine models, but the Armenians soon began to strike out into more original paths. The Armenians became more and more daring in the use of fanciful vignettes and marginal figures, often in the style of musicians or acrobats, and in the introduction of costume detail and of plants, animals and birds more typical of medieval Armenia than of Biblical Palestine. In the miniatures of the Haghpat Gospels, copied near Ani in 1211, the artist depicted the Entry of Christ into Jerusalem as if it were some royal procession in the time of the Armenian kings, with joyous townspeople holding musical instruments, and a number of youths on a balcony, engaged in light-hearted banter with a group of young ladies. From such touches as these, it is only a few steps to still later manuscripts, where Christ is shown in medieval costume, wearing wide trousers and leather boots.

The zenith of Armenian miniature painting occurred in Cilicia in the thirteenth century, with the art of the immortal Toros Roslin, in whose person the advances made by earlier generations of Armenian painters were combined with appreciation of the techniques of Byzantium and Italy. Inspired by an inborn sense of the beautiful and a superiority of technique all his own, Toros Roslin has been hailed as a true precursor of the Italian Renaissance. Though of miniature proportions, his work is comparable to that of Cimabue or Giotto, and merits a prominent place in the history of world art.[38]

Both the Armenians and Georgians decorated manuscripts of lives of saints, lectionaries and other liturgical books. Adventure stories such as the Alexander Romance by pseudo-Callisthenes also gave scope for original treatment. The Georgians went in for illustrated manuscripts of a number of other medieval romances, often translated from Persian. During the seventeenth century, they produced some remarkable sets of illustrations to the romantic epic of Shota Rustaveli, *The Man in the Panther's Skin*, reflecting the taste and style of Safavid Iran.[39]

No account of the arts of Armenia and Georgia would be complete without reference to the highly individual musical culture which has existed there for several thousand years. Even though the very oldest melodies and songs are lost to us, we derive a vivid impression of musical life from archaeological finds, sculptures and frescoes, manuscript illuminations, and references to music and singers in ancient literary sources.

At least two Bronze Age burials in Georgia contain musical instruments. In one case, a little shepherd is buried together with his pipe, carved from bone. In another instance, a tomb dating from the fifteenth century BC was found to contain a delicately fashioned flute, 20 cm. long, made from the tibia of a swan. Georgian musicologists have found that simple tunes can still be played on this remarkable instrument.[40]

Contact with Iran and Greece greatly enriched Armenian and Georgian musical life during Hellenistic times. No king or feudal noble would have dreamed of holding a banquet without the presence of minstrels and singers. There is a famous scene in the *Life of Crassus* by Plutarch where, in 53 BC, a messenger brings the head of the slain Crassus into the hall where the kings of Armenia and Parthia are holding a banquet, and hurls it among the revellers. At this feast, we are told, the *Bacchae* of Euripides was being performed to music.

Another gruesome scene occurred in AD 374, when the Armenian king Pap was murdered at a dinner, when he was gazing at groups of *gusans* or minstrels, who were performing to an accompaniment of drummers, pipers, lyre-players and trumpeters. The chronicler Moses of Khorene specifically refers to information about ancient Armenian kings and heroes such as Aram, lacking in books, being handed down 'by the chants and popular songs of certain obscure *gusans*'.

There is no doubt whatever that the temple rites of Armenia's pagan shrines were accompanied by chanting and by solemn chords on gongs and other instruments. Early Armenian Christian writers inveigh against people who employed lay minstrels to sing at funerals instead of regular priests. One authority commands: 'Let not priests abandoning pious songs, receive *gusans* into their houses', while an Armenian prayer book contains the confession: 'I have sinned by attending comedies, I have sinned by entertaining minstrels.'[41]

The Armenian and Georgian Church Fathers were not backward in competing with the charms of secular music. Around AD 400, we learn that St Sahak the Great was 'perfectly versed in singers' writing'. From the ninth century onwards, we find in hundreds of Armenian and Georgian sacred manuscripts a system of musical signs known in Armenian as *khaz*, which are written in above the line to help the priest in chanting the divine service. These signs, which resemble the *neumes* employed in the West, marked the pitch, nuance, rhythm and cadence, though they appear not to provide a complete system of musical notation.[42] Great progress was made by the Armenian composer Komitas (1869–1935) in deciphering the *khaz* signs and reconstructing the ancient Church music. However his library was destroyed in 1915 by the Young Turks, whose persecutions also robbed Komitas of his sanity.

Great schools of hymnographers grew up in Georgia and Armenia from the tenth century. In Georgia the great names are those of Michael Modrekili and Ioane Mtbevari. The Iviron Monastery on Mount Athos performed pioneer work in adapting Byzantine chants and liturgical works for use in Georgia.[43] In Armenia, a famous composer of sacred poems and melodies was Gregory of Narek (945–1003), and his work was carried on in Cilician Armenia by St Nerses Shnorhali (1101–73) whose surname means 'the Gracious'.

Georgian vocal music is basically polyphonic. The music of the liturgy has features in common with such polyphonic drinking songs as the *Mravalzhamieri*, or 'Toast of Long Life'. In Armenia, the leading genre of Church music is the *sharakan* or hymn; here again, the Church Fathers have not disdained to use popular traditional melodies, a fact which contributes to the truly national character of the Armenian Church. Though polyphony is not unknown, Armenian sacred music is largely homophonic in character, with beautiful flowing melodies and use of cantilena.

Following the destruction of the Armenian kingdom of the Bagratids of Ani, patronage of music and the arts passed to the Bagratid rulers of Georgia, who for a time exercised suzerainty over parts of Armenia also. Medieval manuscript illustrations show that the Georgians, like the Armenians, performed on cymbals, the lute, the tabor and the flute. One striking Georgian medieval miniature shows Gideon and his Israelite band giving a spirited performance on trumpets, putting the Midianites to flight. These trumpets may be a type known as *buki*, a vibrating-lip aerophone looking much like its Central Asian and Far Eastern analogues. Much in evidence also was the *doli*, a two-headed cylindrical drum deriving from the *dhol* of Afghanistan.

When Queen Tamar married David Soslan in 1189, a musical performance or *sakhioba* was given, with the participation of numerous minstrels or *mgosani*, and acrobats. In his romantic epic, *The Man in the Panther's Skin*, Shota Rustaveli mentions no less than fourteen types of musical instruments, indicating that they were in use at the time of Queen Tamar. Apart from those already mentioned, Rustaveli knew of the harp (*changi*), castanets (*chaghana*), the psaltery (*knari*), rattles (*ezhvanni*), and the reed-pipe.[44] Georgian peasants have from time immemorial been expert performers on that international rustic instrument, the pan-pipes (*lartchemi*).

Although there are some gaps in our information, anyone who listens today to the compositions of Aram Khatchaturian or Zakaria Paliashvili, or to the liturgy of Holy Echmiadzin, may be certain that he is enjoying an experience deriving from a musical culture with an ancient and highly distinctive history.

NOTES

ABBREVIATIONS USED IN THE FOOTNOTES

AJA: *American Journal of Archaeology*, Princeton, N.J., etc., 1885–.

ARAB: D.D. Luckenbill, *Ancient Records of Assyria and Babylon*, Chicago, 1926.

AS: *Anatolian Studies*.

Belleten: Türk Tarih Kurumu Belleten, Ankara.

Bronze Age USSR: T. Sulimirski, 'The Bronze Age of the USSR, Bulletin no. 7 of the Institute of Archaeology, University of London, 1968.

CAH: *Cambridge Ancient History* (revised edition of Volumes I and II, in separate fascicles).

Chronologies: R.W. Ehrich (editor), *Chronologies in Old World Archaeology*, Chicago, 1965.

ESA: *Eurasia Septentrionalis Antiqua*.

GIM: *Trudy Gosudarsvennogo Istoricheskogo Muzeya*, Moscow.

Handbuch: F.W.König, *Handbuch der chaldischen Inschriften* Archiv für Orientforschung, Beiheft 8, Graz, 1955–7.

JAOS: *Journal of the American Oriental Society*.

JCS: *Journal of Cuneiform Studies*.

JNES: *Journal of Near Eastern Studies*.

KSIA: *Kratkie Soobshcheniya Instituta Arkheologii*. AN SSSR, Moscow.

MIA: *Materialy i Issledovaniya po Arkheologii SSSR*, Moscow-Leningrad.

Neolithic USSR: T. Sulimirski, 'The Neolithic of the USSR Bulletin no. 6 of the Institute of

Archaeology, University of London, 1967.

OIP: Oriental Institute Publications, Chicago.

PEQ: *Palestine Exploration Quarterly*.

PPS: *Proceedings of the Prehistoric Society*.

SA: *Sovetskaya Arkheologiya*, Moscow.

SAOC: Studies in Ancient Oriental Civilization, Chicago.

Stratigraphie: C.F.A. Schaeffer: *Stratigraphie Comparée et Chronologie de l'Asie Occidentale*, Oxford University Press, London, 1948.

UKN: G.A.Melikishvili, *Urartskie Klinoobraznye Nadpisi* (Urartian Cuneiform Inscriptions), Moscow, 1960.

ZA: *Zeitschrift für Assyriologie*.

I. THE ENVIRONMENT

1 K.W.Butzer, 'Physical Conditions in Eastern Europe, Western Asia and Egypt, before the period of agricultural and urban settlement etc.', CAH fasc. 33 1965; and the same writer's *Quaternary Stratigraphy and Climate in the Near East*, Bonn, 1958.

2 (a) K.W.Butzer, *Environment and Archaeology: an Introduction to Pleistocene Geography*, Chicago, 1964; London, 1965. (b) W.C.Brice, *South-West Asia: a Systematic Regional Geography*, vol. VIII, London, 1967, including a sound general discussion of Turkey.

3 H.Wright, in R.J.Braidwood and B.Howe: *Prehistoric Investigations in Iraqi Kurdistan*, SAOC no. 31, Chicago, 1960, pp. 71–97 (chapter VII).

4 H.R.Cohen and Öğüz Erol, 'Aspects of the Palaeogeography of Central Anatolia', *The Geographical Journal* 135 (3), September, 1969, pp. 388–98.

5 Seton Lloyd and James Mellaart, *Beycesultan* II, London, 1965, especially pp. 3–34. For a provocative but not altogether reliable review by J.V. Canby, see AJA 70, 1966.

6 R.S.Young, 'The Gordion Campaign of 1957: Preliminary Report', AJA 62, 1958, pp. 139–54 and plates 20–27.

7 B.B.Piotrovskii, The Aeneolithic Culture of Transcaucasia in the Third Millennium BC, *Sixth International Congress of Prehistoric and Protohistoric Sciences*, Reports, Moscow, 1962.

8 (a) Hans Helbaek, in *Prehistoric Investigations in Iraqi Kurdistan*, pp. 99–118 (chapter VIII). (b) Helbaek, 'Commentary on the Phylogenesis of Triticum and Hordeum', *Economic Botany* 20, 1966, pp. 355ff. (c) Jane Renfrew, 'A Note on the Neolithic Grain from Can Hasan', AS XVIII, 1968, pp. 55–6.

9 The writer can witness to this, illustrated by a popular story of an iron door on a hillside, underneath which there is said to be a silver door, then a gold door, then – cold water!

10 e.g. Hacilar. See James Mellaart's reports in AS VIII, 1958, pp. 127–56, IX, 1959, pp. 51–65, X, 1960, pp. 83–104 and XI, 1961, pp. 39–75.

11 e.g. the Cilician Gates, used by Alexander the Great.

12 Xenophon, *Anabasis*, Bk IV, chr vii.

13 ARAB I, paras 236–7, 584, 604, 785.

14 (a) For references in Hittite texts, John Garstang and O.R.Gurney, *The Geography of the Hittite Empire*, London, 1959, pp. 33–6. This is in connection with Samuha, here located on the upper Halys (Kizil Irmak or Red River) near Zara, where the river is indeed small. (b) For navigation on Lake Van, the implied evidence of Sarduri I's inscriptions at Van, *Handbuch* I, p. 37 (nos. 1a–c) and pl. 1. (c) For Lake Urmia, Strabo, *Geography*, Bk XI, 13, paras 1–3.

15 T.Cuyler Young, 'The Iranian Migration into the Zagros', *Iran* V, 1967, pp. 11–34, in which a north-easterly approach rather than one through the Caucasus is suggested; see Chapter IV.

16 (a) Colin Renfrew, J.E.Dixon and J.R.Cann, 'Obsidian and Early Cultural Contact in the Near East', PPS XXXII, 1966, pp. 30–72). (b)

Gary A.Wright, *Obsidian Analyses and Prehistoric Near Eastern Trade, 7500 to 3500 BC*, Anthropological Papers 37, Museum of Anthropology, University of Michigan, 1969.

17 R.J.Forbes, *Metallurgy in Antiquity*, Leiden, 1950, pp. 238–40 for tin sources.

18 (a) For the most important source of copper in Anatolia, S.E.Birgi, 'Notes on the Influence of the Ergani Copper Mines on the Development of the Metal Industry in the Ancient Near East', *Jahrbuch für kleinasiatische Forschung* I 1951, pp. 337 ff. (b) For Kanesh, Paul Garelli: *Les Assyriens en Cappadoce*, Paris, 1963; and (c) M.T.Larsen, *Old Assyrian Caravan Procedures*, Netherlands Historical and Archaeological Institute of Istanbul, 1967.

19 Colin Renfrew, J.E.Dixon and J.R.Cann, 'The Characterization of Obsidian and its Application to the Mediterranean Region', PPS XXX, 1964, pp. 111–33.

20 Colin Renfrew, J.E.Dixon and J.R.Cann, 'Further Analysis of Near Eastern Obsidians' PPS XXXIV, 1968, pp. 319–31, where a newly discovered source is mentioned (p. 320). This occurrence of obsidian was found only because of its immediate proximity to the modern highway from Bingöl to Muş. Many other sources in less accessible places most certainly must exist in eastern Anatolia.

21 Peter H.Davis, with J.Cullen and M.J.E.Coode, *Flora of Turkey and the East Aegean Islands*, vol. I, Edinburgh, 1967.

22 (a) H.Helbaek, 'Domestication of Wild Food Plants in the Old World', *Science* 130, 1959, pp. 365–72; and (b) in *Prehistoric Investigations in Iraqi Kurdistan*, pp. 100–115. (c) K.W.Butzer, CAH I, fasc. 33, especially fig. 4 and pp. 12–13.

23 (a) Pliny in the *Natural History* discussed wines (especially in Book XIV), listed ninety-one varieties of grapes and fifty wines and described methods of training vines. (b) D.M.Lang: *The Georgians*, Ancient Peoples and Places, London, 1966, p. 34.

24 H.Helbaek, *Prehistoric Investigations in Iraqi Kurdistan*, p. 116.

25 CAH I, fasc. 33, pp. 8–10.

26 James Mellaart, *Çatal Hüyük*, London 1967, pp. 223–4.

27 *Ibid* and Jacques Bordaz, AS XV, 1965, p. 32; and XVI, 1966, p. 33.

28 *Prehistoric Investigations in Iraqi Kurdistan*, pp. 47–8.

29 (a) Charles A.Reed, in *Prehistoric Investigations in Iraqi Kurdistan*, pp. 119–45 (Chapter IX). (b) F.E.Zeuner, *A History of Domesticated Animals*, London, 1963. (c) Wolf Herre, 'The Science and History of Domestic Animals', D.R.Brothwell and E.S.Higgs (editors), *Science in Archaeology*, revised and enlarged edition, London, 1969, pp. 257–72. (d) Sebastian Payne, 'The Origins of Domesticated Sheep and Goats: a Reconsideration', PPS XXXIV, 1968, pp. 368–84, with a full bibliography.

30 R.J.Braidwood has long favoured the use of 'food-gathering' or 'food-collecting' and 'food-producing' to replace the adjectives 'palaeolithic' and 'neolithic' respectively. For his attitude to the development of early cultures compare *Antiquity* XXXI, 1957, pp. 73–81, with *Prehistoric*

Investigations in Iraqi Kurdistan, Chapters X–XII, pp. 147–84. Such terms as 'epi-palaeolithic', 'proto-neolithic' and 'proto-urban' also appear in the literature on the different regions of the ancient Near East. James Mellaart, *The Earliest Civilizations of the Near East* London, 1965 and Kathleen M.Kenyon, *Archaeology in the Holy Land*, London, 1965, demonstrate the use of these terms.

31 James Mellaart, 'The Earliest Settlements in Western Asia', CAH I, fasc. 59 1967, especially pp. 6–7.

2. THE EARLIEST SETTLEMENTS

1 For a general account of radio-carbon dating E.H.Willis, 'Radiocarbon Dating' *Science in Archaeology* (1969 edition), pp. 46–57. For its applications, E.Neustupny: 'A New Epoch in Radio-Carbon Dating', with bibliography, *Antiquity* XLIV, 1970, pp. 38–45.

2 Braidwood's preference for the higher of two mean dates for Jarmo (*c.* 6,750 BC rather than *c.* 4,750 BC) accords with the archaeological evidence for the absolute chronology of this and related sites, though *c.* 6,250 BC would seem a generally acceptable mean date. For summaries of radio-carbon dates from Jarmo, Jericho, Çatal Hüyük etc., *Chronologies*, pp. 84–8, 124, 248.

3 (a) D.R.Hughes and D.R.Brothwell: 'The Earliest Populations of Man in Europe, Western Asia and Northern Africa', CAH I, fasc. 50. (b) D.A.E.Garrod and D. Bates, *The Stone Age of Mount Carmel* I, Oxford, 1937. (c) T.D.McCown and A.Keith, *The Stone Age of Mount Carmel* II Oxford, 1939.

4 (a) Enver Bostanci, 'A New Palaeolithic Site at Beldibi', *Anatolia* VI 1961/62, pp. 129–78. (b) For a brief report on the 1966–7 seasons at Beldibi, Bostanci, *Türk Arkeoloji Dergisi* 16, 1 1967, pp. 51–4. (c) I.Kiliç Kökten: 'Die Stellung von Karain innerhalb der türkischen Vorgeschichte,' *Anatolia* VI 1963, pp. 59–69.

5 The writer is much indebted to Professor Yampolski and to the other archaeologists of the Azerbaijan SSR who made his brief visit to Baku (April 1968) so rewarding. A full report on the four thousand rock drawings of Kobistan was prepared over thirty years ago, but, after the author's death, was never published.

6 See Chapter I, notes 16 and 20 (Renfrew, Dixon and Cann; Wright).

7 (a) R.S.Solecki: 'Prehistory in Shanidar Valley, North Iraq', *Science* 18, 1963, pp. 179ff. (b) D.A.E.Garrod and J.G.D.Clark: 'Primitive Man In Egypt, Western Asia and Europe', CAH I, fasc. 30, 1965, pp. 19–22.

8 A.Mongait: *Archaeology in the USSR* Moscow, 1955; English translation, Moscow, 1959; London, 1961, pp. 64–7, 83–4. On display in the Georgian State Museum in Tbilisi is a selection of Lower, Middle and Upper Palaeolithic artifacts and associated animal bones.

9 S.A.Sardarian: *Primitive Society in Armenia*, Erevan, 1967, pp. 317–25. See note 47 below.

10 (a) *Archaeology in the USSR*, pp. 74–87, for a summary of the Upper Palaeolithic cultures as then known. (b) For the Palaeolithic sequence in the whole USSR, J.M.Coles and E.S.Higgs: *The Archaeology of Early Man*, London, 1969, pp. 325–56.

11 (a) James Mellaart, 'The Earliest Settlements in Western Asia', CAH I, fasc. 59, 1967, pp. 9–12, with a full bibliography. (b) Robert J. Braidwood and Bruce Howe: *Prehistoric Investigations in Iraqi Kurdistan*, SAOC no. 31, Chicago, 1960, pp. 28, 52–4, 157–9.

12 (a) D.A.E.Garrod: 'The Natufian Culture: the Life and Economy of a Mesolithic People in the Near East', *Proceedings of the British Academy*, 43, 1957, pp. 211ff. (b) CAH I, fasc. 30, pp. 51–4. (c) Kathleen M. Kenyon: *Archaeology in the Holy Land*, London, 1965, pp. 36–47 and pls 1–10.

13 (a) For Suberde, Jacques Bordaz: AS XV 1965, pp. 30–2; XVI, 1966, pp. 32–3. Recently Bordaz has also excavated the Neolithic mound of Erbaba, 10 km. north-north-west of Beyşehir (Mellink: AJA 74, 1970, p. 159). (b) I.A.Todd: 'Aşikli Hüyük – a Protoneolithic Site in Central Anatolia' AS XVI, 1966, pp. 139–63. For dating of this site there is a reference in Renfrew *et al.*: PPS XXXIV, 1968, p. 321. (c) James Mellaart: 'Excavations at Hacilar, Fourth Preliminary Report, 1960', AS XI, 1961, pp. 70–3.

14 James Mellaart, the excavator, has given a general account, with emphasis on the art, in *Çatal Hüyük*, London, 1967. His lengthy and detailed preliminary reports, in scope going beyond what is usually understood by that term, include much not mentioned in the above book. These reports appeared in AS XII, 1962, pp. 41–65; XIII, 1963, pp. 43–103; XIV 1964, pp. 39–119; and XVI, 1966, pp. 165–91, accompanied by pls 3–18, 3–29, 1–26 and 29–63 respectively. The promptness of these reports is to be commended. They describe the results of the 1961, 1962, 1963 and 1965 seasons.

15 (a) *Çatal Hüyük*, p. 224. (b) H.Helbaek: 'First Impressions of the Çatal Hüyük Plant Husbandry, AS XIV, 1964, pp. 121–3. (c) Jane Renfrew: 'A Note on the Neolithic Grain from Can Hasan', AS XVIII, 1968, pp. 55–6. (d) cf. for Beidha in Trans-Jordan, H. Helbaek: PEQ, 98, 1966, pp. 61–6. (e) cf, for Bus Mordeh etc. in Khuzistan, Frank Hole and Kent V.Flannery: 'The Prehistory of South-West Iran: a Preliminary Report', PPS XXXIII, 1967, pp. 147–206, an invaluable source of evidence with stimulating conclusions and full bibliography.

16 (a) James Mellaart, 'Excavations at Hacilar: Fourth Preliminary Report', AS XI 1961, pp. 37–61 and pls VII–XIII. (b) For general conclusions on Hacilar and other Near Eastern figurines (Jarmo, Hassuna, Halaf, Ubaid etc.), Peter J.Ucko: *Anthropomorphic Figurines of Predynastic Egypt and Neolithic Crete with Comparative Material from the Prehistoric Near East and Mainland Greece*, London, 1968, Royal Anthropological Institute Occasional Papers no. 24, especially pp. 343–67. (c) P.J.Ucko: 'The Interpretation of Prehistoric Anthropomorphic Figurines', *Journal of the Royal Anthropological Institute* XCII, 1962, pp. 38–54.

17 (a) *Çatal Hüyük*, pp. 216–17. (b) Mellaart: AS XIV, 1964, pp. 81–4. (c)

For Jericho, *Archaeology in the Holy Land*, pp. 39–57. (d) For the pottery of Jarmo, *Prehistoric Investigations in Iraqi Kurdistan*, pp. 39, 43–4, 49 and pl. 15. (e) For Ganj Dareh, note 66 below. This site comes nearer than almost any other excavated in the Near East to illustrating the origins of pottery.

18 Rodney S.Young: AJA 62, 1958, pp. 139–54.

19 (a) *Çatal Hüyük*, pp. 217–18. (b) Mellaart: AS XIV, 1964, pp. 111, 114. (c) T.A.Wertime: 'Man's First Encounters with Metallurgy', *Science* 146, no. 3649, 1964, pp. 1257–67. (d) H.Neuninger, R.Pittioni and W. Siegl: 'Frühkeramikzeitliche Kupfergewinnung in Anatolien', *Archaeologia Austriaca*, 35, 1964, pp. 98–110. (e) For an even earlier occurrence of metal, at Çayönü near Diyarbakir, M.J.Mellink: AJA 69, 1965, p. 138. The radio-carbon dates from this site, 7,570 and 7,520 BC, are mentioned by Renfrew *et al.* PPS XXXIV, 1968, p. 325. (f) For the 1964 and 1968 seasons at Çayönü, a report in *Science* 164, 1969, pp. 1275–6; and M.J.Mellink: AJA 74, 1970, p. 159. (g) For copper mining in the Diyarbakir region (Ergani) in later periods, Chapter I, note 18 (a).

20 (a) *Çatal Hüyük*, pp. 219–20. (b) H.Helbaek 'Textiles from Çatal Hüyük' *Archaeology* 16, 1963, pp. 39–46 and H.B.Burnham 'Çatal Hüyük – the Textiles and Twined Fabrics', AS XV, 1965, pp. 169–74 come down in favour of wool. (c) An identification as flax is advocated by M.L.Ryder 'Report of Textiles from Çatal Hüyük', AS XV, 1965, pp. 175–6. (d) For linen fragments, cf. G.Caton-Thompson and E.W.Gardner, *The Desert Fayum*, London, 1934, pl. 28.

21 See note 32 below and AS VIII, 1958, pp. 166–7.

22 *Çatal Hüyük*, pls 45–9 and pp. 166–7.

23 Ochre burial had a very long tradition from Palaeolithic times (e.g. Coles and Higgs: *The Archaeology of Early Man*, p. 232). It was to become a feature of the Kurgan culture of the Russian steppes in the third millennium BC and occurs at Marlik (see Chapters III–IV).

24 (a) For the plastered skulls from Jericho, *Archaeology in the Holy Land*, pls. 13 and 14a. (b) For Tell Ramad, Henri de Contenson and W.J.van Liere: 'Sondages à Tell Ramad en 1963', *Annales Archéologiques de Syrie*, XIV, 1964, pp. 109ff; and Mellaart: CAH I, fasc. 59, p. 21.

25 (a) John Garstang: *Prehistoric Mersin*, Oxford, 1953, pp. 11–43. (b) *Chronologies*, p. 87. The higher half-life for radio-carbon dates (5730 ±40 instead of 5570 ±30) is now generally accepted: Mellaart and others have always advocated it.

26 (a) Robert J.Braidwood and Linda Braidwood: *Excavations in the Plain of Antioch* I, OIP LXI, Chicago, 1960. (b) R.J.Braidwood: 'The Earliest Village Materials of Syro-Cilicia', PPS XXI, 1955, pp. 72–76. (c) cf. D.H.French: AS, XVII, 1967, p. 175.

27 Seton Lloyd and Fuad Safar: 'Tell Hassuna: Excavations by the Iraq Government Directorate General of Antiquities in 1943 and 1944', JNES IV, 1945, pp. 255–89. Hassuna IA may represent the easternmost manifestation of the Dark Faced Burnished Ware or may rather belong to a contemporary cultural province extending through the Zagros region south-eastwards (CAH I, fasc. 59).

28 (a) Henri de Contenson: 'Découvertes Récentes dans le Domaine du Néolithique en Syrie – Bouqras', *Syria* XLIII, 1966, p. 152; and Renfrew *et al.*, PPS XXXIV, 1968, pp. 325–6. Bouqras has three levels, with radio-carbon dates of 6290 BC and 6190 BC (Level I) and of 5990 BC (Level III, the latest). (b) For Çayönü, note 19 (e) and (f) above.

29 James Mellaart: (a) 'Early Cultures of the South Anatolian Plateau I', AS XI, 1961, especially pp. 159–72; and (b) his original survey report AS IV, 1954, pp. 175–240, especially pp. 180–6.

30 James Mellaart, 'Çatal Hüyük West', AS XV, 1965, pp. 135–56.

31 D.H.French: successive preliminary reports on each season of excavations at Can Hasan – AS XII, 1962, pp. 27–40; XIII, 1963, pp. 29–42; XIV, 1964, pp. 127–37; XV, 1965, pp. 87–94; XVI, 1966, pp. 113–23; XVII, 1967, pp. 165–78; XVIII, 1968, pp. 45–53. see also M.J.Mellink: AJA 74, 1970, p. 159.

32 James Mellaart's outstanding final publication of the excavations at Hacilar (Edinburgh University Press, 1970) of course gives a full record of the painted pottery.

33 (a) For Yazir Hüyük, Raci Temizer: *V Türk Tarih Kongresi*, Ankara, 1960, pp. 156–64 and pls XLVI–L; and M.J.Mellink: AJA 62, 1958, p. 97. (b) James Mellaart: 'Early Cultures of the South Anatolian Plateau II: the Late Chalcolithic of the Konya Plain', AS XIII, 1963, pp. 199–236, especially pp. 199–207. (c) D.H.French: 'Excavations at Can Hasan: Fourth Preliminary Report, 1964', AS XV, 1965, pp. 87–94.

34 Seton Lloyd and James Mellaart, *Beycesultan* I, London, 1962, pp. 17–26 and 71–115 for the Late Chalcolithic levels, XL–XX.

35 *Ibid*, pp. 280–3 (D.B.Stronach).

36 (a) H.Z.Koşay and M.Akok: *Ausgrabungen von Büyük Güllücek 1947 und 1949* Ankara, 1957. (b) James Mellaart: 'Anatolia, c. 4,000–2,300 BC', CAH I, fasc. 8 1965.

37 The writer is indebted to Professor van Loon for information on the 1968 season at Korucutepe (Aşaği Içme). Most of the levels excavated at sites in the Keban Dam area are of the third millennium BC and later. (a) For these results, from Pulur, Tepecik, Norşuntepe and Korucutepe, see M.J.Mellink's 'Archaeology in Asia Minor', that invaluable compendium of up-to-date news, in AJA 73, 1969, pp. 209–11 and in AJA 74, 1970, pp. 164–5. (b) For an introduction to the work of the expeditions in the area of the Keban Dam, there is an article by Robert Whallon and Sonmez Kantman, *Current Anthropology* 10, 1969, pp. 128–33.

38 C.A.Burney: 'Eastern Anatolia in the Chalcolithic and Early Bronze Age' AS VIII, 1958, pp. 157–209.

39 Edward B.Reilly: 'Test Excavations at Tilki Tepe' *Türk Tarih, Arkeoloji ve Etnografya Dergisi* 4, 1940, pp. 156–78. In the library of the Griffith Institute, Oxford, is to be found a typewritten report on the American expedition to Van (1938–9), under the direction of Kirsopp and Silvia Lake: this deals not only with Tilkitepe but also with Van Kale, Kalecik etc.

40 (a) For the obsidian trade, Chapter I, notes 16 and 20 (Renfrew, Dixon

and Cann). (b) That great late Victorian traveller, H.F.B.Lynch, made a detailed survey of Nemrut Dağ with its crater lake, recorded in his *Armenia vol. II: The Turkish Provinces*, London, 1901; reprinted Beirut, 1965, pp. 298–313.

41 H.Z.Koşay, 'Erzurum-Karaz Kazisi Raporu', *Belleten* XXIII 1959, pp. 349–413.

42 Mellaart: CAH I, fasc. 59, pp. 9–14.

43 (a) For a brief summary of the work at Hasanlu and associated sites, R.H.Dyson: 'A Decade in Iran', *Expedition* 11, no. 2, 1969. (b) For relations with the Hassuna, Halaf and Ubaid cultures, *Chronologies*, pp. 218–19. (c) For Pisdeli Tepe, see note 51 below.

44 Robert J.Braidwood: 'The Iranian Prehistoric Project, 1959–60', *Iranica Antiqua* I, 1961, pp. 3–7 (Tepe Sarab).

45 For brief summaries of the results of the excavations at Ganj Dareh Tepe, Philip E.L.Smith, *Iran* V, 1967, p. 139; VI, 1968, pp. 158–60; VIII, 1970, pp. 178–80. See also CAH I, fasc. 59, p. 17.

46 (a) C.A.Burney: *Iraq* XXVI, 1964, pp. 55–7 and pl. XIII a–b. (b) *Chronologies*, pp. 218, 248. (c) For the 1968 excavations at Hajji Firuz, R.H.Dyson and Mary Voigt: *Iran* VII, 1969, pp. 179–80.

47 S.A.Sardarian: *Primitive Society in Armenia*, Erevan, 1967, pp. 327–31. While the comparisons with other parts of the Near East may be reckoned only partly relevant, the author is to be congratulated on this work with its long English summary (48 pp.), its Russian summary (55 pp.) and its full Armenian text (254 pp.).

48 (a) For radio-carbon dates from Shulaveri I and Toire Tepe (4,295 ±125 BC), *Proceedings of the Academy of Sciences of the Georgian SSR* 6, 39, 1967, p. 353 (see note 54 below). (b) For Şomu Tepe, the reference to the radio-carbon date no. LE-631 (SA no. 1, 1969).

49 Excavations at Tegut have been carried out by Rafik Torosian, to whom the writer is indebted for information at first hand.

50 (a) For Dalma Tepe, T.C.Young, 'Dalma Painted Ware', *Expedition* 5, 1963, pp. 38–9; and Mellaart: *Earliest Civilizations of the Near East*, figs 41–43. (b) For Yanik Tepe, *Iraq* XXIV, 1962, pp. 134–49.

51 (a) R.H.Dyson and T.C.Young: 'Pisdeli Tepe', *Antiquity* XXXIV, 1960, pp. 19–28. (b) *Chronologies*, p. 248. (c) T.Burton-Brown: *Excavations in Azerbaijan 1948*, London, 1951, p. 16 (Geoy Tepe, Period N) and pp. 17–33 (Period M). (d) C.A.Burney: 'Excavations at Yanik Tepe, Azerbaijan, 1961', *Iraq* XXIV, 1962, pp. 134–49, and especially pp. 137–9.

52 (a) A.A.Iessen: 'The Caucasus and the Ancient East in the Fourth and Third Millennia BC', KSIA 93, 1963, pp. 3–14. (b) A.A.Iessen: report on the whole work of the Azerbaijan Expedition, MIA 125, 1965. (c) K.Kh.Kushnareva and A.L.Yakobson: 'Basic Problems of the Work of the Azerbaijan Expedition', KSIA 108, 1966. All the above are in Russian.

53 (a) The writer owes the information on Ilanli Tepe, too recent to have been included in Chubinishvili's article (note 54), to Dr Narimanov, of

the Historical Institute, Baku. (b) For Dalma Tepe, note 50 above. (c) For a later parallel with the 'jabbed' decoration, Chapter III, note 124 etc. (Kurgan I pottery).

54 T.N.Chubinishvili and K.Kh.Kushnareva: 'New Materials on the Eneolithic of the Southern Caucasus', *Proceedings of the Academy of Sciences of the Georgian SSR* 6, 39, 1967, pp. 336–62. In Russian, published in Tbilisi.

55 O.M.Japaridze and A.I.Javakhishvili: 'Results of the Work of the Kvemo-Kartlian Archaeological Expedition (1965–6)', *Proceedings of the Academy of Sciences of the Georgian SSR* 3 1967, pp. 292–8. In Georgian, with a brief Russian summary. This deals with Shulaveri I only.

56 The writer is greatly indebted to Professor Yampolski for taking him to see the sites on the Apsheron peninsula and then the drawings of Kobistan; and to Dr Aslanov for his opinions on the dating of the various styles of rock drawing, with the evidence for a sequence of styles at Kobistan.

57 *Primitive Society in Armenia*, pp. 326–7 and pls XIX–XXXII.

58 O.A.Abibullaev has published reports on his excavations at Kültepe (Nakhichevan): (a) 'Fouilles de Kül-Tepe ... en 1955', MIA 67, 1959, pp. 431–52; (b) 'Some Results of the Study of the Mound of Kül-Tepe in Azerbaijan',SA no. 3, 1963, pp. 157–68; (c) 'Remains of Houses in the Second Level of Kül-Tepe, near Nakhichevan', MIA 125, 1965, pp. 40–64. (d) See also A.A.Iessen: KSIA 93, 1963, pp. 3–14. All the above are in Russian, with brief French summaries of (a) and (c).

3. FROM CAUCASUS TO EUPHRATES – THE EARLY TRANS-CAUCASIAN CULTURE

1 For a brief discussion (11 pp.) of linguistic problems affecting especially the end of the period covered by this chapter, T.V.Gamkrelidze, ' "Anatolian Languages" and the Problem of Indo-European Migration to Asia Minor', *Seventh International Congress of Anthropological and Ethnological Sciences*, Moscow, August 1964. In English.

2 For short summaries in English of the conclusions drawn by Soviet archaeologists from their field work in Trans-Caucasia in the years up to 1963: (a) T.N.Chubinishvili, 'The Interconnections between the Caucasian ("Kura-Araxes") and the Near East Cultures in the Third Millennium BC', *Seventh International Congress of Anthropological and Ethnological Sciences*, Moscow, August 1964. (b) O.M.Japaridze, 'The Culture of Early Agricultural Tribes in the Territory of Georgia' (*ibid*, August 1964). (c) B.B.Piotrovskii, 'The Aeneolithic Culture of Trans-Caucasia in the Third Millennium BC', *Sixth International Congress of Prehistoric and Protohistoric Sciences, Reports* [Moscow, 1962].

3 Chapter II, note 58. A joint publication of all the excavations in the Keban Dam area is planned.

4 A.Palmieri, 'Insediamento de Bronzo Antico a Gelinciktepe (Malatya)', *Origini* I 1967, pp. 117–93.

5 C.A.Burney, 'Eastern Anatolia in the Chalcolithic and Early Bronze Age' AS VIII, 1958, pp. 157–209.

6 It may be noted that these terms are tied more literally to the stages in metallurgical advance than those used, e.g. in Anatolia, by non-Soviet archaeologists. Much depends on the significance attached to pottery and to metal-working respectively.

7 (a) See note 5 above. (b) For the term 'Yanik culture', R.H.Dyson, 'The Archaeological Evidence of the Second Millennium BC on the Persian Plateau', CAH II, fasc. 66, 1968, pp. 14–16.

8 (a) See note 2 (c) (Piotrovskii). (b) E.V.Khanzadian, *The Culture of the Armenian Highlands in the Third Millennium* BC, Erevan, 1967. In Armenian, with a Russian summary (pp. 102–15). (c) E.V.Khanzadian, 'Établissement Énéolithique près de la ville Kirovakan', SA XXXIII, no. 1, 1963, pp. 152–61. In Russian.

9 Burney, AS VIII, 1958, especially pp. 167–72, 206–7.

10 T.Burton-Brown, *Excavations in Azerbaijan 1948*, London, 1951, pp. 34–62 (Period K), with explicit statement (p.36).

11 It must be admitted that the only firm evidence supporting such a low dating for the end of the Early Trans-Caucasian culture in the Van region is provided by the radio-carbon dates from Yanik Tepe. Otherwise it is largely a matter of filling the lacuna before the rise of Urartu.

12 Burney, *Iran* VIII, 1970, p. 164.

13 Burney, AS VIII, 1958, pp. 167–8.

14 See note 2 (b) and (c) (Japaridze, Piotrovskii).

15 With the solitary exception of the stele set up by Tiglath-Pileser I at Yoncalu, in the plain near Bulanik in the upper Murat (Arsanias) valley. (ARAB I, para. 270).

16 (a) I.J.Gelb, P.M.Purves and A.M.MacRae, *Nuzi Personal Names*, OIP LVII, Chicago, 1943, reprinted 1963, for the onomastic evidence, mostly Hurrian. (b) D.J.Wiseman, *The Alalakh Tablets*, London, 1953.

17 The crux of the 'middle chronology' is the date of the reign of Hammurabi (1792–1750 BC). The classic statement of this chronology remains Sidney Smith, *Alalakh and Chronology*, London, 1940.

18 O.R.Gurney, 'Anatolia, *c.* 1,750–1, 600 BC', CAH II, fasc. 11, pp. 24–6, for a description of this campaign and its sequel.

19 E.A.Speiser, 'The Hurrian Participation in the Civilizations of Mesopotamia, Syria and Palestine', *Cahiers d'Histoire Mondiale*, I, 1953–4, pp. 311–27.

20 James Mellaart, 'The End of the Early Bronze Age in Anatolia and the Aegean', AJA 62, 1958, pp. 9–33. For Kizzuwatna, pp. 23–4 especially.

21 (a) *Chronologies*, p. 119. (b) Burney: AS VIII, 1958, pp. 205–8. (c) James Mellaart, 'Anatolian Chronology in the Early and Middle Bronze Age', AS VII 1957, pp. 55–88, especially pp. 66–7.

22 (a) C.J.Gadd, 'Tablets from Chagar Bazar and Tall Brak, 1937–8' *Iraq* VII, 1940, pp. 22–66, with reference to Hurrian divine names (pp. 27–8). (b) AS VIII, 1958, p. 166, note 29.

23 (a) Paul Garelli, *Les Assyriens en Cappadoce*, Paris, 1963, the standard work

on the evidence of the published tablets. (b) Julius Lewy, 'Notes on the Political Organization of Asia Minor at the Time of the Old Assyrian Texts', *Orientalia* XXXIII, 1964, pp. 181–98, for a highly individual interpretation of the evidence. The theory of an Assyrian empire in Anatolia scarcely requires refutation. (c) For a brief general account, James Mellaart, 'Anatolia, *c.* 2,300–1,750 BC', CAH I, fasc. 20 1964.

24 (a) M.Gimbutas, 'The Indo-Europeans: Archaeological Problems', *American Anthropologist* 65, 1963, pp. 815–36. (b) *Chronologies*, p. 487.

25 B.Maisler (Mazar), M.Stekelis and M.Avi Yonah, 'The Excavations at Beth-Yerah (Khirbet el Kerak) 1944–6', *Israel Exploration Journal* 2, 1952, pp. 165–73, 218–29; pls 17–18 and fig. 3 (p. 224).

26 *Excavations in the Plain of Antioch* I, pp. 358–68 (Amuq H), 398–403 (Amuq I) and 518–21; figs 262–3 (p. 347), horseshoe-shaped hearth.

27 *Ibid.*, p. 519.

28 Kathleen M.Kenyon, *Excavations at Jericho I: The Tombs Excavated in 1952–4*, London, 1960, pp. 78–80, 96, 120–1, 133, 160.

29 One opinion is that they comprised 'small groups of itinerant craftsmen', without commitment concerning their ethnic affinities beyond stating their relationship to the Early Bronze Age people of eastern Anatolia. For this, J.B.Hennessy, *The Foreign Relations of Palestine during the Early Bronze Age*, Colt Archaeological Institute Publications, London, 1967, pp. 75, 84, 88.

30 Kathleen M.Kenyon, (a) *Archaeology in the Holy Land*, London, 1965, pp. 135–61, for a general account of the Early Bronze Age–Middle Bronze Age period. (b) *Amorites and Canaanites*, Schweich Lectures, British Academy, London, 1963, especially pp. 6–35.

31 Sherds seen by the writer in 1954 in the museum at Alaca Hüyük form the basis for this opinion. One published sherd could be relevant, though hardly definite evidence (R.O.Arik, *Les Fouilles d'Alaca Höyük 1935*, Ankara, 1937, pl. CXXI, no. 810). For a discussion of similarities between Khirbet Kerak ware and pottery from Anatolian sites (Kusura, Ahlatlibel etc.), Ruth B.K.Amiran, 'Connections between Anatolia and Palestine in the Early Bronze Age', *Israel Exploration Journal* 2, 1952, pp. 89–103. For another aspect, R.B.K.Amiran, 'Yanik Tepe, Shengavit and the Khirbet Kerak Ware', AS XV 1965, pp. 165–67.

32 See note 2 (c) above (Piotrovskii), where a subdivision of the pottery is given, into successive styles named after Shresh-Blur, Shengavit and Elar (p. 7). For Khanzadian's classification, note 59 below.

33 T.N.Chubinishvili and K.Kh.Kushnareva, 'New Materials on the Aeneolithic of the Southern Caucasus (Fifth-Fourth Millennia BC)', *Proceedings of the Academy of Sciences of the Georgian SSR* 6, 39, Tbilisi, 1967. In Russian. For Samele Klde, pp. 350 (with note 35), 356, 359 and plate I (map: site no. 12).

34 *Ibid*, pp. 338 (note 4), 339 (note 6), 357–9 etc. and plate I (map: sites 2, 30).

35 *Ibid*, p. 357 and plate I (map: site 7). See also notes 2 (a) (Chubinishvili) and 82.

36 For Shulaveri, Chapter II, notes 48 and 55. There remains a chronological hiatus extending through most of the fourth millennium BC: this needs to be diminished by further discoveries before any influence from Shulaveri on the Early Trans-Caucasian culture can be substantiated.

37 See note 2 (c) (Piotrovskii). There is a great need for a series of radio-carbon dates from sites in the Armenian SSR.

38 (a) T.C.Young and P.E.L.Smith, 'Research in the Prehistory of Central Western Iran', *Science* 153, 1966, pp. 386ff., especially p. 390. (b) CAH I, fasc. 66, p. 15.

39 Burney, AS VIII, 1958, p. 68. The writer's opinion at that time that the origin of this culture might lie in the Elaziğ-Malatya region is now clearly incorrect.

40 H.Z.Koşay: (a) Preliminary report on Karaz in *Türk Tarih Kongresi* 1943, pp. 164–77, with figs 1–21 and plan. (b) 'Erzurum-Karaz Kazisi Raporu', *Belleten* 23, 1959, pp. 349–413. H.Z.Koşay and H.Vary: (c) *Pulur Kazisi: Die Ausgrabungen von Pulur*, Ankara, 1964. (d) *Güzelova Kazisi: Ausgrabungen von Güzelova* Ankara, 1967.

41 Information given to the writer in Baku. For the remoter areas to the north, including Daghestan, in the Early Trans-Caucasian period, R.M.Munchaev, 'The Earliest Culture of the North-East Caucasus', MIA 100 1961.

42 The pottery from the Muş plain, collected by the writer in his 1956 survey, has not been published. Its general date remains uncertain; it could well be later than the Early Trans-Caucasian culture.

43 S.A.Sardarian, *Primitive Society in Armenia*, Erevan, 1967, p. 332, for the contemporaneity of Shengavit I and Keghzyak-Blur II etc. For a summary of the sequence at Shengavit, *ibid*, pp. 343–47.

44 (a) A.I.Javakhishvili and L.I. Glonti, *Urbnisi I: Archaeological Excavations Carried Out in 1954–1961 at the Site of Kvatskhelebi*, Tbilisi, 1962; in Georgian, with Russian summary; pp. 48 and 62, pl. XXXV. (b) For Kültepe, note 96 below. (c) For examples of metalwork from Armenian sites, note 130 (c) below and Khanzadian, *The Armenian Highlands in the Third Millennium* BC, figs 7 and 10, p. 60, pl. VII.

45 The significance attached to Karaz was a natural result of priority of discovery (note 5 above). For an earlier discussion, W.Lamb, 'The Culture of North-East Anatolia and its Neighbours', AS IV, 1954, pp. 21–32.

46 See notes 32 and 59.

47 B.A.Kuftin, *Excavations in Trialeti* I, Tbilisi, 1941, pp. 168–9.

48 Burney, AS VIII, 1958, sherds nos. 39, 171–3, 222–4.

49 See Chapter II, note 58 (Abibullaev).

50 *Urbnisi* I (see note 44 [a]).

51 See note 2 (b) (Japaridze), p. 6.

52 See note 2 (a) (Chubinishvili), p. 8.

53 But this Circles Building was a unit comprising nine circles within the thickness of its walls and thus perhaps a fortified structure. For a brief discussion, R.B.K.Amiran, AS XV, 1965, p. 167. See also note 25.

54 See notes 44 (a) and 50 above. The writer was fortunate enough to be given a lengthy summary in English of this report. For brief references, D.M.Lang, *The Georgians*, Ancient Peoples and Places, London, 1966, pp. 37, 40.

55 Steven Diamant and Jeremy Rutter, 'Horned Objects in Anatolia and the Near East and Possible Connexions with the Minoan "Horns of Consecration" ', AS XIX, 1969, pp. 147–77.

56 (a) For Kulbakebi and other sites, the important work by O.M.Japaridze, *On the History of the Georgian Tribes in the Early Bronze Age*, Tbilisi, 1961. In Georgian, with an English summary. (b) *The Georgians*, pp. 39–40. (c) C.A.Burney, 'Circular Buildings Found at Yanik Tepe, North-West Iran', *Antiquity* XXXV, 1961, pp. 239–40.

57 (a) Sardarian, *Primitive Society in Armenia*, p. 344 and plan facing p. 180 (Shengavit). (b) *Iraq* XXXIII, 1961, pp. 138–53 (Yanik Tepe): Level 4B (i.e. Level XVII), pl. LXVI.

58 (a) Particularly important among published material of the Early Trans-Caucasian I period, T.N.Chubinishvili, *Amiranis-Gora: Materials on the Ancient History of Meskhet-Javakheti*, Tbilisi, 1963. In Georgian. (b) B.A.Kuftin, *Archaeological Excavations in Trialeti* I, Tbilisi, 1941, especially pp. 168–9. Translation by Henry Field, in *South-Western Journal of Anthropology*, vol. 2, no. 3, 1946: University of New Mexico Press, Albuquerque. (c) G.G.Pkhakadze: *The Aeneolithic Culture of Lower Kartli: Aeneolithic Remains from Kiketi*, Tbilisi, 1963. In Russian.

59 Khanzadian, *The Culture of the Armenian Highlands in the Third Millennium* BC, pls XIX–XX (pottery from Shresh-Blur and Kültepe [Echmiadzin]). The Kirovakan group (pls XXI–XXII) seems to have points of similarity.

60 Burney, AS VIII, 1958, pp. 167–8.

61 A radio-carbon date (P-199) of 2,574 ±146 BC for Geoy Tepe K3, from a sample obtained some years after the excavations from a burnt layer, suggests that the K1 phase dates back well into the Early Trans-Caucasian I period, if not to its very beginning (*Chronologies*, p. 248).

62 See note 38 (Godin Tepe IV).

63 *Ibid*, pp. 168, 179, 182–6.

64 The writer's thanks are due to the University Museum, Philadelphia, for treating the carbon samples submitted from Yanik Tepe. The dates relevant to the Early Trans-Caucasian II period (all to half-life of 5730) are: 2,381 ±62 BC (P-1247), 2,324 ±78 BC (P-1248), 2,621 ±79 BC (P-1249), 2,495 ±61 BC (P-1250).

65 (a) C.A.Burney, 'Excavations at Yanik Tepe, North-West Iran', *Iraq* XXIII, 1961, pp. 138–53 and pls LXVI–LXXV. (b) *Iraq* XXIV, 1962, p. 140. (c) Note 56 (Burney).

66 *Iraq* 24 (1962), p. 141.

67 H.Goldman, *The Excavations at Gözlü Kule*, Tarsus II, Princeton, 1956, nos. 278–9 (pp. 122–3 and pl. 255); and fig. 254. There are also close parallels at Zincirli with the 'red gritty cross-stitched incised ware' of Tarsus.

68 D.B.Stronach, 'The Development and Diffusion of Metal Types in Early Bronze Age Anatolia', AS VII, 1957, pp. 89–125, especially pp. 113–14 stressing the significance of Til Barsip as a metal-working centre.

69 V.G.Childe, *New Light on the Most Ancient East*, London, 1952, especially on 'proofs of diffusion'.

70 It is quite impossible to list all the extensive literature on the *karum* of Kanesh. The most complete general treatment based on the written evidence is Paul Garelli, *Les Assyriens en Cappadoce*, Paris, 1963. This has a first chapter (pp. 31–79) on the chronological problem. The bibliography of works preceding 1963 is very complete, and only a few need emphasis here: (a) Kemal Balkan, *Observations on the Chronological Problems of the Karum Kaniš*, Ankara, 1955. (b) James Mellaart, 'Anatolian Chronology in the Early and Middle Bronze Age', AS VII, 1957, pp. 55–88, in which the 'high chronology' is advocated. (c) J.Lewy, 'Some Aspects of Commercial Life in Assyria and Asia Minor in the Nineteenth Pre-Christian Century', JAOS 78, 1958, pp. 89–101, one of many articles on Kültepe by a scholar of strong opinions. Among works published since 1962 the following deserve mention: (d) Kutlu Emre, 'The Pottery of the Assyrian Colony Period According to the Building Levels of the Kaniš Karum', *Anatolia* VII, 1963, pp. 87–99 (in English). (b) Tahsin Özgüç, 'The Art and Architecture of Ancient Kanesh', *Anatolia* VIII, 1964, pp. 27–48 (in English) and pls III–XXII). (c) Nimet Özgüç, *The Anatolian Group of Cylinder Seals from Kültepe*, Ankara, 1965.

71 (a) For a general description of the Maikop barrow, Franz Hančar, *Urgeschichte Kaukasiens*, Leipzig, 1937, pp. 247–52. (b) For the Maikop culture, here dated *c.* 2,500–2,000 BC, H.H.Formozov, *The Stone Age and Aeneolithic of the Kuban Country*, Moscow, 1965, pp. 64–152. (c) For relations of the Maikop culture with the Early Trans-Caucasian culture, the former here dated to two periods, *c.* 2,500–2,400 BC and *c.* 2,300–2,100 BC, E.I.Krupnov, SA 1964 (1), pp. 26–43. (d) For a rather lower dating of the second period (Tsarskaya etc.), note 153 (b) below. (e) A.A.Iessen, 'Chronology of the Great Kuban Barrows', SA 1950, pp. 157–200.

72 (a) For the dating of Alaca Hüyük on the evidence of the metalwork, see note 68 (Stronach). (b) For one reconstruction of early Indo-European migrations into parts of Anatolia and elsewhere in the Near East, see note 24 (a) (Gimbutas).

73 (a) Tahsin Özgüç; *Türk Tarih Kongresi*, 1943, pp. 393–419; and *Belleten* 1945, pp. 361–400. (b) C.A.Burney, 'Northern Anatolia Before Classical Times' AS VI, 1956, pp. 179–203.

74 (a) T. Özgüç and Mahmut Akok, *Horoztepe: An Early Bronze Age Settlement and Cemetery*, Ankara, 1958. In English and Turkish. (b) T. Özgüç and M.Akok, 'Objects from Horoztepe', *Belleten* XXI, 1957, pp. 211–19. (c) T. Özgüç, 'New Finds from Horoztepe' *Anatolia* VIII, 1964, pp. 1–17 and pls I–II.

75 One feature of the early settlement of Haridj (Artik) is the occurrence of ram's head hearth-stands, comparable with examples from Shengavit Khanzadian, *The Armenian Highlands in the Third Millennium* BC, pl. XVI,

which in turn are in the same general class as plainer variants (*ibid*, pl. XVII, from Mochra-Blur).

76 For Tetri-Tsqaro cemetery etc., G.F.Gobejishvili, *Results of Archaeological Field Work in the Territory of the Georgian SSR in 1958*, Tbilisi, 1959.

77 For the Early Trans-Caucasian III painted pottery of the Malatya and Elazığ provinces, Burney, AS VIII, 1958, pp. 200–208.

78 See note 4.

79 For pottery from Kayakent, Lugovo, Velikent and Novii Arshtii, R.M.Munchaev, 'The Earliest Culture of the North-East Caucasus', MIA 100, 1961, especially pp. 71–131.

80 *Radiocarbon* 12, 1970. These dates were earlier provided for the writer through the kindness of R.H.Dyson.

81 'Painted orange ware' is characteristic of Hasanlu VII, for which the average of five radio-carbon dates is 2,170 ±138 BC, (Dyson: CAH II, fasc. 66, p. 16).

82 See note 2 (a) (Chubinishvili), p. 8.

83 (a) Khanzadian, *The Culture of the Armenian Highlands in the Third Millennium* BC, fig. 15 (p. 64) (Shamlug). (b) *Iraq* XXIV, 1962, pl. XLIV, no. 19 (Yanik Tepe).

84 (a) For graphite burnished pottery from Yanik Tepe (also occurring in approximately contemporary context at Haftavān Tepe), *Iraq* XXIV (1962), pl. XLIV, nos. 17–18. (b) For Tetri-Tsqaro, note 76 (Gobejishvili). In Georgian. Pottery of this graphite burnished ware from Tetri-Tsqaro and Amiranis-Gora is to be seen in the Georgian State Museum, Tbilisi.

85 (a) Henri Frankfort, *Stratified Cylinder Seals from the Diyala Region*, OIP LXXII, Chicago, 1964. (b) H.Frankfort, *Cylinder Seals*, London, 1939, still an excellent general treatment of the subject. (c) For stamp seals (e.g.), M.E.L.Mallowan and J.Cruikshank Rose, 'Excavations at Tell Arpachiyah, 1933', *Iraq* II, 1934, figs 50–1 and pls VIA, VIIA and VIIIA. A stamp seal with swastika design was found in a very early level at Jericho.

86 (a) For Sachkhere, note 98 below. (b) For Tetri-Tsqaro, K.Kh.Kushnareva and T.N.Chubinishvili, 'The Historical Significance of the Southern Caucasus in the Third Millennium BC', English translation from SA 1963 (3), pp. 10–24, in *Soviet Anthropology and Archaeology* II, no. 3 (Winter 1963–4), pp. 3–16.

87 Telemak S.Khachatrian, *The Material Culture of Ancient Artik* (Erevan, 1963). In Russian.

88 The writer was privileged to be taken over the site of Metsamor by Dr Emma V.Khanzadian and other Armenian scholars. (a) James Mellaart, 'Anatolian Trade with Europe and Anatolian Geography and Culture Provinces in the Late Bronze Age', AS XVIII, 1968, pp. 187–202, with a brief note on Metsamor (pp. 200–202). (b) Boris Mkrtichian, 'The Mystery of Metsamor', *New Orient* 3, 1967, pp. 76–8.

89 One opinion is that the metalwork of the Maikop barrow is probably of Iranian rather than Sumerian origin, with Elam as the common source

accounting for parallels between Sumer and Maikop. A second phase of Caucasian metalwork is seen as contemporary with Hissar IIIC and affecting Trans-Caucasia as well as the Kuban basin. One example of metal artifacts said to be of Iranian origin is the range of shafthole axes classified as Type G. (Jean Deshayes: *Les Outils de Bronze de l'Indus au Danube*, Paris, 1960, pp. 414–16). For the origins of Sumerian metallurgy, *ibid*, pp. 408–9.

90 For sources of copper, (a) D.Ghambashidze, *Mineral Resources of Georgia and Caucasia*, London, 1919. (b) R.J.Forbes, *Metallurgy in Antiquity* Leiden, 1950, pp. 302–3. (c) A.A.Iessen, 'The Kuban Centre of Metallurgy and Metal-Working of the End of the Copper-Bronze Age', MIA 23, 1951.

91 (a) I.R.Selimkhanov, 'Spectral Analyses of Metallic Articles from Archaeological Monuments of the Caucasus', PPS XXVIII, 1962, pp. 68–79. (b) E.N.Chernykh, 'Spectral Analysis and the study of the Most Ancient Metallurgy of Eastern Europe', *Archaeology and the Natural Sciences*, Moscow, 1965. In Russian.

92 (a) I.R.Selimkhanov, 'Was Native Copper Used in Trans-Caucasia in Aeneolithic Times?', PPS XXX, 1964, pp. 66–74. (b) H.H.Coghlan, 'A Note upon Native Copper', PPS XXVIII, 1962, pp. 58ff.

93 (a) Ts.N.Abesadze, R.A.Bakhtadze, T.A.Dvali and O.M.Japaridze, *On the History of Copper and Bronze Metallurgy in Georgia*, Tbilisi, 1958. In Georgian, with English summary (pp. 103–8). (b) J.A.Charles, 'Early Arsenical Bronzes – A Metallurgical View', AJA 71, 1967, pp. 21–6.

94 (a) Stuart Piggott, *Ancient Europe*, Edinburgh, 1965, fig. 34 (distribution map) and p. 74. (b) F.Hančar, 'Die Nadelformen des Prähistorischen Kaukasusgebietes', ESA 7, 1932, pp. 113–82.

95 *Urbnisi* I, pl. XXXVI (spearhead, torque, diadem etc.).

96 (a) For Early Trans-Caucasian III metalwork from sites in the Armenian SSR, note 130 below. (b) For Kültepe metalwork, O.A.Abibullaev: 'Ancient Metallurgy in Azerbaijan' MIA 125, 1965, pp. 65–73. In Russian; French summary.

97 For the cemetery at Tetri-Tsqaro, see notes 76 and 84 above.

98 (a) *Stratigraphie*, fig. 293. (b) Lang, *The Georgians*, p. 50. (c) D.L.Koridze, *Bronze Age Finds from Sachkhere*, Tbilisi, 1961. In Georgian.

99 *Stratigraphie*, p. 517.

100 See note 128 below.

101 (a) *Ancient Europe*, pp. 73–75. (b) S.Piggott, 'Neolithic and Bronze Age in East Europe', *Antiquity* XXXIV, 1960, pp. 285–94.

102 For shafthole axes, Deshayes, *Les Outils de Bronze*, pp. 153–230 etc. and maps IX–XI.

103 For one important region, Colin Renfrew, 'Cycladic Metallurgy and the Aegean Bronze Age', AJA LXXI, 1967, pp. 1–20.

104 Personal communication from the excavator, Dr E.V.Khanzadian.

105 S.Piggott, 'The Earliest Wheeled Vehicles and the Caucasian Evidence', PPS XXXIV, 1968, pp. 266–313, for a lengthy discussion with full bibliography (pp. 313–18), an invaluable contribution to this problem.

106 *Ibid*, pp. 296–7.

107 *Ibid*, pp. 302–8.

108 For general discussions of the domestication of the horse, (a) F.E.Zeuner, *A History of Domesticated Animals*, London, 1963, pp. 299–337. (b) F. Hančar, *Das Pferd in frühhistorischer und früher historischer Zeit*, Vienna and Munich, 1956. (c) *Science in Archaeology*, revised edition, 1969, pp. 268–9.

109 Hančar, *Urgeschichte Kaukasiens*, pls XLV–XLVIII.

110 Especially note 2 (b) (Japaridze), pp. 5–6.

111 See note 2 (c) (Piotrovskii, quoting Japaridze).

112 (a) B.P.Lyubin, 'The Aeneolithic Complex from the Cave of Shau-Leget, North Ossetia', KSIA 108, 1966, pp. 49–54. (b) See also note 2 (c), p. 9.

113 *Urbnisi* I, pl. 35.

114 *Primitive Society in Armenia*, p. 346.

115 Khanzadian, *The Culture of the Armenian Highlands in the Third Millennium* BC, Plate I.

116 See note 55.

117 (a) *The Georgians*, p. 53 and pl. 11. (b) *Stratigraphie*, fig. 288.

118 See note 2 (c) (Piotrovskii).

119 *Chronologies*, pp. 471–3.

120 *Ibid*, p. 473.

121 E.Ju.Krichevskii and A.P.Kruglov, 'The Neolithic settlement near the Town of Nal'chik', MIA 3, 1941, pp. 51–63.

122 N.Makarenko, (a) 'Neolithic Man on the Shores of the Sea of Azov', ESA IX, 1934, pp. 135–53. This account, in English, describes the 1930 excavations at Mariupol. (b) *The Cemetery of Mariupol*, Kiev, 1933. In Russian.

123 (a) *ibid*, pp. 477–94 and bibliography. (b) N.J.Merpert, 'L'Énéolithique de la Zone steppique de la Partie Européenne de l'URSS', in *L'Europe à la Fin de l'Age de Pierre*, Prague, 1961, pp. 161–92 (French translation of Russian text).

124 (a) *ibid*, p. 474. (b) M.Gimbutas, 'Notes on the Chronology and Expansion of the Pit-grave Kurgan Culture', in *L'Europe à la Fin de l'Age de Pierre*, pp. 193–200, with a map illustrating the 'tentative distribution and expansion of the Kurgan culture' (p. 199).

125 For the Kurgan III period, (a) *ibid*, pp. 482–8, 492. (b) B.E.Degen, 'Kurgans in the Kabardino Park of the City of Nal'chik', MIA 3, 1941, pp. 213–317.

126 (a) A. P. Kruglov and G. V. Podgaetskii, 'The Habitation Site of Dolinskoe near the City of Nal'chik', MIA 3, 1941, pp. 143–213. (b) For the economy of Dolinskoe and contemporary settlements in the north-west Caucasus and their attribution to the Maikop culture, A.A. Formozov, KSIA 88, 1962, pp. 27ff.

127 A.P.Kruglov, B.B.Piotrovskii and G.V.Podgaetskii, 'The Cemetery in the City of Nal'chik', MIA 3, 1941, pp. 67–147. For Novii Arshti, note 79 above.

128 (a) Piggott, *Ancient Europe*, pp. 84–5. (b) Gimbutas, *The Prehistory of Eastern Europe Part I*, pp. 75–83. (c) On Alaca Hüyük, V.Milojcic, 'Zur Zeitstellung der Hammerknopfnadeln', *Germania* XXXIII, 1955, pp. 240–2. (d) J.L.Caskey, 'Excavations at Lerna, 1955', *Hesperia* XXV, 1956, pp. 147–73, especially p. 160. (e) For Sachkhere, *Stratigraphie*, pp. 516–17 and fig. 293, nos. 1–4. (f) It may be noted that the contents of Kurgan no. 4, Grave 1, in the Kabardino Park cemetery near Nal'chik included a 'crutch-headed' copper pin and a double spiral copper pin (*The Prehistory of Eastern Europe I*, fig. 32).

129 (a) For Maikop, see note 71 above; and (b) Henri Frankfort, *The Art and Architecture of the Ancient Orient*, pp. 115–16.

130 (a) *Ancient Europe*, fig. 37, nos. 5 and 7 (copper adze and axe-adze) (p. 82). cf. (b) items from Sachkhere (*Stratigraphie*, fig. 293); and (c) from sites in Armenia, A.A.Martirosian, *Armenia in the Bronze and Early Iron Ages* 1964, pl. XXXIII (summary chart): V(1), VII(1), XI(1–2). In Russian. (d) For an important aspect, V.G.Childe, 'The Axes from Maikop and Caucasian Metallurgy' *Liverpool Annals of Archaeology and Anthropology* XXIII, 1936, pp. 113ff.

131 *Ancient Europe*, p. 81 (brief statement). The burial customs may point to the steppes, but the contents of the Alaca tombs are essentially Anatolian. The case for Indo-European affinities, through the expansion of the Kurgan culture, is most forcefully (perhaps too forcefully) argued by M.Gimbutas (note 24 (a)).

132 For the theory of an origin of the Alaca dynasty from the neighbouring Pontic region, Mellaart, CAH I, fasc. 20, p. 33.

133 See note 109.

134 (a) For a general description of Tsarskaya, *Urgeschichte Kaukasiens*, pp. 243–7 and pls XXXV–XXXIX. (b) *Chronologies*, pp. 488–9. (c) For a discussion of the chronology of Tsarskaya and other tombs, *Stratigraphie*, pp. 518–24. (d) See also note 138 below.

135 E.V.Khanzadian, 'Lchashen Barrow no. 6', KSIA 91, 1962, pp. 66–71.

136 (a) R.de Vaux, O.P., 'Palestine during the Neolithic and Chalcolithic Periods', CAH I, fasc. 47, 1966, pp. 42–3. (b) E.C.Broome, 'The Dolmens of Palestine and Transjordania', *Journal of Biblical Literature* LIX, 1940, pp. 479ff. The affinities of these dolmens remain enigmatic.

137 A.M.Tallgren, ESA IX, 1934, fig. 19 (p. 21).

138 (a) A.M.Tallgren, 'Sur les Monuments du Caucase', ESA IX, 1934, pp. 1–46. (b) T.B.Popova, *Dolmens of the Stanitsa Novosvobodnaya*, GIM 34, Moscow, 1963, 47 pp., a study of the barrow graves of Tsarskaya-Novosvobodnaya, here dated around 2,000 BC (cf. note 71 above).

139 (a) *Chronologies*, pp. 491–4. (b) Among articles in Russian on the Catacomb culture are those by L.Klein SA 1961 (2), pp. 49–65; SA 1962 (2), pp. 26–38 and by A.A.Ierusalimskaya SA 1958 (2), pp. 34–48. For these and other references, *Bronze Age USSR*, pp. 59–61.

140 See note 138 above; and *Stratigraphie*, pp. 513–14 and fig. 294.

141 (a) Burney, AS VIII, pp. 175–8. (b) Chapter IV, note 25.

4 NEW PEOPLES IN AN OLD WORLD

1 B.B.Piotrovskii, *The Aeneolithic Culture of Trans-Caucasia in the Third Millennium* BC, Moscow, 1962. see Chapter III, note 2 (c).

2 For brief notices of the 1968 and 1969 seasons' results in the Keban Dam area, Chapter II, note 37. The writer understands that Dr R.Whallon (University of Michigan) formed this conclusion also on the basis of his own survey. Nothing from the survey of 1956 (Burney: AS VIII (1958), pp. 157–209) conflicts with this.

3 (a) R.A.Crossland, 'Immigrants from the North' CAH I, fasc. 60, 1967, with extensive bibliography. (b) P.Bosch-Gimpera, *Les Indo-Européens: Problèmes Archéologiques*, Paris, 1961. (c) H.Hencken, *Indo-European Languages and Archaeology*, American Anthropological Association Memoir 84, 1955.

4 V.Gordon Childe, *The Aryans*, London, 1926, p. 195.

5 (a) Crossland: CAH I, fasc. 60. (b) M.Gimbutas, 'The Indo-Europeans: Archaeological Problems', *American Anthropologist* 65, 1963, pp. 815–36.

6 (a) Paul Garelli, *Les Assyriens en Cappadoce*, Paris, 1963; for the Hittite and Luvian elements in the population, especially pp. 133–52. (b) M.T. Larsen, *Old Assyrian Caravan Procedures*, Istanbul, 1967. (c) For a short article, Jaan Puhvel, 'Anatolian Languages', *Encyclopaedia Britannica* vol. 1 1967, pp. 864–5.

7 (a) For a brief but useful discussion of all aspects of Hittite civilization, J.Puhvel's article 'Hittites', *Encyclopaedia Britannica* vol. 11, 1967, pp. 550–60. (b) For a fuller discussion, O.R.Gurney, *The Hittites*, Harmondsworth, 1961. (c) For kingship and law, H.G.Guterbock, in *Authority and Law in the Ancient Orient*, JAOS Supplement 17, 1954. (d) J.G.Macqueen, 'Hattian Mythology and Hittite Monarchy', AS IX, 1959, pp. 171–88.

8 (a) E.Laroche, 'Le Panthéon de Yazilikaya', JCS VI, 1952, pp. 115–23. (b) H. G. Guterbock, 'The Hurrian Element in the Hittite Empire', *Cahiers d'Histoire Mondiale* 2, 1954, pp. 283ff. (c) H.G.Guterbock, 'Towards a Definition of the Term Hittite', *Oriens* IV, 1957, pp. 233ff.

9 (a) This jar is now in the Erevan Museum. For comparable painted ornament, E.V.Khanzadian, 'A Painted Vessel with Zoomorphic Decoration from Elar', SA 1966, pp. 172–5. (b) Examples of the combination of incision on the exterior and painted decoration on the interior of one and the same pot add to the evidence for a degree of ceramic continuity from the Early Trans-Caucasian III period into the Middle Bronze Age. *Primitive Society in Armenia*, pls LXI and LXIX.

10 (a) B.A.Kuftin, *Archaeological Excavations in Trialeti* I, Tbilisi, 1941, p. 156. (b) *Stratigraphie*, p. 500 and fig. 270.

11 (a) Mellaart, AS 18, 1968, pp. 200–2 (Metsamor), with a discussion on the implications for the tin trade with Anatolia. (b) T.S.Khachatrian, *The Material Culture of Ancient Artik*, Erevan, 1963.

12 K.Kh.Kushnareva: report on the excavations at Ouzerlik Tepe, MIA 67, 1959, pp. 388–430.

13 S.Piggott, 'The Earliest Wheeled Vehicles and the Caucasian Evidence', PPS XXXIV, 1968, pp. 266–318. For the dating of the Lchashen burials, pp. 285–6.

14 *Bronze Age USSR*, p. 65, with a reference to D.L.Koridze, *On the History of the Colchidic Culture*, Tbilisi, 1965. In Georgian, with a Russian summary.

15 (a) J.Deshayes, *Les Outils de Bronze, de l'Indus au Danube*, Paris, 1960, p. 402 etc. (b) A.A.Iessen, 'The Kuban Centre of Metallurgy and Metal-Working of the End of the Copper-Bronze Age', MIA 23, 1951.

16 *Archaeological Excavations in Trialeti* I; for a short summary, E.H.Minns, 'Trialeti', *Antiquity* XVII, 1943, pp. 129–35.

17 Three reports by O.M.Japaridze: (a) a summary of his Trialeti excavations in 1959–62, SA 1964, 2, pp. 102–21. (b) *Archaeological Excavations at Trialeti 1957–8*, Tbilisi, 1960. In Georgian, with German and Russian summaries. (c) 'Report on the Trialeti Archaeological Expedition of 1962–3', *Trudy Tbilisi Gosudar. Universiteta* 107, 1964, pp. 65–85.

18 (a) See notes 16 and 17. For general descriptions of aspects of the Trialeti material, (b) Piggott: PPS XXXIV, 1968, pp. 278–85; and (c) *Stratigraphie*, pp. 507–15 and figs 286–92.

19 Piggott: PPS XXXIV, 1968, pp. 295–302 with bibliography.

20 D.M.Lang, *The Georgians*, London, 1966, p. 46, quoting Schaeffer, 'Archaeological Discoveries in Trialeti-Caucasus', *Journal of the Royal Asiatic Society* 1944, pp. 25–9.

21 The precise dates are 2,539 ±120 BC (LE-305) and 2,867 ±230 BC (LE-300), obtained from roof timbers and charcoal respectively (quoted, PPS XXXIV, p. 284).

22 The writer's earlier opinion, AS VIII 1958, p. 176, that this painted pottery is paralleled in the Tripolye culture was never more than a speculation and is no longer tenable.

23 *The Georgians*, p. 53.

24 Burney, AS VIII, 1958, pp. 175–8.

25 The classification adopted by the Georgian specialists groups the Trialeti barrows thus: Group 1 – Barrows IV, X–XI(?), XIX, XXII, XXIV, XL, XLVII; Group 2 – Barrows XXIX (?early), III, IV, VIII, IX, XVI–XVIII, XXXIV; Group 3 – Barrows I, VII, XV, XXXII, XLII. For a chart giving this and earlier, less reliable, classifications, Piggott: PPS XXXIV, 1968, p. 280.

26 A.A.Martirosian, *Armenia in the Bronze and Early Iron Ages*, Erevan, 1964, pp. 47–78 (the Middle Bronze stage), figs 28–32 and pl. I.

27 *Les Outils de Bronze*, Type J4B.

28 T.Burton-Brown, *Excavations in Azerbaijan 1948*, London, 1951, p. 193 (analyses).

29 P.R.S.Moorey, 'Prehistoric Copper and Bronze Metallurgy in Western Iran, with Special Reference to Luristan', *Iran* VII, 1969, pp. 131–53, especially p. 136.

30 (a) W.F.Leemans, *Foreign Trade in the Old Babylonian Period*, Leiden, 1960, pp. 122–3. (b) M.E.L.Mallowan, 'The Mechanics of Ancient Trade in Western Asia', *Iran* III, 1965, pp. 1–7, where a different

location for Magan, along the north shore of the Persian Gulf (= Makan) is proposed, instead of in Oman.

31 (a) *Foreign Trade in the Old Babylonian Period*, pp. 121–2. (b) *Les Assyriens en Cappadoce*, pp. 287, 290, 296 (prices).

32 (a) For the political relationship of Isua and neighbouring regions to the Hittite state, A. Goetze, 'The Struggle for the Domination of Syria', CAH II, fasc. 37, p. 153 etc. (b) John Garstang and O. R. Gurney, *The Geography of the Hittite Empire*, London, 1959, pp. 40–1 etc. (c) The writer's survey of the Elaziğ region made its links with central Anatolia in the Late Bronze Age very clear (unpublished surface pottery).

33 (a) The significance of this incident is stressed by H. G. Guterbock (note 8 (b)). (b) For the information on the 1968 season at Korucu Tepe the writer is indebted to Professor Van Loon.

34 ARAB I, para. 221. The land is not called Isua but Alzi, but the equation of these two names, and Enzite also, is generally accepted.

35 It is not widely known that much Urartian pottery is hand-made. See note 2 and Chapter II, note 58.

36 For the approximate dating of the kings of Carchemish, R. D. Barnett, *Carchemish: Report on the Excavations at Jerablus on behalf of the British Museum* III, London, 1952, pp. 265–6. For the Long Wall, *ibid*, pp. 242–3; and *Carchemish* II, London, 1921, pp. 164–7 and pls B37–B45; and *Carchemish* I, London, 1914, pls B1–B3 etc.

37 Sir Aurel Stein: (a) *Old Routes of Western Iran*, London, 1940. (b) 'An Archaeological Journey in Western Iran', *Geographical Journal* 92, 1938, pp. 313ff.

38 (a) R. H. Dyson, 'The Archaeological Evidence of the Second Millennium BC on the Persian Plateau', CAH II, fasc. 66, 1968, p. 21. (b) For a more recent summary of work at Dinkha Tepe, Dyson, *Iran* V, 1967, pp. 136–7; and (c) O. W. Muscarella, 'Excavations at Dinkha Tepe, 1966', *The Metropolitan Museum of Art Bulletin* 25, 1966, pp. 16ff.

39 Dyson, CAH II, fasc. 66, p. 22.

40 (a) *Chronologies*, p. 172. (b) M. E. L. Mallowan's excavation reports on Tell Chagar Bazar, with Khabur ware among the material, *Iraq* III, 1936, pp. 1–86; *Iraq* IV, 1937, pp. 91–177; and *Iraq* IX, 1947, pp. 1–259 ('Excavations at Brak and Chagar Bazar').

41 (a) B. Hrouda, *Die bemalte Keramik des zweiten Jahrtausends in Nordmesopotamien und Nordsyrien*, Istanbuler Forschungen, Bd. 19, Berlin, 1957. (b) For grey wares from Tepe Hissar etc. see note 97 below.

42 *Excavations in Azerbaijan 1948*, pp. 69–99 (Period D) and 131–40 (Period C).

43 C. A. Burney, 'Excavations at Haftavan Tepe 1968: First Preliminary Report', *Iran* VIII, 1970, pp. 157–71. For the 1969 season, *ibid*, pp. 182–3 and the report due to be published in Iran X, 1972.

44 Dyson, CAH II, fasc. 66, pp. 16–17.

45 See note 42.

46 Dyson, CAH II, fasc. 66, p. 16.

47 See notes 24 and 25 (dating of Trialeti) and note 42 (Geoy Tepe D–C).

48 (a) Chapter III, note 83 (painted pottery of the Early Trans-Caucasian

III period in the Malatya–Elaziğ region). (b) James Mellaart, 'Anatolia, c. 2,300–1,750 BC', CAH I, fasc. 20, 1964, pp. 35–6.

49 Dyson, CAH II, fasc. 66, pp. 24–5.

50 J.R.Kupper, *Archives Royales de Mari* VI: *Correspondence de Bahdi-Lim*, Paris, 1954, letter no. 76, pp. 8, 108–9.

51 ARAB I, paras 405–6.

52 (a) Dyson, CAH II, fasc. 66, p. 5. (b) M.Gimbutas, *Bronze Age Cultures in Central and Eastern Europe*, The Hague, 1965, pp. 47ff. (c) S.Piggott, *Ancient Europe*, Edinburgh, 1965, pp. 137–8, mentioning the fact that in Greece the amber trade reached its peak in the fourteenth century BC.

53 *Les Outils de Bronze*, e.g. axes of Types J4A and J4B, p. 85 etc. For conclusions, pp. 447–8.

54 (a) *ibid*, p. 216. Axes of Sub-Type M1 first appear in this cultural province. (b) *Stratigraphie*, p. 498.

55 *Les Outils de Bronze*, pp. 216–17.

56 *Ibid*, nos. 1524 and 1820.

57 See note 29 above, especially pp. 132–7.

58 *Les Outils de Bronze*, pp. 415–16.

59 *Ibid*, pp. 216–18.

60 *Armenia in the Bronze and Early Iron Ages*, pp. 81–190.

61 (a) A.O.Mnatsakanian, *Bronze Age Cultures on Lake Sevan Coast in Armenia*, 25th International Congress of Orientalists, Moscow, 1960. (b) Piggott: PPS XXXIV, 1968, pp. 285–6.

62 (a) Piggott: PPS XXXIV, 1968, p. 286. (b) P.R.S.Moorey, 'The Earliest spoked Wheels and their Chronology', PPS XXXIV, 1968, pp. 430–2, a valuable note on this problem, quoting (*inter alia*): (c) G.Dossin, *Archives Royales de Mari* I, Paris, 1950, letter no. 50. This is the earliest written reference to a horse-drawn light hunting chariot – cf. note 50; and (d) R. de Vaux, O.P. *Revue Biblique* 74, 1967, pp. 484ff., on the Hurrian role in the early development of chariotry. Moorey claims that 'present evidence suggests that the home of the spoked wheel in the Near East lies somewhere in the plains of northern Syria or eastern Turkey, where it would appear to have been invented towards the end of the third millennium BC, possibly by the Hurrians'. This would reinforce the probability of Mitannian influence on the culture of Lchashen.

63 For the rise of Assyrian power: (a) C.J.Gadd, 'Assyria and Babylon, c. 1,370–1,300 BC', CAH II, fasc. 42. (b) J.M.Munn-Rankin, 'Assyrian Military Power, c. 1,300–1,200 BC', CAH II, fasc. 49.

64 See Chapter III, note 150.

65 (a) A.O.Mnatsakanian, 'Vehicles from Bronze Age Barrows on the Shores of Lake Sevan', SA 2, 1960, pp. 139–52. (b) *Armenia in the Bronze and Early Iron Ages*, pp. 81–113 and pls V, VIII, IX (Lchashen etc.); and pp. 132–60, including fig. 64 (Adiaman etc.).

66 (a) Piggott, PPS XXXIV, 1968, p. 286. (b) *Stratigraphie*, pp. 504–7 and figs 297–8. (c) Martirosian, *Armenia in the Bronze and Early Iron Ages*, figs 77–8 (attributed to ninth to eighth centuries BC).

67 (a) *ibid*, pl. V (encrusted ware from Lchashen, no. 4 being an example of

the twin bowl). (b) For the four groups of Lchashen burials, PPS XXXIV, 1968, p. 285; and note 61 (a) (Mnatsakanian).

68 Wherever oxen were in use as draught animals there was an obvious function for goads, whether bidents or tridents. (a) *Armenia in the Bronze and Early Iron Ages*, pl. IX, no. 10 and pl. XXXV: I, no. 12 (tridents); figs 49(1) and 59(2) and 64 (bidents). (b) C.F.A.Schaeffer, *Ugaritica* II, Paris, 1949, pp. 169–78. (c) In the megalithic house-grave 1 at Tsarskaya occur possible parallels of much earlier date, in the form of a copper bident with hooked points and a decorated copper trident; M.Gimbutas, *The Prehistory of Eastern Europe* I, Cambridge, Mass., 1956, fig. 30 (p. 61). It is doubtful if great significance attaches to parallels with the Lchashen examples.

69 (a) *The Material Culture of Ancient Artik*, p. 45 etc. (b) S.A.Esayan: *Arms and Warfare in Ancient Armenia*, Erevan, 1966, pp. 58–77 (discussion of daggers with classification into six types). In Russian. (c) *Armenia in the Bronze and Early Iron Ages*, pl. IX, no. 8 (Lchashen).

70 See note 59.

71 (a) *Stratigraphie*, p. 500 and fig. 270. (b) For a discussion of Kizil Vank pottery with reference to sources, *Excavations in Azerbaijan 1948*, p. 82, note 6. Among references given is the *Bulletin de la Commission Impériale Archéologique*, Moscow, XXIX; and *South-Western Journal of Anthropology* II, no. 3, p. 341. New excavations at Kizil Vank were planned to begin in 1968.

72 K.N.Pitskhelauri, *The Ancient Culture of the Tribes Living in the Basins of the Iori and the Alazani*, Tbilisi, 1965. In Georgian, with a Russian summary.

73 (a) *Bronze Age USSR*, p. 65, quoting R.M.Abrahamishvili, *Vestnik Gosudar. Muzeia Gruzii* XIX–XXI, Tbilisi, 1957, pp. 115–39; and T.Chubinishvili: *The Earliest Archaeological Remains of the Town of Mtskheta*, Tbilisi, 1957. In Georgian, with Russian summary. (b) *Stratigraphie*, pp. 503–4 and figs. 277, 296–7.

74 (a) In 1960–3 and 1965 excavations were carried out in the Dashkesen area, under the direction of Dr Kesamanli, to whom the writer is grateful for details of his discoveries. In 1901 Ressler excavated a barrow containing eighteen burials. (b) For Haftavān Tepe burials, Burney, *Iran* VIII, 1970, fig. 7 (p. 168) and fig. 8 nos. 4 and 5 (p. 170).

75 See note 17.

76 (a) *The Material Culture of Ancient Artik*, fig. 5 (p. 75) for an example of parallels with Lchashen (open-work bronze birds etc.) (b) Esayan, *Arms and Warfare in Ancient Armenia*, pp. 62–8 etc., for daggers and sheaths. (c) PPS 34, 1968, pp. 286–92.

77 (a) For Metsamor, note 11 above. The writer's visit (April 1968) gave him a vivid impression of this complex site. (b) For references to other aspects of early metallurgy in Trans-Caucasia and beyond, *Bronze Age USSR*, pp. 47–8.

78 (a) V.I.Markovin, 'The Culture of the North Caucasus during the Bronze Age', MIA 93, 1963. In Russian, 152 pp. (b) *Bronze Age USSR*, pp. 63–5.

79 (a) Chapter V, note 106. (b) E.I.Kruglov: 'New Antiquities of the Early Culture of Daghestan ... Investigations in the Cemetery of Tarki, 1947', MIA 23, 1951, pp. 208–25. (c) K.F.Smirnov, 'Archaeological Investigations in the Tarki Region of Daghestan in 1948–9', (ibid, pp. 226–72).

80 Les Outils de Bronze, p. 80.

81 (a) A.A.Iessen, 'The Kuban Centre of Metallurgy and Metal-Working of the End of the Copper-Bronze Age', MIA 23, 1951; for map of sites, fig. 34. (b) For a recently discovered copper mine attributed to the mid-second millennium BC, at Mt Pastukhovaya (2733 m.) in the north-west Caucasus, V.K.Kuznetsov, KSIA 108, 1966, pp. 62–7. (c) The Prehistory of Eastern Europe I, p. 46.

82 (a) Les Outils de Bronze, p. 402. (b) Bronze Age USSR, pp. 63–4. (c) E. Krupnov, 'Contributions to the Archaeology of Northern Ossetia of the Pre-Koban Period', MIA 23, 1951.

83 (a) Stratigraphie, pp. 418–20. (b) M.Gimbutas, 'Borodino, Seima and their Contemporaries', PPS XXII, 1956, pp. 143–72, especially pp. 148–51. (c) For metalwork from the Rutkha cemetery, V.A.Safronov, KSIA 108, 1966, pp. 23–30.

84 See Chapter III, note 132 (a).

85 (a) Bronze Age USSR, pp. 64–5. (b) Gimbutas, PPS XXII, 1956, pp. 148–51. (c) Les Outils de Bronze, Type J4A (Pitsunda axe).

86 (a) For the Koban metalwork and its origins, ibid, pp. 213–16 etc. (including shafthole axes of Deshayes' Type L) (b) The Georgians, pp. 60–3. (c) For imported daggers found in the Koban cultural province, Bronze Age USSR, p. 65; and M.N.Pogrebova, KSIA 103, 1965, pp. 11–18, where three main groups are distinguished.

87 (a) R.H.Dyson, 'Problems of Protohistoric Iran as Seen from Hasanlu', JNES XXIV, 1965, pp. 193–217. (b) Dyson, CAH II, fasc. 66, p. 28.

88 Henry Hodges, Technology in the Ancient World, London, 1970, pp. 123–4.

89 C.Desroches-Noblecourt, Tutankhamen, English translation: London, 1964, pl. XXIA (p. 97).

90 (a) cf. I Samuel 13, 19–22. (b) For a general account, R.D.Barnett, 'The Sea Peoples', CAH II, fasc. 68, 1969, with full bibliography. (c) For the Egyptian records, W.F.Edgerton and J.A.Wilson, Medinet Habu Inscriptions, Chicago, 1936. (d) For the cuneiform records, M.C.Astour, 'New Evidence on the Last Days of Ugarit', AJA 69, 1965, pp. 253–8. (e) For evidence on the Philistines, W.M.F.Petrie, Beth-Pelet I (Tell Fara), London, 1930.

91 C.F.Lehmann-Haupt, Armenien einst und jetzt, Berlin, 1910–31, pp. 889–95.

92 (a) The Georgians, p. 66. (b) Apollonius Rhodius, Argonautica, translated by Edward P.Coleridge, New York, 1960, p. 127.

93 (a) C.A.Burney, 'A First Season of Excavations at the Urartian Citadel of Kayalidere' AS XVI, 1966, pp. 55–111. For arrowheads, p. 79, fig. 21 (nos. 8–12) and pl. XIIIA. (b) For arrowheads from Haftavān, report to be published on the second season (Iran X, 1972).

94 See note 87 (a) and Chapter III, note 86.

95 T.Cuyler Young, 'The Iranian Migration into the Zagros', *Iran* V, 1967, pp. 11–34.

96 T.Cuyler Young, 'A Comparative Ceramic Chronology for Western Iran, 1,500–500 BC', *Iran* III, 1965, pp. 53–85.

97 (a) Erich F.Schmidt, *Excavations at Tepe Hissar Damghan*, Philadelphia, 1937. For Hissar IIIC pottery, pp. 181–4 especially. (b) J.Deshayes, 'Tureng Tepe et la Période Hissar IIIC', *Ugaritica* VI (Mission de Ras Shamra, Tome XVII), Paris, 1969, pp. 139–63. (c) For the argument for a derivation of Iron I wares from north-east Iran, T. C. Young, *Iran* V, 1967, especially p. 24.

98 These sherds from mounds in the Muş plain were collected by the writer during his survey of 1956.

99 T.C.Young, *Iran* V, 1967, pp. 20–1.

100 (a) *ibid*, p. 11. (b) R.N.Frye, *The Heritage of Persia*, London, 1963, pp. 36–49. (c) V.G.Childe, *The Aryans*, London, 1926, pp. 30–41.

101 see note 83.

102 Dyson, CAH II, fasc. 66, p. 31.

103 *Ibid*, p. 29.

104 Burney, (a) *Iraq* XXIV, 1962, pp. 146–7 and pl. XLIV, nos. 24–29 (Yanik Tepe). (b) *Iran* VIII, 1970, fig. 8, no. 1 and pl. IIIC (Haftavān Tepe).

105 (a) T.C.Young, *Iran* V, 1967, especially pp. 22–24. (b) *Excavations in Azerbaijan 1948*, pp. 142–5 (Tomb K). (c) *Stratigraphie*, pp. 406–8 and figs 217, 221, 237 (Agha Evlar).

106 Although not at first stating this opinion (cf. *A Preliminary Report on Marlik Excavations*, pp. 37–8), Professor Negahban has since made clear his belief, one which indeed carries much conviction, that the art of Marlik can be attributed to the Medes. This has obvious implications for the affinities of the Hasanlu bowl, the art of Medes and of Persians (Parsua) being at that time probably indistinguishable from each other.

107 E.O.Negahban, (a) *A Preliminary Report on Marlik Excavations, Gohar Rud Expedition, Rudbar 1961–2*, Teheran, 1964. In English. (b) 'A Brief Report on the Excavation of Marlik Tepe and Pileh Qal'eh', *Iran* II, 1964, pp. 13–19. (c) 'Notes on Some Objects from Marlik', JNES, XXIV, 1965, pp. 309–27.

108 (a) For horse burials in Iran, Clare Goff, 'Excavations at Bābā Jān, 1967; Second Preliminary Report', *Iran* VII, 1969, pp. 123–6; T.C.Young, *Iran* VI, 1968, p. 161 (Godin Tepe); R.H.Dyson, JNES XXIV, 1965, pp. 208–9 (Hasanlu); (b) For a more distant manifestation, in tombs of the eighth and seventh centuries BC, V.Karageorghis, 'Horse Burials on the Island of Cyprus', *Archaeology* 18 (4), 1965, pp. 282–90.

109 *Stratigraphie*, pp. 408–13 and fig. 221 (stag). (b) Note 83 above. (c) *A Preliminary Report on Marlik Excavations*, fig. 15 (triple goblet) and fig. 100 (model oxen and plough). (d) E.Porada, 'Facets of Iranian Art', *Archaeology* 17 (3), 1964, pp. 199–204, with illustration of triple goblet (p. 203).

110 *Stratigraphie*, fig. 217, no. 10; fig. 227, no. 16.
111 (a) *ibid*, fig. 282, no. 7; fig. 283, no. 5 (Beshtasheni Safarharab). (b) Edith Porada, *Ancient Iran*, New York, 1965, p. 236, note 3.
112 Porada, *Ancient Iran*, p. 91.
113 *Ibid*, p. 94.
114 The Hasanlu gold bowl has given rise to wide discussion. (a) *ibid*, pp. 96–102, (b) R.H.Dyson's reports, *Archaeology* 13, 1960, pp. 118–29; and *Expedition* I, 1959, pp. 4–17. (c) E.Porada, *Expedition* I, 1959, pp. 19–22. (d) Pourhan Diba, *Les Trésors de l'Iran et les Vases en Or des Manéens*, Paris, 1965.
115 M.J.Mellink, 'The Hasanlu Bowl in Anatolian Perspective', *Iranica Antiqua* VI, 1966, pp. 72–87.
116 *Ancient Iran*, p. 101.
117 See notes 114 and 106. If not specifically Median, the art of Marlik may very well be in the wider sense Iranian.
118 T.C.Young, *Iran* V, 1967, pp. 24–7.
119 ARAB I, paras. 581, 587, 588, 637.
120 The main sources for the writer's reconstruction of the historical geography of the southern Urmia basin are the Urartian inscriptions, especially the annals of Menua and Argishti I (Chapter V, notes 21 and 40). Dr Louis Levine, formerly of Philadelphia and now at the University of Toronto, kindly allowed the writer to see his most important and stimulating thesis on the historical geography of the Zagros region, in which he suggests a more southerly location for Parsua. Since this term certainly was applied to different areas, there is not necessarily any irreconcilable disagreement. For supporting evidence for the location of Parsua in the Solduz plain, *Iran* V, 1967, p. 17, note 54.
121 D.J.Wiseman, 'The Vassal Treaties of Esarhaddon', *Iraq* XX, 1958, pp. 1–100.
122 (a) T.C.Young, *Iran* V, 1967, pp. 17–19, for a convincing statement of the case against a migration of the Persians from the Urmia basin to Fars. See also note 20. (b) For the theory of such a migration, R.Ghirshman, *Iran*, Harmondsworth, 1954, pp. 118–19.
123 R.D.Barnett, 'Median Art', *Iranica Antiqua* II, 1962, pp. 77–95.
124 T.Cuyler Young, 'Thoughts on the Architecture of Hasanlu iv', *Iranica Antiqua*, VII, 1967, pp. 48–71.
125 *Ibid*. For a short summary of the results of the first three seasons of excavations, R.H.Dyson, 'Hasanlu and Early Iran', *Archaeology* 13, 1960, pp. 118–29.
126 (a) R.D.Barnett, *Catalogue of the Nimrud Ivories*, London, 1952. This deals with the material from the nineteenth century excavations in Assyria by Layard, Loftus and Rassam. (b) M.E.L.Mallowan, *Nimrud and its Remains* II, London, 1966, for the ivories from Fort Shalmaneser. Here a simplified interpretation of the styles of ivory-carving is proposed. Mallowan would in effect deny the existence of a distinct Syrian school of ivory work, which Barnett believes to have been centred in Hamath, leaving only the Phoenician and Assyrian styles.

127 T.C.Young, *Iran* V, 1967, p. 25.

128 C.A.Burney, 'Northern Anatolia Before Classical Times', AS VI, 1956, pp. 179–203. The writer can vouch for this from the surface pottery which he collected during one week in the valley of the Porsuk River, west of Gordion and around modern Eskişehir, at the end of his survey of 1954.

129 Burney, for the first and second preliminary reports, see note 43 above. and especially *Iran* VIII, 1970, fig. 7, fig. 8, nos. 4–5 and pl. IV. For the other burials, the report due to be published in *Iran* X, 1972.

5. FROM THE RISE OF URARTU TO THE BIRTH OF ARMENIA

1 (a) For the trade routes across Anatolia, J.M.Birmingham, 'The Overland Route Across Anatolia in the Eighth and Seventh Centuries BC', AS XI, 1961, pp. 185–95. (b) For the suggestion of Urartian links with the Greek colony of Trapezos, founded by the Milesians (757 BC) (Eusebius), R.D.Barnett: 'Ancient Oriental Influences on Archaic Greece', S.S. Weinberg (ed.), *The Aegean and the Near East*, Hetty Goldman Festschrift, New York, 1956, pp. 212–38, especially p. 229.

2 (a) ARAB I, para. 117; para. 360 (Uradri referred to by Adad-nirari II); para. 487 (Urartu mentioned by Assurnasirpal II). (b) For the earliest Urartian inscriptions, *Handbuch* I, p. 37 (nos. 1a–c) and pl. I.

3 (a) Henri Frankfort, *The Art and Architecture of the Ancient Orient*, Harmondsworth, 1954, pp. 102, 186, 189. (b) For a summary of early opinions on Urartian civilization, *Iraq* XII, 1950, p. 1.

4 (a) See note 2 (b). (b) Nicholas Adontz: *Histoire d'Arménie*, Paris, 1946, p. 145 etc.

5 (a) N.V.Arutyunian, *Urartian Agriculture and Cattle-Breeding*, Erevan, 1964, figs 25, 27, 28, pp. 129–33. In Russian. (b) C.A.Burney, AS XVI, 1966, pp. 88–90 (Kayalidere). (c) Tahsin Özgüç, *Altintepe II: Tombs, Storehouses and Ivories*, Ankara, 1969, p. 77 and pls LIII, 1–4 and LIV, 1–2. The suggestion that these are Hittite hieroglyphs seems improbable.

6 (a) F.Thureau-Dangin, *La Huitième Campagne de Sargon*, Paris, 1912, pp. vi–vii and 17–29 (lines 91–166). (b) For a detailed discussion, K.L.Oganesian, 'The Assyro-Urartian Battle on Mount Uaush', *Historical-Philological Journal of the Academy of Sciences of the Armenian SSR* 34 (3), 1966, pp. 107–18. In Russian. (c) See also note 68 below.

7 (a) Xenophon, *Anabasis* IV, iii (for the Carduchoi). (b) Maurits N.Van Loon: *Urartian Art*, Netherlands Historical-Archaeological Institute, Istanbul, 1966, for a reference (p. 169) to this horse, named Arsibi, quoting an inscription from near Toprakkale (UKN 110).

8 H.H.Von der Osten, 'Die urartaische Töpferei aus Van und die Möglichkeiten ihrer Einordnung in die anatolische Keramik', *Orientalia* 21, 1952, pp. 307–28 and 22, 1953, pp. 329–54. The significance of this painted ware is, however, uncertain.

9 Pottery collected by the writer during his survey in 1956.

10 For the Balawat Gates: (a) L.W.King, *Bronze Reliefs from the Gates of*

Shalmaneser, British Museum, London, 1915. (b) M.E.L.Mallowan, *Nimrud and its Remains* I, London, 1966, pp. 194, 282. (c) For the correct attribution of the bronze bands to Balawat rather than Nimrud, Mallowan, *Iraq* XIX, 1957, pp. 1–3. For the possible location of Arzashkun: (d) C.A.Burney, 'A First Season of Excavations at the Urartian Citadel of Kayalidere', AS XVI, 1966, especially pp. 58–63. (e) J.V.Kinnier-Wilson, 'The Kurba'il Statue of Shalmaneser III', *Iraq* XXIV, 1962, especially pp. 106–8. (f) *Histoire d'Arménie*, p. 81.

11 (a) ARAB I, paras 236 and 270. (b) For an earlier reference, to a victory over 43 kings of the Nairi lands by Tukulti-Ninurta I, *ibid*, paras 144 and 165. (c) *Histoire d'Arménie*, pp. 47–61.

12 W.G.Lambert, 'Shalmaneser in Ararat: the Sultantepe Tablets VIII', AS XI, 1961, pp. 143–58, especially pp. 152–3 (line 57).

13 For discussion of fluctuations in the relationship of Lake Van to its shores, H.F.B.Lynch, *Armenia: Vol II, The Turkish Provinces*, London, 1901; reprinted Beirut, 1965, pp. 46–53. At Adilcevaz the lake appears to have risen in level, submerging mediaeval walls. (Burney, AS VII, 1957, p. 39).

14 (a) *Handbuch* I, nos. 2–12. These inscriptions of Ishpuini include four *in situ* (nos. 8, 9, 10, 12) and two almost certainly close to their original location (6B,7). (b) For a more recent translation and discussion of the Kel-i-Shin stele, W.C.Benedict, 'The Urartian-Assyrian Inscription of Kelishin', JAOS 81, 1961, pp. 359–85.

15 Robert H.Dyson, *Expedition* 11, no. 2 1969, p. 44.

16 ARAB I, para. 718.

17 *Handbuch* I, no. 17. The copy (pl. 18) shows how badly damaged this is.

18 W.C.Benedict, 'Two Urartian Inscriptions from Azerbaijan', JCS–XIX, 1965, pp. 35–40.

19 R.D.Barnett, in *The Aegean and the Near East*, p. 231.

20 Henry Rawlinson, *Journal of The Royal Geographical Society* X, 1841, pp. 12–13. Quoted in a footnote on the significance of Tashtepe (E.M.Wright, JNES II, 1943, p. 179, note 31).

21 Kemal Balkan, 'Ein urartäischer Tempel auf Anzavurtepe und hier entdeckte Inschriften', *Anatolia* V, 1960, pp. 99–131.

22 (a) Ekrem Akurgal, *Remarques Stylistiques sur les Reliefs de Malatya*, Ankara, 1946, especially pp. 108ff. (b) For a recent statement of the same author's views, *The Birth of Greek Art*, translated by W.Dynes: London, 1968, especially pp. 97–100. (c) But cf. *The Art and Architecture of the Ancient Orient*, pp. 128–9 and 247 (note 47) for a contrary opinion.

23 ARAB I, paras 237, 580, 610, 636, 674, 686, 690.

24 (a) For Ali̇şar IV painted pottery, H.H.Von der Osten, *The Alishar Hüyük: Seasons of 1930–32* Part II, Chicago, 1937, pp. 350–410. (b) For the Komurhan rock inscription, *Handbuch*, no. 104. (c) For sites of all periods around Malatya, P.Meriggi, 'Quinto Viaggio Anatolico', *Oriens Antiquus* 5, 1966, pp. 67–109, especially pp. 100–1.

25 (a) For Urartian references, *Handbuch*, nos. 16, 25 and 80. (b) For Assyrian references, ARAB I, paras 476–8, 585, 593, 599–601, 610.

26 ARAB I, para. 593 (the Black Obelisk from the Central Palace of Nimrud, now in the British Museum).

27 (a) C.A.Burney: AS XVI, 1966, especially pp. 58–63. (b) J.V.Kinnier-Wilson, *Iraq* XXIV, 1962, especially p. 104, for a contrary opinion. See note 10 (d–e).

28 (a) ARAB I, paras 236–7, 604. (b) Xenophon, *Anabasis* Book IV, iv, 18; vi, 5; vii, 1–2. (c) J.V.Kinnier-Wilson; *Iraq* XXIV, 1962, quoting G.A. Melikishvili, *Nairi-Urartu*, Tbilisi, 1954, pp. 58ff. and 111.

29 (a) B.B.Piotrovskii, *Karmir-Blur I: The Results of the Excavations of 1939–1949*, Erevan, 1950, pl. 9. (b) B.B.Piotrovskii, *Karmir-Blur II: The Results of the Excavations of 1949–1950*, Erevan, 1952, pl. 18. (c) See p. 143 of R.D.Barnett's summary of *Karmir-Blur I*, 'Russian Excavations in Armenia', *Iraq* XIV, 1952, pp. 132–47; R.D.Barnett also summarized *Karmir-Blur II*, 'Further Russian Excavations in Armenia', *Iraq* XXI, 1959, pp. 1–19.

30 C.A.Burney: (a) 'Urartian Fortresses and Towns in the Van Region', AS VII, 1957, pp. 37–53; and (b) 'Measured Plans of Urartian Fortresses', AS X, 1960, pp. 177–96.

31 H.F.B.Lynch, *Armenia: Vol. II – The Turkish Provinces*, pp. 76–115, for an excellent description of Van in the late nineteenth century.

32 ARAB II, para. 161. Cf. *La Huitième Campagne de Sargon*.

33 (a) Burney, AS X, 1960, pp. 192–4. (b) See also note 21.

34 For general discussions of the Urartian temple: (a) W.Kleiss, 'Zur Rekonstruktion des urartäischen Tempels', *Istanbuler Mitteilungen* 13–14, 1963–4, pp. 1ff. (b) D.B.Stronach, 'Urartian and Achaemenian Tower Temples', *JNES* XXVI, 1967, pp. 278–88.

35 M.Van Loon, *Urartian Art*, pp. 55–6, with reference to M.J.Mellink, 'Archaeology in Asia Minor', *AJA* 67, 1963, p. 183.

36 Tamara Talbot-Rice, *The Scythians* (Ancient Peoples and Places), London, 1957, p. 43, quoting Ellsworth Huntington: *The Pulse of Asia*, Boston, 1919, p. ix.

37 (a) UKN 43–56 (quoted in *Urartian Art*, pp. 12–13). (b) *Handbuch*, nos. 30a–i. (c) C.F.Lehmann-Haupt, *Armenien Einst und Jetzt*, Berlin, 1910–1931, II, pp. 95–109. (d) For Shammuramat, ARAB I, para. 731.

38 Urartian irrigation works would make a worthwhile subject for research. (a) Burney, AS VII, 1957, pp. 51–2 and X, 1960, pp. 194–6; and *Handbuch*, no. 39 (Bostankaya). (b) ARAB II, para. 160 (Ulhu). (c) J.Laessoe, 'The Irrigation System at Ulhu', *JCS*, V, 1951, pp. 21–32. (d) Bruno Meissner, "Die Eroberung der Stadt Ulhu auf Sargons 8 Feldzug', *ZA* 34, 1922, pp. 113–22.

39 (a) UKN 110. (b) ARAB I, para. 405 (Tukulti-Ninurta II) and paras 716–22 (Shamshi-Adad V). (c) B.B.Piotrovskii, *Urartu: The Kingdom of Van and its Art*, translated by P.S.Gelling, London, 1967, figs 7, 8, 30, etc. (d) cf. also AS XVI, 1966, fig. 10 (p. 78).

40 (a) *Handbuch*, no. 80. (b) *Histoire d'Arménie*, pp. 161–7.

41 (a) K.L.Oganesian, *Arin-Berd I: The Architecture of Erebuni – Materials of the Excavations of 1950–9*, Erevan, 1961. In Russian. (b) *Handbuch*, no. 91a.

42 (a) *Handbuch*, no. 80 (sections 5–12). (b) UKN 127. (c) *Histoire d'Arménie*, pp. 163–6, 185–6.

43 (a) B.B.Piotrovskii, *Vanskoe Tsarstvo/The Kingdom of Van*, Moscow, 1959, figs 58, 60, 62, 63 (pp. 209–13). (b) *Urartian Art*, pp. 60–2.

44 *Arin-Berd I* (see note 41 [a]).

45 (a) *ibid*, fig. 38. (b) *Urartian Art*, pp. 65–6. (c) G.Perrot and C.Chipiez, *Histoire de l'Art* II, Paris, 1884, p. 703, pl. XIV. (d) M.E.L.Mallowan, *Nimrud and its Remains* I, pp. 105–6.

46 *Urartian Art*, pp. 166–8 (summary). The distinguishing of this 'court style' is one of the main conclusions of this book.

47 (a) The Erebuni paintings are to appear in *Arin-Berd II*. (b) For a discussion of the Assurbanipal hunting reliefs (now in the British Museum), *The Art and Architecture of the Ancient Orient*, pp. 99–101 and pls. 108–13.

48 (a) For a concise discussion of Urartian decorated shields, helmets, quivers and belts, *Urartu: The Kingdom of Van and its Art*, pp. 43–50. (b) cf. *Urartian Art*, pp. 116–24.

49 (a) *Handbuch*, no. 103 (sections 3 and 11). (b) UKN 155. (c) *Histoire d'Arménie*, pp. 203, 211, 276 (Qulhi).

50 (a) *Handbuch*, no. 103 (section 9). (b) For Kutmuhi and Kummuhu in the Assyrian annals, ARAB I, paras 73, 117, 143 (among early references); paras 221–3, 227 (Tiglath-Pileser I); 360 (Adad-nirari II); 442–3, 459, 480 (Assurnasirpal II); 599, 610 (Shalmaneser III); 769, 772, 785, 797, 801, 813 (Tiglath-Pileser III).

51 ARAB I, paras 769, 785, 813. These accounts telescope the events of the third year (Kishtan and Halpi) and those of the march through the heart of Urartu.

52 (a) *Handbuch*, no. 103. (b) UKN 155. (c) For the original publication of the Russian excavations at Van in 1916, N.Y.Marr and J.Orbeli, *Russkoye Archeologicheskoye Obshchestvo* ..., St Petersburg, 1922. The Turkish name for this rock-cut shrine is Hazineh Kapisi (Treasury Door).

53 *Altintepe II: Tombs, Storehouses and Ivories*, pp. 73–4, figs 29–33 and pls XXVI–XXVII.

54 (a) Burney, AS VII, 1957, pp. 45–7 (where it is called Asbaşin, after the adjoining village). (b) M.J.Mellink, 'Archaeology in Asia Minor', AJA 69, 1965, p. 141; 70, 1966, pp. 150–1, 281; 71, 1967, p. 164, etc.

55 C.A.Burney, 'A First Season of Excavations at the Urartian Citadel of Kayalidere' AS XVI, 1966, pp. 55–111.

56 (a) Note 34 (b) (Stronach). (b) Carl Nylander, 'Old Persian and Greek Stone-Cutting and the Chronology of Achaemenian ... Monuments', AJA 69, 1965, pp. 49–55.

57 For the original drawing of this relief, P.E.Botta and E.Flandin, *Monument de Ninive* II, Paris, 1849, pl. 141. For a reproduction, *Iraq* XII, 1950, p. 21 (fig. 11) and many other publications. For Musasir see also note 34 above, and for Altintepe note 74 below.

58 Burney, AS XVI, 1966, fig. 10 (p. 78) ('belt' fragments), fig. 8 (p. 76) (lion) and pls IX–X. The stylistic parallel with the stone lions, on an

infinitely larger scale, from Tell Tayanat (*The Art and Architecture of the Ancient Orient*, pl. 156) should not be pressed too far.

59 See note 5.

60 (a) e.g. *The Art and Architecture of the Ancient Orient*, pl. 89. (b) For the theory of the derivation of Urartian art from ninth-century Assyria, *Urartian Art*, pp. 168, 172–4.

61 (a) R.D.Barnett, 'The Urartian Cemetery at Igdyr', AS XIII, 1963, pp. 153–98). For K.Balkan's excavations in the Iğdir area, M.J.Mellink, AJA 71, 1967, p. 165. (b) For Alacahan and Evditepe burials, M.J. Mellink, 'Archaeology in Asia Minor', AJA 69, 1965, pp. 141–2 and 70, 1966, p. 151. See also AS XIV, 1964, p. 22. (c) *Altintepe II*, pp. 65–72, figs 4–28 and pls II–XVIII. (d) For Kayalidere, AS XVI, 1966, pp. 101–11 and pls XXII–XXV, Tomb A. (e) *Urartian Art*, pp. 60–4.

62 For the Topzaua stele, *Handbuch*, no. 122 and UKN 264.

63 *Urartian Art*, pp. 19–20, quoting UKN 268 and the supporting opinion of Albrecht Goetze, *Kleinasien*, Munich, 1957, p. 198, note 2.

64 *La Huitième Campagne de Sargon*, p. viii (suggesting Ulhu was at Marand). See also note 38.

65 ARAB II, para. 10.

66 (a) For Assyrian references to the 'mighty Medes', the 'distant Medes' etc., ARAB I, paras 784, 795, 811–2; and II, paras 23, 54, 79, 82, 118, 137, 238, 432, 519, 540, 566. (b) For Deioces (Daiakku), Herodotus I.96 and I.101; and ARAB II, paras 12 and 56. (c) For Phraortes, Herodotus I.102. (d) For a general discussion, R.N.Frye, *The Heritage of Persia*, London, 1963, pp. 68–78. (e) For the account of a first season's work at an important Median site in the Hamadan region, D.B.Stronach, 'Excavations at Tepe Nush-i Jan 1967', *Iran* VII, 1969, pp. 1–20. This report includes an excellent concise account (pp. 2–8) of Median history and the rise of the Achaemenid dynasty.

67 For a modern publication of these drawings by Flandin, Yigael Yadin, *The Art of Warfare in Biblical Lands in the Light of Archaeological Discovery*, London, 1963, pp. 416–25.

68 (a) F.Thureau-Dangin, *La Huitième Campagne de Sargon*, Paris, 1912. (b) ARAB II, paras 140–78. (c) For an account of part of Sargon's probable route, based on first-hand knowledge of the terrain, E.M. Wright, 'The Eighth Campaign of Sargon II', JNES II, 1943, pp. 173–186.

69 ARAB II, para. 166.

70 (a) For the battle on Mount Uaush, ARAB II, paras 152–5 and note 6 (b). (b) See also note 68 (c) (Wright).

71 Leroy Waterman, *Royal Correspondence of the Assyrian Empire*, Ann Arbor, 1930–6, nos. 197, 646, 1079.

72 *Ibid*, no. 197.

73 See note 18 above. For other inscriptions of Argishti II, *Handbuch*, nos. 123–5.

74 (a) R.D.Barnett and N.Gökçe, 'The Find of Urartian Bronzes at Altintepe, near Erzincan', AS III, 1953, pp. 121–9. (b). For the subject

of cauldrons, P.Amandry, 'Chaudrons à Protomes de Taureau en Orient et en Grèce', *The Aegean and the Near East* (Hetty Goldman Festschrift), pp. 239–61.

75 *Altintepe II*, pp. 70–1, for the dating of the tombs, Tomb III yielding two inscribed bronzes with the name of Argishti son of Rusa (i.e. Argishti II). Tomb III is said to be later than the other two tombs. See also Özgüç: *Belleten* 98, 1961, p. 274. In *Altintepe I: Architectural Monuments and Wall Paintings*, Ankara, 1966, it is stated (p. 46) that 'the levels date from the second half of the eighth century BC to the second half of the seventh'.

76 *Altintepe I*, pp. 47–56 and pls I–III, XXIII–XXXII, 1.

77 (a) *ibid*, pp. 44–6 (for the apadana) and fig. 1 (reconstruction of the temple). (b) T.Özgüç, 'The Urartian Architecture on the Summit of Altintepe', *Anatolia* VII, 1963, pp. 43–9 (English version). Cf. note 34.

78 *Altintepe I*, pp. 39–44. See also note 88.

79 ARAB I, para. 774.

80 (a) For the ivories, *Altintepe II*, pp. 78–93 and pls XXXII–LII. (b) For wood-carving, *ibid*, pp. 65–72 and pls XIX–XXII. (c) *Urartian Art*, pp. 137–8. (d) References in the earliest report on Altintepe, *Belleten* 98, 1961, pp. 269ff.

81 (a) *Histoire d'Arménie*, pp. 125–36 and 179–80. The opinion that Urartu was entirely on the defensive after Rusa I's defeat by Sargon II and by the Cimmerians, and that military adventures were eschewed (*Urartian Art*, p. 19), is not obviously borne out by the limited number of inscriptions of Rusa II. (b) For a summary of Urartian sites in Azerbaijan, W.Kleiss, 'Bericht über zwei Erkundungsfahrten in Nordwest-Iran', *Archaeologische Mitteilungen aus Iran*, Band 2, 1969, pp. 20–6. (c) For results to date from Bastam, W.Kleiss's short summaries, *Iran* VII, 1969, p. 188; and VIII, 1970, pp. 176–8.

82 (a) See note 1 (b). (b) For references to Mushki and Hate, *Handbuch*, no. 128.

83 ARAB I, para. 221.

84 *Histoire d'Arménie*, pp. 133–6, with references to sources.

85 Old Testament references to Urartu: II *Kings* 19, v. 37 and *Isaiah* 37, v. 38 (escape of assassins of Sennacherib); and *Jeremiah* 51, vv. 27–8 (prophesying the fall of Babylon).

86 (a) *Urartian Art*, pp. 19–20, 49–50 etc. (b) UKN 268 (inscription recording the city's foundation).

87 R.D.Barnett, 'The Excavations of the British Museum at Toprakkale near Van', *Iraq* XII, 1950, pp. 1–43, especially fig. 22; and *Iraq*, 1954, pp. 3–22.

88 (a) C.A.Burney and G.R.J.Lawson, 'Urartian Reliefs at Adilcevaz...', AS VIII, 1958, pp. 211–17. (b) For the revised interpretation, based on the results of the first season of excavations, Emin Bilgiç and Baki Oğun, 'Excavations at Kef Kalesi of Adilcevaz, 1964', *Anatolia* VIII, 1964, pp. 93–124, especially pp. 116ff. (c) *Anatolia* IX, 1965, p. 19.

89 *The Art and Architecture of the Ancient Orient*, fig. 54 (p. 127).

90 (a) For *Karmir-Blur I* and *II* and English summaries (Barnett), see note

29 above. (b) B.B.Piotrovskii, *Karmir-Blur III: Results of the Excavations of 1951-3*, Erevan, 1955. (c) K.L.Oganesian, *Karmir-Blur IV: The Architecture of Teishebaini*, Erevan, 1955.

91 See Chapter IV, note 43 (Haftavān Tepe) and note 88 above (Kefkalesi).

92 (a) Herodotus I.104, IV.12. (b) *Urartian Art*, p. 16, for the opinion that the distinction between Scyths and Cimmerians is unreal and that the two terms are interchangeable. (c) Against this a more cautious opinion is expressed by R.N.Frye, *The Heritage of Persia*, p. 265 (note 27). (d) T. Sulimirski, 'The Cimmerian Problem', *Bulletin of the Institute of Archaeology, London* 2, 1959, pp. 45-64.

93 (a) Herodotus I.104, IV.12. (b) For action by Esarhaddon against both Scyths and Cimmerians, in Hubushna and Mannaean territory respectively, ARAB II, paras 516-7. (c) For a brief summary of the invasions through the Caucasus, E.H.Minns, 'The Scythians and Northern Nomads', CAH III, Cambridge, 1929, especially pp. 187-96.

94 (a) Note 72: this letter was related to a region not far from Tabal, west of Malatya. (b) For the destruction of Sinope, Herodotus IV.12 (Cimmerian settlement there). (c) For the sack of Phrygian Gordion, Herodotus I,6, 15; and the preliminary excavation reports by Rodney S. Young, AJA 55, 1951 and in subsequent issues.

95 (a) ARAB II, paras 516, 530, 546 (against Teushpa the Cimmerian); paras. 606-7 (extradition of Urartian exiles from Shupria). (b) J.A. Knudtzon, *Assyrische Gebete an den Sonnengott*, Leipzig, 1893, no. 48 (the Cimmero-Urartian threat to Assyria).

96 ARAB II, paras 784-5. (b) Herodotus I.15. (c) D.G.Hogarth, 'Lydia and Ionia', CAH III, ipp. 505-18, for Lydia before the reign of Croesus. (d) The excavations at Sardis under the direction of G.F.Hanfmann (summarized in various issues of AS and elsewhere) are largely concerned with later periods, but are also revealing much of importance of the Lydian city, as well as work in the tumuli of Bin Tepe. (e) R.D.Barnett, 'Phrygia and the Peoples of Anatolia in the Iron Age', CAH II, fasc. 56, 1967, pp. 24-5.

97 (a) ARAB II, para. 1001. (b) R.Campbell Thompson, 'The British Museum Excavations at Nineveh', *Liverpool Annals of Archaeology and Anthropology* XX, 1933, p. 88, lines 138-62.

98 (a) *Urartian Art*, p. 15. (b) UKN 127. Col. V 1.49; and 133, 1.5.

99 (a) For Partatua, *Assyrische Gebete an den Sonnengott* II, no. 29 (marriage of a daughter of Esarhaddon). (b) For the traditional account of the twenty-eight year Scythian rule of 'Upper Asia' (the highland zone east of the River Halys), Herodotus 1.103-7. (c) Another opinion would date this period of Scythian domination to 613-585 BC (*Urartian Art*, pp. 22-25), rather than the orthodox dating of 653-25 BC; but this chronology raises difficulties too. (d) For the cuneiform sources on the fall of Assyria, Cyril Gadd, *The Fall of Nineveh*, London, 1923; D.J.Wiseman, *Chronicles of Chaldaean Kings*, London, 1956. (e) For the change in Scythian support from Sin-shar-ishkun to Cyaxares, J.B.Pritchard, *Ancient Near Eastern Texts*, second edition, Princeton, 1955, p. 304.

100 *Royal Correspondence of the Assyrian Empire*, no. 146.

101 (a) For Samtavro, see Chapter IV, note 73. (b) For Mingechaur, note 126 below.

102 (a) For a treatment of the whole subject, Karl Jettmar, *Le Style Animalier Eurasiatique, Genèse et Arrière-Plan Social*, Paris, 1965, especially Chapter XV (pp. 214–42); very full bibliography. (b) Among earlier works, M.Rostovtzeff, *Iranians and Greeks in South Russia*, Oxford, 1922 is still valuable.

103 O.W.Muscarella, 'The Tumuli at Sé Girdan: A Preliminary Report', *Metropolitan Museum Journal* 2, 1969, pp. 5–25.

104 R.W.Hamilton, 'The Decorated Bronze Strip from Guschi', AS XV, 1965, pp. 41–51. For the Ziwiye treasure, note 125 below.

105 For information on the excavations of 1965–7 at Karaköpektepe the writer is indebted to the excavator, G.S.Ismailov, whom he had the good fortune to meet when in Baku in April 1968.

106 (a) Strabo, *Geography* XI, 4, 7. ('trampling' on the body of a human sacrificial victim). (b) For the Kayakent-Khorochoi culture, A.P. Kruglov, 'The North-East Caucasus in the Second–First Millennia BC', MIA 68, 1958, especially pp. 51–146. (c) T.Sulimirski, *Prehistoric Russia*, London, 1970, pp. 362–3.

107 (a) *Stratigraphie*, p. 527. (b) Against this high dating, cf. *Bronze Age USSR*, p. 65. (c) A Georgian publication with Russian summary, D.L.Koridze, *On the History of the Colchidic Culture*, Tbilisi, 1965.

108 (a) D.B.Stronach, 'The Development of the Fibula in the Near East', *Iraq* XXI, 1959, pp. 181–206. (b) Chr.Blinkenberg, *Fibules Grècques et Orientales*, Copenhagen, 1926. (c) *Stratigraphie*, pp. 502, 527, 533 and figs 275–6. (d) O.W.Muscarella, 'A Fibula from Hasanlu', AJA 69, 1965, pp. 233–40. (e) J.M.Birmingham, 'The Development of the Fibula in Cyprus and the Levant', PEQ, 1963, pp. 80–112.

109 (a) *The Georgians*, figs 5 and 14, pl. 18. (b) Piggott, PPS XXXIV, 1968, pp. 291–2 (Stepanavan 'belt'). (c) R.D.Barnett, 'The Treasure of Ziwiye', *Iraq* XVIII, 1956, pp. 111–16. For a reference to the Akthala bronze 'belt', p. 113 with fig. 1. (d) *Armenia in the Bronze and Early Iron Ages*, figs 65, 85 etc.

110 For Guschi, note 104. For Kayalidere, note 58. For Zakim, R.D.Barnett, 'Median Art', *Iranica Antiqua* II, 1962, pp. 82, 87; figs 2, 4. For Nor-Aresh, Barnett, AS XIII, 1963, pp. 194–8.

111 CAH III, pp. 145–7. The Scythian raid left an echo in the name of Scythopolis (Beisan) in Palestine.

112 R.Campbell Thompson, *Liverpool Annals of Archaeology and Anthropology* XX, 1933, p. 87, lines 121–3.

113 Herodotus I,134, for the organization of the Median kingdom; and I,74, for the Medo-Lydian war, which began with a Scythian alliance with Alyattes of Lydia against Cyaxares (590 BC) and ended with the agreement on the River Halys as the frontier between the Median and Lydian kingdoms (585 BC). Van cannot have fallen later than 590 BC.

114 See note 97.

115 *Chronicles of Chaldaean Kings*, p. 62 (lines 72–3) and p. 64 (lines 1–11).

116 Herodotus I,106.

117 For the evidence for the attribution of these arrowheads to the Scyths, T. Sulimirski, 'Scythian Antiquities in Western Asia' *Artibus Asiae*, XVII, 1954, pp. 282–318, especially pp. 308–13.

118 (a) The writer owes the suggestion about the garrison at Erebuni to K.L.Oganesian. (b) For Scythian mercenaries, *Urartian Art*, p. 25.

119 *Jeremiah* 51, vv. 27–8.

120 (a) Herodotus VII,64. (b) R.E.Emmerick, *Saka Grammatical Studies*, London Oriental Series Vol. 20, Oxford, 1968, pp. 2–3. (c) *The Heritage of Persia*, pp. 43–4.

121 The Sachkhere material is in the Tbilisi Museum. For the Khrtanots cemetery, *Armenia in the Bronze and Early Iron Ages*, pl. XXVIII etc.

122 (a) E.H.Minns, *Antiquity* XVII, 1943, p. 135, quoting B.A.Kuftin, *Archaeological Excavations in Trialeti*, pp. 41–7 and pls XIII–XVI (Beshtasheni). (b) For the Kazbek treasure, A.M.Tallgren, 'Caucasian Monuments', ESA V, 1930, pp. 109ff.

123 (a) On Scythian burial customs, Herodotus IV,71–2. (b) E.D.Phillips, *The Royal Hordes: Nomad Peoples of the Steppes*, London, 1965, p. 72.

124 (a) *ibid*, especially figs 57 (Kelermes mirror back) and 72 (Kostromskaya barrow). (b) *Iranians and Greeks in South Russia*, pls 7–9. (c) K.Jettmar: *L'Art des Steppes*, Paris, 1965, especially pp. 30–3. (d) *Urartian Art*, pp. 175–7.

125 There is a very large literature on Ziwiye, a subject of considerable discussion and controversy over the attribution of different styles and over dating. (a) André Godard, *Le Trésor de Ziwiye*, Haarlem, 1950, is the basic publication, though other items have since appeared. For articles on various aspects: (b) R.Ghirshman, 'Le Trésor de Sakkez', *Artibus Asiae* XIII, 1950, pp. 181–206. (c) R.D.Barnett, 'The Treasure of Ziwiye', *Iraq* XVIII, 1956, pp. 111–16. (d) C.K.Wilkinson, 'More Details on Ziwiye', (*Iraq* XXII, 1960, pp. 213–20); and 'Treasure from the Mannaean Land', *Metropolitan Museum of Art Bulletin* 21, 1963, pp. 274–84. (e) E.Porada, *Ancient Iran*, pp. 113–27. (f) K.Jettmar, *L'Art des Steppes*, pp. 227–30. (g) *The Art and Architecture of the Ancient Orient*, pp. 205–7. (h) *Urartian Art*, pp. 177–8.

126 (a) A.Mongait, *Archaeology in the USSR*, pp. 250–2 and references in the bibliography. (b) For earlier burials etc., dating from the thirteenth century BC till *c*. 700 BC, G.M.Aslanov, R.M.Vaidov and G.I.Ione, *Ancient Mingechaur: the Aeneolithic and Bronze Age*, Baku, 1959. In Russian. (c) Strabo: *Geography* XI, 14,4 (Sakasene).

127 (a) Homer: *Odyssey* XI, 13–19. (b) Herodotus IV, 11–13. (c) Strabo XIV, 1, 40.

128 T.Sulimirski, article 'Cimmerians' *Encyclopaedia Britannica*, 1967 edition.

129 K.Jettmar, *L'Art des Steppes*, pp. 80–141, with references to the publications of S.I.Roudenko, pp. 255–6.

130 (a) Ellen L.Kohler, 'Phrygian Animal Style and Nomadic Art', in M.J. Mellink (ed.), *Dark Ages and Nomads, c.* 1,000 BC, Istanbul, 1964, pp. 58–62. (b) R.S.Young, AJA 61, 1957, pl. 91, figs 16, 17.

131 (a) Herodotus VII,73. (b) Strabo XI, 14, 12. (c) *Histoire d'Arménie*, pp. 322–3.

132 (a) Herodotus III, 93–4. (b) *Histoire d'Arménie*, p. 332, quoting Adontz, *Zeitschrift für Ethnologie*, 1901, pp. 181 and 209.

133 (a) Herodotus VII,73. (b) René Grousset, *Histoire de l'Arménie*, Paris, 1947, p. 68. (c) E.Forrer, *Die Provinzeinteilung des Assyrischen Reiches*, Leipzig, 1921, pp. 80–1. (d) *Histoire d'Arménie*, pp. 125, 316, 320.

134 (a) R.A.Crossland, 'Immigrants from the North', CAH I, fasc. 60, pp. 36, 44, etc., with references in the bibliography. (b) I.M.Diakonov, 'Phrygians, Hittites and Armenians', in *Problems of Hitto- and Hurrology*, Peredneaziatskiy Sbornik, Moscow, 1961, pp. 333ff. and 594ff.

135 (a) Eudoxos (*c.* 370 BC) in his *Itinerary*, quoted by Stephen of Byzantium (fifth century AD) in the *Ethnica*, a gazetteer, under the name 'Armenia'. (b) For the affinities of the Armenian language, the articles by A.Meillet, in *Revue des Etudes Arméniennes* IV, 1924 and VII, 1927.

136 (a) J.Garstang and O.R.Gurney, *The Geography of the Hittite Empire*, especially pp. 36–8. (b) Strabo XI, 14,12. (c) According to Moses of Khorene I,1, chapters X–XI, Haik was the eponymous hero who led the Armenians to conquer their new homeland.

137 (a) For the land of Urme, *Handbuch* nos. 26, 27, 80, 81, 103. Argishti I's campaigns against Urme strongly suggest it lay much further from Van than the Muş plain. (b) *Histoire d'Arménie*, p. 137 etc. (Behistun).

138 (a) Xenophon, *Cyropedia* I,5; II,4; III,1. (b) For the Old Persian text of the Behistun inscription, R.Kent, *Old Persian*, New Haven, 1950. (c) For the significance of the rebellion of Gaumata (Smerdis), *The Heritage of Persia*, pp. 88–93.

139 For Kefirkalesi, Burney, AS VII, 1957, p. 51.

140 (a) Herodotus III,94. (b) Strabo XI,14,4. (mentioning Sakasene as one of the districts of Armenia). (c) *Histoire d'Arménie*, pp. 308–9.

141 For the difficult passage of the Ten Thousand through Carduchian territory before they reached Armenia, Xenophon, *Anabasis* IV, iii.

142 Burney, *Iraq* XXIV, 1962, especially pp, 147–9, 152 and pl. XLV.

143 (a) R.H.Dyson, 'Problems of Protohistoric Iran as Seen from Hasanlu', JNES XXIV, 1965, pl. XLIV: jar described as IIIA, from Agrab Tepe. This is in fact typically Urartian. (b) T.C.Young, 'A Comparative Ceramic Chronology for Western Iran', *Iran* III, 1965, pp. 53–85, for a discussion including Hasanlu, Ziwiye and the Achaemenid village at Susa. (c) R.H.Dyson, 'Archaeological Scrap: Glimpses of History at Ziwiyeh', *Expedition* 5, (3) 1963, pp. 32–7. (d) R.Ghirshman, *Mémoires de la Mission Archéologique en Iran, Tome XXXVI: Village Perse-Achéménide*, Paris, 1954. (e) For pottery of sixth–fifth century BC date from Haftavān Tepe, *Iran* VIII, 1970, fig. 8 (nos. 11–12) and pl. VId.

144 Strabo, XI,13, 1–2.

145 (a) A.H.Layard, *Discoveries in the Ruins of Nineveh and Babylon, with Travels in Armenia, Kurdistan and the Desert*, London, 1853, pp. 394, 400–1, with acknowledgment to Schulz; reference in Gordon Waterfield, *Layard of Nineveh*, London, 1963, p. 214. (b) For Zernaki Tepe, Burney, AS VII,

1957, pp. 49–50 and X, 1960, pp. 185–8. (c) For a full discussion of the site as a whole, with support of its attribution to the Urartian rather than to the Achaemenid period or later, Carl Nylander 'Remarks on the Urartian Acropolis at Zernaki Tepe', *Orientalia Suecana* XIV–XV, 1965–6, pp. 141–54.

6. HISTORY AND INSTITUTIONS

1 Herodotus, *The Histories*, III, 89–94.
2 Herodotus, *The Histories*, III, 73, 79.
3 H.A.Manandian, *The Trade and Cities of Armenia in Relation to Ancient World Trade*, trans. N.G.Garsoian, Lisbon, 1965, p. 36.
4 *Histories*, V, 49.
5 *Anabasis*, III, 5.
6 *Anabasis*, IV, 4 and 5. On the use of drinking tubes for beer and other beverages in antiquity, see E.Herzfeld, *Iran in the Ancient East*, Oxford University Press, 1941, p. 144.
7 C.Toumanoff, *Studies in Christian Caucasian History*, Georgetown, 1963, p. 279; R.Ghirshman, *Iran*, Harmondsworth, 1965, pp. 197–201.
8 Kévork Aslan, *Études historiques sur le peuple arménien*, Paris, 1928, p. 70.
9 Toumanoff, *Studies*, pp. 280, 289.
10 Strabo, *Geography*, XI, 14, 6: 'Artaxata is near the Araxene plain, being a beautiful settlement and the royal residence of the country. It is situated on a peninsula-like elbow of land and its walls have the river as protection all round them, except at the isthmus, which is enclosed by a trench and a palisade.'
11 R.Grousset, *Histoire de l'Arménie*, Paris, 1947, p. 80.
12 Manandian, *Trade and Cities*, pp. 58, 64; G.Kh.Sarkissian, *Tigranakert*, Moscow, 1960 (in Russian).
13 Toumanoff, *Studies*, p. 282. Coins of King Xerxes may be seen in the Department of Coins and Medals, British Museum.
14 K.V.Trever, *Ocherki po istorii kul'tury drevnei Armenii* ('Studies in the history of the culture of ancient Armenia'), Moscow, Leningrad, 1953, pp. 134–7, 142–7 (in Russian).
15 Strabo, *Geography*, XI, 14, 5.
16 G.A.Melikishvili, *K istorii drevnei Gruzii* ('On the history of ancient Georgia'), Tbilisi, 1959, p. 217 (in Russian).
17 M.P.Inadze, *Prichernomorskie goroda drevnei Kolkhidy* ('The Black sea coastal towns of ancient Colchis'), Tbilisi, 1968 (in Russian).
18 O.D.Lortkipanidze, 'Monuments of Graeco-Roman culture on the territory of ancient Georgia', *Archaeologia*, XVII, 1966, pp. 49–79.
19 D.M.Lang, *Studies in the Numismatic History of Georgia in Transcaucasia*, New York, 1955, p. 10.
20 D.M.Lang, *The Georgians*, London, 1966, p. 82.
21 O.D.Lortkipanidze, *Antikuri samqaro da Kartlis samepo (Iberia)* ('The Classical world and the kingdom of Kartli, Iberia'), Tbilisi, 1968 (Georgian text, Russian summary).

22 Ya.I.Smirnov, *Der Schatz von Achalgori*, Tbilisi, 1934.

23 Strabo, *Geography*, XI, 2, 19, and XI, 3, 1–3.

24 See also A.M.Apakidze, *Goroda drevnei Gruzii* ('Towns of ancient Georgia'), Tbilisi, 1968 (in Russian).

25 N.A.Berdzenishvili and others, *Istoriya Gruzii*, I, Tbilisi, 1962, p. 68 (in Russian).

26 Strabo; *Geography*, XI, 3, 6.

27 *Geography*, XI, 2, 13.

28 Theodore Reinach, *Mithridate Eupator, roi de Pont*, Paris, 1890, p. 54; Alfred Duggan, *He died old. Mithradates Eupator king of Pontus*, London, 1958, p. 31.

29 Reinach, *Mithridate Eupator*, pp. 121–211; Duggan, *He died old*, p. 85.

30 Reinach, *Mithridate Eupator*, pp. 405–10; Duggan, *He died old*, p. 194.

31 Hagop Manandian, *Tigrane II et Rome*, Lisbon, 1963.

32 C.F.Lehmann-Haupt, *Armenien einst und jetzt*, I, Berlin, 1910, pp. 381–429.

33 *The Dryden Plutarch*, revised by A.H.Clough (Everyman's Library), II, pp. 219, 225.

34 *Dryden Plutarch*, II, 230.

35 *Dryden Plutarch*, II, 419.

36 H.Pasdermadjian, *Histoire de l'Arménie*, 2nd ed., Paris, 1964, pp. 71–4.

37 Paul Z.Bedoukian, 'A classification of the coins of the Artaxiad dynasty of Armenia', *ANS Museum Notes*, 14, New York, 1968, pp. 41–66.

38 Malcolm A.R.Colledge, *The Parthians*, London, 1967, p. 50.

39 M.J.Vermaseren, *Mithras, the secret God*, London, 1963, p. 23.

40 Colledge, *The Parthians*, p. 51.

41 M.-L.Chaumont, 'L'Ordre des préséances à la cour des Arsacides d'Arménie', *Journal Asiatique*, CCLIV, 1966, pp. 471–97.

42 Grousset, *Histoire de l'Arménie*, pp. 121–27; D.M.Lang, *Lives and Legends of the Georgian Saints*, London, 1956, pp. 13–39.

43 Toumanoff, *Studies in Christian Caucasian History*, pp. 100–1.

44 Lang, *Lives and Legends of the Georgian Saints*, p. 59.

45 G.Radde, *Die Chews'uren und ihr Land*, Cassel, 1878.

46 Lang, *Lives and Legends of the Georgian Saints*, p. 56.

47 Lang, *Lives and Legends of the Georgian Saints*, pp. 36–7.

48 Lang, *Lives and Legends of the Georgian Saints*, pp. 44–56.

49 Sirarpie Der Nersessian, *The Armenians*, London, 1969, pp. 31–2; C. Toumanoff, in *Cambridge Medieval History*, IV, pt 1, 'Byzantium and its neighbours', Cambridge, 1966, p. 608.

50 P. Charanis, *The Armenians in the Byzantine Empire*, Lisbon, 1963. An unsurpassed account of Armenia in the early Byzantine period is now available in N.Adontz, *Armenia in the period of Justinian*, trans. Nina G. Garsoïan, Lisbon, 1970.

51 Toumanoff, in *Cambridge Medieval History*, IV, pt 1, pp. 611–13.

52 Quoted by Manandian, *Trade and Cities*, p. 138.

53 Quoted by Manandian, *Trade and Cities*, p. 139.

54 Lang, *The Georgians*, p. 158.

55 M.Canard, 'Le royaume d'Arméno-Cilicie et les Mamelouks jusqu'au traité de 1285', *Revue des Etudes Arméniennes*, nouvelle série, tom. IV, 1967, pp. 217–59.

56 D.M.Lang, 'Notes on Caucasian Numismatics', *Numismatic Chronicle*, 6th series, vol. XVII, 1957, pp. 144–5. In its corrected form the marginal legend of the coin reads: 'O Christ! David, king of the Abkhazians, the Kartvelians, the Ranians, the Kakhetians and the Armenians'.

57 C.Toumanoff, 'On the relationship between the founder of the Empire of Trebizond and the Georgian Queen Thamar', *Speculum*, 15, Cambridge, Mass., 1940.

58 Toumanoff, in *Cambridge Medieval History*, IV, pt 1, p. 623.

59 'Laws of King George v, of Georgia, surnamed "The Brilliant" ', trans. Oliver Wardrop, *Journal of the Royal Asiatic Society*, 1914, pp. 607–26.

7 PAGANISM, HELLENISM AND CHRISTIANITY

1 N.Y.Marr and Ya.I.Smirnov, *Les Vichaps*, Leningrad, 1931; L.A. Barseghian, 'Les *višaps* des monts Guegham', *Revue des Etudes Arméniennes*, nouvelle série, tom. V, Paris, 1968, pp. 289–93.

2 A.Carrière, *Les huit sanctuaires de l'Arménie païenne*, Paris, 1899.

3 H.Pasdermadjian, *Histoire de l'Arménie*, p. 89.

4 K.V.Trever, *Ocherki po istorii kul'tury drevnei Armenii*, p. 105.

5 Leroy A.Campbell, *Mithraic iconography and ideology*, Leiden, 1968.

6 *Daredevils of Sassoun*, trans. L.Surmelian, London, 1966, p. 93.

7 Strabo, *Geography*, XI, 14, 16.

8 S.K.Chatterji, 'Armenian Hero-Legends, and the Epic of David of Sasun', in *Journal of the Asiatic Society*, Calcutta, vol. 1, no. 3, 1959, p. 205.

9 *Dryden Plutarch*, II, 222.

10 Colledge, *The Parthians*, p. 107.

11 See further J.Hambroer, *Armenischer Dämonenglaube in religionswissenschaftlicher Sicht*, Vienna, 1962 (Studien zur armenischen Geschichte, X); M.H.Ananikian, *Armenian Mythology*, Boston, 1925.

12 Cf. Zabelle C.Boyajian, *Armenian Legends and Poems*, 2nd ed., London, 1958, pp. 65–6.

13 D.M.Lang and G.M.Meredith-Owens, '*Amiran-Darejaniani*: a Georgian Romance and its English rendering', in *Bulletin of the School of Oriental and African Studies*, London, XXII, pt 3, 1959, pp. 454–90.

14 Strabo, *Geography*, XI, 4, 7.

15 Trans.C.J.F.Dowsett, Oxford University Press, 1961, bk I, chap. 18, pp. 29–32.

16 See further O.G.von Wesendonk, *Über georgisches Heidentum*, Leipzig, 1924; M.G.Tsereteli, 'The Asianic elements in national Georgian paganism', in *Georgica*, vol. 1, no. 1, London, 1935, pp. 28–66.

17 D.M.Lang, *The Georgians*, pp. 89–90.

18 M.Ormanian, *The Church of Armenia*, trans. G.M.Gregory, London, 1955, p. 14. For the historical background to the conversion of Armenia, see

Marie-Louise Chaumont, *Recherches sur l'Histoire d'Arménie de l'avènement des Sassanides à la conversion du royaume*, Paris, 1969.

19 G.Peradze, 'An account of the Georgian monks and monasteries in Palestine', in *Georgica*, vol. I, nos. 4–5, London, 1937, pp. 181–246.

20 See the official Calendar of the Georgian Church, published annually at Tbilisi under the supervision of the Catholicos-Patriarch of All Georgia.

21 Trans. and ed. at Oxford, by F.C.Conybeare. There exists a large literature about the Paulicians and Tondrakites, an excellent guide to which is given in *The Paulician Heresy* by Nina G.Garsoïan, The Hague, 1967. In the view of some scholars, *The Key of Truth* is a comparatively recent document: its compiler has been alleged to be an Armenian adventurer of the eighteenth century. (See the article by V.Grigorian in the *Banber* or Bulletin of the Matenadaran, Erevan, V, 1960, pp. 333–44, in Armenian.)

8. LITERATURE AND SCHOLARSHIP IN ARMENIA AND GEORGIA

1 Metsamor is mentioned already in Chapter III above, in connection with primitive metallurgy in Armenia. See further E.Khanzadian, 'Raskopki na Metsamore' ('Excavations at Metsamor') in *Literaturnaya Armeniya* ('Literary Armenia'), 6, 1969, pp. 41–9 (in Russian).

2 K.V.Trever, *Ocherki po istorii kul'tury drevnei Armenii*, pp. 162–74; A. Perikhanian, 'Une inscription araméenne du roi Artašēs trouvée à Zanguézour', in *Revue des Etudes Arméniennes*, nouvelle série, tom. III, Paris, 1966, pp. 17–29.

3 G.V.Tsereteli, 'Armazis bilingva. A bilingual inscription from Armazi near Mcheta in Georgia', Tbilisi, 1942. (Offprint from the *Bulletin of the Marr Institute of Languages, History and Material Culture*, vol. 13.)

4 Shalva Amiranashvili, *Istoriya gruzinskogo iskusstva* 'History of Georgian Art') Moscow, 1963 (in Russian); see further, W.B.Henning, 'A Sassanian silver bowl from Georgia', in *Bulletin of the School of Oriental and African Studies*, 24, 2, 1961, pp. 353–6.

5 Koriun, *The Life of Mashtots*, trans. Bedros Norehad, New York, 1964; Ormanian, *The Church of Armenia*, pp. 17–19; J.Marquart, *Über den Ursprung des armenischen Alphabets*, Vienna, 1917.

6 Eznik de Kolb, *De Deo*, trans. Louis Mariès and Ch.Mercier, Paris, 1959. (*Patrologia Orientalis*, tom. XXVIII, fasc. 4.) The traditional title of Eznik's work is here arbitrarily altered, and the translation composed in a very clumsy form of French, designed to follow the Armenian word by word.

7 G.W.Abgarian, *The Matenadaran*, Erevan, 1962, pp. 35–6; Vahan Inglisian, 'Die armenische Literatur', in *Handbuch der Orientalistik*, I Abt., Bd 7, Leiden, 1963, pp. 170–2. David's *Definition of Philosophy* and his *Interpretation of Aristotle's Analytics* have been edited, with Russian trans., by S.S.Arevshatian, Erevan, 1960, 1967.

8 K.Salia, 'La Littérature géorgienne', in *Bedi Kartlisa: Revue de Kartvélologie*, XVII–XVIII, Paris, 1964, pp. 28–35.

9 Lang, *Lives and Legends of the Georgian Saints*, pp. 115–33.

10 Lang, *Lives and Legends of the Georgian Saints*, pp. 81–93.

11 G.Garitte, *Documents pour l'Etude du livre d'Agathange*, Rome, 1946.

12 V.Inglisian, 'Die armenische Literatur', pp. 177–9. Extracts from Moses of Khorene are given in Zabelle C.Boyajian, *Armenian Legends and Poems*, also an appreciation of his work by Aram Raffi.

13 C.Toumanoff, 'Medieval Georgian historical literature', in *Traditio*, 1, New York, 1943.

14 H.Berberian, 'Autobiographie d'Anania Širakac'i', in *Revue des Etudes Arméniennes*, nouvelle série, tom. I, Paris, 1964, pp. 189–94.

15 An excellent historical map of Armenia, based on the data collected by Anania Shirakatsi, was published in 1960 by Professor S.T.Eremian.

16 *Barlaam and Ioasaph*, trans. Woodward and Mattingly (Loeb Classical Library); *The Balavariani: A Tale from the Christian East*, trans. D.M.Lang, introd. by Ilia V.Abuladze, London, Berkeley, Los Angeles, 1966.

17 *Le Livre de Prières*, Paris, 1961.

18 See H.Thorossian *Histoire de la littérature arménienne*, Paris, 1951.

19 Inglisian, 'Die armenische Literatur', pp. 195–6.

20 Russian trans. under the title *Uteshenie pri likhoradkakh*, 2nd ed, revised by S.S.Arevshatian, Erevan, 1968. See further A.S.Ktsoyan, *Mkhitar Heratsi: XII Century Physician (in commemoration of the 850th anniversary)* (English text), Erevan, 1969.

21 Lang, *The Georgians*, p. 167.

22 Critical literature on Rustaveli is very abundant, most of it being in Georgian or Russian (see D.M.Lang, *Catalogue of Georgian books in the British Museum*, London, 1962, cols. 233–8). English-speaking readers may begin with Marjory Wardrop's prose translation, published by the Royal Asiatic Society in 1912 under the title *The Man in the Panther's Skin*. A blank verse rendering by Venera Urushadze, *The Knight in the Panther's Skin*, appeared at Tbilisi in 1968. Highly recommended is the French version by S.Tsouladzé, *Le Chevalier à la peau de tigre*, Paris, 1964.

23 See *Daredevils of Sassoun* ... by Leon Surmelian, London, 1966; *David de Sassoun, épopée en vers*, trans. F.Feydit, Paris, 1964.

9 ARMENIAN AND GEORGIAN ARCHITECTURE AND FINE ARTS

1 Xenophon, *Anabasis*, V, 4.

2 G.Gaprindashvili, *Peshcherny ansambl' Vardzia* ('The cave complex of Vardzia'), Tbilisi, 1960 (in Russian).

3 Freya Stark, *Rome on the Euphrates*, London, 1966, pp. 82–3, 179, 184, 262.

4 Alexander Mongait, *Archaeology in the USSR*, Moscow, 1959, pp. 226–8; K.V.Trever, *Nadpis' o postroenii armyanskoi kreposti Garni* ('Inscription on the building of the Armenian fortress at Garni'), Leningrad, 1949 (in Russian); Trever, 'K voprosu ob antichnom khrame v Garni' ('On the problem of the Classical temple at Garni'), in *Sovetskaya Arkheologiya* ('Soviet Archaeology'), XI, 1949, pp. 285–304.

5 Karo Kafadarian (Ghafadarian), 'Les fouilles de la ville de Dvin (Duin)', in *Revue des Etudes Arméniennes*, nouvelle série, tom. 2, Paris, 1965, pp. 283–301.

6 Francovich, de Maffei, Cuneo and others, *Architettura medievale armena*, Rome, 1968, p. 78, plates 19–20. This finely illustrated work is valuable for its systematic references to earlier literature.

7 Jules Leroy, *Monks and Monasteries of the Near East*, London, 1963, pp. 140–4.

8 G.N.Chubinashvili, 'Georgia', in the McGraw-Hill *Encyclopedia of World Art*.

9 Denis Cecil Hills, *My Travels in Turkey*, London, 1964, pp. 114–15; Ilia Zdanévitch, *L'Itinéraire géorgien de Ruy Gonzales de Clavijo et les églises aux confins de l'Atabégat*, Paris, 1966, plate 32; David Winfield, 'Some early medieval figure sculpture from north-east Turkey', in *Journal of the Warburg and Courtauld Institutes*, XXXI, 1968, plate 28. There is another graceful Georgian basilica in this region, that of Dörtkilise.

10 However, the recent excavations of Professor David Oates at Tell Arimeh have brought to light early Assyrian mud brick vaults, evidently supported on squinches. Thus, the whole history of this architectural form evidently requires revision.

11 *Architettura medievale armena*, pp. 99–100, plates 54–5, 63–7; Lang, *The Georgians*, pp. 101, 129–30, plates 36, 38.

12 Sirarpie Der Nersessian, *Armenia and the Byzantine Empire*, Harvard University Press, 1945, p. 66, fig. 3, plate VI.

13 S.Der Nersessian, *The Armenians*, London, 1969, pp. 104–6, figs 17, 18, plates 31, 32; *Architettura medievale armena*, p. 102, plates 72–7.

14 J.M.Thierry, 'Monastères arméniens du Vaspurakan', in *Revue des Etudes Arméniennes*, nouvelle série, tom. IV, 1967, pp. 167–86, plates LIV–LXIX.

15 H.F.B.Lynch, *Armenia. Travels and Studies*, London, 1901, I, pp. 371–3, figs 72–4.

16 David Roden Buxton, *Russian Mediaeval Architecture*, Cambridge, 1934, p. 96, plates 94, 95; Lang, *The Georgians*, pp. 134–5, fig. 40, plate 42.

17 J.Strzygowski, *Die Baukunst der Armenier und Europa*, 2 vols, Vienna, 1918.

18 C.Toumanoff, 'The Background to Mantzikert', *Thirteenth International Congress of Byzantine Studies*, Oxford, 1966, *Main Papers*, XIII; Sir Steven Runciman, *A History of the Crusades*, 3 vols, Cambridge, 1953–5.

19 John H.Harvey, 'The Origins of Gothic Architecture: some further thoughts', in *The Antiquaries Journal*, XLVIII, 1968, pt 1, pp. 87–99, plates XXXIII–XXXVI.

20 *Khatchkar*. Collana diretta da Agopik ed Armen Manoukian. (Documents of Armenian Architecture, 2). Milan, 1969.

21 R.O.Schmerling, *Malye formy v arkhitekture srednevekovoi Gruzii* ('Secondary features in Georgian medieval architecture'), Tbilisi, 1962 (in Russian).

22 S.Der Nersessian, *Aght'amar, Church of the Holy Cross*, Harvard, 1965; Edward Hyams, *Dionysus: A social history of the wine vine*, London, 1965, plates 90–2.

23 In Armenia, we have the donor relief of King Gagik at Aghtamar, and the bas-relief of Princes Smbat and Gurgen supporting a little model of the church at Haghpat (*Il complesso monastico di Hakhpat* (Documents of Armenian Architecture, 1.) Milan, 1968, plate 9), and also a number of others.

24 David Winfield, 'Some early medieval figure sculpture from north-east Turkey', *Journal of the Warburg and Courtauld Institutes*, XXXI, 1968, pp. 54–5.

25 *Ancient Arts of Central Asia*, London, 1965, p. 232, plate 214.

26 S.Der Nersessian, *The Armenians*, plate 42.

27 Abgarian, *The Matenadaran*, pp. 20–1; S.Der Nersessian, *The Armenians*, plate 48.

28 Colour reproductions in Tamara Talbot Rice, *Ancient Arts of Central Asia*, plates 241, 242. On Georgian enamels, see Shalva Amiranashvili, *Les Émaux de Géorgie*. Paris, 1962, English edition, *Medieval Georgian enamels of Russia*, New York (Abrams), 1969.

29 G.N.Chubinashvili, *Gruzinskoe chekannoe iskusstvo s VIII po XVIII vek* ('Georgian repoussé work of the eighth to the eighteenth centuries'), Tbilisi, 1957 (Georgian, Russian, English, French, and German texts).

30 Reproduced in the *Album of the Catholicosate of Cilicia*, Antelias, 1965.

31 S.Der Nersessian, 'Le Reliquaire de Skevra', in *Revue des Études Arméniennes*, nouvelle série, tom. 1, 1964, pp. 121–47, plates 1–14. The reliquary is now preserved in the State Hermitage, in Leningrad.

32 Quoted by S.Der Nersessian, *Armenia and the Byzantine Empire*, p. 111.

33 Shalva Amiranashvili, *Istoriya gruzinskoi monumental'noi zhivopisi* ('History of Georgian mural painting'), vol. 1, Tbilisi, 1957 (in Russian).

34 Lydia A.Dournovo, *Armenian Miniatures*, London, 1961, pp. 32–9.

35 Mesrop Janashian, *Armenian Miniature Paintings of the Monastic Library at San Lazzaro*, Venice, 1966, pp. 16–23, plates 1–11.

36 Shalva Amiranashvili, *Gruzinskaya miniatyura* ('Georgian miniature painting'), Moscow, 1966, pp. 12–17, plates 1–12. (In Russian.)

37 Amiranashvili, *Gruzinskaya miniatyura*, pp. 19–27, plates 20–39.

38 S.Der Nersessian, *The Armenians*, pp. 150–1, plates 64, 67, 68, 74; Sotheby and Co., *Catalogue of twenty-three important illuminated Armenian manuscripts*, London, 1967 (describing manuscripts brought from the Armenian Patriarchate in Jerusalem, and now returned there); Lydia A. Dournovo and R.G.Drampian, *Miniatures arméniennes*, Erevan, 1967 (in Armenian, Russian and French).

39 Besides the publications of Amiranashvili, see Basil Gray, 'The Man in the Panther Skin', in *The Bodleian Library Record*, vol. 3, no. 32, Oxford, 1951, pp. 194–8.

40 Gr.Tchkhikvadze, 'La culture musicale populaire géorgienne', in *Bedi Kartlisa*, XXVI, Paris, 1969, pp. 18–20.

41 Other references are given by Professor Mary Boyce, in her article 'The Parthian *gōsān* and Iranian minstrel tradition', in *Journal of the Royal Asiatic Society*, 1957, pp. 11–16.

42 Robert Atayan, 'Armenian systems of musical notation', in *New Orient*, vol. 6, no. 5, Prague, October, 1967, pp. 129–31.

43 Pavle Ingoroqva, 'The lost hymns of Georgia', in *The UNESCO Courier*, No. 5, May, 1962, pp. 24–7.

44 A list of musical instruments referred to in Rustaveli's poem is given in Appendix III to Marjory Wardrop's translation of *The Man in the Panther's Skin*, London, 1912, p. 273.

INDEX

NOTE: Countries and peoples mentioned repeatedly in the text (e.g. Anatolia, Armenia, Asia Minor, Georgia, Caucasus, Turkey) have not been included in this index.

313

Carchemish, 98, 135, 136
Carduchoi, 129, 180
Caria, 183
Carrhae, battle of, 200
Çarşamba river, 18
Catacomb culture, 84, 167, 176
Çatal Hüyük, 4, 10, 12, 18–29, 41, 50
Çavuştepe (Ashbaşin), 140, 150, 160
Cayönü, 25
Ceyhan (Pyramos), 6
Chabarukhi hoard, 170
Chagar Bazar, 49
Chalcedon, 197; Council of, 224
Chaldians, 129, 177
Chalybes, 113–14, 192, 196
Checheno-Ingushetia, 64
Chersonese, 197
Chiatura, 40, 52
China, 188
Chorokhi river, 208
Chosroid dynasty, 206
Chubinishvili, T.N., 39, 40, 65–7, 75
Church, Armenian, 224–5; Georgian, 212, 224–5
Cilicia, 6, 24–5, 27, 48, 62, 183, 198, 211, 213, 215, 236, 256, 260, 263
Cilicia Aspera, 166
Cimmerian Bosphorus, 197
Cimmerians, 80, 113, 129, 141, 144, 147, 150, 157–8, 160–2, 165–8, 172–6, 183, 193–4
Cleopatra, queen of Egypt, 200
Colchis, Colchians, 8, 11, 113, 147, 168, 184, 188, 193–7, 200, 223
Colchidic culture, 93, 103, 111–12, 114, 169, 174
Commagene, 148, 161, 191
Constantine the Great, 204, 233
Constantine Monomachus, 210
Constantine I, Armenian Catholicos, 260
Constantine II, Armenian Catholicos, 260
Constantinople, 208, 211, 229, 243, 254
Copts, 235
Çoruh, 127
Çorum, 7
Cotta, Roman consul, 197
Crassus, 200, 264
Crébillon, French dramatist, 201
Crimea (Krim), 168, 210
Crusades, Crusaders, 206, 211–12, 244, 256
Ctesiphon, 205
Çukurkent, 25
Cyaxares, king of the Medes, 167, 172–3, 179
Cyprus, 235
Cyropedia of Xenophon, 179
Cyrus (Kura) basin and river, 167, 194
Cyrus the Great, 179–82
Cyrus the Younger, 186

Daghestan, 56, 64, 169
Daiaeni (Daia and Dia), 137
Daiaukku (Deioces), Median leader, 155
Dainali, river, 142
Dali, Georgian wood goddess, 223
Dalma, 36–8
Damascus, 136, 201, 208
Daniel the Syrian, bishop, 229
Dante, 239
darbazi houses, 185
Darial Pass, 6, 165
Darius I, Hystaspes, the Great, 177, 179–80, 184
Darius III, Codomannus, Great King of Iran, 187
Dashkesen, 77, 92, 104, 108–9, 170
David the Builder, king of Georgia, 211, 238, 262
David, king of Israel, 204, 208, 230, 236
David of Garesja, saint, 232, 250
David the Invincible, Armenian philosopher, 230
David of Sassoun, epic of, 208, 216, 243–8
David Soslan, consort of Queen Tamar, 211, 265
Deioces (Daiaukku), Median leader, 155
Deli Çay, 132
Demavand, Mount, 221
Derbend Pass, 165
Dersim, 135, 139
Deshayes, J., 103
devs (demons), 219
Diatessaron, 231
Diauehi, 136–7, 141, 144–7, 194
Didube, excavations at, 54–5
Digorian culture, 112–13
Dilijan, 92
Dilmun, Persian Gulf port, 96
Dimitri I, king of Georgia, 259
Dinkha Tepe, culture of, 99–101, 117, 125, 133, 168
Dio Cassius, historian, 204
Dionysius the Areopagite, 238
Dionysius Thrax, 235
Dioscurias, Black Sea port, 193
Divriği iron mines, 8, 9, 64
Diyarbakir, 25, 162, 177, 256
Djulfa, pottery from, 104
Dnieper, river, 78, 175–6
Dodona, oracle of, 215
Doğubayazit, 7
Dolinskoe, North Caucasian site, 80
Don, river, 78, 93, 167
Dubende cave drawings, 40
Dubois de Montpéreux, 63
Dündartepe, 63
Dupont-Sommer, Prof. A., 227
Dvin, 208–9, 252